MANAGING FAMILY TRUSTS

The *Wiley Financial Advisor* Series

Advising the 60+ Investor: Tax and Financial Planning Strategies
   by Darlene Smith, Dale Pulliam, and Holland Tolles
Tax-Smart Investing: Maximizing Your Client's Profits
   by Andrew Westhem and Stuart Weissman
Managing Family Trusts: Taking Control of Inherited Wealth
   by Robert A. Rikoon with Larry Waschka

MANAGING FAMILY TRUSTS

Taking Control of Inherited Wealth

Robert A. Rikoon
with Larry Waschka

John Wiley & Sons, Inc.
New York • Chichester • Weinheim • Brisbane • Singapore • Toronto

Library of Congress Cataloging-in-Publication Data:
Rikoon, Robert A., 1954–
     Managing family trusts: taking control of inherited wealth / Robert A. Rikoon
  with Larry Waschka.
       p.   cm.—(The Wiley financial advisor series)
     ISBN 0-471-32115-X (cloth : alk. paper)
     1. Trust companies.   2. Trusts and trustees.   3. Estate planning.
  I. Waschka, Larry.   II. Title.   III. Series.
  HG4309.R55   1998
  332.2′6—dc21   99-18865

Printed in the United States of America

10 9 8 7 6 5 4 3 2 1

*For my loving wife, Deborah; my devoted mother,
Helen Viteles Rikoon; my shining daughters, Robyn
and Hannah; and to the memory of my father, Howard
Arthur Rikoon, who taught me that in the world of
business, common sense is everything.*

Contents

Acknowledgments   ix

Introduction   xi

PART 1 **The Trust World**   **1**
Chapter 1 Crisis/Opportunity   3
Chapter 2 Deregulation   19
Chapter 3 Expectations and Returns   31

PART 2 **The Art of Trust**   **47**
Chapter 4 Trust Technology   49
Chapter 5 The New Paradigm: Building Trust   57
Chapter 6 What's Compassion Got to Do with It?   67
Chapter 7 Trust Terminology   81
Chapter 8 The Psychology of Inherited Wealth   99
Chapter 9 The Right Stuff   123

PART 3 **The Trust Business: How Business Is Done Now**   **141**
Chapter 10 The Trust World   143
Chapter 11 Trust Mismatches: When the Thrill Is Gone   151
Chapter 12 Why Beneficiaries Don't Move Their Trusts   175
Chapter 13 Matching Beneficiaries with the Right Trustee   185

PART 4   **Trust Busting**   **195**
         Chapter 14 Evaluating the Current Trustee   197
         Chapter 15 Building a Case   209
         Chapter 16 Trust Busting Made Easy   225

PART 5   **Trustworthy Advisors**   **237**
         Chapter 17 Is the Trust Business Appropriate   239
                     for an Advisor?
         Chapter 18 Marketing Trust Services   247
         Chapter 19 Delivering the Goods   257
         Chapter 20 The Trustee Connection   275

PART 6   **Taking Control of Your Inherited Wealth**   **289**
         Chapter 21 Knowing Your Financial Self   291
         Chapter 22 Opening the Door to Change   309
         Chapter 23 If It's Working . . .   327
         Chapter 24 Keys to the Future   337

Appendix   345
Index   357

Acknowledgments

M y first and foremost gratitude goes to my writing mentor and coach, Larry Waschka, whose generosity, good nature, and openness were a constant inspiration and guiding light for me during the two-year period of this book's gestation and birth. As a member of the Council for Independent Financial Advisors (CIFA), I would like to thank the other founding members for their support and encouragement—Ron Yolles, Stewart Welch, Ken Schapiro, and David Citron, who put me up to this project and provided encouragement throughout. I am grateful to Al Snipes of Roswell, New Mexico, who gave me the chance to enter the trust world, and to Stan Fornander of Boise, Idaho, who helped complete my trust education. My work as investment advisor has been made possible by clients and friends: Fred Brown, Larry Taub, William Fell Johnson, M.D., Elise Turner, Steve and Margie Hughes, Sandra Oriel, Lola Moonfrog, Sue Cole, and others who remain unnamed.

Larry and I would like to thank our staffs for their support—particularly Jason Carlten, who provided research support; Lee Moore, who labored through my reckless handwriting; and Barbara London, who provided a thorough and much needed layperson's editorial perspective. Others who helped along the way were Linda, Angie, Jill, and Pat in Little Rock; my brother, Gary M. Rikoon; my mother-in-law Betty Goldsmith; Frankie Greene, Mike Richardson, and other inspirational people in Santa Fe. We want to gratefully acknowledge the support and encouragement of Debby Englander at John Wiley for approaching me to write *Managing Family Trusts*. Finally, I wish to bring into this circle of blessings my teachers and guides along the way: Arthur DaCosta, retired Dean of the Pennsylvania Academy of Fine Arts, and Philip Kapleau, retired abbot of the Rochester Zen Center.

Introduction

As two practicing financial professionals, we know that the business of advising high-net-worth individuals is changing dramatically. What worked well over the last five years doesn't work today, and what is working now will not work five years in the future. This book is addressed to two groups of readers. The first group is *seasoned investment professionals* (SIPs), whom we define as entrepreneurs with one or more areas of technical competence and an intuitive sense for client service. SIPs are accountants, lawyers, planners, advisors, brokers, agents, anyone who has already built a core business in the financial services business. The second group of readers are persons with inherited wealth, particularly trust beneficiaries (TBs). TBs are individuals who have to deal with bank trust departments and who may be inclined to hire some type of expert to help them handle their family wealth

There are few opportunities for those persons of inherited wealth (POWs) who are also trust beneficiaries to exert their personal power and retake control over their assets that are locked up in trust. A central tenet of this book is that inheritors and their advisors receive psychological as well as financial benefits when they take control of inherited wealth, a process we call trust busting and trust building. By *trust busting* we mean breaking down the barriers that keep trust beneficiaries and their advisors from integrating trust assets into the heirs' chosen lifestyle. This includes taking control of and assuming responsibility for choosing investment vehicles, negotiating reasonable fees, accessing funds for normal lifestyle expenses, and appropriate communication among all parties responsible for the beneficiary's assets. *Trust building* is the process whereby SIPs and TBs independently arrive at their own integrated, holistic view of their respective financial desires, capabilities, and constraints. This is hard work! Inheritors and their advisors must be able to communicate and come together in an appropriate match. This will involve setting clear goals and boundaries so that each party in the trust relationship can grow personally and financially.

(A short note on the use of gender-neutral language: We will freely exchange his for her and she for he. No offense is intended if we use one more than another in any particular section of the book.)

If you look hard at the media and mass communications, you will see that much of the financial service industry has become "commoditized." Most people believe that financial advice has become standardized, with no way to distinguish a bank's advice from that of a brokerage firm or a mutual fund company. Investment products, once exclusively distributed by full-service brokerage firms, are now available from banks and insurance companies. Insurance can be bought from brokers or bankers. Discounted products, in every shape and form, are available to the do-it-yourself crowd. On-line purchasing has made it possible for investors to research and buy what they need, wherever and whenever they want.

Family trusts, held hostage by the trust industry, are one of the last vestiges of an era in which freedom of choice and accountability to market forces was absent. That is the main reason for this book: We have the tools needed by so many people who feel they have no hope in dealing with a "Big Brother" bank or a "grandfather" law firm. There is a path for beneficiaries, along with their trusted advisors, to follow in order to assert their rights as inheritors. The choices available to the rest of society should no longer be denied to those families who are constrained by having their assets in trust.

One aspect of the personal financial service industry that can never be commoditized is the person who puts it all together, an advisor with trust expertise whom we call the *trusted advisor*. The successful advisor of the future must distinguish herself from the industry norm. The ultimate aim is to gain a thorough, broad-based knowledge of what people of wealth need, and to have an unmatched commitment and ability to provide excellence of service. The more a seasoned investment professional knows, the more comprehensive services he can offer. This knowledge and its application will, on its own, distinguish one firm from another. The key service that will set an advisor apart from her competition is expertise concerning trusts. If she understands trusts, that advisor will have an edge over her larger, more powerful competitors who are involved with family wealth.

Since the early 1980s, the authors have been dealing with high-net-worth individuals who are also trust beneficiaries. Through our experience working inside bank trust departments, we have seen and been involved firsthand with many trust situations. Because we have been placed in the role of acting as trustees, we understand these matters from all points of view. At times, we have been called on to act as advisors to the corporate trustees, but for the most part we represent beneficiaries. Since the early 1990s, we have been engaged by people all over the United States, Europe, and South America to assist beneficiaries in dealing with recalcitrant trustees. This has led to our role as consultants—helping other financial professionals find fulfilling trust relationships with their clients.

Trust busting and trust building are not about living trusts or revocable trusts. They are about multigenerational irrevocable trusts, which were established to accomplish large wealth transfers and the building of enduring family fortunes. We find that many trusts, both those held at banks and those domiciled with powerful individual trustees, have strayed far from these original goals. Often, these kinds of trustees have a deadening, disempowering, and demeaning effect. Our belief is that trusts can be flexible, durable, and encompassing vehicles that pull together client assets and make them productive and effective tools for keeping families together through difficult circumstances. Our hope is to help put the old-fashioned, irrevocable trusts in sync with the modern world.

People of wealth are often burdened by having to deal with many different professionals, each working independently. Communication between members of the team of advisors is always an issue. We see a strong desire for simplification. Our country's legal and tax considerations are too complicated for loose coordination. People of wealth are bombarded by pitches of every imaginable slant. Everybody now offers the same promises: security, care, performance, customization, value, help, and so on. We believe that inheritors, for whom this book was primarily conceived, prefer to get most, if not all, of their financial services from one source. This is in keeping with consistently expressed objectives, to minimize hassles and reduce stress. In today's world, there are too many decisions and too little time to make them. Wealthy individuals want a financial advisor who personally knows them and makes it easy to get things done. We believe that the SIP who can become a trusted advisor will be able to help his clients make good decisions based on an overarching motivating factor: the client's best interest.

Where We Are Going

The stock market produced record returns in the last two decades of the twentieth century. Many people built wealth through stocks in the 1990s almost by accident. Though not so dramatic as the stock market, real estate prices also moved upward for better than 20 years in some areas. Many families with land moved from working class to middle class to upper class. However, many wealthy families have assets that are out of balance.

While some inheritors feel that they can handle their own investing, most realize they have a need for professional counsel. The person they eventually choose to keep them on track must understand more than security analysis or mutual fund selection. If money management is all a client needs, why not just buy a good index fund? Inheritors' demands for professional help are greater now than they have ever been, because those inheritors realize that their needs are comprehensive; involving tax, estate, and retirement planning, along with family education about financial matters.

Approximately $3 trillion currently resides in irrevocable trusts (ones that can't be changed). Throughout this book, we will be talking about irrevocable trusts, which is where inheritors feel particularly stuck. Close to $30 trillion will be put into new trusts over the next 20 years. This is an astounding amount of money! It is roughly equal to the U.S. economy's total production of goods and services in 1997, plus the total income of everyone in the economy during that year, an amount collectively referred to as *gross domestic product* (GDP).

Most of these trust monies are not managed well. Our goal is to overturn the following traditional attitudes:

- That these funds are the exclusive domain of bank trust departments
- That they are inaccessible
- That they are not subject to market competition as are most other assets

These illusions are purposely perpetuated. Trust money is one of the vestiges of the era of secret deals and good-old-boy networks. Trust funds are still viewed as were bank deposits in the 1960s: poor performers but accepted as part of the system. This, we assure you, is far from the truth.

We hope to pierce the veil that hides trust funds from the scrutiny of inheritors and their advisors.

The common denominator between people of wealth and their advisors is *trust*, a word with many meanings. If you are an advisor who is ready to deal with trust funds, or if you are a trust beneficiary or inheritor whose money is not in a trust but still feel a desire to control your own destiny, read on! After reading this book, advisors will have the vision and knowledge to provide better trust services than most banks or national financial firms. Inheritors and trust beneficiaries, likewise, will be far more knowledgeable regarding trust and investment services, and not likely to be treated in a condescending way by trustees. In the fast-growing trust field, seasoned investment professionals must continue to grow in knowledge and capability; beneficiaries must grow in self-confidence and clarity.

Advisors of high-net-worth individuals reading this book will learn how to get into the trust business, and they will understand what is necessary for building a *trust* relationship in the largest sense of the word—that is, taking care of a client's complete financial life. The trust clients and situations we will be discussing are those with over $1 million in assets. People in this economic band need trusts to avoid taxes and probate, make gifts, help society, and protect their heirs. Trust documents and accounts tie a client's assets together, for better or worse. They are considered an appropriate vehicle for most people with substantial assets. Advisors to inheritors need to be able to help create and run trusts. Once in trust, SIPs will earn annual retainer fees based not on their time or performance (though these are important), but on care, foresight, organizational skill, and long-range efficiency in delivering the final goals of family security.

Trusts create permanent relationships. They reduce anxiety for the parties involved. Clients know that SIPs will be there for them when they are needed, and we SIPs realize that the clients are committed to the relationship as well. Because of the time we invest in doing a thorough job, we come to know and understand our clients as human beings on many levels. Our clients, the trust beneficiaries, understand the value of the services we provide. This means peace of mind, which is worth a great deal in today's hectic world.

There is a need for people in the financial services field to deal with the increased complexity of their clients' personal lives. Tomorrow's successful firms will be those that offer clients a team of totally dedicated financial professionals. If all aspects of an inheritor's financial life can be handled by teams of friendly, competent, and familiar advisors, without waiting in line, that client will be happy. This can be achieved by using a series of strategic trust alliances, which we will describe in this book.

Experienced financial service providers will gain tools that allow them to work with trust beneficiaries as individuals rather than as anonymous holders of funds. Some large financial institutions appear intent on driving the smaller, independent financial advisor's business into the ground. They use the most sophisticated public relations and marketing techniques available and offer a wide choice of seemingly easy-to-use products. These mega-institutions know how to reach a great number of people quickly and efficiently, but most will never know how to personally serve their customers, especially trust beneficiaries. The big firms' prowess in marketing should not be underestimated, and trust beneficiaries should be wary of overblown claims. We hope this book will help advisors who wish to meet this challenge head on. We relish the American ideal of self-sufficient Davids in a world of faceless Goliaths!

To summarize, this book is a primer for financial advisors who see the need to be in the "trust" business. It will work as a model of how to build trust between clients and their trusted advisors. It is essential for professionals to help their clients create the right kind of new trusts as well as to show them how to move existing trusts out of the hands of uncooperative banks or individual trustees. We will show how to find new corporate trustees, willing and able to act as partners with inheritors and their advisors. We will show how to "bust" unworkable trust situations. Each advisor is unique in her talents, as each client is unique in his temperament. We hope to help our peers:

- Become competent in finding and fully servicing high-net-worth individuals.

- Analyze trust situations to see if they can potentially help their clients in an expanded way.

- Show how to move trusts into revenue-sharing situations.

If you are an inheritor, we will:

- Assist you in finding competent help, from both financial advisors and corporate trustees.

- Give you tools to help you decide on the right kind of trusts and where to place them.

- Help you evaluate and promote your own best interests.

Developing expertise in the trust business is an ongoing process. Many people of wealth, specifically those with inherited wealth, have much work to do internally in order to really enjoy the fruits of their privileged position and to be able to establish and maintain successful, nourishing relationships. Seasoned investment professionals have to be constantly developing and reevaluating themselves in order to remain trustworthy advisors. We have divided this book into six working sections so that both groups of readers can find the areas most applicable to their situations.

Part 1, a background of the trust business, explains how SIPs' current position in the financial services industry relates to their probable future success in the trust business. Trust beneficiaries may want to skip over this section.

Part 2 shows how to lay the groundwork for entering the trust business. It is meant to educate financial professionals about what is necessary to be successful in delivering trust services. This should be of particular interest to financial advisors without formal experience in trusts. Part 2 may be helpful to inheritors who have to deal with bank trust officers, accountants, and/or lawyers who are acting as individual trustees. The last two chapters of Part 2 should be of interest to all readers. They begin with an investigation of the psychological aspect of dealing with inherited wealth and conclude with an introduction to the concept of matchmaking between seasoned investment professionals and people who have inherited wealth.

Part 3 describes in detail how trusts get "locked up" and why it is difficult for people to take control of their trusts. Trust beneficiaries as well as SIPs will find Part 3 very informative.

Part 4 is the nuts and bolts of how to "bust" trusts. Busting trusts doesn't mean legally dissolving them, but rather busting the traditional lock hold that banks and some private trustees have over seemingly powerless beneficiaries. However, this book is not intended to disparage in any way the high level of integrity, honesty, and administrative abilities of most people working as individual trustees or as trust officers inside bank trust departments. Having worked in trust departments for eight years, we never found a deliberately malicious, stupid, or lazy person there. We earnestly hope that any ill feelings generated by the material or stories in this book can be transformed into an impetus for generating honest communications between inheritors, their advisors, and trustees.

Part 5 presents a methodology for investment professionals to determine, on a gut level, if the trust business is right for them.

Part 6 is for persons of wealth, be they inheritors or self-made entrepreneurs. These chapters should help them determine what kind of investment relationship would work best for them and how to evaluate which trust-busting strategy would work best from a trust beneficiaries' point of view.

In our efforts to put this material together, we realize that there is a risk of developing a bias, so we would like to thank everyone who guided us toward balance in the writing of this book. Because this book is about balancing the power of money with the freedom that comes from emotional health, we want to direct any merit that comes from its publication to helping us practice what we preach!

Part 1

The Trust World

CHAPTER 1

Crisis/Opportunity

When written in Chinese, the word *crisis* is composed of two characters—one represents danger and the other represents opportunity. We believe that we are facing a great crisis in the financial services industry. However, opportunities are everywhere. Specifically, if you can deliver top-quality, well-rounded, comprehensive services to high-net-worth individuals, you need never be threatened by dangerous opponents. If you are a person with inherited wealth, we can help you take control of your assets and recapture the power vested in you by your ancestors through their accumulation of family wealth inside of a trust shell.

Our modern world is complex and stressful, regardless of how much money we have. The hectic pace of life, the demands that we place on ourselves, and our need to establish an identity in fragmented communities have created overwhelming strains and stresses. On the other hand, these are matched by the great material wealth and abundance enjoyed by many people in the United States. At the end of the twentieth century, because of the passing on of the generation that fought in World War II and created America's dominance on the world's economic scene, a great transfer of wealth, power, and prestige is now taking place. Simultaneously, there is a changing conscience among people about what they want their money to do for them and how they want to live.

3

Danger

The accelerating pace of technology gives us complexity and richness of information, entertainment, and a panoply of choices that beguile most of us. On a material level, we have more, can do more, and are challenged by ourselves and others to make ourselves known, to define our character, and to know ourselves. But we are all so busy. What good is our affluence if we seem to have less time and more stress? We are experiencing America's highest level of material wealth and prosperity, but never before has there been such widespread depression, environmental illness, and chronic fatigue, especially among the wealthy.

The Scope of the Change

Computers have enabled our society at large to be more productive than ever. Corporations are able to maintain high profit margins and increasing market penetration because of computers that increase efficiency and make information work on their behalf. Similarly, large companies are basking in a record string of high profits for shareholders. A new class of information executives and knowledge entrepreneurs are enjoying newly found wealth on a scale that was previously accumulated only by those who could exploit natural resources.

It is difficult to know how powerful and life changing the Internet will be for us. Previous innovations such as the planting of crops, the domestication of animals, development of the written word, the printing press, and the standardization of manufacturing procedures were knowledge-based events that profoundly changed the societies in which they occurred. The twenty-first century will present equally profound changes and challenges for our clients and ourselves.

Financial assets have, over the past 20 years, gained unprecedented stature and value. Wealth based on financial markets has increased more than that of any other field. Individuals whose source of wealth was oil wells, agricultural property, or commercial real estate have seen the investment allure move from natural resources to the stock and bond markets. The introduction of more knowledge-based changes portends continued growth in this shift over the next several decades.

A growing number of entrepreneurs who have created new businesses in America are now wondering how to pass on their wealth in a responsible and charitable way. More people in the United States and the world are starting their own businesses. They wish to use financial assets to provide for their own financial security. As confidence in government programs wanes and the hassles of owning real assets increase, to whom will they turn for counsel?

The Potential Market

It is estimated that there are more than 4,000 families in the United States with net worths over $100 million. There are 100 times as many, or 400,000 families, with net worths between $5 million and $100 million. Approximately twice that number, or 800,000 families, have net worths of $1 million to $5 million.

The upper middle class built wealth by owning their own businesses and then transforming them into ownership of other securities. It is no secret that it is difficult to secure one's financial future by working for someone else. Most people who gain real wealth decide to go out on their own, building their own businesses. This has been made easier by technology. Executives for publicly traded companies can garner real wealth, if they are on the top rung of the corporate ladder. Almost every one of these people has created trusts or will do so in the near future.

The demographic trends of the latter decades of the twentieth century and early decades of the twenty-first century will also create trust markets. One person who has promoted the use of demographics and has worked to simplify the implications of statistics is Harry Dent, author of *The Roaring 2000s* (Simon & Schuster 1998). Dent feels that the economic effect of the baby boom generation approaching retirement will be the most important economic trend of the next 20 years.

Dent believes the economic effects of consumer spending patterns are predictable. Studies show that on average, Americans spend the highest percentage of their income on discretionary goods when they are 46 years of age. The most populous band of the U.S. population is the baby boom generation, and the most prodigious part of that population will be 46 years old sometime between the years of 2004 and 2010. These will be their peak spending years, their peak earning years, and their peak saving years. If Dent is correct, the U.S. economy has a great saving and then spending spree ahead of it, which will impact the value of financial assets and the way people plan for their retirement security. Baby boomers who can afford it will look to trusts to structure their financial future. (See Figure 1.1.)

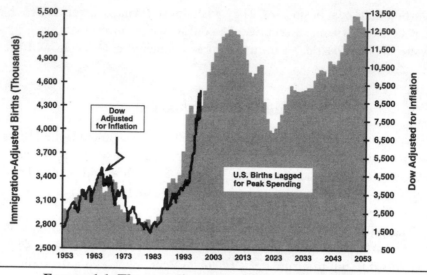

FIGURE 1.1 The spending wave: births lagged for peak in family spending.

Let's begin by explaining how the overall landscape has become more fertile: There are more advisors and more specialized niches in which to show one's talent. The number of wealthy people has also increased. It is now general knowledge that the competitive issue with people of substantial means is service, service, and then more service. The successful independent professional who formerly only had to be a technical expert to have little competition suddenly has 10 competitors, each claiming to be superior in service and expertise.

The Great Transfer of Wealth

There are two relevant trends. First, there is an increased availability of assets to people in the baby boom generation through inheritance. Second, there is a generation of wealth creators through entrepreneurship in high-tech and service industries. These two potential client bases represent outstanding opportunities for the competent advisor. They desire personalized service and have high expectations regarding professionalism and convenience. However, the individuals who comprise these groups have completely different psychological needs and concerns. They may have the same goals, but there are two completely different ways in which they wish to be advised.

We are now seeing the largest transfer of money in the history of the world. It is estimated that over the next 10 years, $10 trillion will be passed from one generation to the next in the United States alone. This is approximately twice the value of all money currently in every mutual fund in the United States.

Inheritors will move most of this money to a new location and to new management. Because this is the opportunity of the century, hoards of people are entering the investment field, hoping to benefit from this unprecedented transfer of wealth. What are the choices for people who are receiving money? To whom can they move their assets? The list is long and getting longer every day. Those who can help include banks who have the history, local insurance agents who have the time, financial planners who understand lifestyle needs, broker-dealers turned financial consultants who have marketing acumen and support, and finally, family friends who have an interest in financial affairs.

Let's say this in a different way. On one hand, $10 trillion will be reallocated to more efficient means of investing. On the other hand, most current advisory relationships will be affected. The traditional relationships between local seasoned investment professionals and their clients will be tested. It is a very competitive situation. The key to survival will be determined by whoever has the best personal relationship.

HOW MUCH MONEY SPECIFICALLY RESIDES INSIDE OF TRUSTS?

By *trust* we mean irrevocable trust accounts held at trust departments, usually connected with banks, where the people who are supposed to benefit from the money do not have immediate access to it. According to the Association of Independent Trust Companies and statistics gathered from the Office of the Comptroller of the Currency, which regulates nationally chartered bank trust departments, there are approximately 950,000 trusts totaling $696 billion. There are probably more assets held privately in trust with family, friends, or law firms, with individual trustees acting in a fiduciary capacity. These groups probably have the same basic demographic profile as trusts held by banks, but it is almost impossible to gather information about them.

Trust Originators

How did most trusts get started?

During the Great Depression and for 40 years afterward, a group of hard-working and honest people stood on the shoulders of their parents, who were first- or second-generation immigrants, and succeeded in establishing themselves in mainstream businesses in America. These were thrifty people with strong family values. This generation of successful workaholics saw the birth of the Internal Revenue Service in 1932—and with it, the introduction of the income tax. There were very few ways to create wealth other than owning real estate or operating a family business, which could be passed down if both the entrepreneur and the heirs lived long enough. Fortunes came and went quickly.

The Rockefellers, Kennedys, Carnegies, Mellons, Bessemers, and other wealthy families of the late nineteenth and early twentieth centuries operated in a different, more rough-and-tumble world. These exploiters of America's natural resources were the fiercest and most successful players of the new industrial age. They formed multigeneration trusts that avoided many of the tax and legal costs that began to plague the rest of the country.

We are concerned with the more modest success stories. The trust benefactors we are referring to here started small businesses, and if they succeeded, they sent their progeny to college. The grandparents of the baby boomers, whom we call *trust originators* (TOs), were well aware of the fact that their wealth came via luck, hard work, and sacrifice. Therefore, the TOs felt that their fortunes should not be squandered away or put at risk. The TOs were self-made businesspeople who were determined to maintain their fortunes for future generations. The TOs had the fortitude, vision, and grandiosity to believe that their assets were as worthy of tucking away as those of European aristocrats (who neatly cached their assets in Swiss banks), or of the more famous and ruthless titans of American industry.

War Veterans: Parents of the Baby Boomers

The trust originators, as young adults during World War I, gave birth to the generation that fought in World War II—those whom we call *war veterans*. Returning from the war, the veterans immediately forged a more competitive economic and academic environment. The successful survivors of the Depression era had established businesses, which they used to help launch their children, the war veterans, into professional fields or businesses. The veterans became lawyers and accountants, doctors or businesspeople, with university degrees. Veterans were also helped by the rise of interstate commerce, which was made possible by the development of efficient highway systems. In an economy with increased telecommunications capabilities, communications and a burgeoning workforce of veterans, educated under the GI Bill, went to work in what they thought would be comfortable and stable careers.

Before they died, the TOs set up trusts to preserve the wealth that they had created, through the aftermath of two world wars, for their children and grandchildren. From the 1920s to the 1950s, people went directly to a local bank trust department, or perhaps set off for the nearest big city to use the more sophisticated services of the bigger banks. People believed in large institutions, because they represented security. Banks generally offered stability in the sense of low personnel turnover and a high sense of ethics. Overall, the trust world was a fairly predictable place. Brokerage firms were not yet acting as trustees; they were too busy making money from a lucrative fixed commission rate schedule.

The trust originators experienced the Great Depression firsthand, and they never forgot those desolate years. Preservation of capital was the watchword of their faith, and the best place to achieve safety was in a bank trust department. Some bought stocks because they believed in entrepreneurship and saw the potential of American blue-chip companies. Although some invested in risky equities, they still felt safe using their local bank and local legal advisor who actively supported the naming of the town bank as trustee for the family trust.

Trust originators and their heirs relied on bank trust departments not for money management services, but for the ability to act as a bona fide trustee for assets. The markets did not move much in those days. Bond interest rates were held steady by the government, and expectations for growth were minimal. Usually, the trust department was expected to hold onto the family stock that the trust originator brought into the bank for safekeeping. The bank was happy with this arrangement, because even if it were not making much money from trust assets, the relationship tied the customer to the institution for loans and deposits. Paying out 2% on savings and trust cash accounts allowed many bankers to work on easy nine-to-five schedules.

Banks were well served by local attorneys who were more than willing to help in this arrangement, because the banks referred clients back to them to draw up the needed documents. Attorneys were glad to use the local banks as trustees because they realized that the bank's primary interest was to avoid lawsuits, therefore protecting the lawyers as well. Sometimes, the attorney ended up acquiescing to clients' pleas to act as trustee. The fact is that many professionals used estates and trusts as "the big payoff" of their careers—a reward for years of service.

When a bank or attorney's name was placed on the trust, family members generally felt that it was inappropriate, rude, or just plain impossible to change trustees. After the trust originators and their most trusted advisor, the attorney, had decided on the efficacy of using the bank as the ultimate manager of the family's wealth and the protector in times of family trouble, that was that! Little did anyone anticipate that banks could be declared insolvent or merge, or that markets would change as drastically as they have. Bank-attorney relationships are still strong, but most attorneys realize that banks are appropriate only in limited circumstances. Furthermore, most of the lucrative paybacks that could be given out by banks are no longer available because of higher regulatory standards, increased competition among lawyers, and a higher level of consumer awareness.

Most trusts set up from the 1920s to the 1970s still reside with the bank trust department originally named in the trust document years ago. More than likely, however, the bank has changed its name and ownership several times since then as a result of a series of acquisitions. The original attorney has passed on or long since retired, but the trust relationship remains at the bank. In these trusts, we often see blue-chip stocks that have done well during the great bull market of the 1980s and 1990s because the bank basically did nothing but hold them for decades. This is fortunate, but come the next bear market, many expert witnesses will point out that diversification was a concept never taken too seriously by the trustee.

The traditional use by bank trust departments of U.S. Treasuries and local municipal bonds has not changed since the 1950s. Municipal bonds are like certificates of deposit. The first bonds were issued by cities to make improvements to schools and roads, which became necessary for the public to keep pace with the rapid rise in the post–World War II population. Typically, bank trust departments have transferred assets into their own internal common trust funds, which are a kind of mutual fund. Blue-chip stocks, favored by trust originators, have done far better than most bank common trust funds. Some trusts were established to provide income for children, grandchildren, and perhaps even for great-grandchildren, so rules regarding trust longevity are one of the few constraints on trustees. We will see how this affects the current situation in which beneficiaries find themselves.

War veterans were young adults during World War II. They reaped the benefits of being victors of World War II and returned home to start families, which they did with great vigor! Some veterans, men and particularly women, were income beneficiaries of trusts set up by their savings-oriented parents, but a far greater number started businesses and created trusts of their own. Their money also went to bank trust departments, because these patriots believed in institutions created by their government. After all, the veterans received ample educational benefits and economic opportunity by playing by the rules. Women also enjoyed some increased occupational opportunities after World War II.

The money that accumulated inside of bank trust departments is now considered to be the largest single pool of noncompetitively managed investment capital in the United States. Most people perceive these funds to be untouchable simply because the trust originators and their heirs considered the bank to be a sacred repository. This image is carefully nurtured and maintained by banks—and for good reason. The perception of non-portability works to their best advantage, but lawyers involved with trusts know that trust documents are not set in stone. Every institution can be challenged, and in an era of consumer rights, trusts have begun to be better known and more familiar, comfortable, and accessible to people who have the rights and abilities to handle their own affairs. Enter the baby boomers.

Baby Boomers (BBs)

By *baby boomers,* we are referring to the segment of the American population born between 1947 and 1962. Most, if not all, BBs dislike having someone else control their personal affairs. There is a stark contrast between the BBs' attitude about banks and their parents' and grandparents' views. Why are BBs more accustomed to having control? The generation that came of age in the 1960s and early 1970s believes that there is a benefit to challenging the establishment. They have their own ideas and want the knowledge and information to create their own way. Lifestyle is key, and believing in an institution such as a bank trust department is antithetical to them. The condescending and secretive fashion in which banks conduct their business does not fit the "me" generation's desire for options, options, and more options from which to choose.

Adding fuel to the fire, the bank trustee sees the situation from a completely different angle. As the only named legal entity responsible for safeguarding assets, the transition from being a relatively sleepy, backwater section of the bank to being a main contributor to the bottom line has placed the trustee under extreme competitive pressure. The arrival of mutual fund sales and the need to provide insurance products and financial plans are part of a trend toward banks' reliance on captive assets to provide an income stream, rather than primarily making money from loans. As stand-alone profit centers, bank trust departments are now being called "money management" or "investment services" to dissassociate themselves from their former sleepy image. The bank trust department's most prized asset is the trust relationship, which is set in stone. Banks feel that their best trust clients are those who are the most quiet. The primary responsibility of today's bank trust officer is to keep the customer satisfied in a fairly noninvolved fashion.

If trust beneficiaries feel that they can't go anywhere else, how motivated is the trustee to perform well? Where is the stimulus to be responsive to the market, to make changes in their policies, or to upgrade their expertise?

Baby boomers are, by and large, not satisfied with below-market rates of investment returns or cookie-cutter brand of service expressed by the "I-have-to-check-with-my-committee" response. Today's trust beneficiaries are not content to leave their money at old-fashioned banks that have maintained a paternalistic or condescending attitude about inherited assets, those which rightfully belong to the family and not to the bank. However, the mental attitude of many people is "that while it may be a bad situation, there is nothing to do about it."

We believe that through various means, this money is going to come out from under the control of bank trust departments into the hands of beneficiaries. This is because trusts are being seen for what they are—a form of legal organization subject to change. We call this process of change *trust busting*. This is not busting the trust in a sense of terminating the trust before its time. *Trust busting is basically busting the lock that the old-line banks had on the treasure of beneficiary rights.*

When a bank is named trustee in a document created by an old family lawyer who was involved with a then-local bank officer, it doesn't mean that the trust has to stay with that bank forever. Almost any trust can be moved, to be placed with a new trustee, especially with trust companies that allow outside investment agents. As with all other areas of modern business, the best provider of specialized professional services should be used, especially when requested by all beneficiaries. Often, beneficiaries arc unhappy with the service being provided by their current bank trustee. They want someone with whom they can identify—someone who truly will be an advocate for them. Trust companies are specialized nonbank corporations whose sole job is to serve as trustee.

As a trust beneficiary, you probably want to know if you can move your trust. Should you try to do it on your own, or hire someone to help you? As a financial professional, you may decide that helping your clients with this part of their financial lives is important enough to take on the long task of trust busting. You can participate directly or subcontract the job to a specialist. Remember, this is not about breaking the intent of the legal document set up by the trust originator or capitulating to unreasonable requests from irresponsible heirs. It is about forcing recalcitrant institutions and individuals to give better service and to get higher investment returns for your client. There are many options available today in terms of professional and corporate trustees.

Most trusts established between 1920 and 1950 are in their last or next-to-last stage. Some trusts were established to bypass estate taxes. In these trusts, the grandchildren or great-grandchildren are the eventual recipients of the assets. Estate tax rates have, like income taxes, gone up and then back down since they were first initiated in the post-Depression years. Because of the high tax cost of transferring assets to heirs, wealthy persons have strived to stay ahead of the government by creating trust documents that reduce the number of times their family assets are subject to reduction by estate taxes.

Trusts Can't Go On Forever

One constraining factor on trusts is the rule that a trust cannot go on forever, that is, it cannot be *perpetual*. The rule states that a trust can last only the length of the lifetime of someone who is alive at the time of the creation of the trust plus 21 years. This rule has been challenged and circumvented in some states, such as South Dakota and Alaska, but has yet to be fully tested in tax court.

In the early twentieth century, estate taxes became a major motivating factor in the creation of family trusts among the superwealthy. The goal of the trust originator and his heirs was not to avoid taxation completely, but rather to extend the estate as long as possible. The conservation of the family business was motivated by the hope that the family would remain intact if they had business dealings with each other. Sometimes it worked and sometimes it didn't. Enter the professional or corporate trustee.

Typically, the youngest person who was alive at the time of the trust creation was the grandchild of the trust originator. We'll assume this grandchild is a baby boomer, who is the last income beneficiary. At the BB's death, the trust assets will be distributed to any surviving children. Sometimes these trusts end earlier, perhaps during the BB's life if the trust terminates on the death of the child rather than the grandchild of the trust originator. In these instances, the assets go directly to the college graduate of the 1960s or 1970s rather than to his children.

If a BB is 40 in 1999, she was born within 15 years of the end of World War II, and chances are that her parents will die within the next 15 years. This generation most often gets an income from a trust that was originally set up by her grandparents when she was an infant, or perhaps she was part of a class of beneficiaries designated but not yet born. If our client, now 40, lives to be 80, the trust will be intact for 40 years. The question is, will it stay with the bank, or go with a seasoned investment professional working in any number of professions. If the BB dies prematurely, leaving a child under age 21, that child will usually receive income from the trust and receive the principal outright on her twenty-first birthday.

New Trusts

Vast new wealth has been created through technology and the financial services industries. Modern-day entrepreneurs are interested in giving the government as little of their estates as possible, just as were the super-wealthy industrialists of the pre-1930s. Trust originators from the 1930s through the 1960s were interested in providing for future generations, knowing that at some point income or estate taxes would have to be paid. Now, BBs are interested in setting up trusts of their own. Many of today's people of wealth are also interested in charitable causes. Our world's social and environmental problems loom ever larger in the public consciousness, and some of these are inadequately addressed by a free-market economy. Our problems are also more complex, and so a whole industry has grown up around charitable trusts.

Many people with a desire to help others wish to use their wealth to make a difference in other people's lives and to contribute to society's overall quality of life for future generations. The result has been the creation of many types of charitable trusts, private foundations, supporting organizations, and the like.

A client of ours named James sold his software company to Microsoft. After reviewing his tax and estate planning options, he founded a private foundation and charitable remainder trust with some of his privately held stock, opting to retain some personally, which he cashed in during the acquisition. James has used some of his personal money to invest in recycling companies, solar and wind energy research, and to support organic producers. His foundation has funded economic development agencies, one of which is on the Sioux Indian Reservation and the other in rural Kentucky.

Unlike traditional trusts designed for the benefit of a particular person, charitable trusts do not usually involve using banks to be implementers of the trust terms. Rather, they are a part of an overall estate plan with various vehicles that fit in with the lifestyle and aspirations of the successful entrepreneur or recent inheritor.

Advisors will be called upon to help clients decide on the designation of an original and a successor trustee. The asset allocation of money in charitable trusts is crucial to the overall financial plan, as is the current investment management program. Younger inheritors want to understand the rationale behind the use of particular mutual funds, individual stocks, real estate, precious metals, venture capital, hedge funds, and the like.

An elderly, heirless client named Evelyn had survived numerous battles with her arch-conservative New York publishing family. Evelyn was determined to find a way to directly impact the lives of other women, especially those suffering poverty and oppression. She asked us to research ways to directly improve the lives of women in Muslim countries. We found the Grameen Bank Coalition, whose average loan of $300 assists women in starting their own home-based businesses. Over the last 15 years, 16 million women have been boosted out of poverty and unemployment. Our client receives a small amount of interest, 3%, on her investment. Evelyn would be happy to have offered interest-free loans or grants, but by supporting fiscal discipline, and rewarding entrepreneurship in the Third World, even more people are being helped.

Research and reporting on socially responsible investments are also important because people with inherited wealth who have a strong sense of ethical use of money often restrict themselves to the use of investments inside established banking systems—simply for lack of knowledge about other options.

There is a network of national community capital foundations that contribute money to low-income families, minorities, and women. This is the same concept applied internationally by the Grameen Bank, which makes loans from $100 to $300 to entrepreneurs in poverty-stricken countries. Organizations associated with Grameen have helped many women start their own businesses in countries such as Bangladesh and Pakistan. Each new business provides employment opportunities for several family members or related parties in local communities. Grameen encourages each borrower to save a little over 5% of the loan, an amount that now totals an estimated $108 million. Additionally, when a borrower accumulates sufficient savings, she is permitted to purchase a single share of the bank, which costs $3. Today, borrowers own over 90% of the Grameen, which posted a $680,000 profit last year. In these poverty-stricken areas, experience shows that six to ten successive loans can lift a borrower out of poverty, often bringing their entire families along. So far, 54% of Grameen borrowers have risen out of poverty, while an additional 27% are about to cross the threshold. The bank is funded by various U.N. agencies, private foundations, U.S. and European governments, and many private individuals.

Can You Handle the Job?

People of wealth need an advisor who is willing to listen and to understand the underlying concerns of their client. For example, many people believe that there is a grave crisis in the way our current use of natural resources is affecting our planet. Although this may be very important to the clients, they may not have discussed it with their trustee. An advisor who takes time to integrate the client's needs, preparing an investment and estate plan that addresses these concerns, will keep that client's assets secure over many generations. It takes knowledge, time, compassion, effort, and organization. The investment professional who focuses only on gathering assets and finding the right stocks or mutual funds will slowly lose out. Do your clients believe that you can take care of all of these demanding issues? Are you set up to handle them?

LINO'S STORY

Lino was a young man who started a small bakery in Philadelphia. Lino's family helped him, and he and his two sisters expanded the family bakery into a chain that served the surrounding suburbs. Through the years, several stock brokers approached Lino with various kinds of speculative investment opportunities, and Lino occasionally traded stocks and options because he was a risk taker and enjoyed the excitement. A national bakery chain came in and offered Lino $20 million for his portion of the bakery business. Each of his sisters stood to receive the same amount. Lino wasn't sure whether he would have enough to do if he sold his business, but he knew that his sisters really wanted freedom from the constant demands of running a family business.

I met Lino by chance on a family trip, and as we talked, it became apparent that the simplest estate planning subject was a mystery and a threat to Lino. Lino had no written will, but his business attorney's firm was preparing one. No one had ever suggested that Lino put his assets (now worth over $20 million) into a living trust, with a companion irrevocable life insurance trust to cover estate taxes. No one had explained to him that if both he and his wife died, his sisters might have to sell the business just to pay estate taxes. None of his brokers had ever mentioned these things because they were concerned with their immediate need to make a sale.

Why hadn't Lino asked anyone about these dangers to his family's financial security, since he obviously had an overriding desire to take care of his wife and children? Why hadn't he asked his brokers about helping him with a financial plan? Why hadn't his attorney put together a trust or series of trusts for his children, his spouse, and several children from a previous marriage? Lino had made a huge and silent assumption, based on his one-sided experience with various advisors, that they probably were not able to handle this complex situation. He didn't feel that they had the background or expertise. Whether right or not, Lino's advisors hadn't positioned themselves to help Lino make the most of his family wealth.

Summary

Situations like Lino's have not gone unnoticed by the big institutions in our industry. Brokerage firms, insurance companies, mutual fund firms, and some money managers are capable of putting together competent financial plans and assisting in their implementation.

Lino's advisors had never spent the time with Lino to discuss his whole financial picture. Lino's hectic schedule left little time to strategize about long-term issues with his financial people. I was fortunate to meet him while on vacation, so we had time to think and talk about the big picture. Lino asked us to assist him in putting together a team to handle these issues, even though he doubted that one person could be capable of doing this.

Lino needs firms that are well-rounded in trust and estate planning, in financial and tax planning, and in investment management services. People like Lino are much sought after but underserved. The strategic decision to approach these high-net-worth individuals is easy to make, but must be followed by a lifetime of study and effort to successfully implement and execute.

Trust beneficiaries are always looking for competent help. A key to success in this endeavor is having a good match between advisor and client. In later chapters, we'll outline simple questions to help trust beneficiaries decide if they need help and how to find it. The overall goal of taking control over one's assets necessitates having confidence in a professional who is set up to correctly handle all aspects of a client's financial life.

CHAPTER

2

How Deregulation Is Breaking Down Barriers between Professional Fields

cathy®   by Cathy Guisewite

This chapter is written primarily for the financial advisor. We will look at where we have come from in the financial service industry and what part trusts will play in the future. Until the 1990s, people went to insurance agents for insurance, to bank trust departments for custody of wills and safekeeping of assets, to brokerage firms for help in analyzing and purchasing stocks, and to financial planners for assurance that all of the threads were pulling together to make a decent fabric of a client's financial life. In short, the financial field was fairly well demarcated.

Occasionally, one player tried to become all things to all people. By and large, this pretty much failed. Bank of America tried to buy its way into new markets. Charles Schwab and Company was then a subsidiary of Bank of America. It was supposed to work through the "bigger is better" theory. Schwab bought back his company from Bank of America because he wanted to provide consumers with a no-frills opportunity to make their own decisions. He was able to take advantage of the dismantling of fixed-commission schedules, which in effect held up competition until the end of the 1970s. Schwab changed everything in the brokerage field by giving his company, and others that followed, the opportunity to unbundle expensive financial services for which consumers had previously paid retail rates. None of this would have happened under Bank of America's roof!

With the advent of negotiated commissions in the brokerage world, brokers did not go out of business; instead, their methods of being paid became harder to track. The rise of limited partnerships, both in real estate and in oil and gas, was a result of an overly complex tax law structure that rewarded convoluted schemers, and a way for salespeople to compensate for the loss of the lucrative system of fixed-commission rates.

Specialists

In the 1980s, salespeople were called upon to explain increasingly complex products from different vantage points. Before this time, brokers were supposed to know only about stocks. There are still some old-timers who really understand stocks, but they are a vanishing breed. The days when you could walk into a broker's office and talk to someone who followed more than the brokerage company's latest mutual fund or picked from a recommended list of stocks is just about over. Brokers are paid to sell, not to do research. In 1963, when the average daily volume on the New York Stock Exchange was about 5 million shares traded, a broker could afford the time to read about what he was selling. In 1973, average daily volume was up, to about 25 million. By 1983, then 1993, average daily volume was about 80 million, then 200 million, respectively. By 1998, the normal number of shares changing hands daily had climbed to 600 million shares. These figures point to an untenable position for any one person attempting to both sell securities and have in-depth knowledge about them.

The reason the largest brokerage firms actively recruit trained salespeople is that they believe it's easier to teach the basics of financial planning and consulting than it is to train people to sell. As a result, investment returns became a hit-or-miss proposition. This worked well until the mid-1990s because until then clients never saw actual performance figures printed on their monthly statements. The current movement to money or asset management services indicates another shift from the specialist to the generalist.

Insurance agents have been specifically trained to gain people's trust, using a combination of fear, guilt, and tax benefits lobbied in during the 1940s, when insurance was seen as one of the few viable alternatives to Social Security or other government aid. Insurance was one nongovernment way of providing families with a secure and independent financial future. Insurance industry experts report that only about 2% of term insurance policyholders ever receive a death benefit. The average universal life insurance policy is held for only seven years. Insurance representatives have been on the main streets of America selling in a traditional way for a long time. The agent's situation has changed because a diverse array of financial instruments are now competing for insurance dollars. Most estate planners and business succession plans view insurance as a necessary cornerstone. This is not because it is a good investment, but because of the unique tax breaks that insurance receives from Congress. It also has one compelling feature: simplicity of payment, and only the specialists understand the actual workings of acturial assumptions upon which payback depends.

Tax accountants and lawyers occupy an important and special place in the lives of high-net-worth individuals. The trust that these professionals garner through years of apprenticeship, along with a high degree of education and sense of ethics, is well deserved. The integrity that comes from a professional code that puts the client's interest first has created a class of advisors who are able to save their clients money. Paradoxically, they have not been compensated to nearly the same degree as salespersons such as stockbrokers or insurance agents. Why is this so?

It is not uncommon to see newly minted lawyers and accountants coming out of school who never intend to practice law or tax preparation. *Today there is one lawyer per 285 people in the United States, which is far above the global average.* Tax accountants and lawyers (except for those few at the top of the legal profession) have much lower earnings potential than do financial advisors. An increasing number of experienced practitioners, from the Big Five firms to mom-and-pop bookkeepers, are looking for ways to augment their income and protect their future.

The lines between tax, legal, investment, and general planning advice are blurred. You cannot do a good job of investing without knowledge of taxes. Likewise, you can't do a proper job of planning for a client's estate unless you understand the likelihood of change in asset class values and

risk versus return. Increasing amounts of information have greatly complicated people's options. Each day in the news, consumers see every
global stock's market performance, gold prices in London, and real estate
prices in Hong Kong. They see Silicon Valley's rags-to-riches stories, and
it is natural to want a piece of the action. We see clients who are more pros-
perous than ever before, and we believe that professionals such as trusted
lawyers and accountants should share in that wealth because their value
added is so dramatic and evident. The disparity exists because we live in a
sales-driven culture, where the motivation to gain outweighs the value of
conserving.

A New World

The wave of mergers between banks, brokerage firms, and insurance companies gives us the feeling that we are entering into a brave new world. Perhaps it will be 2004 when the amalgamation of consumer information and
the ability to target market segments leapfrogs beyond what we previously
envisioned. We know that consumers are increasingly overwhelmed. They
want one secure, stable, knowledgeable, friendly source of information.
They want assistance in making decisions as they weave their way through
the complex morass of options available in today's markets.

Let's take a closer look at who is on the playing field today. Brokers are
now called *financial consultants, financial advisors,* and *money managers.* They offer financial planning services, mortgages, lines of credit,
asset management services, checking accounts, life insurance, and annuities. Life insurance agents are now *consultants* who offer mutual funds,
financial planning, and estate planing in addition to traditional whole and
term life products. Banks are *money managers,* offering insurance, mutual
funds, and portfolio management along with their traditional loan and
deposit products. Is there any difference between them? Aside from regulatory jurisdiction, there is little or no distinction between the players.

The major issue is whether the advisor is doing a good job with the
service the client is getting for his or her money. How secure do clients
feel with their current financial service provider? It is impossible to
know how long a bank employee will be at that particular bank. Insurance agents and brokers are similar in that they are now strictly marketing agents. The individual broker no longer has much influence on how
client accounts are managed, and insurance agents never did! Their job
ends with the sale, implementing the company's model asset allocation.

Insurance agents in particular must live by company rules, which are sta-tistically generated and framed to protect the company's liability. Three-quarters of today's registered independent investment advisors are fairly new to the field and therefore inexperienced with adverse market cir-cumstances. If the average person changes careers three times during his life, then consumers have very little assurance that the person with whom they are currently dealing will be there in the future. If advisors are incompetent, they move on to new fields. There are no longer soci-etal stigmas attached to misrepresentation.

The question we ask prospective trust advisors is, to whom do they owe their first allegiance? We know the expected answer, but isn't it in fact to themselves and their firms? Do employees control firms, or are the firms controlled by an agenda set in another city by a corporate board? This real-ity of modern business presents the consumer with the problem of having an incredible number of choices, but with very little confidence regarding which avenue is best. Certain government actions, such as breaking up the telephone monopoly, are designed to encourage new entrants into the mar-ket, with the hope that consumers will be better served. Is this the result? Regulators and lawmakers are less and less able to supervise the level of quality and integrity of delivery within various financial fields. Poor financial advisors can go unnoticed for years, doing mediocre or even poor jobs. In fact, there is typically little liability for a poor financial advisor except being fired. This is caveat emptor ("let the buyer beware") taken to the extreme. Financial decisions made early in life greatly affect a person's options down the road.

We encountered a portfolio of a Register Investment Advisor who had bought highly speculative leveraged interest-only mortgage bonds for a couple in their 80s. The advisor had no contract, no risk tolerance ques-tionnaire, no documentation, and yet it was the client who was scared to say anything in public for fear of a slander suit!

We are in the middle of a great wave of financial services consolidation. Almost everyone in the United States has witnessed their local banks changing names. The names of the players have changed, and the names of services provided have changed as well. Consumers have to fend for them-selves in this new world, as traditional barriers and ideas about banking, insurance, and securities have disappeared. You may not realize that your insurance agent or mutual fund salesperson in the bank lobby is not an employee of the bank. Does it matter who an advisor works for? When adverse market conditions come, there will be no one around to take responsibility for having given bad advice. The financial consumer is on her own. How can consumers distinguish between quality advice and wasted words? Experience, reputation, proven track record, and consistency of approach are a few of the trademarks of people who have been in the business for a while, but even these aren't enough. The presence of all these attributes may give a consumer peace of mind, but will they be there in the future? Various legislative acts that previously kept players in the financial service industry apart, which were put in place to protect against bad times and to ensure that a major calamity in one service sector would not bring everyone down, are now gone. There is a faith that the markets will take care of themselves and that the government does not need to provide safety nets. The wisdom of this attitude has yet to be tested.

Consumers are confused by the vast complexity of financial decisions. For example, are mutual funds guaranteed by the government? Do government bond funds have a guaranteed return of principal? Is insurance sold by a bank underwritten by highly rated and stable insurance companies? All assumptions now need to be questioned by persons of wealth. Which advisor can they totally trust?

The Trust Officer

The traditional trust officer was generally a middle-aged to elderly man, dependable and not well compensated. His primary emphasis was on protecting the bank from liability. Today, however, the wave of banking consolidations has produced a totally new atmosphere at trust departments. Trust officers are now expected to be marketers, and their performance reviews factor in how well they succeed at this. The trust officer's choice of investment vehicles has expanded so much that the bank's internal common trust fund is now marketed to the general public. This has produced some fairly strange situations regarding trust officers' ability to explain even their own dictated investment strategy. Advisory fees charged by a bank for trust services and mutual fund transactions may consume literally pages of a bank statement. How to understand these complex vehicles is impossible for most people. It is an analogy of how simple things have become so convoluted.

The decisions about what to invest in and how much money to distribute are now rarely in the hands of the local trust officer. Disempowerment at the local level means higher profits for the holding company level. The author worked with the largest bank in Idaho, which was gobbled up first by a Northwest regional bank, then by a West Coast bank, then by a national bank, and finally by a megabank, all within the span of five years. It is hard to determine who is setting the direction for these various trust departments. One thing is clear, though—trust departments are increasingly seen as important contributors to the bottom-line profits of the bank. The trust environment is the same now as for any other investment service provider. Investment management firms around the country have started to create their own trust departments. An array of independent trust companies has arisen to compete with the old-line trust departments.

Large families, such as the Pitcairns and Bessemers, took their family fortunes and the expertise built up handling it and formed their own trust departments, offering their services to a certain level of very affluent clientele. For many years, law firms in Boston and Chicago have very profitably practiced trust business without regulation, guiding clients who can't think of (or don't want to name) a family member as trustee toward naming the firm's senior partner in the trust document. Clients are folded into the law firms' ongoing business structures, which is sometimes a bad mismatch. These attorneys then name their junior partners as successor trustees, thereby creating a succession of individual trustees that generally benefits the law firm at the expense of the inheritor.

How are clients treated in these new venues? Smaller clients, those with under $500,000 in assets, are not given much attention. One set of business owners with employee benefit accounts valued at $500,000 or less received letters from their local bank, which had been taken over by two successively larger banks, stating that the retirement plans of these small businesses were no longer welcome because of insufficient size and that they had just 60 days to place their retirement plans elsewhere. A group of corporate executives in the Midwest decreed that the assets of these formerly loyal bank clients in a Rocky Mountain state were no longer the bank's trouble! It is similar to health insurance companies saying they are discontinuing business in a state because they can't make enough money to satisfy their corporate profit targets, forcing plan participants to go through new waiting periods and disqualification for pre-existing conditions. If you are not a big player, the bank may just drop you.

This insensitivity to local needs and community image will backfire on the larger banks. Seasoned independent professionals who are concerned about their clients and who put together the resources to provide adequate trust services can easily take this business away from the consolidating banks. Many large trust institutions created during the consolidation craze of the 1990s will have their way, write off bad acquisitions, and divest themselves totally of the local trust department market.

What about the trust customers who remain with a local bank's trust department? The trustee, on closer examination, lacking any real investment expertise, has farmed out the major investment decisions to a larger bank or firm elsewhere. The local trust officer can only be following and applying model formulas to her investments inside the local trust accounts. A trust administrator may be available via an 800 number, may visit on a part-time basis, or may even actually be there. However, in all probability, he or she will have little or no authority to make investment or trustee decisions.

Trust Talent

Because of these conditions, trust officers must change jobs to advance. If they are any good, they will be hired away or start their own businesses. The career ladder for trust officers at banks is short! If they are inadequate, it's difficult to get rid of them—like a substandard teacher in public school. In fact, mediocre trust officers are well suited for local banks because they stick around, hold down the fort, and never bend the rules. Why would we emphasize the ability to bend the rules as a good thing? Trust documents are written for future generations by people of the past. They are not set in stone. They are open to interpretation. There is a great deal of discretion in how certain clauses can be interpreted, based on individual family circumstances. If a trust officer takes the time to learn a client's needs, concerns, and goals, and at the same time has the guts to advocate a position on the client's behalf, he is often criticized by compliance-minded superiors. Most trust officers are given too many clients to serve, and their main job then becomes the processing of paperwork. When we talk about transferring trusts, you'll learn what's involved in a typical trust officer's workload.

As you can see, today's trust officer has new business goals as well as an administrative load that would crush a normal person. Being dedicated, hardworking, and underpaid, the trust officer does her best and pays attention to only the most pressing item on the table. She must particularly address those items that might create liability for the bank in the future. This turns out to be a good thing for the seasoned investment professional and the beneficiaries who want to take control of their trust. The fact that the trust officer has no power and no real investment expertise, that she is worried about bringing in new business, and most of all that she is afraid of potential lawsuits, should serve beneficiaries well, if only they know how to leverage these internal mechanisms.

We will discuss later how and why banks pooled their clients' funds and created internal common trust funds. It is discouraging to see the performance of most of them (if you can even get performance data on them). This is one of the first tasks of advisors and their clients.

To summarize, we have a bank that's not local anymore, a trust officer who's not empowered, an investment program that's impersonal, and administrative policies that are designed to protect the trustee against liability. This adds up to giving the trust beneficiary the lowest level of service possible. Delivery of trust services has moved away from the customer relationship, and the quality of personnel has diminished. Trust officers are moving in the opposite direction from the rest of the financial industry. The trust beneficiary now must work with several people within the bank who all have different agendas. The services needed by the beneficiary are fragmented and harder to obtain. The internal profitability of the trust department has ascended to primary importance, so trust departments are now ripe for more consolidation.

Forced restructuring of the trust departments has resulted in a need for mobility for those who are talented: They want to relocate to the center of power. Generally, this is in the larger cities. Smaller communities where fewer services are offered by trust departments receive the less talented trust people. Often, the restructuring of trust departments has resulted in the unloading of trust officers, who are then picked up by local banks. We know of one trust department manager who has been successively laid off by three banks because of poor financial performance—and has been subsequently hired in a more senior capacity by the next bank! Many times, attorneys who can't make it on their own or who cannot deal with the competitive environment end up as trust officers at banks. This is another reason the quality of personnel goes down after restructuring in small communities. Trust departments tout themselves as investment managers, but when was the last time your client received an investment report comparing his portfolio's performance, by asset, to the relevant indexes, net of fees?

Change in the financial landscape will mean that soon clients can have their pick of custodial services and investment managers for their trusts. They may also soon have the power to demand integration of their legal, accounting, and financial planning work. Unfortunately, the average quality of service at the local bank has gone down.

As a result, something of a vacuum was created. Five years ago, there were 20 independent trust companies in the country; today there are over 100; in five years there will be 500. Clients will have an increasing number of options regarding where to put trust assets and how they are handled. The fees charged by banks vary from a minuscule 0.002% or up to a horrendous 2%. This depends on the astuteness of the trust originator in setting up the trust. Did they negotiate with the bank? Have the trust beneficiaries and their advisors put leverage on the bank? Clearly, the consolidation within the industry and the deregulation between the various types of financial institutions should translate into lower fees. In fact, it has not. The consumer is still the one who bears the burden of inconvenient changes, lower service levels, higher costs, and a bewildering maze of administrative paperwork.

Where has all the trust talent gone? It has gone into the bureaucracy—if these people can stand the stress of being inside a banking environment at all. Mostly, though, while good trust officers worked for a trust department at a bank and earned $20 per hour, brokers were selling the same trust services and earning $50 per hour. So, many of the best bank trust officers left to become brokers or investment advisors.

There is now such a plethora of brokerage service providers that consumers cannot tell whether someone is really a financial planner (which used to mean working on a commission) or a fee-only investment advisor. The issue is the level of performance and the breadth and depth of service that is being provided. Brokers who become financial advisors and who turn toward trust services are going to be leading the pack. They have the best marketing skills, support, and training; they appear to have (without actually having) the responsibility for managing the money; and they are taught the latest in estate and financial planning language. These advantages are all appropriate and appealing to most baby boomers. Insurance agents, bankers, traditional investment advisors, and financial planners will, as individual entrepreneurs, be hard-pressed to compete, because traditional lines between financial fields have broken down. The first important task is facing the client and talking the talk. The final task is walking the walk—a more difficult proposition.

Trust Beneficiaries

From the beneficiary's point of view, family trust issues can become very complex. The income and estate tax laws are complicated; family dynamics are complicated; and life in general is incredibly busy. Couples with children are consumed with taking care of their offspring's multitude of commitments. Wealthy people either let their kids attend public school or have to find the right private school. If the children are in private school, there are many fund-raising functions, teacher's meetings, tutorials, and extracurricular activities. In public school, parents who care must help the school raise funds for basic materials and for programs such as art, music, physical education, and sports.

At work, the demands of every business and profession have become more intense. All in all, life is more hectic than it was 20 years ago. Leisure time, when it exists, has to be planned and scheduled and confirmed like everything else. All of this contributes to parents' anxiety about providing future financial security for their children.

Through extensive media efforts, the financial services industry is telling clients that they care, that financial security is within reach, and that answers are available. In most advertising about investments, there's a large discrepancy between our understanding of what constitutes a secure financial life and the reality in our day-to-day experiences. The gap between the two is wide, with no bridge in sight. There are no perfect corporations, just as there are no perfect people. There is a leap of trust involved here, and everyone in the financial service industry knows it. Whatever the particular slant on the market, the person who garners the trust of the inheritor is the one who will fill the breach.

Conclusion

How many wealthy people have the time today to interview, choose, review, and regularly redefine their relationship with various accountants, lawyers, investment advisors, financial planners, and insurance agents? Perhaps some do, but more than likely these people will rely on one trustworthy advisor to recommend other professionals who are competent in their respective fields. Perhaps this trustworthy advisor even offers many of these services. We expect to see the model of the overall personal financial advisor become increasingly popular throughout the United States over the next few decades.

Is anyone capable of delivering on the megafirms' ads promises? Prob ably not. How does a client come to realize this? Usually through experience. Financial service consumers may understand what they're buying and judge whether they are getting value for their money, but it may take two or three years to realize any mistake. There is no "consumer report" on financial service providers. The overabundance of financial information media in all forms merely confuses consumers. The big institutions know all the right words, but the delivery is flawed. Sales acumen does not translate into service delivery.

Clients want someone they can trust who can personally take the lead and orchestrate their financial future. They want someone who is willing to ask the right questions, listen long enough to understand their needs, and deliver results. This is what the new paradigm—building trust—is all about.

Expectations and Returns

"Edna, this is Frank, my happiness, solace, delight, inspiration, comfort, joy, and lawyer."

lawyer: *sometimes called "investment advisor"*

The preceding chapter describes how, in terms of understanding the issues, there is very little difference anymore among the various financial professions. However, there are still wide disparities in how these professionals are paid. It is difficult for consumers to understand the pricing structures for services and products inside the mutual fund, brokerage, and insurance businesses, let alone how people are compensated. Even in the money management and financial planning businesses, where people disclose fees up front, it is difficult for clients to tell whether the fees they pay reflect the value they receive.

We discussed briefly the changing world of trust beneficiaries and predicted that large amounts of wealth will be transferred over the next two to three decades. While the laws that regulate different financial fields have changed, so have both the remuneration level and the expectations of people working in the field. During the 1980s and 1990s, billions of dollars poured into securities as real estate, oil and gas, precious metals, and collectibles lost their allure. The stock and bond markets, scorned during the late 1960s and 1970s, became sovereign.

During this unprecedented flow of assets into financial markets, there has been a dramatic change in the remuneration level of people working with securities. The public's perception of their own level of expertise regarding financial matters is also rapidly changing. With the advent of information technology, which will be covered in the next chapter, the traditional career paths of people working in the field now overlap to a much greater degree. Bank trust officers, once considered to have secure and lifelong positions, are required to become marketers, and even if they're successful, employment security is a thing of the past. We know that most local banks no longer have autonomy. Local and regional brokerage firms, too, have been acquired by larger firms, which leaves the investment industry split between giant brokerage firms and independent investment advisors. This chapter will explore the personalities and pressures that bear down on people working in the financial field. It will help advisors better understand the transition going on in the industry and will help set the stage for determining if the trust business is the right one for his or her financial future.

There are three reasons for the change: deregulation, the amount of money involved, and technology. Many nonfinancial people have seen the potential rewards of being money managers and have started their own firms. There are few barriers to entry, and it takes almost no capital or expertise to get into the business. With 40,000 Registered Investment Advisers as of 1998, and another 10 thousand registering each year, it is important to determine who will survive the next shakeout and how seasoned investment professionals can prepare to take the lead into the next century.

The Old Rules

Traditionally, trusted advisors were split into the salaried, commissioned, and fee-only areas. Accountants and lawyers could be counted on to be competent and operating truly in the clients' best interest because there was no conflict of interest—they did not stand to gain personally from client decisions or situational outcomes other than the occasional naming of themselves as trustee. Commissioned persons such as stockbrokers and insurance agents are consummate and indomitable optimists. The client may never know exactly how a salesperson is being paid, but they know she is doing well. It feels good to deal with successful people. Up until the 1990s, the profit margins in the insurance and brokerage business were extremely high. It takes a certain kind of personality to succeed on commission: someone who can toe the corporate line and sell the company's products. To survive inside big organizations, commissioned people must enjoy dealing with people, must exude confidence, and must appear to have ready solutions for financial consumers' problems.

The fee-only advisor, perhaps the smallest group in absolute numbers, provides an alternative to salespeople. These professionals generally provide services for a flat fee, usually based on a percentage of assets under management. The average fee is 1%, which should cover both the money management and financial planning services. (See Table 3.1.)

Having come out of various other financial industries, most fee-only financial planners used to provide product recommendations and therefore were part of the commission world. Now, however, most planners on the fee-only side are mutual fund allocators or money management consultants.

There are innumerable stockbrokers who have found it difficult to meet their sales goals for individual stocks and mutual fund commissions. As a result, the brokerage industry has positioned itself to become a provider of other kinds of financial products, which now include "wrap" accounts and no-load mutual fund allocation services. "Wrap" accounts allow brokerage firm and large money managers to enter into a cozy agreement whereby the brokerage firm refers clients to an established money manager, and the money manager, who is not an SIP, promises to pay a certain amount of money back through the brokerage firm. The fees are *wrapped*

TABLE 3.1 Typical Management Fee Schedule

Account Size	Annual Fee
$100,000–$249,999	1.60%
$250,000–$499,000	1.40%
$500,000–$999,999	1.20%
$1,000,000–$1,999,999	1.00%
$2,000,000–$2,999,999	0.90%
$3,000,000–$5,999,999	0.80%
$6,000,000–$9,999,999	0.70%
$10,000,000–$14,999,999	0.60%
$15,000,000–$19,999,999	0.50%
$20,000,000+	0.40%

together so a client really never knows what trading costs are involved. Fees for "wrap" or consultant accounts run between 2% and 3% annually. No-load fund allocation services give clients a larger selection of money managers (fund managers) to choose from, but no opportunity to own individual stocks and bonds.

Many brokers are true consultants now, having set up businesses on the side with client trust accounts. This can occur without their employer's knowledge.

Across the country, more investment advisors come into the marketplace daily. Setting oneself up as an independent while simultaneously retaining a brokerage license is not difficult. It takes no capital to enter into the investment advisor field. State regulation of new advisors is relatively lax. The Securities and Exchange Commission estimates that from 1987 through 1997, the number of independent investment advisors grew from 4,000 to 40,000, a tremendous increase.

Financial planners who sell products and money managers who have insurance licenses or pension plan administration businesses are in the minority. There is nothing inherently right or wrong about these arrangements. The point here is that it's impossible to keep track of who is getting paid for what. Furthermore, consumers cannot possibly know what motivates people to hold themselves out as financial advisors. This leaves inheritors confused and somewhat distrustful of the financial services industry.

The inherent conflict of interest between customers and those who are compensated on a commission basis has permeated the car sales business for years. With *Consumer Reports* and other sources offering wholesale and retail price information, retail consumers are better-informed than ever. Therefore, automakers have created yet another tier of hidden charges and rebates for their dealers. Although many consumers come in to buy a car with what they think is the "greater truth," they *still* don't know the whole story. They may believe that they are getting a bargain, but in reality there will always be a hidden layer of compensation rarely seen by the consumer or the retail client. Such is the nature of commission sales.

Fee Business

We recently visited an acquaintance of ours who had interviewed for a job with our firm several years ago. She had started her career in the same bank trust department for which I provided investment management services in the mid-1980s. This person had the ability to get along in a bank trust department while working for some extremely dull and overbearing superiors. She had seemed to grow somewhat meeker over the years that I knew her. After the bank repeatedly changed hands, the local Smith Barney office picked up this trust officer and put her through an expensive training program. Within two years, the reserved, submissive bank trust officer had become an aggressive salesperson, with a knack for dealing with the elderly. While not an entrepreneur type, the broker became adept at selling Smith Barney's products, and she moved comfortably into the committee-laden world of nonprofit organizations. Her work inside a traditional bank environment had prepared her well. Well-dressed and well-heeled, in the middle of a bull market, the broker was enjoying her newfound freedom and greatly increased compensation.

At the same time, the trust department that she had left, once a power-house, fell into disrepair. The trust department manager had been reduced to filling out forms and attending out-of-state committee meetings. The bank gradually lost touch with its base of local trust customers. We helped several of their dissatisfied trust clients move their trusts to a local independent bank that allowed for outside investment management.

At this local bank, now owned by an out-of-state company, the more experienced bank trust officers who had moved into management were drawn into a frustrating zone where the beneficiaries' interests were pitted against the ever increasing financial demands of the more distant trust department management. Eventually, even the trust manager quit. After 20 years of being a yes-man for upper management, he got fed up with the pressure. His former employee, described above, was able to bail out in time, perhaps because she was younger and less tied to the system. This example of two competent trust officers caught in the consolidation squeeze is repeated over and over again in today's trust department environment.

In an era of takeovers and consolidations, no one is sure how long a particular company will be in business with the same employees. It is also hard to know if a seasoned investment professional will remain in the field or succumb to the quickly changing and increasingly competitive nature of the environment. All advertisements say the same thing: "Come to us for financial security; we will listen to you; we know what it takes; we have everything that you need."

The amazing marketing clout of institutions is exemplified by Charles Schwab. Formerly a niche player for do-it-yourselfers, Schwab has grown so much that its breadth of services is vastly greater than a discount broker. Schwab now offers annuities along with referral services to accountants, lawyers, financial planners, and investment advisors. It offers retirement plans, mutual fund advice, and stock research. Schwab also seeks to provide top-tiered services to well-heeled clients.

The concept of gathering assets runs across the board in the financial world. It is turning the hourly wage earner and the commissioned worker into a dying breed. Schwab's entrance into the brokerage field following the deregulation of the brokerage industry drove down commissions of other full-service brokers. Along with many other discount firms, Schwab began offering no-load mutual funds. This service allowed independent investment advisors to build no-load mutual fund portfolios for clients on a fee-only basis. Now, full-service firms like Merrill Lynch are offering similar services with no-load funds from various companies, a development certain to change the face of the independent advisory world.

There is a plethora of no-load products available in every field. Insurance, stocks, funds, investment management, even legal and accounting services can be obtained through electronic means or direct mail. All financial service sector profit margins are headed downward, but commissioned reps are feeling it the most.

Product Business

An individual who makes a million dollars a year selling life insurance or doing commissioned brokerage should be worried about the future. Life insurance remains a favorite vehicle for many tax attorneys, so forward-thinking salespeople are now experts at estate planning. As with the old banker-attorney network, the insurance-lawyer connection provides persons with wealth a sense that estate taxes can be easily handled through the purchase of life insurance. Life insurance is sold on the concepts of replacing wealth lost to the government through estate taxes and providing for one's family. Most agents also sell annuities as tax-advantaged products.

Most people still need help in deciding what to do, and the agents who help people deserve to be paid. The question is one of fair compensation that will keep both the client and the SIP's best interests in mind. Which type of arrangement will reward the SIP and at the same time serve the client? The answer involves an advisory relationship. The trend toward retainer fees and remuneration based on amount of assets is strong. Fee-only service sometimes includes hourly compensation. High-net-worth individuals need ongoing high-touch, high-quality services that are easy to use.

Service Businesses

Accountants and lawyers who come from an hourly rate background are searching for new ways to build a steady revenue stream for themselves. Accountants have traditionally scored higher than all other professions in client evaluations of "trusted advisor" relationships. This is because accountants have worked long hours gathering financial information on all aspects of the client's financial life. Some accountants may have investment expertise, while others specialize in real estate or other business planning areas. In estate planning, the dividing line between a tax lawyer and an exceptional accountant is thin. Top attorneys or accountants may earn well into the six figures. While this is not as much as top insurance agents or stockbrokers traditionally make, they can still leverage the efforts of their junior partners.

This is becoming increasingly hard to do. People are reluctant and sometimes resentful of spending large amounts on hourly fees, so accountants and even some lawyers are entering the field of financial services. Revenue-sharing arrangements are becoming more common, as legal barriers no longer restrict accountants' relationships with their clients. For the first time, certified public accountants (CPAs) can realize commissions in some states. This is an unstoppable trend that will affect the area of financial planning. CPAs can also register as investment advisors and share revenue with money management firms.

Clients should have their priorities in order before they go see a professional who is compensated via hourly billing. Regardless of the amount of help that is received, there is always an element of reluctance to go see a professional whose compensation is based strictly on an hourly rate. If you could tie the fortunes of the accountant or attorney to the success of the client, clients would have less resentment of hourly fees.

Some accounting firms have set up separate subsidiaries to hold themselves out primarily as financial planners. This is a natural extension of the accountant's traditional role as an advisor to families with wealth. The next logical step for a financial planner is to be an asset manager or manager consultant.

Computer programs make it relatively easy for accountants and financial planners or anyone else to show clients what has been the best kind of asset allocation or mutual fund investment based on the past. On-line rating services can pick the "best" mutual funds within different asset classes; thus the accountant now becomes a money manager.

Conservative accountants are reluctant to compromise their objectivity and disturb their trust relationships based on tax preparation and financial advice, while their more venturesome colleagues eye earnings potential two to three times those of tax or audit practice. Many accountants have a standard of ethics, knowledge of the client, and understanding of the long-term results of investment products that far surpasses those of most brokers, insurance agents, and many Registered Investment Advisers. Accountants are not traditionally paid for their expertise in the investment area. To the contrary, as taxes rise and available legal shelters disappear, criticism of conservative accounts sometimes goes up as well!

Accountants have the opportunity to transform their established client relationships into a more valuable asset. It is difficult to make the leap from wage earner to financial advisor. One firm we know set up one partner as a certified financial planner. Then, the planner set up another person in the firm as a money manager. No conflict of interest ensued. Their lack of a track record or money management expertise is not noticed because most clients believe that the accountants will only act with their best interest in mind.

Attorneys interested in managing family trusts are in a different situation. Let us take the example of the best-qualified and most-well-known estate planning attorney in a minor metropolitan area. She has worked for 20 years in the field, gaining clientele and establishing a good hourly wage. The high end of legal rates at best approximates a mediocre life insurance salesperson's salary. Day in and day out, she churns out documents with the help of associates, paralegals, and secretaries, while coping with overhead problems and long hours. Her sales-oriented colleagues at the local estate planning council seem happier, more highly remunerated, and far less skilled; and they also enjoy more leisure time. The difference is the focus on the client relationship.

The sales relationship that brokers and insurance agents take on supposedly involves more risk, so the attorney may console herself in the fact that she has a more stable income or that she has chosen a more intellectually satisfying field. But often, there is a vague feeling of discontent. The client, knowing that the accountants and lawyers have a higher level of expertise, trust them more than their broker or agent. The catch is that the attorney is not sure how to transform the relationship from hourly accounting to an annual retainer. What can the hourly professional do? There is the possibility of setting up as a money manager or as a broker-dealer. Attorneys can joint venture with insurance agents, brokers, or investment advisors. They could simply charge more, but there is a definite market constraint on raising hourly fees. High-net-worth clients who need ongoing advice could be billed on a more systematic basis than is provided under the hourly wage structure. This involves a change of perception for both the legal service provider and the client.

Limits on Service

Top-of-the-line attorneys throughout the country can earn a million dollars a year, that is, $500 per hour. The problem here is that their personal lives are not given adequate time as they have to slave for long hours. Once on top, they have to preside over a pyramidal structure that exploits the time and energy of candidates aspiring to become partners. Finding people willing to go through this grueling apprenticeship is still possible, but clients know that the top accountant or attorney's time is very expensive. This makes clients uncomfortable.

Top-notch attorneys also have another problem. Once they are gone, their clients will move on. Therefore, there is no business equity being built. At a client's death, an estate is settled and the client is gone. At an attorney's death, the client gets another attorney. But what if the attorney is the trustee of a trust? In some large, private law firms in Boston and Chicago, lawyers who have been named as trustees in client wills and trusts are able to perpetuate equity in their companies in much the same way as bank trust departments. They may have to wait a long time, however, to the end of their careers, to benefit from the large fees that are generated in strictly probate situations when there is no ongoing trustee nomination.

Upcoming beneficiaries, the baby boomers, are not going to let this continue. They are fee-conscious and liable to sue for inadequate documentation or representation on matters involving inherited money. Lawyers may be unable to pass on the annuity-like income by naming a junior partner as trustee, as this usually cannot be done without the consent of the beneficiary. This becomes an opportunity for independent trust companies.

One law firm in Chicago went so far as to fabricate a reason to "restate and amend" a trust when the firm stood to lose a series of trust accounts upon the retirement of one particular senior partner who was named in the will. The account, worth over $40 million in 1999, had provided the senior partner with a hefty income for 40 years—and his father before that. What a boondoggle! The lawyers tried to use a current arcane change in the tax code to justify going to the beneficiaries and the court to re-form the trust. It was convenient to put in the court filing an extension of the law firm's tenure as trustee. Fortunately, our client was made aware of this maneuver and we used it to her advantage by calling for accountability where previously there was none.

Lawyers are adept at solving long-term planning issues with their clients, but they are paid on a short-term basis. The client's benefit greatly exceeds what the lawyer is paid. However, the client may suffer later unless the attorney maintains the documents to comply with new estate tax laws or strategies. Higher demands on the attorney's time also create more pressure.

One of my best college friends is a top-tier entertainment attorney in Los Angeles. He has more business than he can handle and can't find enough good younger attorneys to help him deal with all his work, so he is always overloaded. He rarely sees his two young sons and is rarely home to help raise the children. They have nannies and tutors, and his wife spends most of her time in Santa Fe. My friend is caught on a treadmill, hating his work and the lifestyle bifurcation his own brilliant success and hard work has created.

Most attorneys would like to have the option of working on some sort of yearly retainer, and they certainly deserve it. Most clients are not accustomed to this idea, but we expect this to change soon. Attorneys are looking for more lifestyle choices for themselves and their families. It is easier to keep up with technical research and industry developments and case law via computer, so a more flexible work schedule and location is possible. Job satisfaction among lawyers and accountants is way below that of other financial service professionals. It is no wonder that many of them have thoughts about doing something else.

BUILDING EQUITY

After jumping from one law firm to another, a tax attorney friend decided to go out on his own. He lacked the necessary marketing skills to build a practice, so he worked hard for his three largest clients. Eventually, two of the three clients passed away and the attorney decided to go into business with his remaining client. This client was a great salesman and his business was growing. The salesperson lacked what the attorney was good at—organization, structure, and financial management. The most attractive asset the attorney had to offer was his ability to obtain financing for the company's projects, no matter how unusual. This talent had become critical to his former client's success. As a result of the firm's growth, the most attractive aspect of the new relationship that the founder had to offer the ex–practicing attorney was equity in the business, in which the attorney formerly had no share. The attorney let his own practice die and focused solely on his client's business. Though he's making a lower salary, he now has equity and doesn't have to worry about marketing or selling. He has a yearly income stream that renews itself every year. It's no wonder he left his law practice.

The best attorneys we know often express interest in other fields. Why would they want to move out of their protected niche? Good estate planning saves clients hundreds of thousands, if not millions of dollars, but the legal designers and architects are relegated to an hourly wage. There is no chance to relax when one has to log in hour by hour, over and over again, beginning anew each billing period.

The issue to lawyers and accountants becomes the value they create for their clients relative to their own remuneration. Lawyers and accountants have to spend many hours keeping up with their field, both to maintain their certifications and to protect themselves from liability. Can a lawyer or accountant request compensation based on a percentage of a client's assets instead of an hourly wage? Some attorneys are trying this concept. Others are offering a yearly retainer type of service. In some cases, this is working well, but there's still room for improvement and innovation.

Lawyers and accountants can be part of a team that provides comprehensive services, and the value of this cannot be measured in terms of hours. This leads us to the concept of the family office. If enough family wealth can be centralized, the need for expert professional services is recognized, and the persons who can organize the delivery of those services can be compensated on a different scale than an hourly basis. Clients are willing to pay for the relief of being able to relax about their financial affairs if they know that a competent team is taking care of it. Don't get us wrong here—not all inheritors are likely to gravitate toward this kind of arrangement. Clients with short-term horizons may not be suitable, but many people with substantial wealth are interested in having the best possible service with the fewest possible hassles. Enter the trusted advisor.

The New Breed

Trusted advisors are paid to deliver long-term solutions to clients and keep them on track. When no one is looking, the trusted advisor is expected to be there and be square. The goal is to remove anxiety from the client's financial life. When we really want to do a great job, we help with many things outside of our chosen technical fields. When clients come in and present the reality of their lives to us, in both subtle and not-so-subtle ways, we explore all of their concerns and needs as if they were friends or family.

It is tempting to immediately categorize people and then offer them prepackaged programs that are easier to sell, apply, administer, and track than truly personalized approaches. The prepackaged approach does not work with high-net-worth individuals. Inheritors want personal attention and are very capable of intuitively judging whether they are getting it. They desire constant attention to the details of all their financial needs, not just the readily apparent ones.

Any financial professional who has a desire to move into an annualized fee-only situation needs to be willing to sit down with a client and review the following:

1. Spending patterns

2. Family psychological history

3. Current feelings

4. Interactions with spouse and children about money issues

5. Long-term tax situation and retirement needs

6. House and car financing programs

7. An estate plan

8. Current investments

9. Risk tolerance and asset allocations

10. Life insurance

How many families would be unwilling to turn over their legal, accounting, and investment work to a team of professionals who show that this kind of comprehensive care is available through a "family office?" The team must be genuine, sincere, and competent. Most trust beneficiaries could receive such service if they would be willing to pay an annual retainer fee to forgo worrying about all these items. Wouldn't you?

Another connection to make is for inheritors to understand that the advisor's long-term security depends on ensuring the client's vitality. The financial growth of clients' portfolios and the safety of all their assets is vitally important. The client's nest egg is the advisor's as well. At our organization, the goal is for the client to see that our own long-term financial future is intimately tied with theirs. We believe that there is a way to add a large amount of value to both parties in this kind of arrangement. Families need security and desire peace of mind, and advisors need consistency of income and a stable base; these two goals are mutually reinforcing.

There is an overabundance of financial counselors in today's marketplace, but there is no easy money to be made in the long run. Many professionals have picked the wrong time to enter the field as financial advisors. Giving good long-term financial advice takes more skills and more personal commitment than most people can muster. Consumers are not aware of this yet, because many marginally competent people have been shielded from scrutiny by a long-term bull market in stocks.

Major brokerage firms are aware of this situation. While they are brilliant advertisers and can provide comprehensive service, they are hard-pressed to provide personal attention. One major advantage of the local seasoned investment professionals over the largest firms is a personalized image—interdisciplinary rather than amalgamations of out-of-town experts. The building of trust relationships is fairly straightforward. When an advisor is geographically nearby and known to have integrity, a client knows that what the advisor is doing is likely to be right for them and that the advisor will be there for them when needed.

The more complete a service an advisor offers, the more allegiance they will have from their clients. A solid trust relationship can be transmuted into equity for the financial advisor only when he or she has the perspective and the foresight to create an organization that can deliver the kind of service the client needs. This is the foundation upon which client confidence builds, knowing that a high level of service will be delivered now and in the future, no matter what happens to any particular individual in the advisor's organization. The breadth of the advisor's knowledge must be built into the organization by creating allegiances in areas in which the advisor is not a personal expert. No one is an expert in every area. Financial planners don't necessarily make good money managers. Good money managers don't necessarily make great trust officers. Combining the expertise into one seamless product is a challenge.

Building Equity

How do advisors know if they are really building equity in their businesses? They must ask themselves, whom does the client call first? If there's a financial decision to be made—regarding a house purchase, a marriage, a long-term gifting program—are they in on the discussion? If not, they probably don't have the kind of relationship that would last in a merger, acquisition, sale, or transition to a junior partner. All people in the various financial professions want the same thing: to build equity in their businesses. This is accomplished by doing the right thing for the client, which includes providing for continuity of service even if something happens to the founding member of the firm.

I recently had a client who sold a piece of property without telling me. There were some capital losses on the property, and we could have taken some capital gains on stocks to offset that aspect of the tax picture. It didn't happen and I felt bad. The fact that the client lives 3,000 miles away and I hadn't seen him for three years had something to do with it. Nonetheless, I question if I am serving that client adequately. Are his lifestyle and needs for the future being adequately served by my firm? Perhaps not. Is it possible for our firm to service this client? We believe so. The advent of technology allows us to communicate with our clients no matter where they or we are located. It also allows clients to communicate to us about upcoming decisions and events in their lives. Technologies such as voice mail and e-mail have already made many far-reaching changes in our business. This is the subject of the next chapter.

Conclusion

Most large financial institutions need ever increasing profits to satisfy the expectations of their shareholders and to produce justification for top executives' compensation. Institutions have a major disadvantage compared with independent investment professionals who control their own future. How long one person stays as their primary contact is crucial in the eyes of the client. It takes time to establish communication and trust between any two people. The advisor-inheritor bond grows stronger with time if proper attention is given to this personal connection. Trust beneficiaries deserve more time and attention than most institutions can afford to give. This is especially true for newly created trust relationships.

Establishing a trusted advisor relationship requires more up-front, face-to-face, nonbillable time to get to know the client, and it is unlikely that large institutions are willing to provide their employees with tacit approval to give the kind of service necessary in this situation. The SIP has the ability to put in large chunks of time up front to establish new clients. It is worthwhile to spend time to examine the big picture on behalf of the client because that is the way to build trust. An advisor's best hope for a steady future income is not dependent on short-term performance, sale of a product, or billing clients for time, but rather, making a difference in his client's quality of life.

Seasoned investment professionals must have at least one area of superior technical competence, which means that they have been in the field for enough years to earn an honest reputation. This allows advisors to clearly define what they can and cannot do. Strength comes from maintaining integrity in the financial field while dealing with fear, greed, and anxiety. This is what makes great financial advisors. If an investment advisor has stayed in the field and has clients that go back 10 years or more, it is likely that he is well qualified and grounded enough to take on the role of financial quarterback.

Professionals who are paid strictly on commission or hourly fees are unable to leverage their talents and gain long-term equity. Long-term equity essentially means having the ability to be able to put a value on a future income stream in present dollars. There is very little future income stream if a commission has to be earned over and over via transactions. If hourly services have to be scheduled and billed like dentist appointments, equity will consist of customer files and an indeterminate amount of "good will." People who see and understand this come to the conclusion that becoming an asset gatherer and financial quarterback takes technological savvy, compassion, psychological stamina, and integrity.

Part 2

The Art of Trust

4

Trust Technology

"Welcome to First Interactive National Bank!"

Before financial advisors can start helping heirs take control of their trusts from old-line, nonperforming, noncooperative, and noncommunicative banks, they need to figure out how to be available in the way, shape, and form that best suits trust beneficiaries' personalities. They also have to tailor their internal communication in a way that fits the goal of being trusted advisors. Their organizations must be structured to provide high-net-worth clients with whatever is necessary to maintain those clients' lifestyles. The technologies that we will be talking about have to do with machines and software and, more important, how to use them.

Clients' Techno-Habits

Let us start with a general picture of typical days of persons of wealth. These people tend to be very active. They travel to second homes, to foreign countries, to conferences and seminars, and to visit other family members. They go to spiritual retreats, to art events, to schools, to spas, and take more vacations than people without wealth. They fully take advantage of their opportunities to explore a wide range of both professional and business pursuits. Their need for personal attention from a financial advisor comes and goes in spurts. Inside our organization, our own people are constantly traveling for education or personal reasons, as well as to maintain our business. More often than not, we are on different schedules than our clients.

With these divergent schedules of clients and key employees, there needs to be a steady flow of information that completely solves the client's concerns. The purpose of trust technology is to make beneficiaries feel that their advisor is always available. One of the primary concerns of all inheritors, regardless of how much money they have, is that there won't be enough cash available when and where they need it. This is a fear that can be allayed by the proper deployment of technology, particularly in communications.

The technology we use in our organization can be compared with the hub of a great wheel. In our three-dimensional universe, all parts are moving, but there needs to be a constant center. Ideally, that center is the place to which all requests come and from whence all information flows. No matter what the subject, time frame, or responsibility, there has to be a repository for tracking money, information, interpretation, and follow-up on events. This is the techno-version of plain old hand holding.

Techno-Evolution

In every organization, employees sometimes come and go, and our network of related professionals and consultants expands and contracts in an organic way as time goes by. We can bring added amounts of expertise, but more significantly, our clients need to know that they have a constant way of getting in touch with us to ask questions about anything at all, regardless of where they are or the time of day.

For our part, we are constantly updating ourselves on project status—gathering new research and adjusting our methods of implementation of client plans. The investment vehicles that we use may change as our sophistication in evaluation of client portfolios increases. There is always a crisis or two going on in some client's life. How do we keep track of it all? We communicate with the client, with the other professionals involved, and among our own staff. This is what all excellent trust advisors must do. We must ensure that we can fix problems without wasting our client's time and money.

Our "hub" is an integrated computer system into which all information goes; it encompasses much more than a contact management system. We organize our practice based on clients, and we track ongoing projects by client. People are assigned as backups and double backups, with scheduled timelines and follow-up reviews in person and on the telephone. In fact, it is more like a spiderweb or a diamond than a wheel because of the three-dimensional character of the relationship tracking goals of our systems.

The technology that serves this system can respond to telephone calls, faxes, letters, or e-mail. We guarantee to return clients' calls by the end of the day, or at the latest within 24 hours. Our trust technology has to be accessible to our employees and clients seven days a week, 24 hours a day. The Internet is an important part of this and will play an even larger role once security and user-friendly format issues are solved. The speed and accessibility of the Internet is unsatisfactory to many clients, so we pull together many kinds of electronic and personal contact methods. Remember, trust beneficiaries are generally not computer experts. As with a five-star hotel, before we can open our rooms for guests, everything has to be working seamlessly and transparently to the end user. They demand results.

Most people process new information as they do a TV commercial or a movie preview; that is, they pass judgment on its interest and relevance within 30 seconds. This is the method we use initially in our communications with our clients. The use of graphics is essential in meaningful communications to inheritors. It lets them know where they stand and how they are doing relative to the rest of the world, and it shows progress toward their own articulated goals. The burden is on us to communicate to our clients in their chosen way rather than in a predetermined form that smacks of rigidity and demands conformity to understanding arithmetic formulas in a spreadsheet format. Nothing could be further from what people of wealth want or need.

One of our clients requested that we redesign and improve our quarterly statement, which was produced in only one format by our asset management software. He wanted a more straightforward, easy-to-understand format. He wanted to see comparisons to his own goals as set in our meetings each year. We dug in and produced the kind of customized statement he wanted. The client is extremely happy and understands his financial situation better now than ever before. It was a huge amount of work, but we built tremendous trust and loyalty by taking the time to give him exactly what he wanted. The project was very successful, and we eventually found a new client asset software package that can produce statements quite similar to our final design. The client really did us a favor by asking for more—everybody won!

Keeping Up

Since the available technology changes so rapidly, this book does not recommend particular computers or software. The best programs and equipment available are needed to provide efficient and effective client service. It is very important for someone in the advisor's office to keep current on state-of-the-art technology. Tracking tasks is essential to deliver well-rounded and professional trust service. What a difference it makes to trust beneficiaries who have paid for years, sometimes decades, and rarely received much back in return from their current trustees.

It is useful to occasionally share with clients what has been done to upgrade, expand, and maintain the office technology. Clients notice little mistakes. We know that one small problem on the surface usually points to a larger problem underneath. We try from the very start to deal with the little problems so that simultaneous progress is made on the underlying issues. Keeping current on the best way to communicate with the client can be challenging. We try to use each mistake or missed opportunity to communicate as a way to better understand a client's personality, and we provide as much in-depth research as the client wants on any financial matter that interests them, no matter how far afield from their portfolio under management.

One way that we add value for our clients is by trying to keep their financial life simple. We try to follow up on things that our clients may have let slip because it's too easy for them to procrastinate on financial decisions. Trust technology tells us on a real-time basis if the methods of our organization, our commitment to follow up, and the ability to communicate well with our clients are actually working. If not, the system needs to tell us what has broken down.

The actual software that we use in our business—financial planning, asset allocation security research, trading—changes at least annually, if not quarterly. If more than a year goes by without an upgrade, something is not working. We have to remember that the client is not interested in the technical aspects of what we do. They want to know how events affect their situation and if they're meeting their goals. It makes sense that if an advisor invests in an in-house technical analyst or systems administrator, he stands a better chance of taking care of his clients.

This is a personalized, high-tech approach where the SIP—not the client—is required to use technology. If a trust beneficiary wants to get on board technologically, we have methods available that allow her to key into our system, pull up her reports, look at her track records, news, and strategy, and track our progress on the various projects regarding her financial affairs. If inheritors prefer to have a personal phone call summarizing everything for them once a quarter, the technology is invisible to them but essential to the advisor.

Moving On

In the future, we feel that more and more technical aspects of our jobs will be done through using some kind of software-hardware combination. There is nothing mysterious about estate planning, asset allocation, investment vehicle evaluation, or tax analysis. Many people, including trust officers, stockbrokers, and insurance agents, have seen their jobs transformed by technology. We think that the pace of these kinds of changes will accelerate and that technicians in the service industry are moving to the bottom of the food chain. Our point here is that financial professionals who want a long-term commitment from their clients, and for clients who are looking for someone worthy of trust, a willingness to adopt new technology is one of the hallmarks of success.

If you are an investment professional, how can you evaluate the use of technology in your practice? First, ask yourself what new programs, software, telecommunications, and research advances have been made over the last year. Then look at what you have done in terms of changing the quality of communications with your clients, gathering useful research providers, or handling information internally to realize greater efficiencies. Many new products can help you accomplish these goals. Are there some you should be using but don't? What is keeping you from making the change? Money? Time? Internal resistance?

The seasoned investment professional must constantly be upgrading her firm's technological capabilities in order to free up personal time. The most valuable asset of the business is the SIP's time. Trust technology is a focused means of accomplishing this. We will be talking about other ways to help the SIP personally connect with trust clients, but we know that the contact will never be made by a computer. Client contact can be made only by someone capable of taking information from an accessible, comprehensive computer system. This will allow the SIP to know enough about the client's personal situation to meet the client's immediate needs while reviewing the larger picture of trust at each contact.

Occasionally, we know that we have to stretch the client's mind and our own in order to gain new perspectives on a given situation. There is too much information available and not enough wisdom. Inheritors are looking to advisors for personal connection and the ability to make judgments based on a sense of history, using all the information that is available. Advisors are paid well to uncover the underlying personal viewpoints that go into making decisions and to put every detail and task into the context of the client's whole financial picture.

We're well aware that the financial world is changing due to consumers' direct access to financial information on the Internet or by other means. We feel this is a positive development, but we know that few people are able to keep up with current developments, even in their chosen field of interest. Because there are so many choices, we must know what avenues are most appropriate for them.

A money counselor who recently spoke to a group of investment advisors pointed to his own experience in stating that the most important factor for good, long-term relationships is to tailor your communication style to a client's particular needs. Clients need to be brought into the office and shown what technology is available. They may decide not to use a high-tech approach themselves, but they want to know that it is available. Trust beneficiaries are presented with so many choices in the area of finance that it is a blessing to have someone on the other side, willing to scale down or scale up the technological component to meet their personal needs. SIPs need to be able to translate the language of personal finances into an enjoyable experience in a manner that is appropriate.

Promoting Understanding

At the end of the day, trust clients want access to data, information, and knowledge in a way that they find comfortable. If it can't be summed up on one page, it probably isn't useful. The modern mind's ability to retain specific information seems to have diminished as the amount of information reaching it has increased.

Everyone's lives are fuller and more multifaceted with family, business, charities, home, hobby, exercise, sports, recreation, entertainment, travel, news, and politics. The missing ingredient is quiet time for reflection. The advisor's technological mission is to present timely and appropriate facts in a way that provides easy-to-understand options and promotes two-way communication. This is one goal of the trust services field. The seasoned independent professional must be able to consolidate data and communicate information quickly with appropriate, knowledgeable commentary, giving guidance peppered with at least some understanding. Timeliness is as important as accuracy. Events transpire rapidly in the client's life, and the interest level of clients is varied. Technology can provide an appropriate and consistent method to report on the delivery of service and results.

Conclusion

Trust technology will help advisors respond to demands for rapid responses in diverse areas. In the near future, the ability to integrate information from different financial professions will become a central part of serving high-net-worth individuals. As a class, persons with inherited money have unusual needs in terms of reports and methods of communication with their advisors. Technology will never replace face-to-face contact. Remember, most financial decisions are made by the heart and not the mind, based on nonobjective information. The trust advisor needs to know what the facts are and to understand the difference between objective fact and subjective interpretation of data. This is why computers will never take the place of interpersonal communication. It also explains why financial plans and investment strategies based solely on computer programs turn out to be inadequate. The human touch is needed. Investment advisors have to use technology to capture the detailed richness of people's lives and then translate the underlying motives into flexible strategies.

The New Paradigm: Building Trust

This chapter is written primarily for use by financial professionals, but if you are looking for a trusted advisor, you might glance through these pages to see what criteria, skills, and qualities are desirable in an advisor. This chapter may stimulate thoughts about questions to ask a potential advisor. Remember, as an inheritor, choosing an advisor and deciding whether to stay with that person are two of the most important decisions you'll make in your financial life.

As financial professionals, we cannot claim to have all the answers because it just isn't possible to know everything. What is important is intent. If our intent is to be the best that we can possibly be, to live up to the highest standards, and to deliver on the promises we make to our clients, then we have begun our shift. If people come to us and say, "This is my financial life; I need your help," it's our job to give them the breadth of service they need. It's also our job to have the depth of staff and the organization to deliver on our promises.

One major change in the way the financial world works is the movement from sales to service. Now, it is a movement from service to building equity. Equity is about shared goals and about building trust. Before we can do that, let's explore some related paradigm shifts that are taking place in the financial world.

From Money Management to Trust Services

In the money management business, those with long experience in the field know that investors who hire mutual fund companies based on who appears in the *Wall Street Journal* or on television talk programs will not be able to sustain their investment programs through long bear markets. Money managers and people of wealth who take the time to talk to each other directly, who have established a personal rapport, have taken a huge step forward toward building trust and financial security. Increasing the kinds and quality of service offered to clients is another step we'll discuss in this chapter. If you are an investment professional, you need to:

- Build an organized system to track all clients and activities—beyond merely portfolio tracking or cash flow analysis.

- Listen and communicate with the client about all important aspects of his or her financial life, not just those under your management.

- Understand exactly what clients want for themselves, their children, their parents, and their community.

- Build and work with a team of professionals who are already in place.

- Follow up on all aspects of each team member's progress, not just your own.

- Do the right thing for the client, especially when it costs money out of your own pocket.

From the Specialized to the Comprehensive

Money managers, insurance agents, stockbrokers, lawyers, and accountants who desire to be in the trust field all have one thing in common: a specialized background. *Specialization* is the dedication of time and interest to developing mastery in one field. It's as important today as in the past to become a master in one field, but it is far from adequate to be just a competent specialist. All the book learning in the world doesn't help when it comes to real-world applications. There are many Chartered Financial Analysts who have no direct experience in investing other people's money. There are people with Certified Financial Planning degrees who don't have a knowledge of family dynamics. Specialization is necessary, but it is not enough. Some of the most complex estate plans are the result of the efforts of insurance agents who have in mind the sale of life insurance trusts as the best way to maintain large estates. On close examination, life insurance trusts sometimes work and other times they don't. Using a prepackaged approach eventually gets the specialist cornered in a narrow market.

For example, an insurance agent in a small town, who wants to take on clients in a trust capacity, may want to consider pursuing a more comprehensive approach. If the insurance companies she represents do not offer other services such as tax analysis, investment management, retirement planning, and the like, the insurance agent needs to arrange for them herself. Similarly, the tax person or lawyer who wants to be in the financial services business has to create a situation whereby he can deliver money management and financial consulting service in a top-quality fashion to clients. The quality and remunerative potential of long-term relationships depends on a comprehensive approach.

From Commission to Hourly to Equity

Financial professionals are interested in the trust business for the same reason that brokers are becoming investment advisors: Working for hourly wages or on commission is not a viable model for the future for the entrepreneurial advisor. There is too much information, too much anxiety in the world of transactions for commissions, for both sides to feel that they are getting their money's worth. Some attorney-client relationships will continue on an hourly basis. Even for people earning over a million dollars, this may not be satisfactory because of the inherent conflict between pay and performance. Salespeople need to sell to eat, and hourly people must

---

A friend of mine is one of the most esteemed labor lawyers in Los Angeles. We sat on a fire escape at college and smoked cigars together 25 years ago. My friend went on to law school while I went to Europe on a painting fellowship and to buy art as investments for a New York financier. When he graduated from Harvard Law School, offers came from both the public and private sectors. He now stands at the pinnacle of his career, but he has to work unbelievably long hours and is under constant stress. Even with an astronomical salary, it is not a satisfactory situation for himself or his family. Billing at $500 an hour is still working on a treadmill.

log hours to drink. Likewise, there is no real, long-term building of trust for consultants and pure money managers. This is also true for hedge funds and mutual funds.

From Standing Alone to Strategic Alliances to Comprehensive Organization

The inheritor's and the advisor's joint goal is to build equity. Persons of wealth want to protect and increase their assets, and financial advisors deserve a small piece of the action. There is a partnership of interests here. Like all partnerships, it has its dangers. The resources and capacities of the trust service provider have to be wider and more comprehensive than those of specialists. If an advisor's personal equity rises and falls with that of her clients, her commitment will become personal as well as professional. How can a situation be created where a trusted advisor can be responsible for getting the whole job done without necessarily having to be a technician?

Clearly, one person cannot do the job. Every entrepreneur who sets out her shingle must have some great skills. This is not enough, and strategic alliances with other professionals may do it, but in the long run, we believe it will not. Building trust means building equity through having a trust-worthy organization.

Investment advisors are under pressure because mutual fund selection management has become a commodity, much like the sale of insurance. Mutual fund portfolio management services are available through broker-age firms, newsletters, software, and over the Internet. The same may also be true for portfolios constructed by using individual securities. No profession is immune from the cross-marketing efforts of other firms. Today's inheritors need to have their counselor be aware of the cross-fertilization from various areas of expertise. Advisors have to do more and do it better.

As a seasoned professional what is the hub of your company's service? Is it money management, which, like trustee work, involves a high degree of skill, with a massive investment of time up front and more moderate amounts of time to keep things rolling along? Building an appropriate portfolio for clients is not difficult, if you have a good technical background and an honest eye toward what makes money. But does this constitute the whole of your job? If so, you haven't made the transition to a comprehensive trust relationship.

If you are a broker, how much time does it take to sell a mutual fund or money manager service? You have proven the ability to talk and be interested in your client, so now what? Do you know about all of the client's assets? How can you gain confidence so that even if the product fails you are still involved? Insurance agents spend time learning about client's families, then finding a product or two to fit their needs. Not too bad if you stay in close touch, but what about all of the other things you know your client needs?

From Financial Quarterback to Coach

Inheritors, especially trust beneficiaries, need and want a one-stop financial coach. There are too many ways to get into trouble, and it isn't possible to pick the best advisors from many fields without much time-consuming research. Some clients have attorneys and accountants who are their trusted advisors. Often, they have become financial advisors and are told to take care of everything from investments to elder care arrangements. The coach is the person the client calls first with major financial questions. It's the person whose opinion they trust the most. There are now financial advisors who play an important psychological role in the client-family's life. These are the coaches who put players on the field and decide which play to run. Inheritors want to be comfortable with their first and most important decision, who is the coach. They want all services rolled up and delivered to them in a succinct way. When they tell one person something, why should it have to be repeated to others, wasting valuable time and creating more opportunities for errors in communication?

Someone has to step up and say, "I represent you, all of you," and that person becomes the coach. Many of us wish we could say things just once, and by relaying information to one person one time, everyone who needed to know that piece of information would automatically know it. That would be worth some real money. This is the overriding question in the transformation of the financial service industry into the trusted advisor business. Not only is a multifaceted approach necessary, but the client wants every financial decision to be integrated and implemented quickly. It's a big order; whoever can fill it is in a powerful position.

These issues are rarely articulated unless this underlying need is the specific item under discussion. People with inherited wealth go home and think, "there's just too much to do, I'm overwhelmed." The financial professional goes home and says, "How can I get all of this done in as little time as possible?" Trust can take care of details while keeping the big goal in mind. "Do I really have time to take care of these details?" These are the cracks through which trust falls.

The most important skill that money managers have is tenacity coupled with experience. Advisors and beneficiaries need to take the time to communicate properly. When both parties understand what they want, they are at least halfway there. Here are the keys to building a successful money management business into trust relationships with your clients.

From a Disinterested Party to a Congruent Soul

Trustworthiness is a characteristic of a person who will not let his clients down, who will deliver on every part of every promise made to a client. Trust is also the legal formation by which power is vested in someone other than the owner. The person who has this power has to carry through on promises made to the actual owner. Traditionally, trust documents were set up by attorneys to be ongoing entities. In a sense, they have a longer life than that of an individual. They can be multigenerational. They were to cross personality lines and ideological or political persuasions.

The person or entity to be trusted is called a *trustee*. This is an independent, qualified person with a multigenerational vision who looks beyond clients' immediate needs. As a financial planner, insurance agent, or tax or legal advisor, the trustee has to stand in the shoes of the original owner and the future owners. It is an inherently conflicted posture. Being a trusted advisor is a lot like being married. We go in with dreams and expectations and come out, hopefully, with compassion, humility, a sense of humor, and maybe a little wisdom.

The future personalities of our progeny are unknown. In the financial field, putting together trust documents, naming trustees, and specifying trusted investment vehicles are important, but all choices must be open-ended and flexible. This was not the case from 1920 to almost 1990. Trust busting can remedy those situations where there is not true concern on the part of the trustees for the all-around well-being of their charges.

Most inheritors realize that when someone says they know how to beat the market, it is best to walk away. When a salesperson touts the latest tax-avoidance scheme and it doesn't resonate with common sense, some wealthy people ignore it. Likewise, if an insurance agent delivers an old style guilt message, implying that he alone knows the best way to take care of a wealthy family's needs (without explaining the contingencies and uncertainties surrounding his assumptions); intelligent and experienced beneficiaries can instinctively pass on the proposals in a courteous way. Congruence means that your financial persona is understood and resonates with the basic outlook and advice of the trusted advisor.

From Win-Lose to Win-Win

The basic shift here is that the fortunes of the trusted advisor need to be tied to the fortunes of the inheritor. This is somewhat true already in the investment advisory field, but it can and should be more closely linked than it is presently. We call this a *sharing of risk capital.* There are many kinds of capital: money, time, and reputation. Winners in the trust field have a good reputation. Reputation is based on track record, which is based on performance. How reliable the advisor is has some connection to how long she has been in business. Performance comes from capability. Capability is a result of people devoting concern, attention, effort, and long-term commitment. Winning is the ability to help a client family with any financial situation that might come up in the future. It requires the advisor to be capable of mustering resources to answer questions that come up, not necessarily personally, but as an organization with resources in all areas of life. The investment professional must be capable of delivering answers in a format that can be easily assimilated and communicated to all family members.

The advisor's primary concern is financial security. If advisors can be sure their clients know what's going out, what's coming in, and how well things are going with their investments, then it is possible for them to have a sense of security. Without this basic, well-rounded knowledge, a client's life will be based on dreams, wishes, hopes, desires, and assumptions—all of which can cause a general malaise of anxiety from lack of knowledge. The job of the seasoned investment professional is to be there and be square with the client. It is not a question of doing away with uncertainty and misfortune, because these will always be factors. We can prepare a family to handle these events in the same way that we organize our own affairs. To know is to be secure. This is the winner's circle.

The seasoned investment professional realizes that she can offer more than most other professionals, and that she must do so in order to survive. It's an attitude: "I'll take care of it. I'm ready, capable, and available." "I'll do it and then tell you that I've done it."

We recently had a very expensive team-building professional visit us from Houston. He followed the same script used in big corporations, and it was somewhat effective in our small business. He told us what he was going to do, then stumbled briefly when he didn't meet the timeline that he originally committed to, but owned up to it right away. He didn't complain, argue, or worry about getting his fees. He was totally available when he was present. His follow-up stumbled again, but when I needed him, he was right there.

Now, this outside person really didn't do anything for me that I couldn't have done myself. If I wanted to take the time, I could have saved a large amount of money. Isn't this the same for any client? If they really enjoyed financial work and had the time, they could take care of their own financial affairs. Most people don't have the time, interest, inclination, energy, determination, perseverance, or desire to be their own financial managers. That's why they need an advisor. Like my own clients, I just wanted someone from the outside to come in and ease the burden. Although I had never set eyes on him before he arrived, I had signed a contract. After the day was over, I came away feeling happy, satisfied, and content. Now, when crises arise, I can bounce ideas off him and save myself the anxiety of feeling alone, wondering if I am doing something right or wrong. The results of the actions aren't as important as the process. In fact, practically nothing of lasting import came from his visit, other than the lessening of my anxiety.

The second point is that the team-building professional wasn't perfect. He did his best and was honest about everything—including his mistakes. People hire humans and trust humans, especially those who can admit their mistakes. I begin every day knowing that I'm going to make mistakes, and I try to allow for these eventualities. Nothing is accomplished without mistakes, and this is the hallmark of creativity. Mistakes made by artists generally produce the best results.

From Meeting Expectations to Exceeding Expectations

Personal financial services are about the delivery, gaining, building, getting, and keeping of trust. The objective is not just to do what is asked, but to exceed a client's expectations. How do we go about doing this? First, we try asking the right questions, listening, going the extra mile, and then asking more questions. We consider ourselves to be trusted members of people's families. We have a duty to safeguard their assets, to make them grow, to ensure that they are not getting ripped off.

When we accomplish these goals for our clients, we come away at the end of the day feeling tired but good. It is a self-motivating business. When we get up in the morning, we have to feel inspired to do good work. Our clients give that feeling back to us in various ways.

One way in which we are rewarded is with money. Our compensation is limited by the number and type of people that we serve. We strive to match the level of our service and expertise with the needs of our clients. Sometimes they don't match. When we give too much service to a client with too small an asset base, we lose money. That's okay, because we also have high-net-worth clients to whom we sometimes give an enormous amount of service, while at other times the best approach is to let assets and relationships ride. During those more relaxed times, we renew, refresh, and reinvigorate ourselves, using the opportunity to give back to our community and do a great job for clients with smaller assets, who perhaps need us even more than the high-net-worth clientele.

Referrals

The best type of business comes from personal referrals. Referrals come from jobs well done. Our clients know and appreciate our solid base of operations, and they communicate that to their friends. We never ask for referrals, though this is what is taught at marketing seminars. We feel that by proving ourselves through our actions, our clients will have a chance to say, "My advisor did a good job for me." How many of us have found car mechanics like that? Do we go to a garage based on Yellow Page ads, radio advertisements, newspaper flyers, and discounts, or is it because a person who has a similar car recommended the place? If the price is fair, that's where we take our trusted car.

People have a satisfied feeling when they know they can call us for any reason—or their kids can call us, or their grandkids can call us—and we will be there, ready to help. We're not impatient to get back to our portfolio management research; we're not out trying to drum up new business. "I care; I can take care of it; I'll call you back" is the attitude that we promote in our business. This attitude is not that common in the modern world.

Situations have wider implications than what appears at first. Every contact with a client, every envelope that goes out to them, everything that comes up has a broad impact. Our job is to recognize it, anticipate its effects, and then do something about it. We want to let our clients know what we've done has been done in a special way. This leaves them feeling reassured and confident.

Conclusion

How can one price such a service? It really isn't possible to put a dollar amount on it. Our equity is built as our clients come and stay with us for years. When we get referrals who are looking for short-term performance, we send them on their way to one of our hungrier colleagues. Investment performance must be there, but it isn't the most important aspect of our best relationships. Our services involve a great deal of time and energy. When markets turn down, service, not performance, will be more important in keeping people from changing course in midstream, which is the most common of all investment mistakes. With the passage of time, the value of what we do becomes more and more apparent to our long-term clients.

What's Compassion Got to Do with It?

As investment professionals, it is necessary to have both a competitive and a compassionate side to our efforts. In order to be appropriately competitive, we must be compassionate. We know that large, sophisticated, and highly trained trustworthy consulting/accounting firms are getting into the financial advisory business. We know these firms will want to have their arms completely around their client's financial affairs. These are also our goals as SIPs and trusted advisors.

We have to prepare for battle with the megafirms. The criteria on which we will be judged is how much genuine compassion we bring to the situation. Can an employee of a major multinational organization deliver a level of personal compassion comparable to that of a seasoned independent professional? All other things being equal, wealthy people, especially those with inherited wealth, are now looking for advisors with empathy, values, knowledge, reputation, longevity, peer groups, and convenient location.

Let's look at our own level of integrity as investment professionals. How can we deepen and develop our approach, so that we bring our own genuine experiences to the table when we sit down face-to-face with clients? We want to relate what we plan to do for them, and this comes from how we live our own financial lives. How we can help them depends on our own circumspection. Clients need to know that we have thought deeply about every issue on which we purport to advise them. We begin with an assumption that we can be honest about ourselves—admitting that we have made mistakes, many of them, and talking freely and unashamedly about our shortcomings. The lessons we teach come from our hard-earned forays into money matters. We have to be forthright about the degree of our ambition for both fame and wealth. These are difficult but necessary discussions for our sense of integrity.

> The subject of real estate as an alternate investment frequently comes up. The pros and cons are never cut-and-dried, and personal factors always play the most important role. I lost the protection of a vacant lot near my home because I tried to save on commissions by cutting out a politically connected real estate broker. It was shortsighted and miserly, and now I have an unpleasant neighbor to deal with. As a friend said to me, "Lousy neighbors are one of life's truly great curses!" There is a lesson in this for my clients. We have seen clients lose more money, sleep, and precious mental energy by getting too involved with real estate.

Daily, financial advisors have to make decisions about taking on certain kinds of clients and about making employee remuneration fair and relative to responsibilities, effort, tenure, and loyalty. Trusted advisors can be in business out of a spirit of joy, obligation, or just to make money. When you sit down with clients and look them in the eye, what goes on in your mind is apparent. The way that you dress, the way that your office looks, the way that your employees deal with their job are all externalizations of your trustworthiness—the main ingredient of successful trust busting and building.

A woman came to our firm with stories about how she was horribly mistreated by her stockbroker. The portfolio was large and she desperately needed help, so we took her case and established relationships with her other important advisors. Soon afterward, she came up with a scheme to enter into a real estate venture in which her own creative urges and experimental psychodrama played a central role. Our client's home was already overpriced for her neighborhood and she planned to use half of her investment account, which was her only source of steady income, to add to her residence yet again. We pointed out the dangers and made extra efforts to bring her team together to dissuade her from proceeding. She telephoned me with angry accusations. I offered my resignation the next day, despite her pleas. In the end, she spent all of her investment account on the project and now is at her wits' end because she must either sell one of her two dream projects or severely curtail her lifestyle.

In this situation, we did our best, but perhaps we were doomed to failure from the start. Other advisors might have decided after the initial meeting not to take on the client, but I felt it was just another challenge. Because of my shortsightedness, my staff was subjected to pressure and stress, adversely affecting all of us for several days. When I find myself getting hot under the collar, I know I am off balance, and remembering this client helps me move out of that place of anger. When I sit with clients, I am not afraid of their anger, nor do I feel the need to react to it.

Great financial service communicators are rare. The ability to analyze stocks or create astute financial plans based on statistics is quite different than the ability to sense what's on a client's mind and in her heart. What is troubling our clients is a constant concern to us, and we know how to bring our own personal attributes to bear on those issues. We don't normally emphasize the strong emotional aspect of our financial services business. But we believe that this is where the client trust relationship begins and that ultimately it is the factor that determines how long it lasts.

We have a client named Bill who engaged a large accounting firm to prepare his privately owned company's financial statements in anticipation of going public. The national firm gradually interjected themselves in the business owner's estate plan, retirement planning, and employee benefit program. They want to take over his money management work as well. In our meetings with the accounting/consulting executives, they are professional and to the point, friendly and personable. They represent an attractive option because they have high credibility. The business owner, who wants to go public someday, feels he needs their credibility.

On the other hand, these out-of-town specialists do not know Bill's wife, his children, or his underlying values. On weekends or evenings, when Bill gets around to looking at his statements, the firm is not available. We rotate our company pager among senior staff to accommodate client needs. Our competition, especially large institutional firms, will never be able to match that kind of flexibility, directness, and emotional connection.

Whether or not a client decides to go with a particular advisor depends on how well the advisor and his firm seem to fit the client's needs. Once

SIPs have an adequate track record, the organization, and service offerings that fit the client's needs, how do they entice the client to choose them over the hordes of other financial advisors out there? The already crowded field is getting ever more competitive. *Compassion* is the rare offering that allows an SIP to stand out without even trying!

There are an estimated 13,000 fee-based investment advisory firms in the United States. If one figures that each firm has three advisors, there are 39,000 advisors. The assets they have under management have grown over 35% during each of the past five years. There are also an estimated 4,000 financial planning firms. All financial service providers have converged on the concept of gathering assets and using fee-based remuneration on a retainer basis. Everyone wants to provide comprehensive service so that they are number one in the consumer's eyes.

Turning Competition into Compassion

How one manifests competitive urges is an internal issue. How do we as advisors sense the nature of our competitive urges? How do we interact with other people in the field? I recently met an insurance salesman/stock-broker turned investment advisor. It was at a luncheon on socially responsible investing, a topic he ostensibly writes about in the local newspaper. His articles are canned, however—provided to him by his broker-dealer network, which uses this type of investing as a marketing ploy to get green-leaning baby boomers to invest their assets in the network's mutual funds. I immediately challenged this person, saying there is no such thing as a "clean corporation," just to see his response. Rather than engage me, he walked away to schmooze with a prospective referral. How is it possible to alert the public to the difference between what we as advisors with two decades of experience in the socially responsible investing field do and what this much more suave and convincing man is doing down the street? How do we let inheritors know that we mean what we say and we say what we mean, especially when it contradicts the hype in the media? The buzzwords are all the same: diversification, cost efficiency, alpha, beta, risk, return . . . The key to winning is, for me, to exhibit genuine compassion to my clients. We don't need to worry about rubbing out the competition down the street, although I may sometimes want to. In truth, it doesn't really matter if there are other providers of financial services in my area, offering what appears to be exactly the same service. What we offer is totally different than anyone else's approach because we are different people from another advisor, appropriate for different persons of wealth and their families.

We ask our prospective clients to share with us their fears and concerns, their dreams and nightmares regarding family issues of money and financial security. It is an opportunity for us to share our views on how to integrate the field of investments and financial security into our lives. We teach by example; we learn by watching what people do, not what they say.

In every city, there are more persons of wealth than there are trusted service providers. We talked in previous chapters about the size of the trust and inherited wealth market and how new wealth is being created through entrepreneurial activity. Although the number of people who can trust a professional with their financial affairs may not be huge, clearly, many people with wealth would benefit from having a trusted financial advisor, both from psychological and investment return points of view. The time, energy, effort, and technical knowledge needed are beyond most people. Few people benefit by preparing their own taxes or drafting their own living trust.

We know that the commitment to a client's goals begins with the first meeting. When clients sense that we want to help, that their interests always come first, that we are oriented in the conduct of our life to sharing with them, then a bond of trust can begin to be established. This is the heart of the matter. In the investment management, financial planning and consulting, and mutual fund selection business, it is the structure upon which one-stop financial service delivery can be built. Two types of compassion need to be developed: personal and business.

Personal Compassion

How do we develop personal compassion? This is not a book about personal growth, but if you are a financial advisor, it is important to discuss and consider (for yourself and your staff) where and how to best develop your internal capacities. There are many excellent programs for executives and salespeople in the financial services industries. All of the self-realization or interpersonal communication methodologies have some basic similarities.

Let's look at some of them. First, there is a willingness to take time to know what you are feeling and to try to honestly articulate it in front of another person, no matter how scary that might seem. Then there is the development of the ability to frame your communication in a way that establishes clear ownership of the issues involved. Requesting confirmation that your message was received exactly as sent is important, as is establishing your personal boundaries in terms of family time, work time, and time for self. All of these tools are necessary to establish a happy, healthy, and balanced life. Having a firmly grounded sense of who we are enables us to help our clients. The client is working on developing these parts of his own personality (sometimes called *self-actualization*). Can we bring the necessary ingredients to bear on our client's situation? Can we balance our financial needs and goals, fear and greed, and bring this to bear on our client's issues? Our years of experience in the financial industry confirm that connecting to clients by relying on these internal resources provides the most satisfying and successful relationships. If you really care about the client, caring for yourself will follow. How do we accomplish this?

Compassion and Empathy

We translate compassion into action when we ask our clients what they want and how they feel, and by listening attentively to their responses. We then prepare actions based on their answers, not on what we think they need. This is not easy to do. We must ask questions on a person-to-person basis. We must treat client views as we would the best Wall Street opinions, not on a condescending "I know the answer, you haven't got a clue" basis. It is very difficult to really listen to other people with compassion in one's heart. I do this by trying to transport myself into the day-to-day world of the person speaking. Where did they come to our office from, where will they go after our meeting is over? I make decisions for my clients as if I walk in their shoes. To do this, I must imagine the pressures on them. What do I dare ask them about how they feel on various levels? Can I respond with my feelings, doubts, and worries? Can my organization take action in a way that addresses their concerns? It is not the outcome but the intent that makes the difference.

Often, people do not know what they need or cannot say what they want. They may be fearful of looking stupid. One simple question can dredge up years of money-related emotional baggage. Clients may just be too busy to have time to think through the consequences of their financial actions. If we help them formulate the right questions to ask, in a context that makes sense to them, then they can connect to us confidently.

We have to respect our clients and treat them as if they were members of our own family. This doesn't normally happen, because we can focus on only one part of the financial picture at a time. In serving high-net-worth individuals who have trusts at banks, we find they have much in common. There may be anger because an ancestor has delegated family responsibilities to an institution. A certain kind of low self-image is fueled by the way banks communicate with heirs. There's often a low level of personal belief in effecting change and regaining control, a result of obscure legal language.

It is easy to ask probing questions of clients and then to ignore the answers. Listening without taking each story into one's own heart is a habit we humans have, occupying ourselves instead in mentally preparing what to do about the situation, as opposed to just taking it in. All of us would like to be taken care of in some ways. It's our job to help as many people as possible. We have to provide service with an understanding that attentive listening and putting the client's needs above our personal goals are aspects of developing compassion.

When two human beings meet together to face the reality of the world of money, how do we best deal with the vast uncertainties? Our feeling is that we bring forward humility and humor. Our investment strategy is based on research, discipline, patience, openness, and a willingness to change strategies should the need arise. Ego must be honed down. We try to forget about ourselves when we're with our clients.

Client anxieties and concerns usually build up to a certain level. When clients encounter us as calm, clear, and understanding of their situation, they relax and open up. What we do is help them appreciate the wonderful things that they have in this particular moment. If they can do that even for a minute, then the feelings of ease, relaxation, and freedom from anxiety are seen not as a fixed goal to be reached only by one path, but as a mutual interdependence that exists here and now. It is a spiritual thing, although we don't refer to it as such. We believe this is the essence of a trusted advisor. Compassion is insight or empathy in action. We think of it as the ability to manifest and tap into the powerful forces that created us and will take us away as well. Being in touch with these forces and choosing to communicate our own experience of them determines the kind of trust clientele we can build.

Values

One of the first elements of establishing clear values is to acknowledge the truth of where we are at the present moment. Bringing the realm of personality development and communication skills into the financial service process is essential.

What can we do to solidify our compassion into a set of communicable and measurable values in a direct way? Taking time for oneself is important. This is often the first casualty of busy, hectic schedules, especially for hardworking type A advisors. Relaxation and meditation techniques are easily learned and can be practiced in 20 minutes per day. I always start my day with a quiet, sitting, focused meditation period. My mind may wander aimlessly during meditation, but without it, the stress of a normal day would get to me much more than it does.

There are other ways to take time for oneself: walking or lying down with a conscious effort to be aware of our breathing, in and out, in a pure and simple way. I find that painting landscapes or drawing the human figure is not only fun, but helps my ability to relate to my clients' needs. The perspective gained from art or music or helping those less fortunate than ourselves helps us approach just about everything with a better sense of humor.

We all need to have our own form of relaxation and communion with powers greater than ourselves: being in nature, going to church, playing sports, relating to our spouses, or walking the dog. We, as advisors have a strong need to reflect, to renew and refresh ourselves; and putting a high value on these activities is an important element of developing compassion. It is difficult but necessary to take this time. This is the primary focus of one of the country's leading management consultants to the financial services industry.

How can we develop compassion for ourselves that allows us to take this quiet time for internal nurturing? One way is keep this old admonition in mind: "No one ever lay on their death bed and wished he had spent more time at the office!"

We can look to our individual cultural backgrounds to find some form of reflective practice. Every tradition in every country has one. Making this commitment to psychic health, we reestablish the harmonious relationship between different aspects of our lives. We gain distance from the normal swirl of thoughts and emotions about obtaining more security for ourselves, more success for our firm, and so on. We remember that the sound of a bird, the sight of leaves fluttering in the breeze against a blue sky on an autumn day, the pungent smell of fires burning in the clear, cold air of winter are all direct expressions of the unity and beauty of life just as it is right now, lacking nothing. I remember that people all over the world share my wishes for decent food, shelter, clothing, and family life. These commonalities supersede all differences. The desire for challenge, advancement, entertainment, travel, interaction with other people, self-expression through art, music, drama, or just sitting and relaxing motivates not only myself, but also my peers, my employees, my competitors, and most definitely our clients. For me to succeed, my clients must succeed, without the pressures of acquiring more assets out of greed or insecurity or because they fear loss of lifestyle.

If this kind of discussion seems out of place in a book about managing family trusts, we beg to disagree. We must be in touch with these aspects of ourselves on a regular basis in order to be healthy. We must be healthy in order to deliver a complete and responsive service to inheritors. Inheritors, by and large, see this as the point of taking control of their inherited wealth.

What place does competition have in this model? Various levels of our personalities are operating at all times. The reptilian part of human nature is always looking for safety and security. It perceives competitors as threatening and wants to wipe them out or to flee from them. This is healthy in the proper context; it is the survival, fight or flight, mode. Investment professionals need to develop the ability to stop regretting accounts that don't come their way, to avoid berating themselves for clients who leave because they found someone else with whom they communicate better, and to cease being so hard on themselves for choosing an occasional fund or company that turns out to be an underperformer. This is about forgiving ourselves, whatever the reason.

In terms of financial success, we must own up to our desires and the attendant insecurities and fears about not obtaining them. When we examine our own family histories about how money was treated, how it may have been used as a control button, and how it may have become a measure of our self-worth, then we take a real step toward understanding and assisting our clients to resolve their underlying issues. *These* obstacles, not declining markets, stand in the way of financial security. How many of our clients really are enjoying the financial security that they already have?

The compatibility of values between a financial advisor and her clients determines the strength of the trust bond, and this determines the duration of the relationship. Integrity, intimacy with each other, honesty, compatibility of lifestyle, and communication are the elements that bind the SIP to her clients.

Business Integrity

What are the business aspects of compassion? What can we do in our business specifically to better serve our trust clients? One of the first points that I try to make with all new clients is that I am not any smarter than they are. In fact, in many cases, they have more technical expertise in some area of the business than I do. Without a doubt, if most clients chose to take the time, they could become proficient enough in the investment area to do an adequate job for themselves. I tell them that I do not have any special access to information. Some firms promote themselves as being on top of the next great deal, but that is not the financial advisory business—it is the transaction business.

While private deals, venture capitalists, and hedge funds can make large amounts of money (and lose it as well), this is not the main goal of long-term strategies that rely on diversified investing. Being in on the latest deal doesn't have much to do with building trust or ensuring a family's long-term financial future. The truth is that advisors don't know what the future holds, and they don't have access to special information. As human beings, we are doing our best with the knowledge we have at the time. That is all we can do. This is the homely message we send out, and it doesn't fit many prospective clients' desires. If clients want 15% to 20% growth per year, we send them on to someone else. By primarily emphasizing performance, whether of a particular fund or individual stock, or even of an entire firm's history, improper expectations are created. Returns are crucial, but unless they are presented with caveats and downplayed compared to the trust issue, the next extended bear market (and I'm talking about several years) will see an implosion of business and personal relationships that were established on the wrong basis.

Knowledge, Reputation

The establishment of trust and helping inheritors gain control of their family's wealth has to do with more than making money. Advisors have the knowledge that in good times, they should take the excess appreciation or the accumulated returns over historical norms and put them away for the eventual lean years. This means psychologically preparing clients for the downside years. No matter how difficult it is to bring this up in conversations, it is a necessary part of helping clients obtain financial security. There will be a time, perhaps an extended period of time, when money will be lost or will cease to grow.

We know that it takes more than a good track record to keep clients during downside markets. The way that we do this should set the tone for the rest of the relationship. Our firm compares the market indexes to our own investments, which is fine, but this is not nearly enough. We constantly reemphasize the overall picture—that the family's lifestyle is not going to be much impacted by cyclical market downturns. Our clients want to know that we are watching their accounts. We have a concrete way of expressing to them, over and over, that we know how events in the world are affecting their future.

The 1980s and 1990s have, by and large, been a period of wealth accumulation. We caution our clients, however, about the possibility of an equally long period of depreciation and the accompanying risk to their lifestyles. No market operates on a constantly upward trend. But overall, the general level of wealth is increasing worldwide. The advancements of technology and the increased motivation, productivity, and knowledge of so many people living on our planet is astounding.

By nature, I am an optimist. Investing is a good and necessary component of preparing for the long term, but I always want to prepare for the next disaster. Our job is to help prepare our clients for this future pain that inevitably must come. In the trust world, our reputation is built on solid preparation. Anticipating the worst is a necessary part of long-term estate planning. While we make plans to deal with future disasters, we want our trust beneficiaries to feel the power and joy and abundance that their current holdings represent.

Our reputation is formed by the kind of promises we make to our clients, either by outright statements or by omission of stating what could go wrong. We talk, as most advisors do, about historical time periods for stock returns and about our expectations for the future. Are we trying to convince clients to use our firm and to invest in stocks or higher-yielding bonds out of a need to prove ourselves, or is our advice intelligently based on what is necessary to meet their financial goals? Our goal is to deliver more than we promise. We try to keep financial expectations low and service expectations high, because we know we can deliver superb service.

When the market drops 50%, will there still be a need for investment professionals? When bank savings accounts look better, in terms of investment returns, than the most sophisticated and more expensive managed account, what kind of value do we bring to our clients' lives? I believe we can manifest the kind of compassion that will allow our clients to feel comfortable with the vagaries of the market and the crises of their financial lives. We try to be there for them in times of need, just as they are there for us and pay our fees during times of low investment returns. Inheritors are willing to share some of their wealth in order to be able to enjoy the bulk of it. When going on a trip to a strange place, people are willing to pay for a guided tour so they don't have to figure out where to eat, which car to rent, or what to see. The world of trusts and investments is a foreign country for most people with wealth. The complexity of the instruments, the plethora of information, the difficulty of pulling it all together—this is why our clients need us. We have been doing this since 1983 and still have most of our original clients. Our reputation is firmly established.

Like-Hearted Peers

There are alliances available to help us develop compassion. It takes interacting with experienced teachers, peers, and mentors. We have found peers in our field who have the same values and who connect with their clients in the same way. As a small firm, it is necessary to reach out. We cannot be everything to everyone, but our connection with our clients is helped by the assistance of other professionals, especially money counselors, accountants, and lawyers who share our internal values.

The optimum size of an organization that can deliver comprehensive, compassionate, and cohesive financial services is unknown. While the banking industry is consolidating, small organizations are teaming up through strategic alliances. The basis of these alliances is trust. No amount of paperwork can produce the spirit of cooperation that's necessary to get things done for clients in today's world. The best deals are created by a handshake, most likely a telephonic one, where both parties feel that their honor and lifestyles are enhanced. This leads to a commitment to follow through. There are bumps along the way, as in all alliances, and communication is sometimes difficult, as it is in any marriage. But our complex world demands many different skills, and so requires various alliances. For example, we have always thought of insurance agents as competitors and lawyers as allies. Neither statement is categorically true. Anyone can be an ally if their service is based on internal compassion. We find like-minded people in our communities by putting out feelers and by letting our compassion show. Personal contact is essential. We have a wonderful relationship with a financial planning firm in another city. Every so often, we get eyeball-to-eyeball, and it always serves to benefit our connection. As with our clients, we get to know one another better, and to understand each other's growth and change, when we occupy the same physical space on a regular basis. And as we reinvent our firm and let experience shape us, our investment philosophies adapt. Similarly, as our clients' family situations change, we need to see them in person. Our like-hearted peers and clients can live and work at great distances from us if we maintain these nurturing connections with occasional in-person visits.

Once systems for communication have been set up and enough time has been spent in person up front, how often do we need to see people to maintain empathy and compassion for their situations? It depends partially on people's preferred methods of communication and their comfort with phones, faxes, and e-mail. If we know emotionally what our clients and peers want, we can be there to help them at short notice. A relationship *can* be maintained over long distances, and perhaps even with long periods of no personal contact. The compassion we have toward our clients and peers is evident by who we bring in with us as part of our team. The issue is the level of connection. Our deep compassion and respect for other professionals lets us deliver excellent service. People need us, and we need them. In a world of mutual interdependence, it is important to articulate this connection, to acknowledge it, to honor it, and to manifest it every day, both in work and play.

CHAPTER

7

Trust Terminology

I f you're not an experienced cook, one of the most frustrating aspects of
trying to use a cookbook is not being familiar with the terminology or not
having the proper utensils. Likewise, if you're new to the trust business
or generally uncomfortable with technical jargon, the words themselves can
be intimidating because of strict legal interpretations or the meaning of particular phrases. Once you understand the basic building blocks, you can put
it all together and develop an adequate plan for retaining control of a trust.
Preparing an enjoyable meal doesn't mean you have to be a gourmet.

To provide trust beneficiaries and investment professionals with an adequate background in the language that is used in trust situations, the basic
concepts used in the trust field are divided into four sections:

1. The players

2. Types of trusts

3. Trust assets

4. Rules of the game

Within each section, the terms are arranged alphabetically. If you have a
question about the meaning of a term, this will allow you to quickly find its
definition. If you're already familiar with the technical aspects of trusts, you

may want to skip this chapter altogether. Newcomers and persons intimidated by trust bankers, lawyers, and business in general may wish to use this chapter as a primer to get acquainted with the general concepts of the trust world. Other readers may find that only some of these terms are of interest.

The Players

This section provides a description of the parties and controlling entities involved in trust situations.

Administrative trustee   The person responsible for paperwork and custody assets.

Beneficiary   Someone who has a right to enjoy the fruits of a trust situation. The beneficiary is the person for whom everything is ostensibly created.

Beneficiary under disability   *Disability* can be determined by a doctor's certification that a person is not able to make financial decisions for him/herself. A trustee can also make this kind of a judgment.

Conservator (guardian)   A person or entity appointed by a court to handle the business and/or personal affairs of a legally disabled individual.

Contingent beneficiary   A person who receives income or principal only after some event occurs, such as the death of a current beneficiary or on attaining a certain age.

Corporate fiduciary   A corporate fiduciary is a corporation that can act as a fiduciary. Formerly, this was typically a bank but now includes nonbanking organizations which have been set up specifically to act as the responsible parties in handling trust matters.

Cotrustee   When there is more than one trustee, each is called a *cotrustee.* The language of the trust may create circumstances where a cotrustee's power is subservient to another cotrustee's. Depending on the expertise and personality of the cotrustees, one or more cotrustees may assume a secondary role when it comes to making decisions.

Current beneficiary   A person who receives income at the present time, either automatically or at the trustee's discretion.

Descendant   A descendant is someone who can be traced either by bloodline or adoption to a person with either a present or contingent interest in the income or principal of a trust. It can also be otherwise defined in a particular document.

Executor or personal representative of the estate   These terms refer to a person or company named in a will as the responsible party, that is, the one who will act as a fiduciary in disposing of and taking care of all financial matters regarding the deceased person's financial assets according to a will.

Fiduciary   A *fiduciary* is someone who is responsible for acting for the benefit of another person. Fiduciaries are held to a higher standard of behavior than average businesspeople, and they are expected to put the interest of the beneficiary first.

Grantor   See definition of **Trustor** below.

Guardian ad litem   Party appointed by the court to represent the interests of a minor or incompetent person.

Guardian (natural)   A guardian is a fiduciary. A legal guardian can be appointed by a court when the natural guardian (i.e., the parent) is not around. Remember, the guardian of the person is different from the conservator of the estate. The guardian generally has responsibility for personal care, while the conservator has responsibility for financial decisions.

Heirs at law   Those who inherit assets of an estate in the absence of a written trust or will. This is the state's way of distributing assets for those who die intestate (i.e, without a will or trust).

Income beneficiary   A person entitled or chosen to receive trust income.

Investment trustee   A person or institution responsible for making investment decisions.

Issue   This terms means *children, grandchildren, and more distant progeny*. It can be further defined in a will or trust to include or exclude adopted persons.

Nominee   A person or firm who agrees, for convenience, to hold title to the assets of another party. The nominee is restricted to use that asset only for the benefit of the person who really owned it. A brokerage firm that holds stock for someone else and collects dividends is a good example of a nominee. The brokerage firm doesn't really own the stock, but holds it in the firm's *street name* for the real owner. In this way, dividends of the stock can be processed in bulk.

Operating and nonoperating foundations   These are two kinds of charitable organizations. Nonoperating foundations give money to other charitable organizations. Operating foundations are those involved in delivering services to the public.

Personal trustee A person or an institution whose sole responsibility is to make decisions regarding the distribution of assets to beneficiaries.

Per stirpes A formula for distributing assets to descendants of an ancestor.

Principal The assets (*corpus*) in the trust. This sometimes includes capital gains or any increase in intrinsic value, both realized and unrealized. Principal is the counterpart to income: Principal is the tree; income is the fruit.

Principal beneficiary The person who actually gets the *corpus*, or principal, of the trust. When either the trust is terminated or the beneficiary has reached a certain age or a certain event has occurred (graduation, marriage, etc.).

Private foundation A charitable organization created to distribute money contributed by an individual, family, group of people, or noncharitable organization (for example, a publicly traded company) to other charities. Foundations (private or public) are usually set up to obtain current income tax deductions and estate tax benefits as well as to control the timing and use of charitable contributions. There are greater limitations on the ability to obtain income tax benefits when money and appreciated assets are given to private foundation.

Public foundation A nonprofit charitable organization supported by contributions from the public (e.g., United Way).

Remainder person The same as a principal beneficiary. The remainder person (old term, *remainderman*) refers to the one who gets the remainder or actual assets after a predesignated time period or event.

Substitute trustee Well-drafted trusts include provision for a trustee who stands in line to take over for the first trustee if the asset owners are not happy. This is the *substitute trustee*. It also refers to a person or firm who takes over the trust if a bank resigns or is removed. In general, the substitute acts in the event of resignation, disability, death, or refusal to act.

Successor trustee A substitute trustee who takes over due to his/her designation in the trust document.

Trustee Someone who has the title or legal ownership to property. This does not mean the trustee has the right to enjoy the fruits of ownership. The trustee is the person or entity, as an *individual trustee*, or the corporation (as a *corporate trustee*) who acts as a fiduciary. The trustee is to act in a responsible fashion, with the interest of the beneficiaries at heart.

Trustee appointer A person named in a trust document who can appoint a successor or a substitute trustee.

Trustee remover A person who decides if unhappiness with a current trustee is justified and who can take action to remove the acting trustee.

Trustor Synonymous with *grantor, trust originator,* and *donor.* The trustor is the person who is giving up legal title to her assets to the trustee. The agreement between the trustor and trustee is called the *trust document.*

Types of Trusts

This section is an introduction to the different kinds of trusts.

Annuity An annuity is a stream of income and/or principal that comes out of a trust and for a predetermined time.

Asset protection trusts These trusts are set up to reduce exposure to lawsuits. Assets must be moved in well before any trouble starts, as it is considered fraudulent to anticipate creditors' (bill collectors') claims and to try to avoid them by using trusts.

Blind trusts Set up by public figures during their tenure as officeholders. The trustor has no say in what happens to the assets, so that no conflict of interest or influence peddling can be alleged, at least in regard to the assets in the trust!

Charitable lead trust A *charity* is a nonprofit organization set up to benefit the public domain. *Lead* means that some amount of money (usually a set amount of income) goes to charity for a certain period of time (the charity being first in line to get a benefit). After the designated period of time is over, the trust distributes any remaining assets to other designees.

Charitable remainder annuity trust (CRAT) This trust is for the benefit of a charity and also the grantor, or donor; i.e., the person who set up the trust. Annuities were explained above. Here, the annuity is a defined stream of income where the amount to be paid out to the person who set it up is constant. A 5% CRAT will distribute 5% of the original principal of the trust each year, whether it is earned through dividends and interest or not earned at all. If the value of the trust goes up or down due to appreciation or depreciation (bad stock market), the amount and timing of the payment to the donor is totally unaffected. Assets left in the trust at its ending date go to the charity.

Charitable remainder trust   This is the reverse of the lead trust. The charity gets the benefit of the trust, but only the remainder part. The *income* from a charitable remainder trust is paid to someone other than the charity, normally the person who set up the trust, or her children. The amount remaining after a set amount of time is paid over to the charity.

Charitable remainder unitrust (CRUT)   Charitable unitrusts pay out a fixed percent of the market value of the trusts assets on the first or last day of the year. The percentage is set when the trust is created, but as market conditions change, the actual amount of money distributed will vary. In order to qualify for favored tax treatment, charitable trusts must strictly comply with numerous requirements set forth in the Internal Revenue Code and federal tax regulations.

Charitable trusts   The four basic types of charitable trusts are charitable lead annuity trust, charitable lead unitrust, charitable remainder annuity trust, and charitable remainder unitrust (CLAT, CLUT, CRAT, and CRUT). Generally, in a *lead trust*, the charity gets income for a certain period of time, after which the trust assets are paid to a party that is not a charity. The reverse is true with *remainder trusts*. The income gets paid to someone other than a charity, normally the person who set up the trust, or his children, for a fixed number of years, and then the trust assets are paid over to a charity.

Credit shelter trust (CST)   This is sometimes called the *credit equivalent trust* and is established to save estate taxes by utilizing, to the greatest extent possible, the "unified credit" of both a husband and wife. The unified credit is a dollar-for-dollar credit that offsets the federal estate or gift tax that would otherwise be payable on property transferred to nonspouses. The amount of property protected from estate or gift tax by the unified credit is commonly called the *exemption amount* or *exemption equivalent*. The exemption amount for people dying or making lifetime gifts in 1999 is $650,000.00. This amount will increase to $1 million by 2006. Who knows what Congress (in its wisdom) will change it to in the future? A common estate plan is, when the first spouse dies, to put the exemption amount into a credit shelter trust for the benefit of the surviving spouse and/or others. The rest of the deceased spouse's property is left to the surviving spouse in a way that qualifies for the marital deduction, which shields it from estate tax. When the first spouse dies there will be no federal estate tax. Usually, the terms of the credit shelter trust allow the surviving spouse or others to use the money in the trust, if needed. When the surviving spouse dies, and this is the important part, the amount in the credit shelter trust is not taxed as part of his or her estate. This includes any appreciation of the assets in the trust. The surviving spouse's estate is taxed only on the amount by which the marital deduction property received on the first spouse's death, plus the amount of the other assets of the surviving spouse, exceeds the survivor's exemption amount. Note, if the first spouse to die had left all his or her money to the surviving spouse, his or her marital deduction would still have shielded that property from estate tax; however, the inheritors would only have the benefit of one unified credit amount, not two, which is why this type of planning is so popular. Note that this type of planning is useful if it is anticipated that when the surviving spouse passes away, his or her assets would exceed the exemption amount had no credit shelter trust been created on the first spouse's death. Moreover, this type of planning will not work if too many of a couple's assets are jointly held in a way that such assets pass to the survivor "outside" of the provisions of a will or trust.

Decedent's trust   This is the same as the credit shelter trust.

Dynasty trusts   Promoted by the abolishment in some states of the "rule against perpetuities," dynasty trusts are supposed to be able to last indefinitely, thus providing families with a longer-lasting trust and possible savings in estate taxes.

Education trusts   Trusts set up to benefit minors and young adults by providing funds for their education. These trusts are usually structured so that transfers of property to the trust are *annual exclusion gifts*. Annual exclusion gifts are exempt from gift tax because they qualify for the gift tax annual exclusion. Currently, the gift tax annual exclusion is $10,000 per donee per year ($20,000 per donee per year if a spouse consents to one-half of the gift being treated as having been made by the consenting spouse). One commonly used technique of qualifying transfers to a trust as annual exclusion gifts is to give the beneficiary the right (for a short period of time) to withdraw all the assets of the trust at age 21. If (as the grantor hopes) the beneficiary does not exercise his or her right to withdraw, such right expires and the trust can continue beyond the beneficiary's reaching age 21.

Family trust   A trust created for the benefit of multiple family members that is not intended to qualify for the estate or gift tax marital deduction. *Credit shelter trusts* are a type of family trust.

Generation-skipping trust   People can leave a certain amount of money to generations below their children without having two different estate taxes to pay. This is helpful because if all the money is left to the children, there is estate tax to be paid both at the death of the person setting up the trust (the grandparent) and another estate tax is paid when the parents die. The current maximum amount that can be put into this kind of trust is $1 million per donor, no matter how many heirs are named. Generation-skipping trusts are created for the benefit of persons two or more generations below the person creating the trust. Persons in such lower generations are called *skip persons*. Prior to the enactment of the generation-skipping tax, property in any amount could be transferred to skip persons in ways that avoided transferring property first to the closest lower generation and a second transfer from the first lower generation to the skip person. This avoided the possibility of estate or gift tax being paid on both transfers. Now, the generation-skipping tax effectively taxes gifts to skip persons in excess of $1 million per transferor. The tax collector treats overages as though the property gifted had first been transferred to the first-closest generation and then transferred by that generation to the second generation down, or skip person. The generation-skipping tax is the highest tax rate (55%)! So, estate planners now recommend putting the generation-skipping tax exemption amount into a separate trust.

Grantor retained annuity trust and grantor retained unitrust (GRAT)   These trusts pay either an annuity or unitrust interest to the grantor for a period of years. At the end of the annuity or unitrust period, the property is transferred (or kept in trust for the benefit of, and later transferred) to members of the immediate family of the grantor. Because the annuity or unitrust interest kept by the grantor has a recognized value (which varies depending on the annuity or unitrust period and the applicable interest rate), the value of the property transferred to such trusts, for gift tax purposes, is less than the fair market value of the property transferred. Provided the grantor survives the period of the retained interest, the tax law allows the value of the interest transferred to others to be removed from the grantor's estate at a reduced gift tax value. However, if the grantor dies before the annuity or unitrust interest expires, the tax benefits are lost. Like their charitable brothers and sisters, to qualify for beneficial tax treatment, these trusts must also strictly comply with numerous requirements set forth in the Internal Revenue Code and federal tax regulations.

Irrevocable trust   *Irrevocable* means that a trust can't be changed. The tax authorities allow a "freeze," or setting point, for the values of gifts/transfers made to irrevocable trust. Because people will not be able to change their minds, it means they have given up control of these assets. Once gift or estate tax is paid on the initially transferred amount, any growth that occurs later is not subject to gift, transfer tax, or estate tax. Another advantage of giving up control is protection of assets from lawsuits, called *protection from creditors*.

Life insurance trusts   Life insurance is put inside a trust so that if and when the insurance policy pays off, the insurance proceeds are not taxed, but pass free of estate taxes directly to a designated person. Life insurance trusts are irrevocable and are generally funded in the same way as are educational trusts—that is, with the dollar amount that can be given by a parent to child, a family member to another family member, or from a friend to another friend free of tax reporting requirements (i.e., $10,000 per person per year).

Living trust   Revocable or irrevocable trust set up during someone's lifetime. See **Revocable trusts** for further detail.

Marital trust   Sometimes called marital deduction trust, this is a trust set up for the sole benefit of a surviving spouse in a way that qualifies the assets for the estate or gift tax marital deduction. As is indicated in the discussion of the credit shelter trust, under certain circumstances, this type of trust can be very useful in avoiding estate taxes when a spouse dies.

NIMCRUT/NIMCRAT   Acronyms for *net income makeup* CRUTS and CRATS. If there is not enough income to make the annuity or unitrust payments, these trusts are allowed to make up the distributions in future years when there is adequate surplus to make up for the previous shortages.

Offshore trusts   Irrevocable trusts set up in foreign countries and with foreign trustees. These trusts are most often created by people who are in high-risk businesses (businesses having a high potential for lawsuits that could result in large judgments against the owner—for example, doctors and lawyers) to protect their assets from their creditors who might obtain judgments against the grantor after the trusts are created. The law is still evolving in this area, so anyone thinking about setting up one of these trusts needs to understand that experienced experts should be consulted when creating them; such trusts are not absolute protection against creditors; and there are risks in putting assets in foreign countries and in the hands of foreign trustees.

Qualified personal residence trust (QPRT)   A trust in which personal residence is placed, for estate planning purposes, in order to be transferred to the trustee and then later to the heirs at a reduced value for gift and estate tax purposes. These generally last at least 10 years, and in order to work, the original owner must remain alive for the full length of the trust. Only primary and secondary homes are allowed in QPRTs.

Qualified terminable interest property (QTIP) trust   Property in trust where the income is set aside for the use of a second (or later) spouse, but eventually reverts back to the children of a first or previous marriage.

Rabbi trusts   A kind of retirement plan that takes the place of salary that is not subject to current income taxation. They are set up by religious institutions to benefit clergy.

Revocable trusts   These are set up during a person's lifetime and their terms can be changed at any time. The trustee and designated beneficiary are usually the people who set up the trust during their lifetime. There are no tax benefits to setting up a revocable trust. Assets titled in the trust's name do not have to go through the probate process upon the death of the grantor.

Special (supplemental) needs trusts   Trusts created to supplement government benefits (Medicaid, SSI) without disqualifying the beneficiary from receiving or continuing to receive such benefits.

Trust Assets

This section defines different kinds of trust income, expenses, and taxes.

Accrual and adjustments of income   *Accrual* means keeping track of what is due to come in but has not yet been received. An *adjustment of income* means a change in the calculation of income to be distributed from a trust.

Accumulation as additions to principal (undistributed income)   This formidable phrase refers to the decision on the part of the trustee *not* to distribute all the income that has been generated by a trust. If the trust's perceived obligation is to not give beneficiaries the maximum amount possible, the trustee can add that undistributed sum to the principal corpus, or ongoing body, of the account. When this happens, income loses its character and becomes part of principal.

Annual (gift) exclusion   The amount per year that any one person can give to an unlimited number of other people free of transfer or gift tax.

Capital and surplus requirements   The total amount of assets required for a bank or independent corporate trustee to qualify to act as a trustee. These clauses are generally left out of modern trusts because there is essentially no difference between the safety factor and amounts of insurance carried by all corporate trustees today. Even when commercial (loan-making and deposit-taking) banks fail, no trust assets are lost, because trust assets are never comingled with bank assets.

Capital gains   Term used to describe the change in value due to appreciation or growth in the marketplace.

Computation of trustee fees   Trust service organizations must provide regular schedules of fees to all persons who have an ownership interest in the account, whether they are income or principal beneficiaries or whether they have a current or future interest. Fees can change at the trustee's discretion and can be a major source of abuse by trustees. Some states' laws govern trustee fees.

Discretionary distributions   Trustees often have wide latitude when it comes to distributing money to a beneficiary. Some trust documents include guidelines for making payments that support the living style to which the beneficiary has grown accustomed. Many subjective judgments come into play regarding discretionary distributions.

Distribution of tangible personal property   This refers to the distribution of personal property other than securities. Personal property is not usually of particularly large monetary value, but may be important from an emotional point of view.

Diversification   This refers to the tenets of modern portfolio theory and asset management procedures whereby assets are distributed among diverse markets to achieve an ample spread of risk within and between asset classes. For example, a stock portfolio of $1 million is undiversified if it is made up of only four companies. A diversified portfolio might include large U.S. companies, small U.S. companies, international companies, and some bonds.

Estate tax   In some states called *inheritance tax*, this tax is levied on the transfer of property resulting from a person's death. In both the federal and state estate tax systems, there is an amount that is exempt from the imposition of the estate tax, often referred to as the *exempt amount*.

Taking into account the exempt amount, the federal estate tax rate starts at 37% and goes as high as 55%.

Expenses This refers to charges against income or against the principal itself. Rules regarding allowable expenses are spelled out in the trust itself and/or by state laws.

Extraordinary fees This is a very loose term, subject to wide interpretation. What constitutes "extraordinary" should be negotiated ahead of time by trust originators and the eventual beneficiaries. When challenged about past performance, trustees can threaten to charge the trust for their extra time in defending themselves as trustee. These fees can be challenged.

Fee calculations These can be done in one of two ways. An annual percentage can be taken based on the total value of the trust assets. This runs from 0.002% up to 2% per year. You can calculate this by taking quarterly fees charged, multiplying by 4, then dividing by the value of the trust. This is an interesting exercise because it usually surprises people to see how high their fees can be if the originator did not hold the bank to a fixed fee. Another type of fee is called an *income fee*, collected by the trustee as income accrues to the trust. Income fees generally apply to oil and mineral interest and to some real estate properties.

Flower bonds These are U.S. government bonds that can be redeemed at face value if they are held by someone at the time of his or her death. These bonds were purchased specifically to pay estate taxes, but they are no longer being issued.

Gift tax This is a tax levied upon transfers by gift during a person's life. A person's gift of property to another individual of up to $10,000 per year (*annual exclusion amount*) is not subject to gift tax. A person can make such tax-free gifts annually to as many different people as he or she chooses. Gifts of property to any individual in excess of $10,000 per year are subject to gift tax. When an individual has made lifetime gifts in excess of the exemption amount, gift tax must be paid. The exemption amount for gift tax purposes is the same as the estate tax exemption amount. The gift tax rate is the same as the estate tax rate (37% to 55%). The federal gift and estate tax systems are said to be "unified' because a person's lifetime and death transfers are aggregated before the gift or estate tax is imposed, and the same tax rates and exemption amounts are applicable in computing the tax. As previously indicated, lifetime gifts remove the postgift appreciation of the property from one's estate and control. A second benefit is that any gift tax paid is also removed from the estate if the person making the gift survives for three years.

Growth   This is an occasional but not constant characteristic of some assets such as stocks, real estate, and natural resources to increase in real value. *Appreciation* and *growth* are synonymous. Until an asset is sold, growth is referred to as *unrealized*, or *paper profits*. When assets are sold, the growth is then "realized" and then taxed, usually at a lower rate than money received as income. The growth is not taxed until assets are sold.

Hold uninvested   This implies that the trustee is allowed to invest money in cash, at his or her discretion.

Income   This is an asset thrown off or paid by another asset. Real estate throws off rent, stocks throw off dividends, and bonds throw off interest. Income is the fulfillment of an obligation by someone who is using your money. That person or firm must pay you something on a regular basis for the privilege of using your capital.

Investment without being limited by statute   This implies that the trustee is allowed to invest in undiversified and high-risk holdings. Trustees like this clause as they are not held liable by the trust beneficiaries for keeping inherited stocks or for putting the money in their own mutual funds.

Lifetime interest in property   This is the right to enjoy property only during an individual's lifetime. Individuals so constrained do not have the right to designate who gets the asset when they pass on. The right to use property ends upon their death.

Low-cost-basis property   Assets that have been in family trusts for generations retain, for income tax purposes, a low tax basis. Because of its low cost and high current value, there is a large capital gains tax to be paid if low-cost-basis property is sold.

Net income   Income is what comes in on a regular basis, no matter how the value of the assets change due to the market's rise and fall. Income can be money that's paid out by companies as dividends or interest. Rent, some oil royalties, and so forth are all income. *Net income* is what remains after all expenses paid from income have been deducted, including administrative fees, taxes, and operating costs. Often, money is held back for future unanticipated expenses, which reduces net income.

Other sources of income of the beneficiary   This is a factor used in determining discretionary distributions of trust monies. When considering other sources of a beneficiary's income, the trustee should also consider a proper diversification scheme that will allocate assets between growth and income. If a beneficiary lacks sufficient income from other sources, the trustee may have the responsibility to give out more assets.

Principal distributions   These are distributions of the corpus or body of the trust.

Principal fees   These are fees paid to the trustee out of principal which are calculated on the amount of assets in the trust.

Productivity of assets   This concept assumes that assets should be producing income for the current beneficiary. Often, we see a clash between people who have opposing interests in a trust. Some people want income to enjoy now; others want the trust to grow for later use. Sometimes, trusts can be split if siblings cannot agree on the direction for a trust.

Prudent investor rule   The prudent investor rule holds that fiduciaries, such as trustees, are held to a higher standard in dealing with trust assets than they would be with their own money. This led people to be conservative and many trustees missed out on the great bull market of the 1980s by investing too heavily in bonds. This rule has recently been revised so that trustees are evaluated on how well they diversify their portfolio overall. Trustees cannot be criticized if they invest some money in very risky assets, such as emerging markets or real estate, if the majority of trust assets are invested intelligently between various types of assets.

Schedule A   This is an attachment to a trust. Schedule A is usually a list of property or money going into a trust when it is first set up.

Schedule K-1   This is the form beneficiaries use to prepare their personal tax return showing what taxable income they received from the trust.

Securities   Assets such as common stocks, preferred stocks, bonds, debentures, notes, warrants, and rights are publicly traded and therefore liquid, which means they can be easily turned into cash. Closely held businesses are generally illiquid, as are insurance contracts, real estate, leases, and commodities. These are the typical assets that are placed in trusts.

Tax returns   Tax returns are required to be filed on all trusts. All beneficiaries, both income and principal, have a right to see them.

Termination fees   These are fees charged when a trust is moved or ends. Banks often see termination fees as a way to discourage the movement of trusts. They are a windfall for the trustee when the original grantor is no longer around to object. These fees are definitely negotiable. Termination fees may be reasonable during the first two or three years of a trust. After that, trustees may ask for reimbursement of extra transfer expenses or if they are required to make special court appearances or accountings.

Trust capital gains tax   Upon the sale of stocks at a gain, the trust capital gains tax is paid out of principal, since the principal remainder persons and not the income beneficiaries will benefit from the growth in value.

Trust income tax   This is the tax paid on earned income from assets that stay in a trust. If all income is paid out to a beneficiary, there is no income tax obligation inside the trust because the person who received the income distribution has to pay the tax.

Trust records and papers   These are documents that relate to decisions made by the trustee regarding the use of the trust assets for the beneficiary (that is, how monies were handled, invested, or not invested). These include tax documents and discretionary decisions made by the trustee regarding issuance of monies to the beneficiaries.

Trustee's extraordinary fees   These are fees charged when the trustee is required to perform extraordinary services. Because reasonable people can differ on the meaning of the term *extraordinary*, the circumstances under which the payment of such fees is authorized and the amount of such fees (reasonable) should be negotiated up front by trust originators and trust service organizations. When challenged about past performance, trustees may threaten to charge the trust for the additional (extraordinary) services they render in defending themselves. Such fees should be challenged.

Rules of the Game

This section is to help heirs understand common phrases found in trust documents.

Acts made in good faith are binding   Trustees are not responsible to predict the future, but only to use all the information available to make logical and rational decisions.

Annual reports required to be given to beneficiaries   All people who have a present or future interest in trust assets have the right to receive regular and usable documents from the trustee concerning the trust's management.

To appoint between various beneficiaries   This is the power to leave assets by last will to a class of people (e.g., those in the bloodline) if there are multiple claimants.

Ascertainable standards "health, support, care, maintenance, and education"   This is a popular guideline for trustees in making distributions as defined in discretionary distributions of income and principal.

Best interests of a beneficiary   This phrase is an open door to conflicted interpretations, as the best interests of people change throughout their lives.

Delegation of trustees duties   Trustees can employ agents, including lawyers, accountants, investment advisors, and other specialists, regarding the assets for which they are responsible. This authorizes the trustee to hire professionals in areas in which the trustees themselves are not experts.

To determine what is income and what is principal and to decide how capital gains shall be treated   When assets are sold at a gain or loss, the trustee has the power to decide whether the income or principal beneficiary is to receive the benefit of realized gains. When assets are received that may be income or principal (e.g., a stock dividend), then the trustee has to determine who receives the benefit of that asset.

Disclaimer and renunciation   This defines the right of a named beneficiary to renounce the income and/or principal of a trust. It allows those assets to pass on to someone else, generally the disclaimer's children, or to whomever is indicated in the document to receive assets as if the renouncer had predeceased the event that triggered the distribution.

Domicile   The location of trustor or beneficiary; a person or entity's permanent residence.

Donor not eligible to act   This is the choice of a person to set up a trust and then not act as trustee of an irrevocable trust. The originator has to give up control over assets for the trust to qualify as a bona fide transfer of assets for tax purposes.

To establish and adjust reserves to pay estate taxes   This is the right of the trustee to hold back money in order to pay future expenses.

Examination of records   All people who have an interest in the trust have the right to examine all trust documents and past reports.

Exclusion of descendants by adoption   If a trustor so chooses, he or she can disallow adopted children from being eligible to receive income or principal distributions.

Full acquittance and discharge   The person acting as trustee no longer has any liability for acting upon trust assets and is released from liability by the beneficiaries or a court for actions of the past.

Furnishing bonds   Fiduciary insurance or bonds are sometimes required to protect against possible wrongful acts of the trustee.

Judgment that net income is insufficient   In examining other sources of income of the beneficiary, this process determines whether a budget prepared by a beneficiary is reasonable. It includes a request for adequate disclosure of all other assets and income so the trustee can determine if more income should be distributed from the trust.

Lawful issue of the body   A person related by blood in a lower generation.

Limitation on power of beneficiaries who are acting as cotrustees   Just as a donor may be excluded from certain decisions regarding trust property in order for the trust property to be deemed outside the donor's estate, so too the beneficiary may be prohibited from exercising certain kinds of control to prevent the trust property from being included in the beneficiary's estate.

Majority determination   A voting procedure on trust decisions.

Mandatory distributions   Trust documents can tell the trustee specifically how much of the principal or income to give out at a particular time.

No liability for loss except for negligence, default, or misdeed   This is a concept that trustees are not personally liable for poor decisions unless they are the result of gross neglect or willful deceit.

Power of appointment   The power to decide who gets assets held in trust after the current beneficiary.

Probate   The court process of validating a deceased person's last will and testament.

Pro rata   Pro rata means fairly and evenly distributed. The trustee must take previous amounts given to any person into account when equalizing benefits of a trust.

Revocation   The power to change the trust terms or to dissolve the trust.

Rule against perpetuities   State laws that limit the duration of trusts.

Situs   *Situs* means location. It defines which state's laws will be applied if disputes arise regarding trust property or if court interpretation of the trust document is required.

Special-needs limitation   Government benefits to beneficiaries are often reduced when outside sources of income, such as those from a trust, are available. The special-needs limitation allows trust assets to be held out of and not be considered as part of a beneficiary's assets. In this way, the government's determination of whether benefits should be received by disabled or minor persons is not affected by the trust.

Spendthrift provision   A common clause stating that trust assets may not be used or promised to anyone ahead of the time of distribution and beneficiaries of trust cannot pledge or transfer a bequest or trust asset as collateral for loans. If an heir's loan is in default, the lender cannot look to the beneficiary's interest in a trust for payment if a spendthrift provision is in the trust document.

Sprinkle   The right of the trustee to give one beneficiary more income or principal than another, according to the trustee's own judgment of what is best.

Trust amendment   A change in the provisions of the trust document. It is similar to a change to a will, which is called a *codicil*. Amendments can be done so that a whole new trust does not have to be drawn up.

Trustee resignation   Good trust documents have a mechanism whereby the current trustee can resign without going to court for approval. Some states require a summary court proceeding for certain kinds of trusts.

Written consent of cotrustee   A trustee may need to get written permission for investments or distributions from the individual who was named by the trustor as cotrustee.

Conclusion

This chapter is neither intended to give legal or tax advice nor to serve as a legal or tax reference. The definitions are provided for laypersons. If, in the interest of simplification, we have omitted some of what an expert technician might have included, so be it. The purpose here is to give people who are put off by the complexity of the worlds of law, tax, accounting, and business a starting point for getting comfortable with trusts and trust lingo. We as trusted advisors adhere to the tenet that simplicity leads to clarity. There is nothing in the world of trust that persons of ordinary intelligence can't grasp. The lexicon of trusts has traditionally been a way to keep power from beneficiaries. Hopefully, this chapter will help return the power to where it belongs.

CHAPTER
8

The Psychology of Inherited Wealth

*"Everything I have, son, I have because your grandfather left
it to me. I see now that that was a bad thing."*

This chapter is designed to give inheritors and advisors a look into the world of two high-net-worth individuals who have encountered great difficulties along with their wealth. This chapter will provide insight and help advisors understand some of the particular difficulties of many baby boomers who grew up with inherited wealth. Please understand that there are many healthy, wealthy families whose problems are no different in tenor and degree than any well-adjusted middle- or lower-class American household. Some of the personality traits of the dysfunctional families portrayed here: obsessive control, excessive spending problems, or difficulty in integrating the meaning of money with issues of self-esteem may also apply to entrepreneurs who have created a great deal of wealth for themselves. Early contact with large amounts of money, amounts that most people are never exposed to, can create special problems for some people of wealth. Again, we focus here on the more dramatic illustrations without meaning to imply that most trust beneficiary families succumb to these pressures of inherited wealth.

The chapter will follow two cases of people who inherited large amounts of wealth—enough so they will never have to create a livelihood for themselves. (The names and details of the stories have been changed. Any resemblance to people we know and love is coincidental.) No two families of origin are alike, and no two people have the same psychodramas going on inside their heads. Still, we feel that certain patterns are prevalent throughout the world of wealth, in particular among baby boomers raised in America in the latter half of the twentieth century. Our two individual stories run parallel to the currents of popular culture. Our main characters' consciousness of changing events is related in important ways to the politics of peace and women's movements, as well as to Eastern and Western spiritual renaissances.

Case Study: Edgar

Childhood

This is a story of one of our clients, Edgar, whose wealth actually makes normal problems worse. This happens because, unfortunately, it is easy to hide behind money. Most people prefer to sweep unpleasant situations under the rug and hide behind a facade of luxury and enjoyment.

Edgar grew up in a very wealthy family in the Boston suburbs. His grandfather had started a chain of car dealerships, now one of the most successful in the United States. During Edgar's early childhood, he rarely saw his father. His mother was an alcoholic. His father was driven by the need to surpass Edgar's grandfather in the amount of money that he could make. Edgar's childhood had some brief bright spots. In a parade of mansions that the family maintained—Cape Cod, Vermont, Boston—a steady stream of nannies took care of Edgar during his early childhood years. Until he entered school, most of Edgar's memories were of these surrogate parents. Some left for better jobs; others were fired because of racial tensions or as scapegoats for the emotional guilt felt by his parents.

During Edgar's childhood, he was insulated and removed from normal family life. Because of his family's great wealth, no expense was spared in exposing Edgar to the arts. Literature was especially revered by Edgar's mother, who was financially supported but emotionally neglected by his father. Attended by private tutors, Edgar traveled around the United States and Europe, and so came to an early appreciation of social injustices apparent everywhere outside his family's wealthy neighborhoods. Edgar knew that he was privileged but was unsure why these privileges had been bestowed upon him rather than others. Other students at the private schools Edgar attended did not have the vast wealth of Edgar's family. Edgar's sense of values was influenced by his aversion to his father's endless dedication to the pursuit of money. As in many wealthy American families, there was a dysfunctional commitment of time and energy to things outside of the family. Achieving, maintaining, and increasing the level of wealth was the measure of self-worth for Edgar's father. Edgar hated his father's absences and disliked himself for not having the same values about money as Edgar's grandparents.

On the other hand, Edgar's mother was dedicated to the women's movement, peace in Vietnam, and free speech for minorities. The family was divided over social issues. Edgar's younger sister began experimenting with drugs, which nearly incapacitated her for life (though eventually, after a long period of rehab, she did manage to attain some stability in her life).

Adolescence and Early Adulthood

When Edgar was in his teens, his parents divorced and his father married a secretary with whom he worked. Subsequently, he had two additional sons. The family was split, and over time, his father's second wife ensured that her two sons, who remained in their father's good graces, were groomed to take over the chain of car dealerships. Edgar was out of the picture and glad of it. He detested cars. He wandered about, pursuing Eastern religion and art—

which made it even more unlikely that he would be part of the family succession plans.

During the 1960s, Edgar lived in several communes. At one point he rejected money from one of the family trust funds. He "abdicated" in favor of his sister. Because Edgar refused to learn about money or take any interest in it, he was reluctant to look at anything with numbers and, in fact, suffered a kind of dyslexia concerning financial matters.

It can be difficult to psychologically account for money that you have not earned. It is a painful process to look and see what you really are doing with your money, either on the spending or the earning side. Through the money door, you see an uncompromised view of your own reality of fear of loss, of the constant need for more, or a combination of the two. It is deemed unclean and uncouth to discuss these issues except with a psychiatrist! Underneath all of the enjoyment, there is the nagging suspicion that since you did not earn the money, you may not be worthy. If this is so, then you are living a lie or a farce. At times, all inheritors feel this way, and it is very scary. It's an awesome responsibility for the financial advisor, because until clients can look at their money and acknowledge where they stand in relationship to it, no good long-term financial planning or investment program can be put into place. Edgar's experimentation with drugs and alternative living styles during the 1960s has contributed to his family's distrust of him. He is still basically excluded from the majority of financial decisions. In the areas of estate planning, his opinions and desires are not given the weight of those of his sister's husband, a doctor.

The 30s and 40s

Edgar's energies, instead of being devoted to making money, went into volunteer work, particularly for animal shelters. Seeing himself as abandoned, helpless, and nonverbal, Edgar relates deeply to the suffering of animals. They do not challenge Edgar's sense of self-esteem, nor do they threaten the self-imposed isolation that has surrounded him since childhood. Jessie H. O'Neill, in *The Golden Ghetto: The Psychology of Affluence,* writes about abandonment issues and surrogate parent problems when there is not a present, sustaining, long-term adult relationship in the development of the child.

Edgar's tutors and friends changed rapidly when he was a child because hardly anyone could remain in the family's good graces, given the emotional turmoil present, along with the extremely high standard of living that the family took for granted. Edgar became isolated not only from his peer groups and his family, but from the money, which he began to inherit in his mid-30s. That first distribution of trust money served to create a barrier that precluded much contact with other people his age, since he didn't have to work for a living. There was no regular interaction between Edgar and others, except when Edgar initiated contacts himself, and always on his own terms. As a result, Edgar became obsessed with small details about life. He worried constantly.

This kind of obsessive-compulsive behavior is typical of people with much time on their hands who seek meaning and order but who have little experience of the physical demands of working for a livelihood. Self-generated stress then fills up their time. While the animal shelter work holds Edgar's interest, often he is too sick to fulfill his obligations as a volunteer. The proliferation of chronic fatigue syndrome and environmental illness among wealthy people may be symptomatic of a weakened constitution, a result of being a prisoner in "the golden ghetto." People can scoff at the seriousness of these problems that affect the ultrawealthy, but their unhappiness is real and their suffering is genuine. How can advisors help people deal with these aspects of life? We must try to become fully cognizant of them, as well as trained to deal with them in a variety of ways.

Edgar exhibited a high level of sensitivity to many social equality issues, but, like many inheritors, he desperately needed verification of his value to society. It had always been difficult for Edgar to maintain relationships, but when his peers started to build their families, his isolation became more pronounced. Now in his 40s, Edgar wanted to have children, but he is not sure of his ability to commit to a particular path with one partner.

He is unsure of his ability to provide for his family, though ample trust fund monies for this purpose were set up through his grandfather and his father. Edgar's sister did get married, but unsuccessfully, to a bully who was interested in using the family money to start his own business. The family's mistrust of outsiders has become a self-fulfilling prophecy. The family's older advisors and trusted friends at the bank are no longer around. Edgar's mother died when Edgar was 45, leaving half of the family's assets in a trust controlled by a bank in the family's hometown.

At this point, on the brink of a breakdown, Edgar went through extensive counseling, which provided some validation that his problems were not rich-kid fantasies, but real. This sparked Edgar to search for a meaningful path that would be helpful to himself and others. He decided to go back to school to become a counselor. There has always been a gap between Edgar's abilities and his self-image. Because Edgar was raised in an environment of money, he did not learn many basic skills such as completing assignments. In short, he is hampered by lack of preparation for hardship in the world. This has not served him well in his attempts to achieve adulthood.

Edgar is judgmental about the lifestyle of others because he is even more judgmental of himself. It is very difficult for Edgar to accept himself, because no one has accepted him for just being himself.

Another common trait of people with inherited assets—and Edgar is a stellar example of this—is an inability to deal with paperwork. Each detail of everyday life has intense significance for someone who doesn't have the outside pressure of a job or family. To compensate, Edgar has an obsession with doing things "right." He has created a morass of records and is unwilling to throw anything away, lest it not be dealt with properly. There is a frozen quality to not being able to make decisions and agonizing over mundane details. There is no view of the forest, only endless trees.

Several therapists have helped Edgar deal with his problems, but with only some success. His inability to prioritize is a direct outgrowth of the lack of boundaries Edgar experienced as a child. Because he was allowed to do whatever he pleased, he did not suffer consequences for his wandering attention, and he did not have to deal with what would now likely be called attention deficit disorder. Edgar was given the sense that everything would be taken care of, no matter what he did or didn't accomplish. This was debilitating because it left no room for his personal responsibility. The ability to keep track of time, to keep appointments, and to be reliable becomes a daunting task without these early adulthood skill-building lessons.

Edgar is bright, compassionate, loving, and generous, but is overwhelmed by the world around him. In his mind, he always has too much to do: taking care of the animals, keeping up the house, meeting charitable commitments, and dealing with his family politics. The same is true of many people from dysfunctional wealthy families. There are many well-adjusted heirs who are leading productive lives. However, overcoming the problems of extreme wealth during early childhood is much more difficult than you might think.

As a result of Edgar's dysfunctional relationship with paperwork, it is almost impossible for him to locate anything. This makes financial and estate planning difficult. How can a financial advisor truly analyze someone's ability to take risk and help get their affairs in order for someone with a paperwork intolerance? The ability to process technical information, to read background data about companies, and to think through the ramifications of investment policies does not really make sense to Edgar.

It is not that he lacks intelligence or is incapable of understanding terms. Nor is it that he doesn't have the time or that he doesn't want to take the time to learn or to be involved in these kinds of decisions.

Growing up, Edgar received no training in financial affairs, and now he cannot be motivated to care. Rather, there is a dreary benign neglect about the details of responsible stewardship. Edgar has not filed tax returns for several years. He receives income from several trusts, but his records regarding donations to charity are a mess. Edgar would like to make a difference in the world, to use his wealth to be part of a constructive, healing process for the earth. But his intolerance for paperwork and lack of in-depth knowledge about his own financial picture make him unable to really grasp the magnitude of his wealth. Edgar is unable to move forward to determine what portion of his money he doesn't need. He is unable to give away substantial amounts to charity. Gifting is a potentially liberating activity in which the advisor can be of great assistance.

Edgar's spiritual life is a hodgepodge of different interests. Although he dabbled in Eastern religions during his teens and 20s, he was unable to stay with any one tradition. He does not have a sense of discipline or the experience of delaying gratification in order to master any one subject. As a result, he rushes from one seminar to another, from one diet to another, well intentioned and open to suggestions, but finally unable to incorporate any real, long-lasting, profound changes in his own lifestyle.

As you can imagine, Edgar is a very lonely person. With no community of coworkers, no family, no real need to interact, his life is busy but without structure.

People who work for Edgar, tending his plants or helping with his animals, are generally there for only brief amounts of time. It is difficult for them to come into contact with Edgar's vast wealth without being envious. Edgar basically distrusts people because of his sister's experience with her first husband and because of the way that Edgar's family treated the hired help—with distrust and disdain. Most people think that life without financial worries would be bliss. In fact, it can be a kind of a hell. Giving away all his money so that the demands of "normal" life come into play is not a viable option for Edgar, because he really has no workplace skills. Edgar's quality of life has not been enhanced by his money. The would-be joys of the many trips he takes and the material comfort that surrounds him are generally overshadowed by an ever present sense of shame and anxiety.

A sense of shame is common among inheritors. There is a private feeling that they are living a lie by enjoying the fruits of money they haven't earned. Additionally, there may be a kind of shame in how the wealth was made in the first place. Having a keen natural sense of social justice, Edgar understands well that his grandfather abused labor and dealt underhandedly with his competitors in order to establish a successful car business during the early part of the century.

Edgar's strong need to control his environment is a displacement of his natural compassion and affection for others, transferred somehow into an attitude of irritation that things are not working right at his house, a rambling antebellum mansion overlooking a large lake. Edgar is constantly upset about workers not showing up or things breaking down. Other members in his family disdain Edgar for his inability to get organized. It is true that Edgar is unable to stick with one subject for very long. He does have deep insight into the motivations of family members, and his suggestions about ways that the family money could help others through the use of charitable vehicles are quite good. Edgar is an outspoken advocate of social causes, carrying on a tradition established by his now-deceased mother.

Edgar is trapped by his past because he constantly relives family embroilments and traumas. Arguments between his mother and father concerning what is best for the family are now revisited between Edgar and his sister. He is deeply wounded that his father leaves him out of business decisions, though previously Edgar never took any interest in these matters.

Edgar's strongest desire is to get out from under the emotional baggage he carries around as a result of his family's wealth. He has feelings of guilt, shame, and inadequacy regarding his contribution to the family, and he mistrusts the emphasis on appearances. He wants to do the right thing at all costs. Edgar knows about meditation and wants healing, but he never seems to find time because his life is continuously buffeted by small events.

By looking at the underlying issues of Edgar's life, we can see things that may be helpful to advisors in understanding many people with inherited wealth.

The 1960s Era: Freedom

Edgar's most formative years were the 1960s, when he came of age. Many of his current opinions about himself and his place in society were molded at that time. As a descendant of a wealthy family, it was necessary for Edgar to hide his wealth, because wealth was associated with business; business was associated with war; and war was associated with the Establishment. The 1960s were decidedly an antiestablishment time. If you weren't a young Republican, you were part of the larger mass of freedom-seeking, free-thinking young people who were outraged by the Vietnam War.

Society's doubt about its right to wage war in Vietnam was reflective of the questions about self-worth already on the minds of people like Edgar. Having dirty clothes and long hair and giving expression to anger and rage were appealing to discontented wealthy young people, who had already seen the vacancy and lies behind the American dream. The American dream was independence, self-sufficiency, and wealth, but those who had these things were not happy. What a joy to be part of a group and to experience free love, sensual indulgence, and classless camaraderie.

The presidency of Richard Nixon served as a perfect forum for people like Edgar to externalize anger about the hypocrisy of their parent's lives. Appearances are all-important for the wealthy. Looking perfect made it seem that everything was all right, that there was a calm, peaceful, connected feeling inside Edgar's family. In fact, his home life was fractured, wrought with alcoholism and neglect. Using the military, industrial, business, and academic worlds as a foil, Edgar lashed out, left home, ignored his education and his inheritances in order to find himself. After the resignation of Nixon and the withdrawal from Vietnam, the preeminence of American power was challenged in the 1970s by the Arabs and the Japanese. This was, in a way, vindicating to people like Edgar. Internally, Edgar sought to see the dismantling of his own family "establishment" because of the stifling effect it had on his own personal development.

Traditions became irrelevant in the 1960s, with persons of Jewish or Christian ancestry delving into Eastern religions, becoming Muslims, Bahaists, Sikhs, Buddhists, shamans, whatever! Many young people in the 1960s were into anything that wasn't like their family's traditions. It was a time for personal expression outside the boundaries of traditionalism. Many people with inherited wealth were drawn to this kind of expression because they were finally equal in the eyes of their peers. It became much easier to slough off the shackles of prep schools, Ivy League colleges, and exclusive clubs. The rejection of and rebellion against authoritarianism included their own wealthy families. Dictates such as "get a job" and "get married" were seen as empty expressions of traditional morals, out of touch with the times. The commonly held judgment by the counterculture that traditional society was bad made it easy for Edgar to reject everything that society held dear, including parents and family money. It was a liberating time for Edgar, perhaps one of the happiest times of his life.

The freedom of movement exemplified by hitchhiking, a common activity when Edgar was in his early 20s, was exactly what he needed. Hitching a ride was a way for Edgar to lose his identity, travel without class lines, and experience the aliveness of being out on his own. Edgar's questioning of all that was held sacred by his parents and his rejection of wealth was a liberating experience, allowing him to live life firsthand rather than being protected and sheltered by his parents. Edgar's rejection of the Establishment and his distrust of authority were translated into a dislike of institutions in general. Individuality is of key importance to Edgar, and this will play a large role in what kind of trust organization is best suited to handle his needs—and by extension, the needs of other baby boomers with inherited wealth.

Understanding Edgar's discomfort with the stigma of wealth and his desire for an egalitarian lifestyle is essential in understanding the decisions and motivations for many of today's and tomorrow's trust beneficiaries. What is important to people is not being seen as the wealthiest person on the block, but rather integrating their lifestyle decisions with deeper needs and exploring their personal capabilities—"raising consciousness," in other words. The experiences of the 1960s have not been forgotten, but rather, they have been transformed and made real in the choice of inheritors' life interests. The financial advisor who is able to understand the underlying desires of people of wealth, and to arrange for convenient and understandable strategies, will garner a great deal of loyalty.

The 1970s: Loss of Power

The 1970s began with the admission that the United States was not undefeatable and ended amid a crisis of high oil prices, high inflation, and public hysteria against the Soviet Union, the "evil empire." Personal expression, so prized in the 1960s, gave way to a deep anxiety about what the world was coming to. Pop music turned harsher, and economic reality started to creep back into the American consciousness. With the oil crisis of 1973 and rising inflation, we seemed to be embarking on a course of uncertainty.

Edgar dropped out of college during this period to explore alternatives and to find a sense of personal identity. He lived in several religious communities, never staying long in one place. Edgar turned back to a childhood interest, pottery, which had also been one of his mother's pursuits. He attended a community college, studied pottery, and then set up a studio in a rural area far from his home. During his hitchhiking period, Edgar visited the West and settled in Colorado during the 1970s. Colorado was a "mile high," clean, clear, fresh, and provided fertile ground for his aspirations to make a new start.

Edgar enrolled in a four-year college, this time with the idea of becoming a teacher in the public school system. This didn't work out for a variety of reasons, so Edgar went to live in his own place in the country, a ramshackle homestead with character. He wanted a stable lifestyle from which he could evaluate his family's history and establish a separate identity from the old-line money pressure to conform.

The fact that America's dominance in world business was being challenged was a sort of comfort to Edgar, since he himself believed that his own family's business was without any redeeming qualities, a rip-off of the general public. Edgar's interest in Eastern religions developed into a pursuit of Eastern diets, and he eventually became a vegetarian, experimenting with macrobiotic cooking. This further distanced him from his family. On his infrequent trips back to Boston, he became even more of an outcast in the family's eyes.

The move to Colorado was good for Edgar because at that point, many people in Colorado showed concern about maintaining a "natural environment." The swift increase in oil prices allowed Edgar to feel justified in owning a small car rather than one of the behemoths his family had been selling for generations. Edgar's new sense of identity allowed him to look at his family's financial situation for the first time. His mistrust and ignorance of where he stood had led to a gift of funds to his sister, a transfer that he now questioned. He felt that his judgment during the 1960s had been clouded by his exuberance for experimentation. Edgar resented not the loss of money, but that his sister did not acknowledge the intent and magnitude of his gift, which her ex-husband had blown in business ventures. She was living in denial about the emotional cost to the family of that experience. This lingering resentment about the gift continued to come between Edgar and his sister. Years of counseling would be spent on the issue of fairness.

The 1970s saw the stock and bond markets plummet. The traditional trust investment strategy of buying long-term U.S. Treasury bonds was a complete failure. Beneficiaries' costs of living skyrocketed while the value of portfolio holdings plummeted. Only real estate assets were appreciating. Edgar was totally ignorant about what kinds of assets were in his trust, and this was probably fortunate. His bank trust departments were scurrying to adjust to the new era of deregulated interest rates, and stockbrokers had to adjust to negotiable commissions. The good-old-boy networks were starting to break up.

This was the period when Charles Schwab sold his company to Bank of America and then bought it back again. The U.S. securities investors were in a panic. Mutual funds had crashed, to be replaced by newfangled money markets, pesky usurpers of the banks' bread-and-butter savings accounts. The banks were also saddled with large fixed-interest loans. The real estate crisis of the 1980s was in the making as investors rushed to get into oil and gas deals, real estate, limited partnerships, or anything else that would beat the ascending rate of inflation.

Inflation caused fear that no matter how much money you had, it might not be enough. The decline in purchasing power of the U.S. dollar was expected to get worse. At the same time, the end of the world's oil supply seemed just around the corner. Population pressures and a multitude of environmental hazards came into the public's consciousness. Edgar felt vindicated in his rejection of the "system." His sojourn into psychological independence during the 1960s had allowed him, in his mind, to escape the worst of the crisis now beginning to manifest.

Edgar was still embarrassed and ashamed to ask about his trusts. Even if he had, he wouldn't have been told much. His various trust departments were losing money alarmingly in long-term bonds. As interest rates skyrocketed, the value of his trusts plummeted. By the late 1970s, banks realized they needed to adjust to the new environment, but there was little competition on the horizon and few ideas about how to protect portfolios against rampant inflation. IRAs and other retirement plans came into existence. Japan's stock market began to rocket up and international stocks, though not on the radar screens of U.S. investors, began a meteoric rise.

Edgar's foray into graduate school to become a teacher came to an end when he realized that he wasn't going to be able to use the radical methods that he believed in inside the public school context. Nonetheless, Edgar had become an established part of the community around Boulder, a community that included many people like himself—disenchanted middle- and upper-class rebels. Edgar's peers were marrying and starting families. How would he find a mate who could relate to his issues? Edgar was hardly able to articulate the deep, unresolved family problems beneath his eccentric lifestyle. Edgar's uneasiness about his future and the meaning of his life was slowly and silently growing.

The 1980s: Return to Traditional Values

Beginning with Ronald Reagan's election to the presidency in 1980, America took a sharp about-face. Edgar disdained the political sparring between the Soviet Union and the United States, but the public's increasing concerns with business and stopping inflation thrust a new kind of peer consciousness into the spotlight.

The Reagan Administration policy to build up our military capabilities during the 1980s sparked the beginning of a boom in the U.S. economy, much as the production of arms for World War II marked the end of the Great Depression. This translated into higher trust account values and more choices of investment vehicles for people like Edgar. Banks came out with interest-bearing checking accounts in an effort to compete with the burgeoning world of financial service companies.

Edgar's friends were settled down now and committed to careers. Edgar married and fathered a child with a local woman of Hispanic descent, whose ancestors had arrived in Colorado with the Spanish Jesuits in the 1600s. This rootedness warmly attracted Edgar. They met in a bar, and Edgar figured that if she could drink with him, she could live with him, but this did not turn out to be the case.

Edgar's brief marriage ended in divorce. His former wife took their son and moved to Denver to pursue a beautician's career, paid for by a settlement from Edgar's trust. One impact of Edgar's becoming a father was that reconciliation became possible with his own father, who took a major interest in his first and only natural grandchild. Edgar's deep attachment to his young son led him to commute regularly to Denver from Boulder. As Edgar became cognizant of the responsibilities and opportunities that his trust money might provide for his son, he began to take an interest in the trusts.

Meanwhile, Edgar's two younger half brothers were allowed to take over the family car business. Edgar was left out of this decision completely, and he was deeply hurt, alienated anew from the family who showed disdain and distrust for his lifestyle. Edgar's portion of his father's business was put in trust with a local bank. The half brothers and the car dealerships were big customers of the same bank, so the trust officers had split loyalties. Although they hired an outside consultant to make decisions that would protect Edgar from his brothers' mishandling of the family's wealth, the person they hired was a friend of Edgar's siblings. The local attorney who had helped Edgar's father set up the trust was also beholden to the half brothers. Thus the interests of Edgar and his sister were compromised.

Back in Colorado, Edgar was splitting his time between looking after his young son while his ex-wife established a career, keeping up his interest in pottery, and volunteering with local environmental groups. Like the culture around him, by the late 1980s, Edgar was beginning to appreciate the importance of traditional values. Relations with his ex-wife were not good, although Edgar joined the Catholic Church to help convince his in-laws that he was not totally irresponsible. His interest in learning more about his assets continued to grow, although Edgar did not know what power he might be able to exercise now or in the future. As his son approached school age, Edgar began thinking about the years of financial responsibility ahead of him. He wanted the best for his son, but felt powerless to affect his own destiny.

The 1990s: Taking Back the Power

We have followed Edgar through the 1960s, a period of self-expression and experimentation. During the 1970s, Edgar's disillusionment with traditional values was muted by his reentry into mainstream society through marriage and the birth of his son. Edgar's inability to settle into a career led him, in the early 1990s, to counseling in a desire to heal himself. He joined several support groups, one specifically for persons with inherited wealth. He also joined Alcoholics Anonymous, which has given him for the first time a sense that he is not really so very different from others.

The problems that Edgar struggled with for 30 years, from the age of 15 to 45, kept him isolated. The trust funds in Boston have taken on increased significance to Edgar, because now he not only wants to help other people, but also to have a balanced life for himself and his son. He needs money to fund his own endeavors and to ensure that his child doesn't grow up in the same emasculating circumstances as he himself did.

Edgar wants information about his trust and he wants to make wise decisions. The trust department back in Boston, which has been sending him money for 25 years, has changed dramatically. Edgar feels unable to establish a personal rapport with any of the new trust officers. While he is now able to articulate his need for input, the trust department's management has changed from local to regional and now to national. The new cor-

poration's people, policies, and procedures have little relation to the original workings of the trust.

Edgar desires control over his assets, but he is frustrated by the bureau-
cratic procedure he must go through to make even the simplest changes in
his account. His interest in becoming a responsible member of his Colorado community has motivated him to make anonymous donations to
local causes. There is a large amount of inherited stock in his trust account
with very low tax basis. He is aware that it is possible to transfer those
assets, currently invested in companies whose ethics are antithetical to
him, into higher-income-producing instruments. He also wants his favorite
charities to have an endowment fund sometime in the future. Edgar is
stymied by his trust officer's lack of guidance about accomplishing this
goal. He knows that he is the rightful owner of the assets, but does not
know how to assert his control. He has attended seminars regarding investments, but feels insecure about his own assets.

A sea change has taken place in the attitude of Edgar's peers. People are
expected to be knowledgeable about money affairs and markets. The go-go
years of the 1990s saw Edgar's trust value explode, tripling along with the
market. The death of an aunt resulted in several additional trusts for Edgar's
benefit as well. One of these trusts distributed assets to Edgar in the form
of inherited stock. For the first time, Edgar has his own account and can
move forward on his own, dealing with his own advisors on issues such as
charitable trusts. Edgar now has his own sense of identity regarding money,
and he can proceed to make charitable contributions to his community. His
sense of self-esteem has risen accordingly. Although he doesn't make a
great deal of money from his pottery, the joy of creativity gives him an identity in his own eyes and among his peers.

Behind the sense of accomplishment, there remains a huge sense of
emptiness. The negative self-esteem foisted on Edgar from his parents' emotional neglect remains, and true enjoyment of his money still eludes Edgar.
More information is now forthcoming on his trust. The bank's investment
philosophy has been to use their own common trust funds rather than to keep
Edgar's low-cost stocks. This turned out to be a big mistake from rate-of-
return and tax perspectives. Edgar would like to choose his own investments—in socially responsible funds such as Ben & Jerry's, Hasbro, Idaho
Power and Light, and other socially responsible companies.

The current trust situation is not meeting Edgar's needs. The bulk of his
assets are locked up in trust, some of them for his entire lifetime. Knowing

that his son will receive a large inheritance, Edgar is determined to do something for other people and to exercise what control he can over his assets, both inside and outside of his trusts. He needs to integrate the management of those assets with his highly developed sensitivity for social responsibility. The institutions that he is dealing with do not understand this, nor are they interested in his personal life. This is where the trusted advisor plays the most important role. Later in the book, we will discuss how to evaluate the current trustee and strategize the best way Edgar can exert his rights on the assets in his trust. Edgar's father recently passed on, and Edgar made an effort to reconcile himself with his half brothers. He is now in a position to have some influence on the family business through a private family foundation set up by Edgar's father in his will. Edgar knows little about the workings of nonprofits and has little time or inclination to be involved in the day-to-day operations with siblings, who live far away and have completely different values and views.

The main constraint in Edgar's life now is time. He is busy and stressed out. He needs more income from the trust. His trust's equities have grown in value, but the decline in interest rates from the mid-1980s throughout the end of the 1990s has greatly reduced the amount of income available to him. The bank is reluctant to manage the trust assets for Edgar's benefit, refusing to use Colorado municipal bonds or anything that might increase Edgar's after-tax income.

2000 and Beyond

Edgar has established a budget that is likely to require increasing levels of cash flow. He has a sense of identity that includes being a philanthropist. Being involved as a coach for his son's teams gives him less time to devote to the family foundation or dealing with the old-line trust department back East. Edgar's goals in life are clearer now. He wants to have quality time with his son and to develop as a person. The psychological wounds of his childhood and the inherited assets in the form of intimidatingly complex trust funds remain formidable obstacles. Edgar would feel successful and happy if he had an advisor who would allow him the opportunity to express his interests and give input to the investment process. He also needs someone who will be a strong advocate for him—organizing, formulating, and implementing a strategy to get his financial life in shape. Edgar wants help in addressing all these issues, but they have to be carried out in a way that is not stressful to him. These are the challenges that face the advisor who wishes to help this inheritor take control of his family wealth.

Case Study: Louisa

Background

Louisa came into money partially through her deceased husband's family, although her own mother had some family trusts as well. Louisa was raised in the South, steeped in old southern plantation tradition. There was a long-standing denial about the ongoing drain of money from the family fortune, which originally came from tobacco. Her family was disordered. Her older sister received most of the attention, being a genteel sort of debutante in a way that held little appeal for Louisa. Louisa's intellect and curiosity exceeded her sister's, and she was sent away to be educated at girl's boarding school throughout her adolescence. The overall attitude was chauvinistic: Louisa and her sister should be kept, pampered, and cared for in every way. Anything to do with her assets, however, and the family land managed by her uncle was off limits. Being a strong-willed person, this was not a tolerable situation in Louisa's eyes.

After attending a small, Christian girl's college, Louisa rejected her affluent background and became a social worker. She moved north. Dealing with the incredible red tape, she became depressed about the delivery of social services to the poor in New York. Louisa then moved out West and established herself as a horseback-riding instructor, working on dude ranches and for wealthy transplants from the East Coast and California. Finally, locating herself in Santa Fe, Louisa married a handsome Swiss immigrant named Emilo. They had two sons before her husband's life was tragically cut short by an auto accident, leaving Louisa with two children under five and an incredibly complicated estate. Her husband was heir to several European trusts as well as two trusts that had been set up in New York. Louisa was about to enter the world of private trustees and to tangle with family members she had never met.

Her Conflicts

Emilo's family lawyers in New York had named themselves as trustees of the largest trusts. The attorneys had set up a separate legal partnership to administer the trusts, creating a sort of professional dynasty within their law firm. The oldest attorney, resident curmudgeon and son of the attorney who drafted the original document in the 1930s, refused Louisa any financial support from her husband's trusts for six years while he ostensibly tried to determine what her standard of living should be.

Concurrently, some of Louisa's own family money had been transferred to one of the largest corporate trustees in New York, who promised to look after her children's investments. When Louisa tried to exert control over these assets, which she herself had put into trust, the bank of her own choosing forced her to go to court! The trustees did this in order to relieve themselves from liability, to take a full termination fee, and to slow down the return of assets to Louisa, which would allow them to collect fees for an additional year or so. The expense to Louisa was well a full year's living allowance.

Louisa's life became a morass of legal wranglings. At one time, she was in three separate legal disputes: one with her deceased husband's family over who should receive Emilo's former income; the second with the lawyer of the trustees who were taking a hard-line, adversarial role, as they attacked her lifestyle decisions regarding the children's upbringing; and the third with her own trustees in New York, who appointed an unnecessary guardian to represent the children's interest, even though the only issue was a change in trustee.

Initially, Louisa's conservative upbringing made it difficult for her to challenge the male authority figures of the attorneys, trustees, and relatives. However, her strong-willed and independent nature prevailed. She is extremely busy, raising two children and running a horse operation at the same time. She has built several houses, moving on to the next project as she completes each one. A consummate bargainer, Louisa inherited a shrewd sense of business from her mother, who had inherited income from her family late in life.

Louisa's needs in a trusted advisor are for simplicity of communication and advice about how to directly confront anything that stands in her way. She is an attractive woman who has been married several times since the death of her first husband. These relationships were mostly with people who were willing to take a supporting role to her various interests of children, horses, and real estate development. Louisa is unwilling to subject her children to any negative influences, and so has unfortunately insulated them from the realities of their financial situation and the legal struggles and stress that she herself has undertaken as the family provider. Louisa may well have unintentionally perpetrated, for her progeny, the unhealthy sheltering that she herself experienced as a child.

Louisa enjoys face-to-face communication with people who care about her trials and tribulations, who understand the emotional pressure that has been brought to bear by her and Emilo's families and their lawyers. She wants to protect her children's interests, but she is also concerned about having enough for herself.

The Advisor's Challenge: Relationship Management

A good illustration of how a trusted advisor might work with someone like Louisa would be to communicate with her in a time frame and by methods that fit in with her busy lifestyle. She likes to drop in and see the boss. She wants letters drafted for her, reviewed, typed, mailed, and copied. In fact, she wants to have a kind of family office without bearing the direct expense. She is not unreasonable, but once in a while, she challenges some minutia concerning her expenses while missing out on the big picture. When a minor detail takes on major importance for Louisa, it is best to deal with that item as if it were the most important thing in the world, as if the fate of all issues rested on the resolution of this one detail. Paying or not paying a wire fee may make the difference between her having a good or a bad day. This kind of control is not unusual for people who were disempowered as youths. Because she has never had a job, she feels inside that she must prove her acumen and sharpen her wits on inconsequential matters.

She does not like a lot of written information, preferring only a summary of what needs to be done. Louisa expects to know ahead of time the odds of achieving her objectives. She does not like bad news and is unaccepting of market fluctuations in her portfolio. She only likes to see her investments appreciate. When the market is up, she wants to be in it, but when it goes down, she expects to be out. This kind of unrealistic expectation about investments goes along with a lack of education or interest in securities. It is results that count, but the results that really matter the most are those on a personal level. Louisa will never run out of money, so tailoring a portfolio to her emotional needs is as important, perhaps more so, than doing well against an index. Her own estate planning has been neglected, but she hates to pay lawyers. What's an advisor to do?

Regardless of her family's wealth, Louisa does not want to be relegated to a one-dimensional status symbol because she has beauty, brains, and bravado. Like many others in her generation, she wants to be seen as her own person, acknowledged for the tribulations she has been through as a single mother in our culture. She would like to know that she is not sought after for her money. Louisa has a need to know only occasionally what is going on with her affairs, and on the spontaneous days when she feels like delving into these matters, she has only short amounts of time to be informed about her situation. She wants to be listened to by her advisor.

Having all her options clearly spelled out and having as many options as possible is extremely satisfying to Louisa. She wants to make the final decisions and have other people implement them. She wants to be respected for her experience and knowledge. She wants to know picky details about obscure issues and perhaps forgo more important topics if she doesn't feel like talking about them. She wants to be assured that her decisions and lifestyle are not adversely affecting the environment, so she will go to great lengths to see that her real estate development projects are in keeping with her sense of conservation. Her intentions are to be the number one caring contributor to her children's sense of self-esteem. Louisa is determined not to have the same break between her and her children as happened with her parents and her siblings.

Louisa believes her children are not yet ready to handle or even know about their money. This is a reflection of her misgivings and insecurity about handling her own money. There is a certain sense of miserliness about her activities. The sense of entitlement that comes along with generations of money in her family is suppressed on little things, but comes out in grand statements about what she and her children absolutely must have. She has a sense that if she can save a few dollars on small things, the good things in life will naturally come her way, which they have, and that she has a right to them. The result of habitual conflict over inherited money has been isolation from her current husband and a sense of malaise about the future.

As in Edgar's case, Louisa has difficulty in sensing her own intrinsic self-worth. She is preoccupied with past injustices, whether real or imaginary. Louisa spends a great deal of psychic energy trying to justify her position as being "right," and the strong sense of entitlement with which she grew up now takes the format of being angry at those who withhold from her what she believes is her due. She wants to be reassured that she is making wise choices and that she is in the right. Louisa needs enormous amounts of emotional support to wage battle on the world around her.

Louisa spars with private trustees in New York and battles with the children's grandfather (who went to court for visitation rights). She even harbors resentment against her sister who received a larger portion of their father's estate. Conflict is a big part of Louisa's inheritance.

Emotional Support

Louisa needs a team of advisors who all understand the psychological aspects of her battles. To coordinate such a team is difficult in today's environment. We believe it will be a hallmark of the successful SIP of the future to put together a system of coordination and communication among a team of professional advisors. This will save Louisa time, money, and armor. When the team of professionals talk to each other, Louisa may be best served by constant updates of the time and cost involved.

The future for Louisa is bright, as she takes good care of herself and is likely to live well into her 80s. While abhorring risk and detesting any declines in the value of her account, she realizes the need to diversify into equities but is psychologically unable to bear even the smallest of temporary losses. On the positive side, she is aware of how much she is earning from the various trusts. Moreover, never having been told "no" as a child, she is now incapable of living within a budget. In the back of her mind, Louisa contemplates the possibility that her children will leave home and take away the income from assets that she has protected for them over the years since her first husband's death. She is adamant about not being dependent on another person, and most of her partners have been financially weak.

It seems that women are more likely to ask for help in dealing with inheritance issues than are men. Women live longer and tend to control more wealth because they tend not to blow their money on egotistical ideas that promise great riches quickly. Men tend to think they can do it all themselves, and their egos are more tied up in being savvy. One grave danger to herself is her tendency to switch advisors every few years: be they attorneys, accountants, realtors or consultants. She is susceptible to guile; because of her low self-esteem, she can turn vindictive and punishing on former advisors who are not completely subservient and accommodating to her wishes.

Louisa has a great deal of anger toward the attorneys who set up their self-serving, self-perpetuating empire with her husband's trust funds. These trustees, and other private trustees we have seen in Boston and Chicago, generally try to make beneficiaries feel guilty and unwise about withdrawing principal. Louisa is strong enough to stand up to her advisors. She has a sense that what she wants for her children takes precedence and that it is not the trustee's place to determine how she should raise them. The definition of standards of support for health, education, and welfare are broad. In her case, the trustee has been so difficult that Louisa has to show receipts in order to get reimbursed.

Many women see that they do not have to put up with the paternalistic attitudes of trust officers who judge requests by their own narrow life experiences. The traditional role of a woman's place as being at home is unacceptable to many women, so child care and providing money for extracurricular activities for the children are desired. If Louisa believes a trip to Paris is essential for the education of her sons, so be it. If there are ample funds, and the trustees are feathering their own pockets by retaining hundreds of thousands of dollars in income that could have been distributed over several years, Louisa is ready to fight for her rights.

When Louisa's father died, he left several trusts for Louisa and her sister. By design, the trusts were not distributed equally; a larger portion was given to Louisa's sister because of her father's feeling that Louisa's children would be amply provided for by their inheritances from her deceased husband's side of the family. Louisa's sense of injustice about this situation has never really been resolved between her and her sister. This is not a question of needing the money, but of feeling cared for, counted, and acknowledged. It is seen as a reflection of who is loved more, concretized in how gifts are distributed and how estates are passed on. Lasting family damage could have been avoided by discussing these issues among the three of them before her father passed away. On every side, Louisa is involved with conflict. Her substantial assets do not provide peace of mind—why?

Conclusion

From our two stories, we can surmise that people of wealth are not different from most of us, but that their problems manifest themselves in different and often more difficult ways. Wealthy people want to be loved and appreciated and to contribute to the world by helping other people around them. The emotional liabilities of growing up with inherited wealth is well presented in Jessie H. O'Neill's book, *The Golden Ghetto: The Psychology of Affluence*. They describe, from the inside, the particular strains and stresses of growing up in wealthy families.

Regardless of the fact that wealthy people are no more neurotic, nor happier or sadder than any other class of people, the types of isolation, problems of lack of self-confidence, and difficulty in establishing self-esteem are endemic among people who will not ever have to work for a living. This presents special problems for financial advisors who seek to deal with inheritors in an effective and compassionate way.

It is clear that the majority of employees of large institutions (i.e., trust officers) are in no way equipped to deal with the deeper psychological issues so important to the happiness and well-being of those they are supposed to be assisting. Many professionals who seek to give beneficiaries advice about how, where, when, and in what way to invest their inherited assets can totally miss the boat if these underlying issues are not addressed. Fred Brown, in his book, *Money and Spirit,* perceptively points out many of these signs of this submerged agenda.

Most people want to feel good about themselves and to contribute to the welfare and happiness of others. When large amounts of money are present, it is more difficult to form this sense of identity by the normal methods of working through issues of education, work experience, or proving you can make your own way in the world. People with inherited money find that their artistic talents and spiritual interests hold greater promise for defining who they are than do answers to the standard introductory question, "What do you do for a living?" For most people, spending long hours studying, overcoming difficult tasks, and facing unknown and scary challenges form character. This is not true for the person who has inherited wealth, who must discover internal motivation not fueled by material need.

In both case studies, we find that dealing with emotional scars and unresolved issues will be a central factor in the relationship between people of wealth and their advisors. Relating to their personal makeup and cultural experience not only brings rapport but also influence. As trusted advisors, our role is not merely, or even primarily, technical. Nor is it just to handhold and trivialize problems as they occur. The moral of these stories is that both inheritors and advisors must be willing to look hard at recurring psychological blocks that stand in the way of the inheritors' true enjoyment of their lives. It is not a simple assignment.

The Right Stuff

"Won't you please welcome Edwin Nells—accompanied, as always, by his attorney."

attorney: *one breed of "trusted advisor"*

This final chapter of Part 2 will round out our description of the underlying elements that make up the art of trust. We have described systems, motivations, and internal strengths, and we have introduced the language of trusts for both advisors and inheritors. Every advisor should determine whether he or she has the personal characteristics that are prerequisites for entering this field. We'll provide a litmus test to help.

We believe that several definitive psychological traits are necessary for an SIP to be a successful trust advisor. We outline 19 specific attributes that will serve you well in this field, with its incredible stress and concurrent rewards. These standards of thoughts, feelings, and actions embody the kind of trust services that people with inherited assets desire. They are the nutritional part of the relationship, and clients want, need, and deserve all of these. Together, they provide a litmus test for the "right stuff."

Acceptance

Acceptance is the first key to becoming a trust advisor to people with inherited wealth. We must try to accept our potential clients as whole and complete people, just as they are, without judging them for their shortcomings. This is not a hollow platitude. It takes lifelong effort. We must do the same for ourselves.

It is easy to look down on people who have never had to work for a living. This may be difficult for an investment professional who has been working 70-hour weeks. There's a tendency to envy or denigrate those who haven't worked for the material goods they have. It may be difficult for inheritors to accept an advisor if the advisor comes on too strong because of his ego. These are problems to which every successful person in the financial services field is prone because as advisors, we cannot do a good job unless we have a strong belief in ourselves. Our self-confidence has to be high to cut through the mire of financial figures and news that comes our way, and to boldly state, "This is how I recommend you deal with the future." At the same time, however, we must approach our clients with an open heart. This begins with our attitude toward ourselves. Exercising empathy for clients comes from empathizing with ourselves and knowing our true values.

How will people know if we are capable of accepting them? Studies show that 95% of communication takes place on a nonverbal level. This means that eye contact, body language, and other subliminal messages tell our clients the truth about what we are feeling toward them.

Are we *really* paying attention to them when we speak? Do we allow enough time to interact with them? There are many programs for business-people to learn how to set priorities, establish goals, develop their career paths, and organize time. These are helpful on an intellectual level. But we also need to take time to be in touch with ourselves and make sure that our business is aligned with our personal life. This is the only way that we can accept each service occasion as a chance to fulfill our deepest desires: to be successful, to provide service, or whatever we strive to achieve.

Inheritors need to feel valued, even though they may not know anything about money or may not have an earnings capability of their own. There is a strong likelihood that unreconciled family conflicts have been generated over money issues. These may not be articulated or conscious, but they nonetheless create anxieties concerning finding the right advisor and doing the right thing.

Particularly if they have inherited assets, wealthy people may not feel, and in fact may not be, capable of choosing an advisor based on the right criteria. When an advisor accepts herself and accepts prospective clients' decisions without pressure, it goes a long way toward diffusing the emotional trauma of past experiences with money experts.

There needs to be an acknowledgment between the advisor and inheritor about the kinds of issues raised in the stories of Edgar and Louisa. By accepting clients, an advisor establishes herself as a member of the team, no matter what personality traits or idiosyncrasies the clients manifest. Misconceptions and prejudgment come up for all parties. In many ways, the relationship between the trusted advisor and the client is like a marriage without the romance. To be healthy, the relationship must be approached from a healing, nonjudgmental point of view. This is the basis of true acceptance.

Patience

We all know that patience is a virtue, but we recognize that there are few virtuous people in the world today! Patience is a natural result of giving up greed and ambition. This is predicated on making the space and time available to be present. Also, we must have the energy and presence of mind to deal with a client in an appropriate way. To do this, advisors must give up their habitual concerns about whether an inheritor will become a client or whether they are performing well enough to keep a client. Patience is the ability to sit quietly and wait for the exact opportune time to proceed with an appropriate activity. By their ability to embody patience, seasoned investment professionals give the client something they sorely need—

peace of mind. Even a slight reduction on our part of the endless stream of stress that crowds peoples' minds, no matter how much money they have, is a palpable step in the right direction.

The advisor's psychological makeup and spiritual motivations are definitely important when dealing with people, especially inheritors with trusts. A psychological match and a spiritual connection is important if he is to do an adequate job as the trust advisor. Clients who see a financial advisor with patience are more likely to see that person as someone who has the capability to coach them on long-term financial health.

Validation

Inheritors need validation from their advisors in the sense that they wish to hear approval from advisors. To persons without an area of technical expertise or business acumen, the expression by a trusted professional, acknowledging that there are many ways to find true meaning in life, is validating and important. At the most basic level (and this is similar to what we receive from our own profession), achievement is the recognition that we have been able to help others. Wealthy people often do this in the form of volunteer work, action on behalf of the environment and animals, participation in the arts, preserving cultural heritages, and involvement in socially responsible investing. We, as advisors need to let our approval show and to acknowledge the value of these activities—much as we do for our own employees when they do a good job. When employees do well, it makes us look good and it makes life easier. It is the same when inheritors contribute in their own way.

Support

Inheritors need to be at the center of the advisor's universe when we are with them. This does not mean pandering. It is a matter of empowering the person we are talking to by really putting them first. When people are put first, they are generally able to let go of selfish and egotistical desires for short-term results. It is a mysterious phenomenon that when one person lets go of an internal knot or tension, those in their presence immediately feel the effect.

It is critical for us to support our clients by defining their alternatives in ways that they can understand. It also means giving them permission to change their minds. It is important for us as trusted advisors to acknowledge that we make mistakes, and that this is a natural part of every process that takes place. Inheritors need to feel that they have the freedom to change their minds even if it means no longer retaining us as their advisor. They need to be given alternatives and support to explore each and every option, no matter how long it takes. This is exactly what they were not given as prisoners of affluence, when everything was structured for them. Support for our clients means that we are there for them at each step, defining their choices and interpreting how those choices will affect their future.

Most wealthy children are told what to do, when to do it, and how to behave. This is in stark contrast to people who grow up in poverty, whose parents are working or just missing altogether; they have no standards set. The opportunity to be the maker of your own destiny is tremendously empowering. This freedom to fail is lacking in many uptight, wealthy households, where surface appearances and fitting in with people of similar social class are important. In Europe, wealth is not the only determination of social status. There, aristocratic lineages and purity of bloodline are separating factors among otherwise similarly economically situated people. In America, almost all of us are of mixed heritage, so our class distinctions are purely monetary without the ancestral purity issue.

Articulate Lifestyle Values

As advisors, we need to make sure our clients, who are inheritors and trust beneficiaries, know that we understand their underlying values and how they have chosen to live their lives. It is difficult for us to acknowledge that we are aware of our profession's responsibility to the ecosystems, which are increasingly being taxed. This is not an alarmist view. It is clearly indicated by the dwindling number of plant and animal species present today and the increasing measures we must all take to ensure decent and healthy food, water, air, and space. We must address these issues in our own lives and be willing to look our clients in the eye and say, "This is what I've done and this is our company's policy regarding recycling paper, and so forth." Clients will respect and acknowledge your honesty and position.

Persons with great wealth often have guilty feelings about their power and ability to affect the material world. People in pursuit of money are often insensitive about the effects of their lives and work on the environment. It is difficult to find a truly socially responsible publicly traded company anywhere because of the compromises every large corporation has to make to turn a profit.

We help clients do proactive environmental investing if they want to do so. Many people don't even think about connecting their personal financial security with a concern about the planet. While most people acknowledge their uneasiness about the future of the world, they may not know what to do with their concern. We must echo our clients' concerns about these issues and acknowledge that their concerns are real. Our clients have a right to know how their financial and investment decisions affect the environment.

Value Alignment

We define people with inherited wealth as those who have enough money to ensure their standard of living without working for the rest of their lives. They also have ample funds for their children's education and reserves to help their kids start careers. These people have privileges, comforts, and lifestyle choices that surpass those enjoyed by royalty in previous times. This is true not only on a material level, but also regarding information access, entertainment, and the ability to choose where, when, and how to go anyplace they wish. Today's inheritors are faced with psychological problems similar to those of the royalty of old: overstimulation and potentially self-destructive overindulgence.

In pure numbers, there are many more people with inherited wealth than there ever were persons of royalty. Now, the entry key to the upper class is generally money, not birthright. We see peer groups being established and the beginnings of some understanding of the pressures of having been set aside as a chosen few. Isolated from their economic inferiors, people with great amounts of inherited wealth can find validation by being placed in a contextual situation that acknowledges the trauma of having too much. Like a minister who provides education and advice, the empathetic advisor must allow the person with the royal scepter to make final decisions. Living with the results of decisions, both good and bad, is one of the healthiest steps and a new experience for many people with inherited wealth.

In the context of investing and planning for the future, the inheritors' life-value decisions will affect their family's future probably more than anything else. The ability to affect the world through charitable contribu-

tions is one route to self-esteem. A good and purposeful life through helping others directly is another. Whether these kinds of actualization take
place depends on making good decisions. And this depends on the quality
of advice received from an astute and tuned-in trusted advisor.

The personalities of most people with inherited wealth are created by
their family origins and by the privileged environment in which they grew
up. Portfolio management and financial planning become all the more
important because of the presence of that wealth. The difficult psychological problems that attend everyone in the modern world are painful because
of their internal nature. It is easier to fix something physically and get a
sense of accomplishment and self-worth than to make progress on emotional issues.

Inheritors, like royalty, need to be conscious of what they are doing and
how it affects other people. When too many wealthy people move to an
area, locals are often pushed out. Our job as advisors is to help inheritors
bring their money and actions into congruence with their values. More
often than not, the intent is to help others and give back to the extended
community. As objective, long-term counselors, we need to be ready to
give good advice on avenues that will best accomplish these goals.

People who inherited their wealth are taking the stored-up energy
handed down to them through their families and defining how they want
that energy to go constructively into the future. This kind of work is the
logical step for the generations who come after the accumulators. After the
basics of life have been taken care of, after we have satiated ourselves with
enough material goods and comfort to bolster our sense of being successful, and after we have surrounded ourselves with people who acknowledge
our success, what is the point of having more money? Most inheritors *do*
see the benefits of giving. Comments made by religious leaders concerning the difficulty of owning assets while obtaining spiritual awareness
point to the fact that, while not being mutually exclusive, to have great
riches and to enter heaven is somewhat difficult. When someone who has
either inherited or earned wealth has attained a certain level of accumulation, giving up some of it will provide rich rewards on deeper levels. Many
of our clients have reached that point in their own lives. They have more
than the royalty of old, but without the accompanying public acknowledgment or civic duties. It is our job as advisors to "minister to the royalty" in
a way that clarifies these issues and helps them make decisions that match
their values.

A client decided to set up a private foundation after many years of turmoil within her family. In keeping with our client's desire to repair and maintain relations with her two sisters (all three lived in different parts of the country), she forged a private foundation, funding it with low-tax-cost-basis inherited assets, in which they all shared an interest. The most amazing effect of this, aside from its impact on the organizations that received the money, was the way in which it drew the family together. Our client was transformed. Instead of worrying about money and conflict within her family, she now spends time researching and becoming involved with the organizations to which she gives.

Another client worked for 30 years with his wife to establish a biotech company. The business increased in value and was sold following the couple's divorce. He turned for meaning in his life to helping entrepreneurs in inner cities obtain low-interest loans and technical assistance, some of which he provided himself. In his own mind, the fact that he created employment opportunities for large numbers of people in what were previously thought to be unworkable economic zones was the most worthwhile and rewarding achievement of his business life.

Keeping Informed

It is critical for clients to be kept informed about events affecting their lives. This includes not only financial items but topics of personal interest to them as well. Because we are connecting with them on more than a financial basis, we have to be well-rounded in our research. We can note their concerns and help keep them up-to-date in a way that they can easily understand.

For example, one of our clients is interested in low-income housing. We make a special effort to search the Internet for the latest developments on projects around the world and share how our client can participate. We cut out and mail articles to our client, who thus feels that he is relieved of some of the burden of keeping up with the media. We are in touch, which frees him to do other things with his time.

Clients with inherited wealth want to know how their investments are making a difference in the world. This client, by investing in low-income housing bonds, feels that he is able to help others less fortunate than himself while still getting an adequate and sometimes superior rate of return.

This can be quite involved. He once asked about the kinds of wallboard used in a particular low-income housing renovation project. He was concerned about toxic materials used in standard gypsum board, and he knew about alternatives to this harmful material. We talked to those in charge of the project, and it was the first time they had heard of this matter. Only by getting down to the most detailed level of information on some issues can clients feel that their money is working in concert with their underlying values.

Listening

Listening is a more important and more difficult skill than speaking. Most people talk out of nervousness, trying to prove a point or cover up anxiety. Information that we really need to impart can be delivered in short, simple sentences. We need to ask clients to explain their views and tell their story. The more we can listen, the more credibility we have, because listening is a concrete example of caring. Often, we wish to educate and our clients wish to learn. This does not take place until the conflicting ideas banging around in everyone's heads and the baggage from clients' past experiences have been expressed and dealt with. This involves asking questions. Listening is the best way of learning about people, and it must be done frequently. Our chance to speak, as advisors, occurs when our client asks us a question. Often, we must initiate the dialogue because trust beneficiaries and inheritors can be embarrassed and ashamed about their own lack of knowledge. We may initiate, but the client leads the dialogue.

Responsiveness

Our clients wish to be involved but not overwhelmed by their financial matters. Our philosophy is that we return every call from every client within 24 hours, no matter how small a matter it may involve. This holds true for holidays, sick days, vacation days, and staff meeting days. There are few areas in people's lives where they experience total responsiveness from someone. This is an area in which our staffs are well trained and in which we excel. It is another palpable way of showing clients that they come first.

Clients have a need to air their wishes and articulate their desires. Any item they bring up has to be of utmost concern to us because it represents a possible source of anxiety for them. When clients know we are on top of an issue, their stress levels go down. Our job as trust builders is to be stress busters. Our ability to respond in a timely and complete fashion assures clients that when the market falls or someone dies or there is any kind of trauma in their lives, we will make sure that everything possible is being done and that their psychological peace of mind is our concern.

Clarity

Trust advisors must help clients get clear and concise information. When people want to know if they are doing well, if they are going to have enough money, or if their lifestyle is at risk from some event or another, we try to answer with elegant simplicity. We go directly to the point behind what is often a multilevel inquiry. Clients appreciate straightforward answers, even if bordering on bluntness. Without being abrasive, we try to communicate that many of the thoughts causing them concern are fabrications of media input and are fundamentally unimportant. Inheritors can stop worrying about most financial events they hear about because, working together, we have been clear about our goals and risk tolerance; and safety measures are already in place.

Budgeting first and only then implementing an investment program that they can understand is key. Everyone is anxious about whether they have enough money. By constantly distilling the essence of their plans, showing that the basic assumptions are solid and intact, we allow clients to let go and enjoy. Our clients want to know when major events change our views on the markets. They wish to be shown the history of investment returns and the impact of rising costs on their budgets.

Basically, all that people with inherited wealth really want is clear and convincing reassurance that they are financially secure. If they are not going to be secure, they want and need to know this as soon as possible. Obscuring bad news and making excuses or assigning blame is inappropriate. Information should be conveyed directly, evenhandedly, and simply. When uncertainty about the future is acknowledged and recognized by the advisor and the heir, it simplifies everyone's choices. Emotional connection can now take place between the inheritor and her trusted advisor.

Straightforwardness

When news is bad, we immediately try to communicate on the phone with our clients. It is difficult to say something unpleasant, even to our closest friends. We try to deal with our clients believing they want to know any bad news as soon as possible. Usually they don't shoot the messenger! Our ability to tell clients the hard facts in straightforward terms is greatly prized because so few people are willing to do this, especially among the superwealthy. People with inherited assets do not want to be treated with kid gloves. They don't want things sugarcoated or glossed over. In fact, the sheer magnitude of their assets may make bad news irrelevant from a financial point of view. When clients overspend or their stocks go down, they deserve to know. By acknowledging bad news honestly, we show that we respect our clients and that we have the fortitude to take on whatever may happen.

People with inherited wealth do not wish to be idealized or admired. They wish to be called by their familiar names and to be regarded as peers. Friendly banter and a relaxed, informal atmosphere do wonders for our clients. Pandering to clients involves setting up distinctions that imply separateness. We are trying to dissolve the separateness they feel everywhere else in our culture and to make their experience with us special. Straightforwardness is a refreshing change for many people of wealth.

Interpretation

Trust advisors should be able to interpret current financial news for their clients and communicate its relevance to them. We must know how to speak to them. Once inheritors have made a commitment to a certain lifestyle, they adopt a kind of vocabulary and way of looking at the world. We must understand the subtle nuances of this kind and pass financial information about their current and future situations through this filter.

Scientists like technical language backed up by statistics. Writers appreciate an approach that incorporates intellectual discussion with a contextual description of what is occurring in the financial world. A single style of communication does not work for everyone. This is why canned newsletters, generic seminars, and institutional presentations are not effective with many high-net-worth individuals.

In Chapter 10, we will examine how the providers of trust services have changed. Large institutions are having trouble retaining good people who can deal with inheritors in a flexible way, because they themselves have become more rigid. Interpreting data cannot be done without knowing what is going on with clients, their families, and their overall lives. The ability and willingness to customize services is one of the great strengths and advantages that small firms have over large organizations.

Family Involvement

After personal security, the next priority for most people of wealth is providing for their heirs and resolving family issues regarding wealth. Trust advisors must be willing to take on intergenerational issues and to help strategize and implement plans to pass wealth between clients and their children, grandchildren, and charitable beneficiaries. This involves a knowledge of taxes, trusts, insurance, and family dynamics.

To accomplish this, we need to get to know other members of the family. By spending time with each person, we gain insight into their particular personalities—strengths and weaknesses, interests, and aversions—that will likely affect how well various family members will handle their money in the future. This allows the advisor to give good advice to the current owner of the assets. Our job is to help design the most effective way of maintaining purchasing power for the family for many generations.

How can a family ensure that its younger members' aspirations and motivations are not blunted by having too much money too soon? What will prevent them from having a false sense of entitlement to family assets? How do we keep wealthy heirs from insulating themselves from the world, which eventually prevents them from being part of it?

How do we let the older generations know that they can let go of assets with assurance that their heirs will have an opportunity to gain self-confidence? It is a fine line we tread, because much support is necessary to establish a place in the modern world.

Inheritors would like their connections with their progeny to be as free as possible from the emotional baggage which they themselves may have suffered from their parents' and grandparents' actions. They also want to know that their money will be safe and productive. They don't want their progeny to have to depend on trust officers to make discretionary decisions or to follow legal documents that may well become outdated. Most specific directives written 30 years ago in trust documents have little relevance for today.

It is difficult to imagine all the factors that may need to be considered to make future trusts appropriate to the lives of children and grandchildren. People wish to provide for their heirs in a healthy way, to empower them, and to preserve their sense of self-confidence. Poorly drafted trusts stuck in large institutions are the cause of much dissatisfaction and disempowerment. Advisors must help clients understand all their options. To do this, they must be involved with the clients' families.

The Glaze Factor

How many times have we sat down in meetings and found ourselves glazed over because too much information is presented to us in an uninteresting way? Every person's particular way of learning and absorbing information is different. As advisors, we must reject boilerplate reports and standardized meeting formats. Clients want knowledge, hope, and wisdom. Often, advisors give them only data that they may or may not turn into usable information. The kind of condensation or reformatting that is done is all-important. There are only a few basic questions to be asked, but many ways of answering them. We know when we have hit on the appropriate presentation when a client's eyes stay bright during our meetings with them. If not, we have succumbed to the glaze factor.

Being a Conduit

Our job as advisors is to be a clear conduit through which all of the multiple facts about the clients' situations can be integrated, distilled, and presented back to them in a way they can absorb. Clients want to be involved but not overwhelmed. Clients need help in understanding the multiple tax and legal ramifications of estate planning. Financial management and budgeting for future lifestyles are mathematical exercises, but their implementation is wholly human.

Clients need to feel in charge in all of these areas. How can advisors take all the information that relates to clients' financial lives and present it to them in a way that has integrity? This is the challenge, then: to filter but not unduly influence, to advise but not take over. *Taking control of inherited wealth is the job of the inheritor; the advisor is there to help manage it wisely.* We must be careful that our judgments are articulated and identified as such. This is an ego-effacing process that does advisors and our clients with inherited wealth much good.

Counseling

We know that communicating with clients regularly and in accordance with their styles is of paramount importance. How do we know which methods they prefer and in what detail they wish to be kept informed? We ask them! This has yielded some very surprising results: Many clients do not wish to be bothered with most of the nitty-gritty details because their lives are already too full. They want information in various formats, fed to them when *they* think it's important.

We always try to find out our clients' desires and to give them the power to turn off the volumes of paper they receive. They want space and control, not more clutter. Clients want to be involved in their big decisions. It is sometimes difficult to communicate with clients because of their underlying fear of potential losses, conflict with other family members over money, and lack of clarity about their own personal goals. Many people with wealth know exactly what they want and have clarified their family issues; they wish only to be left alone to enjoy their lives. However, even these clients have a great deal of anxiety about whether they are doing everything "right." This is a common anxiety. They can never have a solid enough grasp on their financial world because they've never had to struggle to make money; feelings of accomplishment are transient.

We acknowledge this by saying that the issues most important to our clients are also important to us. We then ask them to share their views. In response, we generally get a torrent of stories about inappropriate investments, broken promises, misplaced trust, family feuds, personal regrets, and so on. We then try to acknowledge this in a way that neither self-aggrandizes us nor cuts down on the validity of the wounds of the person relating these stories. In fact, we acknowledge the strength that it takes to bring all these issues forward, and we try to be of assistance in sorting them out. We refer many clients to professional counselors, especially if a therapist who specializes in financial issues is available.

The need for interpersonal relationships between inheritors and their advisors is evident. The trusted advisor can provide living examples of freedom from the fear and greed that surround money issues.

Convenience

Part of a trusted advisor's job is to reduce their clients' levels of stress. The quickest and easiest way to do this is to save them time. We try to save people time by doing things for them. This is high on the list of services desired by wealthy individuals.

In our firm, we try to make things convenient for our clients. We are willing to make calls, write letters, do errands—whatever we can to make our clients' lives easier. We anticipate what is necessary for trips. When things go wrong, we are there to help right them, even if we don't bill for it. People with inherited wealth prefer professionals and their office staff who can save them time and insulate them from hassles.

Insulate and Protect

As financial advisors, we try to protect our clients against unscrupulous salespeople. It is easy to gloss over the difficulties of staying abreast in financial matters. We have systems in place to protect our adherence to our stated investment discipline. On a practical level, we can drastically reduce paperwork generated by our own firm, and we can protect clients from mail, phone calls, and solicitations that they receive from custodians, banks, and the other purveyors of financial services.

We take on the responsibility of filling out all kinds of paperwork whenever possible. This is not to say we try to put blinders on clients by insulating them from facts about difficulties in the markets. We do try to interject a sense of history and of the long-term nature of our plan to give clients an overview of the screens we erect to protect them from being overwhelmed with too many choices. Decisions today regarding spending, asset allocation, and estate planning greatly affect their futures.

Overall, the displacement of worry and anxiety is crucial. Nick Murray, in his book, *The Excellent Investment Advisor,* makes a statement that we often hand out to our clients: "We absolutely forbid our clients to worry because in a very real sense that's what they are paying us to do."

If clients are going to pay for investment counsel and then worry about it, they haven't really accepted the advice being offered. This in effect means that there is no real trust between the advisor and the client. We cannot handle client assets on that basis because it wouldn't be fair to either the client or ourselves.

For a trust relationship to exist, the SIP must hold up one end of the bargain: "It is my job to know about asset allocation, market history, and the latest developments in the financial world; therefore, you don't need to worry about these things." The client's part of the bargain is no less important: "I will inform you in an honest and straightforward way when I am worried about my spending patterns. I am willing to be an adult and to be told that I'm spending too much." Our clients understand that all final decisions rest with them. If we do our jobs well and if society as a whole doesn't fall apart, then they will by and large have financial security. What more could anyone ask for?

Humility

We do not tell clients that we are geniuses or have special access to information. Perhaps business clairvoyants exist who are ahead of the curve and can foretell the future of interest rate changes, company earnings, or macroeconomic changes—but we've never met them! This is not to be confused with hard work and research. Most seasoned investment professionals know that they are better off to confess at the start that they are neither smarter nor better than others when it comes to predicting the future. What trusted advisors do have is the honesty and integrity to deliver favorable long-term results.

By taking this humble approach, we sense the inheritor's anxiety level going down. By choosing to work with us, clients must believe that there is no longer any reason to watch the market on a day-to-day or week-to-week basis. The best sign that a successful trust relationship exists is that both parties are up-to-date, informed, communicating, and comfortable with the long-term program. Clients accept the reality that we don't know all of the important answers. We try to know most of the important questions, however.

Conclusion

To summarize, we feel that trusted advisors must carefully examine their own resources and motivations. If the qualities and traits covered in this chapter are not present in your personality or are not embodied in your firm, then you must either change your focus or admit that the trust arena is not an appropriate field for you. Client-advisor relationships that have the most long-lasting value are those in which mutual respect and understanding are first and foremost in both parties' minds.

As with any close relationship, we need to reveal ourselves in all of our faults and glory so that our clients can decide if they wish to move forward in an open, honest relationship. There is too much anxiety in the world already. We need not bring more into play by attempting to establish inappropriate relationships. Overall, as advisors, our ability to be on our clients' side, to walk in their shoes, and to reduce the stress in their lives, is determined by our ability to manifest the previously noted psychological attributes and bring them to bear on inheritors' situations. As we move on to Part 3, analyzing existing trusts and learning how to move trusts, we must keep in mind that without these personal attributes, there will likely be disappointment and disillusionment for both parties.

We believe that communication on a personal level is the key to establishing the bond of trust between the client and the advisor. The commitment to making the relationship work has to come from both parties. We also know that the trusted advisor has to be willing to admit mistakes and pay for them when they occur—not *if* they occur but *when* they occur. In the perfect world, services would be delivered precisely and on time. In the real world, this doesn't happen. By connecting on a personal level, we are prepared with humility and integrity to pay for our mistakes out of our own pockets: Our clients know that their interests come first.

Part 3

The Trust Business

Part 3 examines the specific world of trustees, both trust departments and individuals, and summarizes their relationships with beneficiaries. Chapter 10 gives an overview of the size of this market and provides profiles of trust service providers.

Chapter 11 explains the different types of beneficiaries, the reasons trust relationships go awry, and what to do about it. Chapter 12 explores the difficulty in facing up to dysfunctional financial relationships. Chapter 13 discusses in detail expectations and methods that can be used to establish goals for desirable trust situations.

The Trust World

Studies show that the largest transfer of wealth in history is taking place as the baby boomer's parents (described in Chapter 1) pass on. The value of assets moving down to the baby boomer generation is, by some estimates, around $10 trillion. How does $10 trillion become meaningful? It is 10 times the size of all the assets in Merrill Lynch, by far the largest brokerage firm in the United States. It is five times more than all the money currently held in all bank trust departments.

Much of these transfers will be in the form of liquid assets, as family businesses and real estate holdings are sold. Baby boomers, now in their 40s and 50s, don't want to live in the same place as their parents, so residential turnover will be high. This could signal a weak market for real estate in some areas. We estimate that approximately half of this $10 trillion will be in the form of securities.

Trust Money

It is difficult to ascertain exactly how much money is tied up in *irrevocable* trusts. In Chapter 7, we described irrevocable trusts as accounts that prohibit the trust originators from changing their minds and withdrawing funds at will. Irrevocable trusts are almost always set up to involve a third party who is to act as an unrelated trustee.

We know that the trusts held by state and federally chartered banks represent only a portion of total trust money. Bank trust departments are required to file forms with the Office of the Comptroller of the Currency, which is the organization responsible for supervision of national bank trust departments. By reviewing the combined totals of the reports of these institutions, we came up with the following figures: 900,000 trusts, with an average size of $250,000, or a total of $225 billion in trust at national banks. This does not include trusts held by independent trust companies or private trustees.

In addition to bank-chartered institutions, many independent trust departments now file reports with state organizations or with the Office of Thrift Supervision. There are fewer of these trust organizations and they are smaller in size than the bank trust departments. However, they comprise a growing portion of the market, and many private trust companies are finding it advantageous to aggressively pursue this field, which was formerly dominated by large banks.

If the number of trusts is about a million, the number of trust tax returns filed annually with the Internal Revenue Service by beneficiaries is, at last count, approximately 2 million, or about 1% of the U.S. population. Approximately the same percentage of the U.S. population makes up the upper class, defined as those earning over $100,000 per year. Private trusts make up 50% of all trusts, and by our unscientific sampling, they are much larger than the trusts held by banks.

The trusts we are talking about here are all irrevocable. There are innumerable *revocable trusts,* ones that *can* be changed by the person who set them up. This is a common estate planning device used to avoid probate on assets that are inside the revocable trust. These trusts do not live past the life of the grantor—unless at that time they become irrevocable trusts.

The number of irrevocable charitable trusts is growing rapidly. It is one of a few estate planning devices remaining where wealthy people can avoid estate tax and still direct their family assets to causes of their choosing. We might well ask how much money is likely to be put into new irrevocable trusts over the next two decades. If one-tenth of the wealthy population chooses to avoid paying estate tax by creating a trust, that would create 200,000 new trusts averaging 1 million dollars each.

Every major financial firm in the nation is well aware of these projections, and they have created private trust departments in order to attract this trust money. The increase in the number of people working at financial services companies is staggering. The uniformity of their message is,

"Come to us and we'll take care of you and all of your assets." There are some similarities here with the evolution of automobile advertising. When the major car manufacturers realized that people were buying lifestyle decisions and not specific features, talk about 365 overhead cams with dual exhausts gave way to a softer sell, where looks, comfort level, and reliability were the lead topics.

In the financial services world, fees are the last thing to be clarified, and relative investment performance is way down on the list in terms of criteria by which most people pick trustees or trust advisors.

Trust Players: Who Are They?

There is no appreciable difference between the strategic plans of banks, brokerage firms, insurance companies, mutual funds, financial planners, and investment advisors. All these players realize that it comes down to who gets out in front of inheritors with trust needs first. The words, products, and services each player uses are essentially the same. The issue is who can make a case that they are an appropriate match with the personality and lifestyle of the client. The expertise of individuals and their warmth, compassion, and level of personal involvement with clients are features that differentiate between good and not-so-good practitioners. Clients are, by and large, unaware of differences in technical skill, and all of their prospective advisors seem to have compelling cases that their investment approach is the best. Here are brief descriptions of the player. Inheritors are keenly tuned in to the persona of the advisor they end up choosing.

Money Center Banks

The largest players in the trust world are the money center banks. Located on the East and West Coasts in major metropolitan areas, these megabanks are so large that they have a governmental feeling. These players have been created by merging with former competitors. They are superregional or national franchises. Their combined strength is mostly on paper. The trust and investment services provided by these banks has been compromised by their rapid growth. These banks have several generations of common trust funds. They have their own publicly traded mutual funds. They represent themselves as professional money managers and are very strong in providing multiple services, such as commercial lending, real estate, lines of credit, insurance, and business planning. The money center superregionals are very appropriate matches for entrepreneurs who are expanding on a national scale. Money center banks, many with internationally recognized names, are unable to keep persons of great talent because of the relative anonymity of their functioning, the remoteness of the client-advisor relationship, and the relatively low salaries paid to bank employees.

Private Banks

Old-line banks, such as Bessemer and J.P. Morgan, have focused on serving inheritors investment needs for many years. They have branched out into underwriting securities for new companies, and they provide financing for deals around the world. Old-line private banks are like their European counterparts. They strive to present an image of upper-class refinement, exclusivity, and status. The investment resources at their disposal are good, and they are able to develop practical expertise in specific areas such as foreign or small-company investing because of their acquisition of private investment firms. The old-line, private banks are set up to be in line with the needs of people of wealth. They have experience in seeing multigenerational planning through to conclusion. Their services are very expensive, and they are consciously selective in taking only profitable clients.

Professional Dynasties: Law Firms

Another major provider of trust services is what we call a *professional dynasty*. In the larger cities, such as Boston, Chicago, New York, and San Francisco, where old family wealth abounds, attorneys and accountants have successfully established themselves as alternatives to banks. Through legal loopholes, written by and for their industry, law firms act as "company" trustees without being registered with any authority or regulatory supervision. These upper-crust firms have a major advantage over banks in that they are constantly in touch with people and have an intimate knowledge of the inheritors' family financial situation. More often than not, when people create trusts, they will have been working closely with an attorney. A confidential relationship springs up, which the most forward-looking attorney wisely guides toward an ongoing fiduciary relationship, first by naming themselves as trustees for clients who can't quite decide which family member, if any, to use as trustee. Attorneys have ample opportunity to be especially persuasive in explaining that only they can put up with the pressures of fighting heirs; therefore, their own firms' members are the most attractive and natural choice.

We have seen some real abuse in the actions of professional dynasties. After the trust originator and the original trusted legal advisor have passed on, a professional dynasty can become an out-of-control nightmare. We have seen one of the oldest law firms in Chicago violate basic reporting and fee-disclosure requirements. They feel justified in double-billing the account for both legal services and fiduciary fees. Professional dynasties tend to be more distant and rigid than banks. They are not held up to any sort of public scrutiny and are not subject to public shareholder meetings or regulatory oversight.

If a personal relationship existing between the attorney and originator passes down to junior partners and heirs, it is possible for the beneficiaries to feel a more personal connection with a professional firm than with a bank. This primarily occurs with the smaller-size professional dynasties, and the principals are often more highly motivated than the employees because they stand to benefit handsomely from continued good trust relationships.

There is a great loss of power but continued psychological comfort and familiarity in these situations. In the investment area, law firms have no in-house investment expertise. They generally find an associated investment firm that will refer legal business to them in exchange for management of the accounts for which the law firm acts as trustee. For the most part, professional dynasties' trust assets are sent to large brokers. Why? Because large brokers have the most potential clients to refer back to the large attorney firms. This is very understandable.

Expanded Family Offices

The expanded family offices of wealthy families also provide trust services. Family offices were created by moneyed families who got tired of paying separate attorney, accountant, investment management, bank, personal assistant, and other management fees. By bringing all of these functions in-house, wealthy families created their own business entities whose sole function was to manage wealth on behalf of family members. Some families (for example, the Pitcairns) decided they were so pleased with their family office that they would offer it to other wealthy families. The advantage of these organizations is that they work exclusively with wealthy families and thus understand their clientele's emotional problems and idiosyncratic needs. On the other hand, many lack expertise in the markets. By and large, family offices are a good alternative to private banks for people who want a more intimate setting.

Regional Conglomerates

Unlike the gigantic money center banks in major metropolitan areas, some regional banks have followed pretty much the same line as their big-city brethren in terms of consolidation and reorganization. It is hard to say how many banks will be left in this category, because they are neither small nor mammoth. Fleet Bank in the Northeast and First Security Bank in the West are two examples of the players in this middle-size market. They have neither excellent investment departments nor close personal contacts with clients. The regional conglomerates are generally what people get stuck with when their local banks are taken over—unless, of course, the local becomes part of a national chain.

Local Bank Trust Department

Local independent banks, whether long established or newly created, are able to provide minimal investment services. They are usually associated with another bank or an outside firm that acts as a subcontractor. In these situations, clients can have a great deal of personal contact, but it will be with someone who is unlikely to stay at the bank in that relationship for very long, and investments will be canned and delivered en masse. The pressure on local banks for immediate profitability is not that great, and they do understand that face-to-face communication is important to people in small and midsize towns. Local banks have neither investment expertise nor the ability to do in-house financial or estate planning, taxes, or high-end analysis. However, they are able to be part of a local team, and for older inheritors, it is comforting to know that the traditional trust officer still exists, at least for now, at some locations.

Local Independent Trust Companies

These companies are being established around the country. The Association of Independent Trust Companies (AITCO), based in Chicago, can provide a list of local companies that are set up primarily to provide trust services. AITCO can be contacted by phone at (312) 527-6735, or by mail at 401 North Michigan Avenue, Chicago, IL 60611. Independent trust companies vary from new start-ups with very little capital and experience to amalgamations of experienced trust officers who have raised millions of dollars of capital in order to get a National Trust charter.

Independent trust companies fall into two categories. In the first are wholesalers of trust services to independent advisors, planners, brokers, and insurance agents. These trust companies act as *nominal* trustees, which means that they hold title to the assets but do not take actual custody or make investment decisions. Their primary function is to review the fiduciary appropriateness of the investments of another financial advisor and to maintain the books. This has the advantage of allowing people to keep their own financial advisor or broker acting in the larger capacity of overall coach for clients' financial situations. A client needn't have to go to a trust officer who is thinking only of the one particular trust under his tutelage. Instead, trust beneficiaries using independents can go to the person who is thinking of the client's big picture. These nominal corporate trustees are price-sensitive. They are not available for clients to lean on in hard times. They are able to provide corporate trustee services at a low cost, which in turn enables financial advisors to be compensated. Our firm has established relationships with independent trust companies all over the country. They allow us to help heirs gain control over their assets. The best trust companies also provide electronic download capability to a variety of advisor portfolio management software programs.

The other category of private independent trust companies acts as a full trustee. In effect, they are substitute family offices for persons of wealth who don't have the capital or desire to start their own. The amount of assets it takes to successfully create a private family office is in the $50 million range. It takes at least $200 million to start a private trust company that serves other families. Some independent trust companies are extremely responsive and well managed. Others appear to be fly-by-night operations seeking to take advantage of the unraveling of trust services at local banks. We visited one such company that had no experience in trusts, no management capability, and no trust business. Yet this firm was planning an incredible expansion, targeting advisors who might not know the difference. The regulatory climate for independent trust companies varies from state to state.

Individual Trustees

The final player we will discuss in the trust market are individual or private trustees. These are usually lawyers, accountants, or family friends who have accepted appointment as trustee and maintain close contact with the family members. The downside of using these individuals as trustees is that they generally have expertise in only one area. People who choose individual trustees are totally dependent on their trustees to find outside providers of the ancillary services that will most definitely be needed by the trust. Private trustees are the hardest to rein in, and they generally do not perform well in the investment area.

Conclusion

This initial lineup of trust players lays out some important considerations in understanding who might best serve an inheritor. It is a first effort to pull together the reality of the business world of trust providers with the emotional and psychological needs of inheritors. We will return to this subject in Parts 4 and 5, after we show how to change an existing subpar trust relationship.

Trust Mismatches: When the Thrill Is Gone

N ow that we have outlined the types of trust service providers, we will explain the different personality types of trust beneficiaries. Before exploring mismatches in detail, we will look at some examples of clients who are not well served by their current trust server providers. The more background an advisor has in recognizing the problems that most people of inherited wealth experience with their bank trustees, the quicker she will be able to identify the shortcomings of the situation as well as the psychological factors at play under the surface complaints.

When previous generations set up trusts there was usually some kind of bond between themselves and a financial institution. Perhaps it was the local bank trust department, chosen because the bank president and the family founder were close friends. Perhaps a business associate or an attorney became trustee. This arrangement was fine while both parties were alive. Now, there is a second or third succeeding generation of bank officers, or junior partners grown to be of senior status, who operate under a different environment. Concurrently, there are new beneficiaries, with different values, and so the personal connection is barely reminiscent of the original. The period when the trust department or friend was able to provide a high level of individualized service because of personal knowledge of family personalities is over. Today, bank trust departments are managed from afar. Their primary motivation is profit, which means reducing personnel and increasing the standardization of investments and services as much as possible.

Out of fear and insecurity, some trust beneficiary personality types don't want to disturb the relationships set up by a beneficiary's parents, grandparents, or great-grandparents. Others, perhaps out of ignorance, don't understand that they *can* change the relationships. The first type of reticence to approach problems is perpetrated by the trustees themselves. They have the attitude that trust beneficiaries can't do or say anything about the quality of the trust service provider. *The prevailing attitude is that the bank or lawyer has a permanent, unshakable, and legal right to their job as trustee for the term of the trust, that beneficiaries are stuck with them, and that there is no choice in the matter. This is absolutely not the case!*

Trust Beneficiaries: What Do They Need?

The lifestyle habits and sensitivities of inheritors have been the subject of some study because of their large amount of investable funds. If you are a member of this class of people, you can be sure that your habits of spending, the kinds of media that you read and watch, and the particular style of language and advertising that appeals most to you have been dissected by marketing firms. Your thought patterns have even been divided into "do-it-yourselfers" and "delegators" by financial service companies, who are gearing up to provide trust services to at least one if not all of these new classes of inheritors.

This chapter identifies the different kinds of trust beneficiaries so that in later chapters we can match personality types of beneficiaries with the varying capacities of service providers. The classifications that follow offer a general description of the kind of personal characteristics of dissatisfied inheritors that might belong in each class. Please note that we are highlighting the problems here to be helpful, not to create rigid characteristics that stereotype real people. As a beneficiary you may be interested in identifying the behavior class that most closely describes your stress behavior. Then you can determine which kind of trust provider might be most suitable for you to help deal with those issues that relate to your family history.

- Caretakers

- Avoiders

- Drivers
- Worriers
- Entrepreneurs
- Status seekers
- Socialites
- Accumulators
- Technocrats
- Philanthropists

Caretakers

Caretakers are above all, nice people. They are the givers in the codependent relationships. They prefer to stand on the sidelines if there is a dispute and do not generally like to make decisions about financial matters. The caretaker is slightly uncomfortable sitting in on meetings regarding financial affairs and prefers emotional interaction to discussions about making money. The caretaker is a fun person to be with and tends to worry about other people's happiness. Caretakers are responsible, diligent, and generally put themselves last when it comes to spending time on their own personal interests.

Trust service needs of the Caretaker

Caretakers need a solid presence on which they can lean because they are being leaned on themselves by a variety of family members or friends. Caretakers want an empathic presence who is accessible and can converse with them on many different subjects, mostly non-business-related. The caretaker needs money on demand and does not want much information about investment particulars. Caretaker types need someone who will help them take care of paperwork. This includes establishing their estate plans and coordinating their tax returns as well. They can have insightful comments about investment opportunities because they are not misled by paying attention to the financial media.

Avoiders

Avoiders are people who rarely get around to thinking about their financial affairs. They are worried that looking at their statements may bring up painful memories of how they were insulated from and uneducated about their family's wealth during their formative years. Money issues can bring a lack of confidence within themselves about their own accomplishments. The avoider is amenable, flexible, and nondemanding. Any sign of conflict can threaten their sense of peace. Avoiders may get into trouble because they do not look at how much money they are spending versus their income. There is an assumption on the avoider's part that something will eventually turn up to take care of future money problems. The avoider enjoys the good things in life and is likely to be jovial and congenial. Avoiders do not have a desire to do the work needed to understand investments. As long as the assets are intact, the avoider is content. Avoiders can follow an investment program with diligence and discipline, as they rely heavily on their advisor.

Trust service needs of the Avoider

The needs of the avoider are many. There is an underlying, unspoken anxiety in the avoider's life regarding long-term planning and family security. It is difficult for large institutions to provide personalized service, and the avoider fits well into such institutions because he does not complain or rebel against neglect. The institution does not proactively give or explain information to the avoider, nor does the avoider proactively take the time or effort required to ask the institution to analyze what is going on in the account.

Avoiders need someone who will take the lead and say, "This is what is going on with your assets. These are the dangers, and this is the reality of your financial life right now." Avoiders need someone who will make them stick to a schedule of discussions about money, help them do budgets, and assist them in looking at the reality of the family dynamics regarding money.

Drivers

Drivers are people who want, above all, to be in control. They must understand and be involved in every decision. Drivers think that they are essential to getting it right. They are totally up-to-date regarding the family financial situation. In the past, drivers were predominately male. Drivers like to choose their own investments. They won't hesitate to switch attorneys, accountants, or advisors to find the most aggressive person, someone who will follow the driver's own approach. Drivers can be their own worst enemies by making frequent investment changes. They want large amounts of information so they can make their own decisions. Drivers can drive other people crazy. They may be isolated and remote. They often miss out on enjoying life because their time is spent poring over details rather than enjoying the fruits of their labors.

Trust service needs of the Driver

They need control and directness. Drivers want to make the decisions, but they are happy to have a map if it is formatted in an acceptable way. They need not only information but also tools to effect their own transactions. They pride themselves on being able to stay up-to-date on the latest developments in the legal and accounting fields. Drivers need to have many more meetings than do avoiders or caretakers. They need to be in charge of those meetings as well. Drivers tend to ignore the nuances and long-term ramifications of their decisions because they move quickly and decisively. Many drivers tend to be influenced by offhand comments made by their peers regarding investment opportunities. They are very demanding of their professional trust advisors. Drivers chafe at rigid policies and procedures. They require flexibility and accessibility to top people—on their own time frame. Drivers need the most up-to-date technological perks, and they work best with advisors who don't mind taking a back seat at appropriate moments.

Worriers

Worriers are people whose lives are occasionally filled with anxiety about almost everything. Regarding inherited assets, the worrier is fearful, which prevents him from understanding the basic mechanisms of what he has, what it will and will not provide. The worrier can be a victim, and salespeople take advantage of his concerns. Worriers believe in many different approaches but have difficulty settling on one path. Worriers can be persuaded to move from advisor to advisor because they are unsure if they've ever made the right decisions. The worrier is unclear about what he wants out of life. The worrier listens to the day's news and is concerned that current events will adversely affect his lifestyle.

All this contributes to the short-term horizon of the worrier. Little comfort is gleaned from his assets as worriers are constantly trying to think of alternative plans to deal with the disastrous circumstances in which they are sure to find themselves. Worriers tend to be deferential in their treatment of others, because every person they meet becomes an expert who knows more than they do. A beneficial characteristic of worriers is that they tend not to be as greedy as other people, as "caution" is a watchword of their personalities.

Trust service needs of the Worrier

First, worriers need a solid, consistent, low-key personality with whom they can deal. Constantly reassuring worriers that they have done the right thing is necessary. They need to be told that they are on the right track, that they have ample assets (if this is so), that the world is not about to disintegrate. It is difficult for worriers to accept optimism, but they need to hear it often. Someone calm must be present in worriers' lives in order to provide a balance to their anxious energy.

Entrepreneurs

Entrepreneurs are bright, capable, and extremely confident in their ability to deal with the future. The entrepreneur, by definition, likes to take risks and therefore is an aggressive player in the financial markets. Many entrepreneurs have little time to spend on their personal financial situations because their own ventures consume much of their energy. For this reason, entrepreneurs quickly and easily delegate matters that are peripheral to their areas of interest. However, entrepreneurs can feel that they have a better approach than their advisors. Entrepreneurs seldom take time to tend to details, and therefore rarely address estate and tax planning, unless it's presented aggressively to them as a way to decrease or avoid taxes.

Trust service needs of the Entrepreneur

The needs of entrepreneurs include a fast-paced, highly condensed, educational, and technical approach distilled to a minimum to fit into their busy schedules. Entrepreneurs need someone to manage all aspects of financial matters outside of the entrepreneurs' own areas. Entrepreneurs like to communicate at their own convenience. They will go for long periods of time with no demands, an attitude of benign neglect, and then jump into the scene with pointed questions, only to move on again after the dust has settled. They are capable of ignoring the whole trust scene until once again, it comes to the forefront of their attention. Entrepreneurs often are quite accurate in their assessment of investment opportunities, particularly those in the technical areas of their expertise.

Status Seekers

Status seekers are people with inherited wealth who feel the need for external verification of their own worth. They seek comfort in the company of others in the same socioeconomic class. Status seekers like the security of brand-name recognition. They like to feel liked in public. Status seekers are willing to be named on boards of directors and admired for their artistic, spiritual, or charitable accomplishments. Status seekers want to have at least one of the top-performing investment vehicles at all times. Status seekers can be brutally demanding on subordinates and staff people. They have highly honed social skills. They are very loyal to those who meet their criteria of acceptability and as such make good clients.

Trust service needs of Status Seekers

Inheritors of this type need stroking. They need constant assurance that their investments are the best ones possible and that recognized experts confirm the validity of the approach being used. They like stories, but not much technical information, to reassure them that they are in with the best and brightest. The trust would is usually acceptable to them as long as proper acknowledgment and deference is paid to their status by the trustee and advisor.

Socialites

Socialites need to have the security of stable assets and they want assurance it will last forever. Because they have external value systems, socialites tend to spend freely and don't want to be told much about where their money comes from. They are active in charities and the arts. They have difficulty with intimate relationships, even though they have many friends. Socialites are not very demanding of their advisors, but neither do they take responsibility in following up on budgets or estate planning meetings. Socialites like to discuss many topics at length —but do not necessarily bring up the things that are really troubling them. Socialites are very verbal in their support of advisors who help take care of them.

Trust service needs of the Socialite

They need solid, methodical programs that act as an offset to their diffuse energy. Tasks and accountability are not things socialites like, but things they do appreciate. There is an underlying anxiety inside a socialite personality that the bottom might drop out of the stock market or any other investment she might be in; thereby, threatening the stable and secure life so important to the socialite.

Socialites make a strong effort to have an effect on society through their charitable work. They are persistent and have a refreshing optimistic attitude. They do not need reinforcement by others for the validity of their actions. But they need close attention and much personal service in the financial arena; and the security of wealth makes them feel happy.

Accumulators

Accumulators gather money without spending or enjoying it. They need to be in control and worry that they will not have enough money. They tend to be conservative investors. Accumulators are worried about the future and concerned that they will be taken advantage of. Accumulators like dealing with people who have technical certifications and expertise. They expect to receive the highest-quality service for a moderate cost. Accumulators are difficult people for advisors to deal with because they are unrelenting in their attention to detail and expect a special reduced price.

Trust service needs of the Accumulators

Accumulators need expansive, long-range planning that will help them feel comfortable that the future is adequately profiled. This helps them relax and not obsess about changes and risks in the financial world. The best medicine for accumulators is information that points out how their diversification program is working. They need concrete proof that all aspects of their financial lives are being considered and that every detail is being reviewed on a regular basis. Accumulators like frequent and detailed reporting. They do not like face-to-face contact.

Technocrats

Addicts are obsessive-compulsive personalities, who sometimes have a latent desire to gamble. They have a high regard for their own abilities and tend to focus on one small aspect of their financial lives. Technocrats can be exciting to be around when their attitude is positive—and difficult when they are discouraged. Technocrats like to have access to all the details. They insist on making their own decisions, directing their advisors.

Trust service needs of the Technocrats

Technocrats need someone to temper their one-sided and exuberant enthusiasm when they are right and to allay their desire to totally change financial direction when they, or the markets, are down. By being shown an integrated approach to planning, technocrats' behaviors can be mollified and their anxiety reduced. Technocrats want formal reports only irregularly, but they must have a constant and immediate source of information.

They make good investors because they understand the changing nature of the market, and losses do not faze them.

Philanthropists

Philanthropists are usually people who have made or inherited tremendous amounts of money. Philanthropists also tend to be interested in self-development, putting energy into activities that will make them better, healthier, or happier people. Philanthropists are concerned about other people, animals, and the impact of their investments on the world. They appreciate efficiency and effectiveness so their expectations are of excellent service.

Trust service needs of the Philanthropist

Philanthropists need knowledge and not information. Communication needs to be formatted simply so they can understand it quickly and go on with the more interesting parts of their lives. They need to feel directly the effect of their gifting to the world. They do not need the most up-to-date technological access to information nor do they necessarily like sophisticated presentations. Philanthropists like to read, to be well informed, but not be under pressure to make decisions in time frames other than their own.

Matching Inheritors and Beneficiaries with Appropriate Trust Providers

When you, an inheritor, know which type of investment psychological profile you fit in, see if you recognize one of our profiles of trustee descriptions. You then need to consider whether you are satisfied with your current partner. Why is it that you may not find peace of mind in your current relationships? People with inherited money in trusts often do not realize that they have a choice of trustees. We will explain your choices and then show you how to make a change if it is necessary. It is up to trust service providers to choose those potential clients for whom they wish to provide trust services. This will depend on the kind of people with whom they are most adept and comfortable. Most trust beneficiaries feel that they cannot choose their own trustees. If they are unhappy, they feel nothing can be done. We hope to show unhappy inheritors and trust beneficiaries how to figure out why they are unhappy, and what can be done about the situation.

Persons who have created wealth on their own need to know what kind of trustees to look for so that the mistakes and horror stories of the past are not repeated in the future. The surviving spouses and children of the wealthy families who participate in private foundation decisions, and corporate executives nearing retirement should research all possible options in the trust world. By now, beneficiaries should have an idea of what kinds of players (i.e., trust service providers) are available in the market place and who might best serve the family trust. The next step is to match the trustee players with the different types of trust beneficiaries. See Table 11.1.

Caretakers are the easiest to please and could be served well by almost any of the trust service providers. They need to have a personal connection, so large institutions tend to be the least effective. However, if caring people find themselves attached to a large institution, they may stay there, as change is not comfortable for this type of beneficiary. Caretakers form strong relationships and are loyal clients. They do not wish to be in another direct relationship, so using private trustees is not a healthy option. Private family offices, local independent trust companies, or local banks are the best choice for caretakers.

Avoiders prefer to be minimally involved and enjoy turning over their affairs to others. Avoiders tend to choose the first person who comes along or who is referred to them by a friend. Not being businesspeople, avoiders don't have a clear idea of whether they are being well served or not. Sometimes they worry that they are not making as much money as other people. Avoiders like to be given structure in which they can see that someone is applying the financial discipline that they so strongly desire but are unable to implement themselves. Though they're not disciplined themselves, they want advisors who are. Private trustees and professional dynasties are happy to take on work for the avoider. Private trustees and professional dynasties are willing to assume responsibility for all aspects of other people's financial life because it is the most profitable part of their business. Regional and money center banks tend to be poor choices for the avoider, but they are in a good position to get that business because of the avoider's reluctance to do research. All trust service providers will do well as long as they don't insist that avoiders make their own decisions regarding their financial affairs.

Drivers are best served by family offices, local independent trust companies, and professional dynasties. Because drivers want to get involved and make decisions, money center banks, regional banks, and local banks are not good choices—their cumbersome procedures and committee structures would be too constraining. Private banks and family offices may be willing to take on drivers if enough wealth is involved. The professional

TABLE 11.1 The Beneficiary Profile

Classify yourself (or your client) to determine which match is the most appropriate in choosing a trustee for your trust or inherited assets. Knowing your fears and strengths will help you decide on the right trust service provider for your situation. Types of beneficiary personalities are matched to compatible trustee types.

Beneficiary Types	Trustee Matches
Caretakers ■ Easy to please ■ Enjoy personal connections ■ Desire a strong coordinator ■ Need constant education	All but money center and regional banks
Avoiders ■ Dislike being involved ■ Not great detail people ■ Not sure if they are being served properly ■ Avoid discipline but appreciate others who can provide it ■ Spending limits unclear	All okay, but the best are smaller institutions
Drivers ■ Need to get involved occasionally ■ Like to make decisions ■ Require access to decision makers ■ Busy—very time conscious ■ Volatile—change their minds often	Not the large, medium, or small banks
Worriers ■ Don't like to lose any money, anytime ■ Want confidentiality, stability, and little risk ■ Need constant reassurance and protection ■ Require much individualized attention	Independent trust companies, money center banks, or regional conglomerates all acceptable. Not professional dynasty or individual trustee
Entrepreneurs ■ Not likely to delegate authority but easily share responsibility ■ Like one-stop shopping—total service for one price ■ Demand respect and admiration ■ High desire for information on demand	Can fit with any except independent trust companies and local bank trust departments

(continues)

TABLE 11.1 The Beneficiary Profile (*continued*)

Beneficiary Types	Trustee Matches
Status Seekers ■ Image is of high importance ■ Desire for personal contact ■ Opportunities for networking ■ Like narratives—not numbers	Most likely not independent trust companies, local bank trust departments, or individual trustees; okay with money center banks, regional conglomerates, family offices, private banks, or professional dynasties
Socialites ■ Not focused on numerical returns ■ Need reinforcement of their relative standing ■ Desire complete service ■ Not price-sensitive ■ Sophisticated sensibilities	Same as status seekers, above
Accumulators ■ Very price-sensitive ■ Conservative investment philosophy ■ Technological capability important but often not used ■ Detailed supervision of accounts ■ Prefer written to personal contact	Professional dynasty is a possibility, local bank or independent trust company is best fit
Technocrats ■ Information is key ■ Technology access is crucial ■ Highly emotional ■ Need to have final say ■ Hate bureaucracy	Not money center banks, regional conglomerates, or individual trustees; others may be okay, maybe not
Philanthropists ■ Artistic and spiritual temperaments ■ Unfocused on money for long periods of time ■ Socially responsible and alternative projects interests ■ Desire personal and comprehensive services	All will do, but if small independent trust companies or local bank trust departments, they must have top talent

dynasty has the ability to give a driver the needed strokes to keep the client happy and often are in the most visible position as drivers use many attorneys to handle many aspects of their financial life.

Worriers don't want to lose money, and they can find security in large institutions. They desire confidentiality, stability, and as little risk as possible. Money center banks, regional conglomerates, and private banks provide this kind of security and are set up to be helpful in allaying this kind of anxiety. Smaller institutions may be perceived as risky by the worrier. The possibility that an individual trustee or professional advisor might die also causes concern to the worrier.

Entrepreneurs are best served by private banks, family offices, and professional dynasties. Entrepreneurs are likely to be happy when they can delegate responsibility to other individuals who seem equally competent. The lack of personal contact at banks is an inhibitory factor for entrepreneurs. On the other hand, entrepreneurs like one-stop shopping. If a private bank can provide business financing and commercial services, it may be a good fit. Entrepreneurs like to feel as if they are dealing with people who appreciate them. A passive trustee personality works best. Acknowledgment is very important to entrepreneurs, which makes an independent trust company an unwise choice. Entrepreneurs like to change their strategy on a moment's notice, so adopting a new investment direction has got to be acceptable to the trustee. Entrepreneurs should use smaller institutions, not larger ones, because that is where flexibility is highest.

Status seekers are best served by private banks and family offices. Associations with old, well-known names work well for status seekers, who enjoy being well looked after. Large banks and newly formed local independent trustees lack cachet and are unlikely candidates for status seekers.

Socialites prefer the high-profile firms in their communities. Socialites tend to focus last on investment returns, and don't pay much attention to the comprehensive financial services that might be best provided by family offices. Professional dynasties and private banks are well suited to the needs of socialites.

Accumulators believe they can never have too much money in their accounts. They need institutions that can promise them the highest returns at the lowest cost. You might expect high-tech money center banks to be appealing, but they are often thought by accumulators to be inefficient. Private banks and professional dynasties are too expensive, as are the extended family offices. Local and independent trustees have a good chance of obtaining this kind of inheritor/beneficiary. Accumulators are often focused on immediate goals and sacrifice higher investment returns for lower fees. The private bank is not a candidate because status is unimportant to this type of person. Results are what count. Law or accounting firms' advisory arms sometimes get the accumulator's work, but only if a deal can be cut. Local bank trust departments and individual trustees are usually where these people end up, because such organizations are clearly the low-cost, low-service alternatives, willing to work on an hourly or off a cut-rate wholesale fee schedule.

Technocrats who want constant activity are best served by local banks that can put them into a discount brokerage program. They may do well with a particularly flexible private bank that is willing to put up with the constant demands. Private trustees and professional dynasties tend to be too slow, inefficient, and expensive for the technocrat. This kind of wealthy person quickly tires of the bureaucracy in large institutions and therefore may also be a candidate for a local independent trust company.

Philanthropists are best served by trust players who can offer the most personalized and comprehensive services. These include private banks, family offices, professional dynasties, local independent trust companies, and individual trustees. Philanthropists tend to like a high degree of personal touch, which tends to preclude national and regional banks.

Now, let's look at some detailed case studies of the various types of beneficiaries.

Case Study: Caretaker

Delia comes from a family whose holdings included vast tracts of land in Texas. Among other things, her grandfather helped start a bank chain in Texas. Each bank used an independent charter, so every trust department was its own small fiefdom. The bank president and Delia's grandfather arranged for the family to basically run their ranches and oil businesses inside some trust shells to avoid estate taxes, and to keep outsiders from unduly influencing the family founder's daughters. In addition, a charitable trust was set up in the 1970s by the family's estate planning attorney in Dallas. Oil stocks were deposited in a charitable remainder trust. By the 1980s, oil stocks in major companies (Exxon, Texaco, Atlantic Richfield, Amoco, Chevron) made up the bulk of the assets in the charitable remainder trust, while the family operating company still managed the ranches as closely held businesses. With real estate values of over $20 million, the family was cash poor and land rich.

The charitable trust had the income-producing asset as well as highly appreciated stock.

During the 1990s, with the grandfather and fortune founder long gone, the local bank acting as trustee merged twice. The new trust department assumed that the charitable trust was locked up, and the bank proceeded to sell all the individual stocks to reinvest in bank common trust fund (i.e., mutual funds). The family trusts, with the ranches, were now seen by bank management as nuisances, not moneymakers. In fact, they were even seen as potential liabilities to the new bank.

Delia's parents still lived in the same town and used the same bank to maintain their ranch loans. Slowly, Delia's dad was selling off the ranches, piece by piece, to keep up his standard of living. Although the charitable trust threw off some income to the family, the bank, now with many national branches, completely ignored the income beneficiaries, one of which was Delia.

By the time we met Delia, she was thoroughly disgusted with the bank's condescending attitude that was forcing her family to sell off assets when it could have reallocated the mixture of investments in the charitable trust. The bank refused to split the trust for Delia and her two brothers into three portions that would customize the holdings according to each sibling's individual tax bracket. In addition, the bank had outsourced all of the real estate management to a firm in St. Louis, where the regional conglomerate was based. The bank persuaded Delia's father to swap out some of the land in the family trusts in order to reduce the trust department's workload. Some monies were finally set aside in the family trust for Delia and her two brothers. One brother had graduated from agriculture school and was running the ranches—with substantial annual losses. The other brother had entered the oil and gas business, which was now in a nosedive. All of these children desperately needed to parlay the family's holdings into more productive property. Delia, now in her 40s, was a free spirit, making a little money by buying, refurbishing, and selling homes. The trust remained her primary source of income. As interest rates declined during the years from 1988 to 1994, her trust income declined proportionately. Her oblivious trust officer could neither relate to nor keep up with the changes in Delia's personal life. There was a gross insensitivity to adjusting the income-producing capabilities of the trust. Because of the family's extensive ties with the bank, the charitable trust had to remain there. However, as Delia's trusted advisors, we were able to leverage on the political relationship between the father and the bank and on the charitable trust tie-in to the family trusts to force the bank to resign. This allowed Delia's trust to move to a local independent trust company in her new hometown. There was a horse trade going on when breaking up this bad trust relationship. This is often how situations are concluded, when we find something the bank needs from our client. During this whole process, we strove to keep the client focused on his or her own needs, not on the hurt feelings of others. Clearly, Delia was a caretaker.

Case Study: Driver

Sam's family wealth came from the Detroit auto industry. His grandfather told him about traveling on vacation to the Southwest in the early part of the twentieth century by private automobile, a true adventure back then. His grandfather fell in love with Colorado and decided to retire there. At that time, his Detroit fortunes were strong, so he bought several hotel properties to have something to do. By the end of the 1990s, the hotel properties were valued in the tens of millions of dollars and are now the only remaining assets for the extended family. The family's original source of wealth in Detroit dried up as that city's fortunes changed.

The hotel properties went through different phases and now are malls, anchored by high-class retail chain stores. A local bank serves as trustee for the properties. After the death of Sam's grandfather, the bank was bought out, then sold to a group of local investors. The local bank has almost no management skill within the trust department, and no skill managing real estate. The lives of four families, Sam's and his sister's three surviving children, all of whom have several dependents, are reliant upon the rental income from these properties. The family hired an attorney friend to request that the bank do a better job of management. However, no results transpired from all the letters cajoling, pleading, and threatening. Can a bank trust officer, responsible for computer systems and getting checks out on time, manage a multimillion dollar real estate operation? Hardly. It is a bad mix. But the bank is unwilling to contract out the real estate management because it is extremely profitable.

This particular trust has another complication—Sam is now in his 70s, with two ex-wives by whom he had a total of five children. His third wife is in her late 40s, and they also have two children. This surviving spouse will most likely live well past Sam's death. She has no means of support other than Sam. It is likely that she will be thrust into the position of having to depend on the generosity of her children who, because the trust was poorly drafted, will be pitted against their half siblings in a battle for control of the properties. This is an untenable situation. Sam, being a driver, has fought with his first two sets of children in an attempt to get them to pledge the future trust income to his current wife. Once Sam dies, the trust will distribute the income to all his children equally, and none to his surviving spouse. Disastrous results will occur when Sam dies as the undivided property gets split into 14 parts, not a workable scenario.

The bank has done nothing to help with estate or financial planning for the income beneficiaries nor to prepare the remainder people for their eventual real estate management challenges. The local bank trust department is understaffed, underpaid, out of touch with the beneficiaries, and struggling to handle a multimillion dollar real estate rental business.

Everyone realizes that trouble is brewing. Unfortunately, Sam (the income beneficiary) and his children by his first two marriages (the remainder people) are unable to discuss these matters openly. This works to the bank's advantage. When a trusted advisor was called upon to become a mediator, it was necessary to get the parties to sit down and go through counseling. The money center bank, regional conglomerate, local bank trust department, and independent trust company are ill equipped to do this. Most trustees will be happy to ignore the situation, as they have a vested interest in keeping things wrapped up in silence.

Drivers—and Sam is one—are unlikely to put up with this kind of situation. Most banks have the attitude that the trust document dictates a status quo—that is, "Keep your hands off." Sam consulted with outside advisors who gave him the hope that trusts are, in fact, portable. With proper leverage, *any* trust can be moved. In this day and age, no assets are held inviolably captive by any institution. Financial advisors are likely to come into contact with many people with inherited wealth who are unhappy with their current trustee situation.

Case Study: Worrier

Adrian, a cultured woman in her early 40s, placed a trust with a New York money center bank when her first child was two years old. This was to be a revocable trust, and Adrian expected to be able to draw on it at will. She started it for investment and safekeeping purposes. At some point, she became unhappy with the low level of personal service of the New York bank, which changed the account administrator who was Adrian's only contact, every 18 months. The bank could not keep top-notch people in their lowest-level posts. When a totally unresponsive person was assigned to handle Adrian's constant requests for reassurance, she finally asked that the trust be moved to Arkansas so it could be closer to her. She also wanted the assets to be handled by her family's investment advisor. The New York bank flat-out refused to cooperate.

Our worrier was completely chagrined that all the promises and power that had been given to her by her expert lawyers in the document had been usurped. The bank was unrepentant, charging her $50,000 for something that was covered in the trust document, which clearly outlined her right to change trustees. Adrian had no choice but to go to court, which took two years of hassling, not only with the bank but also with her own attorneys, who saw her as a captive audience. All the events she had worried about came to pass because she put the trust with an inappropriate service provider. Her financial advisor placed the trust, once it was available to be moved with an independent trust company that committed not to take any termination fees should she decide to move it again in the future. This was a huge bone of contention between the New York trustee and Adrian. Adrian had no leverage on the first trustee because her original attorney had neglected to specifically address the fee issue in the irrevocable living trust.

Termination fees are charges levied by a trustee at the end of a relationship in order to compensate that trustee for the cost of setting up the trust and for the "extra work" involved in distributing the assets at the end of the firm's tenure as trustee. Termination fees are like the discretionary amounts charged by some attorneys who have an opportunity to take advantage of their right to charge large fees when a trust originator dies. When attorneys' fees are charged like trustee fees, many corporate trustees are prone to feel unfettered to charge "standard" termination fees. The normal published fee schedule for banks is usually raised incrementally on a regular basis, and currently a 1% fee is standard. This is true even if the trustee has no more management responsibilities than before a death or termination date.

There have been some class-action lawsuits against corporate bank trustees over termination fees. Even if banks state that termination fees are part of their standard fee schedules, they were probably not in place when the original grantor or donor set up the trusts. The language inside most trust documents reads "normal and customary fees." This allows an unspoken agreement between old-time lawyers and bankers to take unnecessary fees at the end of a trust relationship.

Drivers and entrepreneurs are not likely to put up with this status quo. Their trusted advisor can help prevent banks from getting away with cavalierly taking unearned and unreasonable termination fees.

Case Study: Entrepreneur

Recently, the father of one of our clients in Florida, owner of several successful beer distributorships, anticipated the issue of termination fees. He didn't want the bank to take advantage of his family or himself. His attorney, however, had colluded with the bank, and the legal directive to waive termination fees ended with the grantor's death. His two sons were stuck with onerous fees (well into the six figures) from both the bank and the attorney, who had named himself a coexecutor and cotrustee with the bank.

Our client's father had also negotiated a discount commission rate with an outside brokerage firm for transactions in his trusts. Upon the death of the grantor, the bank continued to trade through the brokerage firm at five times the negotiated rate. The careful planning done by the father did not benefit his sons. They were constrained by the fact that their father's attorney, who received referral business from the bank, was not willing to take up the sons' side and ask the bank to step down without termination fees nor to negotiate the trading commissions. The sons had no idea if it was even possible to negotiate with the bank. One of their financial advisors was able to step in and arrange a settlement that was less than the bank's normal fee. The entrepreneurial spirit lived on in the sons, who researched the overcharge by the broker and made the bank reimburse the account the overcharged amount.

Case Study: Accumulators

We have a client whose family was stuck with an accountant in Denver as trustee. Over the course of three years, he had received over a million dollars in fees for handling estate planning, taxes, and routine oil and gas matters. Our client's father, the trust originator, had been enticed and entranced by the personal attention and aggressiveness of this professional dynasty, so the accountant became the hub of this oilman's empire. The trust originator turned over powers of attorney to the accountant, naming him trustee and personal representative of his estate. The accountant did good work at a fair market rate during the originator's lifetime. After the originator died, however uncontrolled fees became the norm.

The family's heirs hired us to do thorough and extensive detective work on the accountant's actions. We were able to find overbillings, inaccuracies, inconsistencies, and evidence of self-dealings in his performance of his fiduciary duties. The professionals on his staff obviously lacked breadth and experience in many parts of the trust field. Finally, we arranged to take control of the assets. The next phase involved negotiating a settlement with the former trustee, who wanted several hundred thousand dollars just to let go of the records of the trust. Our persistent efforts to prebuild a case, along with some intimations of disclosure to the accountant's review board, helped move those trusts along to a new trustee.

Once burned, twice shy. The family prenegotiated a separation agreement with the new trustee before moving the trust. This is the trust equivalent of a prenuptial arrangement.

Technocrats

Technocrats represent a growing portion of newly created trust wealth. The baby boom generation has many more technocrats and philanthropists, so we will describe their matches in greater detail. Technocrats need control and a plethora of information. They are not served well by the professional dynasties, who tend to take a low-key, hands-off approach. Regional conglomerates tend to ignore technocrats, providing a modicum of information in a format that falls short of being useful. The local independent bank trust department is unable to provide information at the speed needed by the technocrat. Banks, by and large, are reluctant to act as a clearinghouse in which inheritors can make their own decisions. This new breed of beneficiary wants technology and sophisticated communication links that will keep them up-to-date at all times.

Private banks, family offices, and the independent trust companies should be the first to reach the technological aristocrats' goal of electronic convenience. They stand the best chance of attracting the technocrats' business. Successful professionals and doctors in particular enjoy playing the market themselves. They need flexibility to bend the traditional fiduciary rules on investing. Traditional trust department approaches will be increasingly inadequate for technocrats. When this type of heir is unhappy, they tend to withdraw and to get emotionally violent. This presents a problem for established trustees, while offering opportunities for new types of trustees who are willing to invest heavily in client-usable communication systems. With the advent of e-mail trading for individual investors, web sites, 24-hour access to information on accounts, research, and market commentaries, technocrats will transform their segment of the trust business into a unique niche that can successfully be served by only a few of the best-capitalized and forward-looking trust companies.

Philanthropists

As baby boomers inherit wealth, there is an explosion of interest in private charitable vehicles. Because of this, philanthropists want community connections and a chance to directly do good work. Trust service providers that don't offer this opportunity are regional conglomerates and money center banks. The money center banks have high profiles in New York, Chicago, or San Francisco, which may provide a good fit if the philanthropist is oriented toward opera or national charitable organizations. However, private banks and family offices offer a better sense of connection with philanthropists. They actively support philanthropists' efforts to give away part of their wealth. Local bank trust departments make a poor choice for the philanthropist unless the inheritor is interested in giving mainly on the community level, in established ways. Independent trust companies are poor choices for philanthropists because of their low service level. Private trustees and professional dynasties provide more flexibility by allowing for creative uses of charitable funds and assisting heirs in finding suitable organizations to receive charitable gifts.

Case Study: Philanthropist

The family of one of our clients had established a large trust for their three daughters in Connecticut. Over the years, each of the daughters moved away. While the parents had ample wealth, the trust set up for the three daughters was growing only slowly. One of the daughters became interested in environmental causes in the Pacific Northwest. She decided that she wanted her trust to be used, in part, to fund alternative job opportunities for Native Americans. We helped move the trust from the family bank to a private independent trustee. The new trustee offered some upscale family office services. This daughter was then able to sell some of her inherited assets which had a very low basis. She sold stock of companies whose practices she found objectionable: tobacco, gambling, and nuclear power. She set up a charitable trust with the proceeds and was then allowed to direct the distribution grants. The independent trustee was very cooperative, whereas the family bank had refused to proceed with this plan, a plan that made good sense from an income and estate planning point of view. An unhappy trust relationship ended without too much fuss, in part because the other two daughters stayed with the family bank.

Another reason the bank was willing to let go of our client's trust was that it still had the parents' trusts. While they lost a couple of million dollars of assets, they held on to 10 times that much by being cooperative. When the parents pass on, they stand to lose the rest.

Conclusion: Why Are There So Many Mismatches?

For most of the twentieth century, people did business with local banks. The bank trust department slowly gathered assets and began to be a source of fee income for the bank. In the 1970s and early 1980s, bond market action obliterated traditional trust department portfolios due to rapidly increasing interest rates. The banks had become dependent on bonds, and only slowly increased their allocations to stocks. Few trust departments held on to the stocks originally deposited in the trusts. They moved their clients' holdings into common trust (mutual) funds during the 1980s. If, by chance, they did hold on to the family founder's original stocks, which had done nothing much from 1968 to 1982, the bank trust department's assets would have easily quadrupled in value by 1997. Fee schedules were raised concurrently, and by the late 1980s, some bank trust departments were making more money than the loan departments. Over the past decade, with mergers and acquisitions, bank trust departments became stand-alone profit centers, known by a different title perhaps, but purveying much the same unimaginative fare.

After the mid-1990s, most bank trust departments were no longer managed or owned locally. The ability to discuss investment strategy moved from a local to a regional to a national level. Most national banks then started stand-alone money management units outside of their bank trust department to compete with the Fidelitys and Vanguards of the world in attracting nontrust business. Everyone was making money. The number of mutual funds climbed to over 8,000 by 1998. Banks were having trust beneficiaries pay both mutual fund management fees and trustee fees, a situation that caused such an uproar that the banks were forced to pay back some of their management fees.

Nonlocal banks lost their personal touch. They no longer consistently exhibit the ability to deliver trust service on a face-to-face, first-name basis. Previously, local banks had mediocre investment returns, but they did have a high level of individualized service.

Top money managers who can successfully manage mutual funds stay away from banks because of mediocre pay and the reputation that banks have for investing. Anyone who was very good in her work at a bank usually left to start her own money management firm, a venture capital fund, or a hedge fund. Some top managers landed higher-paying positions at private family offices. Regional conglomerates have ended up with mediocre talent and mediocre service. At the same time, they have raised fees; therefore, they have many dissatisfied clients.

We have pointed out that the highest level of investment expertise and personal service is delivered by private banks and family offices. The professional dynasties have been unable to keep up in the investment field. They have not incorporated the latest technology necessary to deliver high-tech services to their clients, who would like that kind of communication.

The majority of irrevocable trusts have local or regional bank trustees. Many persons of wealth with trusts are also connected in some way to seasoned independent professionals. They are most likely to have trusts with regional conglomerates or local banks. These are the institutions least able to provide high-quality, high-touch service.

These are not $100 million trusts, but in the $300,000 to $3 million range. This is understandable, because a trust that started with $50,000 in 1968 would now be worth over $1 million, without any effort on anyone's part, just by letting blue-chip stocks sit there. The great majority of trusts that eventually get distributed to middle- and upper-class people (not the superwealthy) are with regional conglomerates.

The rising consciousness among inheritors about their own responsibility in fixing these dysfunctional trust situations is increasing. Communication and counseling between spouses is widespread. It used to be that only sick people went to therapists, but now it is a sign of health and awareness. This willingness to face difficult situations is now being used in dealing with family finances as well as emotional dynamics.

This is the groundwork on which taking control of inherited wealth, which we sometimes call trust busting, is based. People, especially baby boomers and those who follow, are not willing to accept placidly the dictates and investment return of banks. There have always been unhappy trust beneficiaries. For the first time, it is generally accepted that beneficiaries have a right to ask for what they want. One effective way of doing this for the future is to draft trust agreements that include the appointment of trust removers and trust appointers. In this way, the power to change the corporate trustee stays within the family—and later their beneficiaries. Astute estate planners should include clauses that prohibit trustees from taking unearned termination or transfer fees at their own discretion.

Why Beneficiaries Don't Move Their Trusts

While matching a beneficiary to the right trustee is a necessary first step in managing a trust, even more crucial is recognition by the heir that there is a problem. This sounds simple but rarely is.

Not unlike the situation faced by married couples who are not communicating, it is a major step to simply admit that one is not happy. The obstacles to making this acknowledgment are huge. Like love and romance, money and finances bring up our deepest and darkest shadows, the hidden parts of ourselves that are painful to even think about. As trusted advisors, we have to know what is lurking beneath the surface. In our pursuit of complete client satisfaction; we, as trusted advisors, are called upon to uncover their hidden fears, many of which are well founded and remain unspoken.

Lack of Knowledge

It's not a great intellectual mystery why most beneficiaries don't move their trusts when they're unhappy with their current trustee. They simply don't know it can be done. Fortunately, this is easy to remedy. No matter what personality type the beneficiaries may be, they are probably not like the family founder's spouse or first-generation heirs in the sense of being accustomed to keeping quiet. Most often, heirs hesitate to change because they lack basic knowledge about alternatives. Our job is to inform them that they can retake control over their financial lives. Beginning forbidden discussions concerning money is often accompanied by sharp psychological barbs for many people if guilt, anxiety, frustration, anger, or rage was associated with money in their families when they were children. This may have created a sort of multilevel unhappiness with the past that seems to incapacitate people when it comes to their trusts. When you help people gain control of their trusts; they will have to deal, at least in part, with the trauma of their family of origin. As an advisor, you must be prepared to deal with, or find help for, that aspect of their lives if it comes up.

Most trust inheritors, along with lawyers, accountants, brokers, investment advisors, insurance agents, and even most bankers, don't realize that it is possible to change one corporate trustee for another. More often than not, the actual trust document is silent on the subject. However, with ample preparation, a case can be made to the current trustee that it would be best resigning because the interests of the beneficiary are better served by an alternative corporate trustee. People honestly seem surprised when we tell them that they are not locked into a bad trustee. This is a huge step.

Most people think that their family bank is the only possible corporate trustee. In fact, people often don't even have their basic trust documents. The bank may be reluctant to share everything in the file with the beneficiary because there are gray areas in most older documents. These may be areas in which the bank has erred, and it does not wish heirs to know about its mistakes.

Most beneficiaries don't know how to find an alternative to the current trustee. The financial advisor is in a good position to advise clients about corporate trustees available both in and out of state.

Avoidance of Conflict

Most people, caretakers and avoiders in particular, don't want to make trouble because any conflict involves pain. The original trust creator was probably an entrepreneur, an accumulator, or a driver. The trust originator's children are likely to have much different personality types, perhaps to compensate for neglect they may have experienced or the unbalanced lifestyle of their successful ancestors. If an heir does turn out to have the same kind of drive as the family founder, she usually has an unhappy life, always trying to outachieve the original achiever. This is often a frustrating challenge. Intuitively sensing this and without the driving pressure of poverty, many children of abundance grow up avoiding conflict. Any disturbance can be a reminder that a shaky peace at home may have been purchased with deep unhappiness on the part of people whose personal lives were sacrificed on the altar of building and maintaining the family fortune.

For these reasons, trust heirs most often fall into the caretaker, avoider, worrier, status seeker, socialite, or philanthropist categories. It is helpful for advisors to know that our individual business personalities and practices require us to specialize; in the sense that we cannot be everything to everyone. We must recognize and choose the inheritor and beneficiary character types that most aptly match our own. This is the key to success in the trust business.

The unwillingness to bring conflicts out into the open is prevalent among inheritors. Heirs®, Inc., in Valley Forge, Pennsylvania, is a support group to help heirs who feel that they have been unjustly treated by bank trust departments. The possibility of pursuing class action suits is one of their main projects. Standish Smith, founder of Heirs has put out an informative booklet, *The Heir's Handbook.* Several examples of checklists regarding preparing for conflict are included as an appendix in this book by permission of Heirs, Inc.

Loss of Security

Most trusts that were set up at local banks were done so with the help of a local attorney. The attorney probably felt it was in the best interests of the client to receive the security offered by traditional banks. This was an accepted practice, and no thought was given to how the bank's form or content might change. "Bigger is better" has turned out to be a fallacious theory in banking. Big banks and large attorney firms are the most expensive, but they are not able to retain the most qualified employees.

Today, many functions of the traditional trust departments are performed by computers. Smaller banks have farmed out management of assets such as mineral and real estate properties, even stocks. With the removal or distancing of the local trust officer, and with fewer real services located where the client can see them, people are asking why they should pay more for less. Clients want to interact with the trustee devoted to their case. Yet it is common for trust officers to change account assignments every two years.

From a financial security point of view, how secure are bank trust departments? There is a great deal of confusion on this point. Many trusts were written during the 1980s when banks and savings and loan associations were failing. Lawyers wrote in a requirement that the originating firm carry minimum net capital of several million dollars to ensure that it will remain solvent and that trust accounts placed there will be secure. This is a faulty approach to trust security. Trust assets are, by law, kept separate from the commercial assets of a bank. There has never been a situation where a bank trust department holding trust assets has put beneficiaries at risk due to the failure of the commercial or loan making side of the bank.

All independent trust companies, private banks, and family offices hold trust assets in depository accounts kept separate from their own. Trust assets are *never* available to be used for loans, collateral, speculation, or anything other than the use of the beneficiary. This protects clients' assets; there is essentially no difference in the amount of security provided to trust assets between any two corporate trustees. As long as adequate errors-and-omissions insurance, liability insurance, and the safeguarding of securities by a third party in segregated accounts are kept in place, the client is equally protected on all fronts. This is *not* true for professional dynasties or individual trustees. These people are not regulated, and thus separate-account safety is not assured.

Because of strict corporate trust regulations, any new trust company—even one with no assets—has the same level of security as the largest money center bank in New York. Sometimes, local independent institutions purchase additional insurance so that they can say that they have the power of major insurance companies behind them. Clients often confuse size with safety and security. Fear of loss due to administrative or fiscal failure is unfounded. However, fear of loss because of poor investment performance is a valid concern.

A much more important issue is the beneficiary's relationship with the person inside of the institution. The trust departments of large banks are divided into marketing/sales, service/administration, tax, and investments. This four-part segmentation does not serve the client well. The split of trust responsibilities has come into play because trust administration is a different skill than trust investing. Unfortunately, neither the trust investment officer nor the administrator really has the time or inclination to pull together and manage information regarding all the assets of the beneficiary. This is a serious shortcoming, and the client's security and best interest are not looked after. The bank is secure because its specialists are focused on covering the bank's exposure to potential liability.

Bad Manners

It is decidedly bad form to get down to brass tacks too early in a trust negotiation. Many people with inherited money, which they have not earned and over which they have little control, exhibit an attitude of resignation: "Don't worry about those assets. There's nothing we can do about them." The bank reinforces this attitude in its condescending way. Bank written statements and reports are superficial, and the attitude prevails that the beneficiaries are not competent and do not need to evaluate the performance of the trust as they might for other financial service providers. For socialites, status seekers, caretakers, and avoiders; this is a workable attitude, a mutual tacit understanding that serves both sides. It is assumed by all that the trust is secure; nothing else is worthy of discussion.

Patience Is a Virtue

It is not true that banks live forever. The fiduciary powers vested in the trustee are serious, and all banks take them seriously. We give bank trust officers credit for trying to do the right thing. As we have discussed, local bank trust departments are much less common now. Microbanks, which have risen to fill the need for community loan services, do not yet offer trust services. Trust beneficiaries are among the first to get lost in the bank shuffle toward "bigger is better." While our clients are patiently putting up with deteriorating service, the trustees' profits are going up.

Obscure Results

Most people with trusts don't have information about the bank's amount and calculation of trust fees levied on the accounts. They don't know the performance of the bank relative to readily available indexes or alternate investment vehicles. All of this information is legally attainable by beneficiaries, regardless of whether they have a current or future right to interest or principal. However, the reports they receive are obscure and inadequate.

Banks can make it difficult for people to see their performance by making it mandatory for trust assets to be part of their internal common trust funds. A common trust fund is another name for a mutual fund run by the bank. These are profitable devices for banks, since they do not have to spend any time on the individual accounts. Generally speaking, if clients have below a certain threshold amount, say $500,000, they are moved into a common trust fund and their assets are pooled with everyone else's. Common trust funds have many disadvantages and only a few benefits. The benefits are that economies of scale are present and that more attention can be paid to a limited number of stocks. Nevertheless, bank common trust funds generally have mediocre performance.

One of their disadvantages is that any trading done inside the common trust fund is passed through to the individual trust, without the beneficiary's consent. Like mutual fund owners, this causes adverse tax consequences for the heir, quite outside the control of the trust beneficiary. Pooling of money in a bank's common trust fund has an illusion of safety. It is difficult to keep in touch with the performance of banks' common trust funds. Banks report their returns infrequently, and they don't appear on the regular statement. Many trust heirs would have been better off if the original stocks put in the account by the family founder had been kept intact rather than sold and reinvested in the bank's common trust fund. While investment performance and loss of personal service are some of the reasons that some beneficiaries may be unhappy with banks, it is difficult for beneficiaries to know how poorly they may be doing because of the overall lack of performance-poor data communication between banks and clients with changing needs. In Chapter 13, we will explore how financial advisors can meet the needs of trust clients.

Legal Agony

Fights over changing trusteeships rarely come out in the open. They are usually resolved in negotiated settlements. Unless the bank or the trustee needs something, the burden of proof and the initiation of the threat of legal action lies with the beneficiary. Banks are aware that people would like to move trusts. For anyone who dislikes dealing with litigation attorneys, which includes most people, the onerous chore of proving abrogation of fiduciary duties is not one to take lightly. One of the bank's main desires, in the face of challenges to their past actions, is to obtain an agreement from the dissenting heirs on all past actions holding the bank "harmless." This document is very important because it absolves the bank from future liability. This should be one of the last documents that the beneficiary signs to get a trust moved from a nonperforming trustee. As we will describe in Chapter 13, there are various stages of negotiating with the current trustee.

Banks can make it an arduous task to prove that their fees are too high, that their investment performance is too low, that they don't have in-house expertise in some of the areas that a beneficiary needs, or that they have failed in their duty to communicate regularly and be knowledgeable about the beneficiary's personal financial situation. Another legal hurdle is getting all members of a family to sign off on a variety of letters and documents that will be needed to move a trust. It can be emotionally draining to deal with sisters, brothers, and cousins. To reach unanimity on anything is never easy; on financial matters it is most often difficult.

Threat of Retaliation

We recently dealt with a client whose family had a large number of related trusts with a New Jersey bank. Some of the heirs were living in California. They could not afford to buy a house in San Francisco's expensive Bay Area. The husband whose family had created the trust was an art therapist. He stood to receive over a million dollars when his aunt died. The aunt, who was in her 80s, wanted the bank to go ahead and distribute the principal early since she had no need for it. The bank refused.

The bank was also unwilling to advance funds as a loan or to buy, as a trust asset, real estate in another state because of the hassles involved. The trusts, which were quite old, were originally set up in a confused fashion. All of the trust originator's heirs by blood shared in the combined value of all the trusts on their date of distribution. This created a morass of cross-purposes and served the bank well, because it was impossible to get total agreement among all heirs, some of whom hadn't seen each other since they were children.

The bank was aware that it could have extended some kind of advance or loan to the set of heirs needing a home, but decided against it. It didn't help that all the trust beneficiaries were unable to present a united front. After a year of wrangling, the bank turned around and reallocated assets toward growth and away from the income that the family needed. The bank's intent was to keep the trust as long as possible, under the guise of honoring the wishes of the original family members.

One of our clients had to deal with a private trustee in Philadelphia. She was unable to get child support for her two children after her husband died. He had been the beneficiary of a trust, from which their children were now entitled to income. The individual trustee, a crusty old lawyer, gave our client such a hard time that she had to hire expensive attorneys in Philadelphia, who managed to eke out a promise of some money for this woman and her children. Try as they might, her attorneys were unable to force payment in arrears for the six years it took the trustee to agree on her right to *some* of the income. The private trustee continues to refuse to pay. Adding insult to injury, the professional dynasty that was set up has gone to court at our client's expense to further extend its dominance over the trust. The firm used the pretense of changing tax laws to try to extend its power. We called a temporary halt to these antics, but at great expense. As part of our legal maneuverings, we uncovered the attorney's neglect of the cash position building up in undistributed income during the eight years of wrangling. From 1991 to 1999, over $2 million was sitting in a money market fund. In fact, it was the wrong kind of money market—*taxable,* instead of the tax-free option that could have been used.

Up-Front Expenses

Most people are intimidated by the potential cost and emotional difficulties involved in moving trusts. These concerns are warranted because banks use high termination fees to lock in assets. But these fees may be unjustified and could possibly be overturned in court. As in divorces, unless the parties can reach an early agreement to part amicably, it can be an expensive and gut-wrenching experience.

The situation is made worse by the bank's threat to fight any change by using *the trust's own money.* This does not have to be the case, because if the bank has made some mistakes and there are bona fide reasons for moving the trust, the beneficiary can demand that the bank return any excess charges it levied. If trusted advisors can show that the bank is protecting its own interests and not those of the client, the bank has a weak position to take extra fees.

Divide and Conquer

Banks can attempt to divide and conquer beneficiaries in an active way, by soliciting dissenting family members against moving the trust. There is a general lack of legal information given to beneficiaries about their rights under the law. This makes it difficult for individuals unless they hire someone to get all the background documentation—or fight the battle themselves. The fear of loss of access to income and principal distributions, which are discretionary and up to the trustee, is a common fear.

Fighting the bank's assertions is not easy or inexpensive. Banks have certain standards that must be met, and they really have no choice but to make distributions, but we have seen people have to go to considerable trouble to get them. Professional dynasties are the greatest culprits in this area, as evidenced by our widow's story. Trustees can be quite arbitrary in their interpretation of standards used to make distributions.

Conclusion

There are no easy answers in deciding whether to move a trust. A full analysis will be presented in Chapter 14. It's important to note that none of these obstacles are unconquerable. When the relationship is right for the inheritor and her advisor, taking control of one's family's wealth is a once-in-a-lifetime event.

Matching Beneficiaries with the Right Trustee

"I'm not quite ready to order. My lawyers are still studying the menu."

lawyers: *aka financial advisors*

W e have described the trust world—its opportunities and attendant problems. We have also introduced the emotional background of many trust beneficiaries and an outline of the kinds of persons and organizations that are set up to serve trust beneficiaries. At this point, we would like to help the beneficiary and her advisor quantify some of the measurements of satisfaction of current matches. We hope this will guide the choice of new trustee should the situation warrant changing.

Our earlier descriptions of different beneficiary types should help you (either as a beneficiary or trust service provider) evaluate your current relationship. Here, we offer a detailed list of questions to gauge the satisfaction level of the trust beneficiaries and the service level of the trustee. Finally, we'll examine the appropriateness of the expectation level of inheritors and make suggestions regarding how positively to influence clients' attitudes about past and possible future trustees. The goal is to build a successful trust relationship.

The Trustee Profile

Let's profile the particular beneficiary and current trustee mix. Into which classification does the current trustee fit? We have included several questions to help you decide. Some may be more worthwhile than others, but all have the potential of providing you with crucial information for preparing to bust or build trusts.

Questions for the beneficiary to answer:

1. Is your trustee located within an hour's drive of your residence? Does this matter to you?

2. How often do you see a person from the trustee's office?

3. Is this often enough?

4. Does the trustee communicate with you in a way you can understand?

5. What don't you understand?

6. What topics never get discussed that you feel are important?

7. Has the ownership of your trustee organization changed in the last two years? If yes, has your service changed since the change?

8. Is your trustee representative likely to change again in the next two years?

9. How well do you know your trustee?

10. Does your contact at the trust service provider have a strong presence?

11. Can you talk freely with your contact?

12. Does your trustee contribute to causes you think are worthwhile?

13. Is your trust professional someone to whom you would give your personal money to invest?

14. Has your trustee ever asked to see your personal tax return?

15. Would you share it if asked?

16. Does your trust service provider have local administrative personnel dedicated to servicing your account?

17. Do trust employees seem energetic or overworked? Happy or stressed?

18. How flexible are employees in terms of availability to talk to you?

19. Can you send e-mail messages to your contact?

20. Do you care about e-mail?

21. Is the trust provider part of a conglomerate or a larger organization?

22. Do you know who owns your trust department? Does it matter to you?

23. Does the trustee provide you with understandable investment performance reports?

24. Do you have to ask or are investment returns provided as normal procedure?

25. Is it a struggle to get that information?

26. Does your trust professional show you your portfolio's performance broken down by asset class performance versus relevant benchmarks?

27. How willing is the trustee to negotiate fees?

28. Have you ever asked your trustee to negotiate fees?

29. Do you know what fees you are being charged?

30. How sophisticated are the trustee's services regarding holding investments other than his own common trust funds?

31. Do you want to have any input regarding what investments are used?

32. Do you want access to your account information electronically?

33. Do you read the bank statements you get?

34. How could they be improved?

35. Does the trust service provider have a personal connection to your family? Did it ever?

36. Does it matter to you whether it does?

37. Does the trustee have other business connections to your family?

38. How long has this relationship been in place?

39. How often is the trustee willing to talk to you?

40. How would other members of your extended family react if you put pressure on the trustee to change some aspect of his handling of your trust?

From our experience in the industry, the following service standards are to be expected:

1. You should be offered input into your own asset allocation.

2. You should be offered a choice of quality ratings for your bonds.

3. You should be offered the option to own individual bonds in lieu of or in addition to a common trust fund or mutual fund.

4. You should expect to be taught about the different kinds of stock markets around the world.

5. You have a right to be educated by your trustee about the difference between individual stocks and bonds from mutual funds.

6. The trustee should explain the criteria and give you the tools for evaluating the bank's common trust fund performance.

All this information has to come together and an evaluation made regarding the trust's performance.

Whether you are the beneficiary or the trusted advisor, you may want to use the preceding questions to help you prioritize what's most important to you as beneficiary or what is in the client's best interest as an advisor. List your top 10 needs and compare this list to the one that follows. This will help a great deal in deciding if you and your trustee are a good match.

The following questions will help you and your advisor place the current trustee in context. This will help you both to strategize about how to get what you want with a minimum of hassle. Please remember that very few people ask these questions of their trustees, even if they are very unsatisfied. As the beneficiary, you have the right to know the answers, and it is reasonable to expect your trustee to give you this information. You deserve (and are paying for) personal time and attention to be devoted to your situation.

Questions for the trust service provider to answer:

1. How many clients are served by your department?
2. How many clients do you, the administrator, handle personally?
3. How much in assets does that represent?
4. How long have you been in this position?
5. Do you provide services other than trust administration? Which ones and for how long?
6. Do you have an in-house attorney?
7. Do you create comprehensive financial plans for your clients?
8. Do you have an in-house accountant?
9. Do you have in-house investment experts?
10. If so, how many people? What is their experience and track record? If they are not in-house, who does the investing?
11. Do you have experience with complicated estate planning situations?
12. Are clients' accounts looked at individually? How often?
13. Have you set up charitable trusts?
14. Are you willing to share information about your past investment performance?
15. Can you provide information about your performance against the indexes, broken down by asset classes?
16. Are you willing to work with an outside investment advisor?
17. Are you willing to let clients direct trades to brokers of their choice or make alternative investments as long as they are fiduciarily acceptable?

18. Are you willing to use socially responsible investments?

19. Are you willing to negotiate your annual fees?

20. Do you have termination fees?

21. Will you customize your statements if requested?

Now match answers to these questions from both your clients and the trust providers. Do they mesh well, or is it likely that another type of provider would be better suited for this trust situation?

Expectations of the Beneficiary

Now that a basis has been established for knowing the kind of beneficiary and the kind of trust service provider you are dealing with, let's see if the client's expectations of the trustee are reasonable. Here is a list of questions that will help:

1. Do you understand what assets are in your account now?

2. How much is in stocks/bonds/cash?

3. Is this the right mix for you?

4. Do you want to be involved in setting the mix?

5. Will you be disappointed if you are not involved?

6. What kind of income do you feel you should be getting from the account?

7. Are you getting enough now?

8. Is the trustee doing enough to increase your income?

9. Would the trustee work harder at it if you asked? Have you asked? Were you pleased with the response?

10. Has the account grown satisfactorily in your estimation?

11. How much did it grow during the last full year?

12. What is your expectation for the future growth of the account?

13. How would you like to be contacted? How often?

14. Has your trustee asked you any of these questions?

15. Are you able to get your trustee to listen to special requests that you feel are reasonable?

16. Does the trustee act quickly enough?

17. Are documentation requests to you reasonable?

18. Is the trustee available at tax time to help answer questions about your tax return?

19. Does the trustee get your tax forms (K-1) to you on time?

20. Does the trustee help you get ready for estimated payments?

21. Will the trustee give you advice on financial matters other than your trust?

22. How much are you paying your trustee?

23. Is this too much or too little?

24. What additional services, if provided, would make you feel better about the fees?

25. Could any service be added for which you would be willing to pay more?

26. Are there any services you could do without in order to reduce fees?

We can separate beneficiaries and their level of expectations into three groups: those people who expect reasonable services for the amount they are paying, those who expect too little, and those who expect too much. We are now ready to evaluate the inheritor's total satisfaction level and compare it with the current trustee's willingness to change either the service level, the performance, or the fees. The advisor must ascertain whether the client's professed expectations are real and also whether the beneficiary knows how well or how poorly the trustee has done for the fees collected.

Is the trust inheritor satisfied with overall administrative service? With the investment performance? With the fees? With the amount of risk being taken to reach the investment performance? How does the fee level compare with those of alternative trustees? Can the income level be changed if the beneficiary so desires? Is the client satisfied emotionally? Has enough personal attention been paid to him?

We know that most trust officers are far too busy to make proactive calls to their clients. Beneficiaries may not be aware that the preceding criteria are areas in which they can and should have high expectations of their trust providers. Now we know whether the inheritor is highly satisfied, satisfied, unsatisfied, or very unsatisfied with the trustee. We also know whether the client's expectations and demands are reasonable, so the trusted financial advisor can decide whether to deal with this particular situation.

Trust advisors are best able to help those beneficiaries whose reasonable expectations are not being met. Advisors must gather information to help educate clients about what they can reasonably expect from their next trustee.

> Please remember that the emotional connection with the previous trustee may be strong. It may be negative, but there still can be a strong sense of attachment because of the family history. Our clients need to feel that we are on their side no matter what. Especially at this information-gathering stage, the financial advisor cannot be out for personal gain. During this initial phase, beneficiaries need an objective third party to help them to determine if they should move forward and take on the emotional work of changing trustees.

Expectations Gone Awry

In trust situations, expectations are often too low. There are six classes of beneficiaries who may not expect much of trustees: *caretakers, avoiders, worriers, status seekers, socialites,* and *philanthropists.* They may well be satisfied with subpar performance. It is the advisor's job to point out what the client really deserves and to raise the beneficiary's level of demand.

On the other hand, *drivers, technocrats,* and *accumulators* may expect too much. Their criteria for success may be impossible to meet. *Entrepreneurs* are in a class of their own. They may be straightforward in terms of high demand, but they are willing to pay for it. In terms of low demand, they're knowledgeable enough to ask for a fee concession. Some entrepreneurs may have unrealistic expectations and feel they deserve special consideration. But this is the exception.

It is the trust advisor's job to decide whether the inheritor can have his or her needs met by anyone, including the current provider. Negotiating with the current provider is one of the options we will discuss. At this point, we must try to ascertain what is best for the beneficiary and who might be available to allow the client his or her unique way. This is a slow process that is not for the fainthearted advisor in a hurry to gain a new account. For the beneficiary, it requires some soul-searching and mental stretching to take ownership in the financial issues bound to surface.

Trust Attitude Adjustments

One of the ways we try to give people some awareness about their level of expectations and the reality of what is possible in the trust world is to use peer group discussion as an educational tool. There are a number of support groups for inheritors, and many seminars are geared toward high-net-worth individuals. The peer support groups are designed to help people deal with the trials and tribulations of inherited wealth. There are also newsletters for beneficiaries. By attending conferences or making contact over the phone, beneficiaries can be emboldened and heartened by the fact that they are not alone. Prisoners of wealth share many common traits, from childhood trauma to adult depression. People of wealth who built their own fortunes (as opposed to inheriting money) should be equally interested in these groups because their children will also bear these pressures.

How does a trust beneficiary differentiate between what is normal and customary and what constitutes neglect or abuse of power on the part of a current trustee? This is a very difficult question and there is no one broad answer. While it is not difficult to know what kind of investment performance or fee schedule is reasonable, it is difficult to ask key questions. Oftentimes, advisors must take the lead in forming questions to be asked of the institution or private trustee. By now, you know full well that much of what goes on is emotional. Fear and trepidation must be articulated if they are not to derail the process. Not only might the trustee react adversely, but other founding family members may decide that the disgruntled beneficiary is getting too uppity. The advisor may be accused of interfering. Nonetheless, the simple criteria of service, performance, and fees are all reasonable questions that, if asked in the right way, should serve to strengthen family ties, not weaken them.

Case Study: Kerry

A client, Kerry, asked me to go to Los Angeles to meet her mother's attorney and visit with her brother Alex about their ailing mother's choice of trustee for the family trust that was to be created upon the mother's death.

Alex and the bank were named as cotrustees. Kerry detested the bank's heavy-handedness, which she experienced as insensitivity to her ethical concerns. The bank had sold the existing family stock and bought shares in arms manufacturers, oil companies, and tobacco firms. The brother treated Kerry with extreme condescension. With our help, Kerry articulated her concerns about the bank. Alex shrugged off the inquiry after promising to tie down the bank's future fees for Kerry. We asked the attorney to pursue the matter. He shrugged it off as well, saying it was something in the range of a one-time 0.005% to 1% charge, plus an annual fee. This amounted to over half a million dollars! It turns out that both the attorney and the brother stand to draw fees based on the bank's schedule, which is why our client, who asked the right professional questions, was given the cold shoulder. Our questions gave Kerry a clear indicator of the true character of her brother and her mother's attorney.

Conclusion

Looking at trust situations in this way, you can see that there are concrete criteria by which to evaluate whether you are satisfied, whether your trust provider is the appropriate organization, and whether you should explore taking control of your inherited wealth, even if it means having to fight.

Part 4

Trust Busting

This is the section of the book that "type A" readers have been waiting for! The next three chapters provide a step-by-step guide to figuring out how to take trust accounts away from banks or other nonperforming trustees—in short, the guts of trust busting.

Whether you are a beneficiary or an advisor, you need to take the time to gather the information described in Chapter 14. Chapter 15 is a methodology for building your case for change by focusing on the current trustee's mistakes. Chapter 16 is the training manual on how to win the battle for control of trust assets. We hope that this approach will build your confidence sufficiently to pursue trust busting.

Evaluating the Current Trustee

**"I'm sorry, but you don't get frequent flyer miles
for regularly investing in high risk securities."**

This chapter is a step-by-step guide for the advisor to follow to help ben-eficiaries start the trust-busting process. Beneficiaries, also, may be keenly interested in this chapter, particularly the questions on page 205 about the level of commitment to change.

We assume at this point that there is an unhappy beneficiary who would like help in changing the trust relationship. This chapter is designed to help you gather the many details needed to ascertain how to approach the current trustee. You will need to go through each step of this process to have confidence in the inheritor's ability to take control eventually of their trust assets.

Gathering Information

The first step is to evaluate the current trustee's performance in various areas. Always remember that you have a right to know where you stand. It may take several months to complete the first phase of gathering information. Trustees will be recalcitrant upon the first request for this information, because they will immediately know that you're contemplating a move. Trusts are cash cows for the trustees. If the trust has been with them for a while, they have probably come to take it for granted. When the trust was first set up, many promises were made. Now, the less effort trustees have to expend, the more profitable the account is. When an advisor or beneficiary starts asking for background information, the trustees will see a red flag and prepare to defend themselves. Their first response is to do whatever they can to allay your fears and concerns. Expect phone calls (nice ones at first) asking what can be done and perhaps giving you some of the personal attention that's been missing for so long. Expect partial responses to your requests for information. The trustees will have reasonable excuses for the delays and incompleteness, which are part of their initial strategy to slow things down.

We can't emphasize enough the need to document all your requests in writing. Don't ask for paperwork over the telephone. If you send anything by fax, keep a confirmation that the request was made. When the trust officer realizes that you are serious, he will begin to give you the information piece by piece. One of his first defensive responses will be to put pressure on you, possibly through other family members. The trustee will want to find out the extent of your problem and see if he can mollify your concerns.

Gathering information is the first step. You will need three years of monthly transaction statements and a list of assets at the end of each report period. These asset and transaction lists should include a breakdown, if possible, of fees taken, estimated tax payments made, and a record of the trust's investment performance by asset class. (For example, what did the portfolio's large-capitalization U.S. stock do versus the S&P 500?)

Ask for the complete trust tax returns for the last three years. You probably have been getting only the beneficiary's distribution form, an IRS form called a K-1, which is akin to a 1099. You have the right to see the entire trust tax return. This will yield information regarding the amount of trading done in the account, the amount of total fees taken, and other expenses that may be hard to find on the regular bank statements or the K-1.

Prepare a net worth statement so you can see what percentage of the beneficiary's total assets the trust makes up. Get out three years of personal tax returns. Find out how dependent the beneficiary is on the trust for income. Has the income been increasing or decreasing? Prepare a monthly or yearly expense report showing how money is spent. Determine whether any life insurance policies exist—are they term, universal, or whole life. What else is being supported? Have credit card debts been built up?

Obtain copies of all correspondence between the beneficiary and the trustee. See if the beneficiary can remember the phone conversation when he was asked about his tax bracket, preference for types of investing, risk tolerance, and the like. In essence, you are trying to see if the trustee has done as thorough a job as you would do with your clients. Whether you work on a commission or fee basis, you should know details about your client's lives and their goals. Find out if the trustee has asked the same kinds of questions.

Obtain copies of the trust documents and any amendments. Prepare a summary so that you thoroughly understand what the trust says and can refer to the relevant sections. When and how do different people get access to their funds? Investigate the resignation and removal clauses of the trust document. Seek out and speak with local attorneys to find out the likelihood of the bank having adverse public exposure if they have treated the trust beneficiaries unfairly. Get a family tree from the beneficiaries. Make contact with each member of the inheritor's family if you as the beneficiary decide to move ahead.

Prepare and complete a risk-tolerance questionnaire to determine whether the investments in the trust account are appropriate. Worksheet 14.1 on pages 200–201 is an example of a brief risk-tolerance questionnaire.

What are the overall asset allocation needs if the beneficiary is to maintain his lifestyle? What are the expressed as well as implied estate planning goals? Does the beneficiary have any special concerns regarding compa-

Worksheet 14.1 Risk Tolerance

1. How would you describe your outlook for the U.S. economy over the next 12 months?

   _____Very positive   _____Moderately negative

   _____Modestly positive   _____Very negative

   _____Neutral   _____Undecided

2. How would you like your returns to be characterized?

   _____Emphasize interest and dividends

   _____Emphasize capital gains

   _____Emphasize total return (i.e., all of the above)

3. Which paragraph best fits your investment risk tolerance?

   _____Safety and conservation of capital is of primary importance. Accordingly, the risk level of my entire portfolio should be low, although it is appropriate for some components to be subject to market fluctuation.

   _____High-quality investments providing an opportunity for modest growth of capital are essential. While my portfolio as a whole should project a generally conservative identity, limited use of aggressive investments is permissible for diversification.

   _____Moderately aggressive growth of capital is of primary importance. Therefore, my portfolio can accept reasonable exposure to greater volatility in the pursuit of above-average long-term rates of return.

   _____Aggressive growth of capital is of primary importance. My portfolio can accept the commensurably higher degree of overall volatility associated with an aggressive growth objective.

4. If 1 represents one-year CDs and Treasury bills and 10 represents options and future contracts, how would you grade your investment threshold?

   Lowest risk   1 2 3 4 5 6 7 8 9 10   Highest risk

5. What do you think is a fair rate of return on your portfolio's assets for the following time periods?

   Next 12 months   Over the next years

   _____6% to 8%   _____6% to 8%

   _____9% to 11%   _____9% to 11%

   _____12% to 13%   _____12% to 13%

   _____14% to 15%   _____14% to 15%

   _____over 15%   _____over 15%

6. Given the rate of return and time period you selected, what is the maximum level of *loss* you can accept during any 12-month period of time?

_____ 5% decline

_____ 10% decline

_____ 15% decline

_____ 20% decline

_____ 30% decline

_____ over 40% decline

---

nics that he does or doesn't like. See if the inheritor had a desire or made any effort to give input to the trustees in the past that was blocked. Evaluate the trustee's performance. Has the trustee accomplished the overall goal of the trust, to provide and support the client no matter what? Has the client's interest always come first?

TRUST-BUSTING CHECKLIST:
WHAT YOU NEED TO GET STARTED

1. Three years of transactions and investment statements
2. Date of acquisition and cost basis on all assets
3. Personal tax returns for three years
4. Performance analysis of account by asset class versus the indexes
5. Trust tax returns—complete set for the last three years
6. Net worth statement
7. Monthly or yearly expense budget
8. Beneficiary's life insurance policy copies or relevant information contained therein
9. Correspondence to and letters from the trustee
10. Trust document and any amendments
11. Family tree
12. Beneficiary's risk-tolerance evaluation
13. Asset allocation target
14. Special concerns of beneficiary—constraints on investment vehicles
15. Goals of the account—income needs, tax bracket info, cash reserve needs

Inquiry and Analysis

Once the basic documents have been gathered, it is time to ask questions intended to determine if the trustees are aware of any areas in which they have failed to perform their services. By asking these questions, we also will be laying out the standards by which the beneficiary will judge current or future trustees.

Service Questions

1. Has the trustee sent the reports with the right amount of detail and at appropriate frequencies?

2. Has the trustee asked about the beneficiary's tax bracket and other investments?

3. Has the trustee asked about other investments owned by the beneficiary?

4. Has the trustee asked about the client's risk tolerance?

5. Has the trustee done a good job diversifying the portfolio?

6. Does the trustee disclose and explain the bank's common trust funds to clients?

7. Does the trustee have the right mixture of taxable versus tax-free bonds for the beneficiary's tax bracket?

8. Does the trustee have a mixture of U.S. and international stocks?

9. Has the trustee held onto low-cost-basis stocks for years? If so, are they charging a full or discounted fee on these low-cost-basis stocks?

10. Is the trustee holding too much cash?

11. Is there a mixture of small- and large-cap stocks?

12. Has the trustee explained his investment philosophy and how it will fare in a long bear market?

13. Has someone been assigned to your account that you know personally?

14. How often are you contracted?

15. Do you know how your fees are calculated?

16. How long does it take to get a return call from your trustee?

Performance Management Questions

1. Does your trustee show quarterly and annual performance against appropriate benchmarks?
2. Do you feel that your trustee has a high level of investment expertise?
3. Does the trustee show performance net of fees?
4. Are you satisfied with the performance of the account?
5. Have you ever made any suggestion regarding investing to the trustee that was implemented? Ignored?
6. Is the trustee holding large amounts of inherited stock?
7. Do you feel you should have a say in how the account is invested?
8. Is the trustee billing on the inherited stocks at full charge?
9. Have you ever asked for a discount? Used an outside investment expert?
10. Has the trustee presented a diversification plan for large holdings?
11. How often does the trustee go over your account with you?
12. When was the last time any of the investments was changed?
13. Do you understand what you are invested in?
14. Do you care?
15. Do you have the fee schedule applied to the trust?
16. Does it seem fair to you?
17. Do you think you have any say in how the trust is being handled?
18. Do you want to?

Accessibility

1. Is your trustee following the trust document and communicating it to you?
2. Have you been given an explanation of your rights as a beneficiary?
3. Has the trustee explained its procedures and criteria for making discretionary distribution decisions?

4. Do you feel that you have to go through undue stress to get extra distributions?

5. Have you asked for and received a written explanation in plain English of the trust's provisions for distributions and final termination?

6. Have you ever had a request turned down by the trustee? What was it?

7. Why did the trustee turn you down?

8. Are you still disappointed by the trustee's response?

9. Do you feel that you have any avenue to appeal a trustee's decision that you don't agree with?

The Beneficiary's Goals

The beneficiary should be able to answer questions regarding what he or she wants from the trust.

1. What do you really want from the trust?

2. Do you feel that you can get this from the current trustee?

3. What kind of reports do you want?

4. Is your trustee good at explaining them to you?

5. Does your trustee know about your outlook on things?

6. What kind of personal contact do you want? How often? In person or by phone?

7. What amount of distributions do you need? Are you getting it?

8. Will your trustee listen to you and change things?

9. Do you want to have input?

10. What kind of investment performance do you expect?

11. What are you basing your expectations on?

12. Describe the perfect relationship with your trustee—what would that look like?

13. As the beneficiary, what are you willing to do to get what you want?

Beneficiary's Level of Commitment to Change

By now, you and the beneficiary are well acquainted with the trust situation and the degree of confidence, trust, and satisfaction (or lack thereof) that the beneficiary has with the current trustee. The next phase is to ascertain how tenaciously the beneficiaries will pursue the course of moving or busting the trust. You should first determine that busting the trust is in fact an appropriate course of action. The next step is to know the depth of your client's commitment to changing the situation. It is best to find this out before you proceed any further. Your client's answers to the following questions will give you an indication of what lies ahead.

1. Are you willing to hurt someone's career inside the bank to get what you want?
2. Are you willing to fight in court for what you want?
3. Insofar as your family goes, are you willing to exert pressure or be pressured regarding these issues?
4. Are you willing to pay money in advance for professional help to get things changed?
5. Are you willing to express your dissatisfaction in front of people who have always been nice to you?
6. Are you willing to take the time necessary to make the change?
7. Do you have patience?
8. Are you willing to let other people who might gossip hear your story?
9. Are you willing to challenge the authority figure of the trustee?
10. Are you willing to reconcile with (or alienate) other members of your family to get this done?
11. Are you willing to go all the way up the corporate ladder with your grievances?
12. Are you willing to go to the media with information about the bank's nonperformance, overcharges, or administrative mistakes?
13. Are you willing to have your name brought to public attention (which entails acknowledging that you do have a trust account) to get the trust moved?
14. Are you willing to put in some personal effort to get the trust moved?
15. Can you get your family members unified behind a strategy?
16. If one member breaks ranks when the bank starts to fight back, will family members drop the whole issue to have superficial peace in the family?

Many of these questions may never have to be asked. Some answers may indicate that the beneficiary is hesitant to proceed. These issues don't necessarily have to be set in stone for the inheritor and his advisor to proceed. But it's better to know up front how hard the fight might become.

Trustee Options: Alternative General Strategies

Strategy 1: Staying Put

We tell our clients that the first option is to negotiate with the current trustee. It is possible for the current trustee, with proper disclosure and sign-offs by the beneficiaries, to allow reallocation of accounts, to increase income, and to allow a financial advisor to direct the trust, making distributions, loans, or changing the way the trust is handled and charged. We are looking for the appropriate way to attune the trust to the client's overall financial goals and needs. It is possible for a trustee to reduce the fees and to perform only custodial and administrative duties.

You can stay with the current trustee and request these changes. You can ask for more income, more control over the investments, better returns (by mixing investment options) more and better reports, and lower fees. If a bank agrees to these requests to the satisfaction of the beneficiary, then certainly you should consider leaving the trust where it is and simply changing the way the trust is run. (Just one caution: I personally have never seen any of this happen.)

A trustee with a golden goose is unlikely to willingly let the goose out of the coop. Once the beneficiary asks for changes and is turned down, the possibility exists that the beneficiary may be in a worse position than ever, at least for a while. At that point, the trustee will be wary of the beneficiary and the relationship will be strained. This may be good in the long run, because the trustee will start paying more attention to the trust. But remember, there may be an emotional price to pay for this kind of better service.

Strategy 2: Friendly Move

Sometimes, the trustee does not want to change his approach but is willing to let go of the trust because the beneficiary would be better off having it at a more appropriate place. This is what we hear from some banks. When they take on new trusts (e.g., as the result of a merger), this attitude is helpful in acquiring the business. However, they generally have a vastly different attitude about their older trusts, which they consider to be a vested part of their permanent asset base and income stream. We are dealing with older trusts here, because the leverage of a financial advisor, an accountant, and an attorney can definitely change the recalcitrant attitude of the trustee.

We strongly suggest doing all of the strategizing before letting the current trustees know that you are about to make new demands of them. You do not want them to know that you are planning a move until the decision has been made. You may need to call on the resources of new trustees to counter the defensive strategy of the current trustees. As a start, existing trustees may reposition assets, send out tax and risk questionnaires, and basically try to rectify past mistakes due to their neglect. In short, they will try to fix things up to stay on good terms with the heirs.

Strategy 3: Forced Departure

When a trustee-beneficiary relationship is not salvageable, it is necessary to gather ammunition for a potential fight. Only rarely do these kinds of fights end up in court. Besides drawing up transfer papers, you may not have to pay legal fees to get a trust moved. If your case is well prepared, the advisor and beneficiary can do most of the work. However, when trustees are recalcitrant and inflexible, you will have legal fees.

Unfortunately, I've seen many cases of abuse of power with trustees who make it onerous for the heir to do anything without paying many expenses. Nonetheless, moving a trust is possible. Armed with information, it's time to gather political and family firepower to stand up to the trustee.

Once the commitment to move has been solidified, you must move forward and find a suitable successor trustee. We have explained where to begin looking for a successor. Every trust situation is different and will have its own best choice for a successor trustee. Chapter 20 will offer more advice on finding a successor.

The successor trustee should help prepare the documents to send an unmistakable signal to the current trustee that the trust will eventually move. It may take months or even years. There may be costs involved, but the trust can likely reimburse most of the costs. At this point, the committed beneficiaries need to give the trusted advisor latitude in finding legal representation on the current trustee's home turf. This will convince the trustee that you are very serious. You are now ready to move on to busting the trust.

CHAPTER

15

Building a Case

You must now review the assembled documents described in the last chapter to find where the trustee erred. You can approach this formidable stack of paper with confidence, because, make no mistake about it, the trustee has made some mistakes. Everyone makes mistakes, and usually they can be fixed. Every mistake, and we won't cover all the possibilities here, has been made by most trustees. Many trustees are competent, honest, hardworking, and well-intentioned. This is not about blaming any particular person. It is about getting leverage on the trustee, whatever is necessary. The proper administration of trusts and the full execution of fiduciary duties is so exacting and encompasses such a broad range of services that almost no one is capable of doing it completely right unless tremendous effort and time are expended. In the past, trustees were not expected to do most of the research that is now accepted as being essential for long-term investment success.

You must understand that many of the errors, omissions, oversights, and shortfalls of complete service are not causes for legal action against trustees. They may serve to point out that the trustee did not do a complete job. You want to set the stage for proposing that if the beneficiary's interests were foremost in the trustee's eyes, then the trustee will need to acknowledge shortcomings. Shortly, we will describe the most likely trustee reactions to our findings.

In addition to the statement of transactions and investments, you should already have looked at the personal and trust tax returns, a net worth statement, the monthly or yearly budget, a summary of life insurance policies owned by the beneficiary, a record of all correspondence between the beneficiary and the trustee, and the trust document, including all its amendments. You should have asked for and received a family tree to make it easier to follow the trust document. You should have received a clear indication, in writing, of the beneficiary's tolerance for risk and any preferences, constraints, needs, or goals for the account.

In doing this, you will certainly have come across things that the trustee has overlooked. There may have been things the trustee was supposed to do but didn't. Conversely, perhaps the trustee did things that weren't appropriate for the client's overall situation. At the very least, you will uncover the flaws in the trustee's communication with the beneficiary.

1. Has the trustee reviewed, on a quarterly basis, the performance of the account against its relevant indexes?

2. Has the trustee made regular inquiries into the standard of living of the beneficiary?

3. Has the trustee done his best to minimize the tax impact on distributions from the trust?

Armed with these documents, the financial advisor and beneficiary are ready to move on to the next step. It's time to search each document for evidence of errors, poor judgment, oversight, and mistakes—all of which will help build the case for moving the trust.

Finding Trustee Errors

Let's turn to the documents you have gathered and discuss the most common mistakes found in each. There may be additional documents not listed here, as well as mistakes not related to documentation. Be open-minded about the sources of information that will help build your case for busting the trust.

Last Three Years of Statements

Look first at the three years of monthly or quarterly transaction statements and asset listing from the trust.

1. What are the trustee's fees? Do they seem excessive given the work involved?

2. Are additional fees being paid to outside attorneys, accountants, and cotrustees?

3. Are double fees being charged? A red flag should go up if there are bank common trust fund fees in addition to the bank's overall management fee.

4. Are there sweep fees for moving money in and out of money market accounts?

5. In reviewing the investment statements, how much activity has occurred?

6. Has the trustee done nothing and charged a full fee on low-cost-basis assets?

7. Has the trustee sold blue-chip stocks and invested in its own common trust funds, which have then vastly underperformed the stocks that were sold?

8. Is the trustee using a taxable land fund for someone in a high tax bracket?

9. Does the client pay high state income tax because the trustee has defaulted to the trustee's own state's lands or land funds?

All of this takes digging. It may involve getting year-end statements as far back as the beneficiary can find. In any case, the trustee is required to keep records, and requests should be made in a nonobtrusive manner, through the beneficiary or his accountant, for older year-end statements.

How have investments been allocated? Has the account been diversified? Are corporate bonds included, or has the trust been mired in Treasuries forever? Is the trust overly allocated to stocks or to bonds? Have the bank's common trust funds or stock choices lagged the market? To answer these questions, either the advisor or the trustee must produce an individual account analysis, just as an outside investment advisor, a pension fund consultant, or a mutual fund company would do if called upon to defend its record. There should be no acrimony here, but the trustee may be shocked to realize that he is not immune from the pressures faced by any other money manager. There is a perception that trustees needn't produce the same competitive investment performance as other people in the financial services industry. This is categorically untrue. Many of the fees trustees charge are for investment services. They must produce the same kinds of records regarding performance as everyone else. Being a fiduciary involves more than just circumspection.

Trustees charge a fee for investing on all assets. Some of the assets may have been in the account for over five years. Assets that have not been changed should be the topic of a sell-versus-hold analysis every two years. If this has not been done, the trustee is out of line in charging a full fee on those assets. Nine out of ten trustees have no documentation regarding this kind of review. If assets remain unchanged to capture tax advantages, the beneficiary should sign off on that approach and a steep discount should be applied to those assets.

> Most trustees provide as little information as possible and almost no inter-pretation of data sent to the beneficiaries. In 1993, one large bank in Delaware began to provide benchmark index data along with a breakdown of results into various asset classes. This bank does not, however, break out inherited assets from the ones it chooses. It is a commendable start and a standard to which all other trusts should be held.

It is common for trusts not to make principal distributions in a timely fashion. When someone turns a certain age, the trustee will often not inform that person of the rights to withdraw the funds. Trustees often hold onto the assets well past their designated distribution time. It may be diffi-cult for some people to tell, but there is a large difference between trust accounting, which uses income and principal cash, and regular accounting. The trustee has to be extremely careful about which monies are put into income and which are put into principal, as it may affect the fairness of later distributions. Serious mistakes are often made in this area.

Underperformance in the investment area is common for bank trust departments. The situation is even worse for professional dynasties and individual trustees. The key to doing this kind of analysis is being able to break down the trust holdings into meaningful asset classes. You can then get an accurate sense of how much trading activity has occurred in the account. One private trust company we work with goes so far as to re-create the exact investment performance of an account by entering 10 years of transactions into its own computers! The company is then able to show the beneficiaries how poorly the current trustee has done in a completely compelling way. Most trust portfolios suffer from overemphasis on one area and concurrent underperformance relative to benchmark indexes. This is a result of plain neglect on the part of the trustee. Using common trust funds for bonds as opposed to going to the extra work of using individual bonds is another extraordinarily weak point of trustee behavior.

Trustees can argue this point, saying that common trust funds provide greater diversity than individual bonds, and this may be true. However, there has not been a sustained rise in interest rates since the 1980s. Bank trust departments were badly hurt in the 1970s when they held long-term U.S. Treasuries and interest rates started to rise. The next time long-term interest rates rise, the effect on their common trust funds will be just as devastating. The common trust fund is a convenient method for the bank to make money. It serves the client to a very minor extent and only in limited circumstances.

Have the fees on the trust gone up? What were the trust charges when the grantor or family founder was alive? Is there anything in the document that restricts the fees? In virtually no other business can one party raise fees without the other's consent. Trustees wantonly do this. Has the trustee involved the beneficiary in the investment of assets? Probably not. Trustees deem themselves to be the owner and feel their judgment is sufficient. Does the trust have real estate that is managed directly by the trustee? How is the performance of that real estate on an after-tax, after-fee basis? How does it compare to the returns possible under an independent real estate manager?

All of these issues depend on the assets in the trust and the language of the trust document. Nine times out of ten, by careful examination of the records and by asking the right questions, you will gather sufficient ammunition to embarrass the bank and provide grounds for moving the trust.

Trust Documents

Reading the legalese of long trust documents takes patience. After reviewing the trust document and its amendments, organize the issues of importance and draw several lines of inquiry to follow to see if the trustee has fulfilled its duties. Has the trustee properly calculated net income and distributed it on time? Has it made the required principal distributions in a timely fashion?

Has the trustee complied with all the provisions of the trust document? Almost no trustee reviews the document regularly. Due to increased standardization of trust administration services and the larger size of the banks, there is an increased caseload on each trust officer. Beneficiaries are categorized into the type of trust document and the investment mix of the account, whether it be conservative, moderate, growth-oriented, or aggressive. After that, everything gets lumped generically into the same funds that everyone else has, perhaps with a somewhat different mix. Has the beneficiary received a summary accounting in an understandable form? Are the investments in keeping with his or her long-term capital growth or current needs? If not, the trustee has not done its job.

Some trusts actually have what we call *portability language.* This means that the beneficiary has the right to move the trust from one trustee to another. We hope that in the future, no trust document will be written without this kind of language. Another way to balance the trustee's power is by use of a trust remover–trust appointer system. This allows concerned individuals to watch over and ensure that no trustee misuses its power.

The beneficiary is legally permitted and should be a member of this group along with the advisor. The group is able to remove the corporate trustee and appoint another one as long as certain criteria have been met.

Another provision to look for in a trust document is any mention of a successor trustee. Often, there is a mention of successor trustee's rights, responsibilities, and assignments, but no mention of how a successor trustee can come into being. This allows an opening for the beneficiaries to assert that the person who set the document did contemplate a future change in trusteeship. Most of the time, details regarding how to install a successor trustee are not forthcoming, perhaps because of the influence of the early attorney-banker relationship.

Beneficiary's Tax Return and Net Worth Statements

When you review the personal tax returns of the beneficiary, you find the income distributed by the trust carried onto the personal tax return. Is it the right kind of income? More often than not, trust departments have invested in municipal bond income for people in low tax brackets or in taxable income instruments for people in high tax brackets. The beneficiary loses in the form of excess tax paid or lost income. The vast majority of trustees never consider buying municipal bonds in the beneficiary's state of residence. The excuse you may hear is they just can't find any good ones. This is unacceptable! They are just too lazy to look, and you can bring them to task for this cavalier attitude, which costs the beneficiary, who then has to pay excess state taxes.

Has the beneficiary had to delay filing the tax returns because of the trustee? Have interest and penalties ever been paid to taxing authorities because of these delays? Have delays in the beneficiary receiving the K-1s from the trust caused the beneficiary extra tax preparation fees? Has the trustee overpaid estimated taxes for the next year's trust tax returns, resulting in a loss of income to the trust and therefore to the beneficiary? Has the trustee ever kept income inside of a trust, resulting in a higher income tax rate being paid than if it had been distributed to the beneficiary and taxed at lower personal tax rates?

This issue of tax returns speaks of the inequality between trust income tax rates and those governing individuals. In order to discourage setting up trusts for income tax avoidance or reduction, the Internal Revenue Service code has lower thresholds for trusts. This results in higher incremental tax brackets for trust income. The upshot is that all trust income should be distributed annually unless the beneficiary is already in a high tax bracket. Has the trustee ever asked for a net worth statement from the beneficiary? Has the trustee ever refused to distribute sufficient income to sustain the beneficiary's customary standard of living? Has the trustee ever refused to make a loan or buy real estate for a beneficiary who does not own his own home? Did the trustee sell closely held companies or real estate properties in order to simplify the job? Was this done in opposition to the beneficiary or grantor's wishes?

Monthly or Yearly Expense Budget

Has the trustee ever requested a monthly or yearly expense budget? Was assistance provided in preparing it? How does the trustee determine the proper distribution of income and principal if the document allows for discretion regarding this issue? Has the trustee ever helped the beneficiary do a financial plan to see if he or she will have enough money for retirement? Has the trustee helped the client put an estate plan in place so that the assets in trust might pass on in the most tax-efficient way? Probably not. These issues are not cause for dismissal of a trustee. By asking these questions, you point out that you know the trustee hasn't done a thorough job.

Beneficiary's Life Insurance Policy Copies and Annual Reports

Review all life insurance to see if it makes sense in the context of the client's needs. Should the trustee change the owner of the policies to a trust?

Correspondence with the Trustee

These documents often disclose unfulfilled trustee promises, admissions of mistakes, and background material regarding difficult issues. Nothing works as well to bust a trust as a damaging statement made on bank stationery.

Family Trust

This document will serve to help understand the trust document and map out which important people to solicit for support in moving the trust.

Beneficiary's Risk Tolerance

This provides insight into the appropriate investment mix for the trust.

Some Common Errors

- Trustee failed to provide information in the past that the beneficiary had a right to receive.

- Trustee made accounting errors.

- Trustee charged more fees than agreed to by the original grantor.

- Trustee failed to communicate about important issues regarding trust assets.

Preparing Your Position

Now that you have the information lined up, you should have found several areas in which the trustee failed to perform adequately. You are ready to proceed with assembling the case and strategizing about how best to present it. You need to have found a new trustee that you can work with, and the new trustee should be available to help you prepare the documents necessary to move the trust.

It is our experience that it is helpful to have the new trustee's involvement when preparing to approach the current trustee. You're still not ready to tip your hand, but strategy sessions need to begin as soon as the decision has been made to move the trust. A new trustee has to be willing to work with the inheritor's advisor in a way that will serve the beneficiary's interests.

Lining Up the Beneficiaries

Getting the beneficiaries to agree that moving all or part of the trust is the desired course of action is the first step. They must be willing to stay the course until the process is finished. You may want to get commitments to this essential position in writing before embarking on the next steps. Getting more than one person to agree to commit is often one of the most difficult parts of the process. Beneficiaries have been intimidated by their trustees for many years. In most families, there is often some kind of discord over money issues. Those entitled to receive income or principal may well have different ideas about the right course of action. Keep in mind that there will be many emotional as well as financial issues to deal with.

We advise getting all relevant beneficiaries lined up and signed off before starting the change process. If there is only one income beneficiary, and there are principal remainders who are not in the same branch of the extended family, you can often proceed with just the income beneficiary's approval. However, it is better to bring on board everyone who may be involved later on. How many beneficiaries are there? Do they get along? Do you understand and have enough history about the emotional relationships between the beneficiaries? This is important because the bank will use whatever methods possible to derail the process. This includes going to dissident family members to try to dissuade a move to another trustee. This is the bank's first line of defense.

If the beneficiaries are not in agreement about moving or busting the trust, can a case be made for dividing the trust into separate trusts for the different parties? Even if the document doesn't specifically address this issue, it can still be accomplished. Banks often divide multibeneficiary trusts into separate trusts for their own convenience, but it is not often that beneficiaries ask for these kinds of reorganizations, because they are not generally aware that it can be done. Splitting trusts into components has many advantages. It allows for individualized negotiations to take place whereby a beneficiary who wants to move agrees not to influence other members to join the exodus, thereby giving the trustee something in exchange for the beneficiary's freedom to move.

If a group of beneficiaries agrees to move, they need to designate one person to be their spokesperson. All the other heirs must stand by the strategy of not speaking with the trustee except through the designated spokesperson. This is very important, because the trustee will certainly try to divide and conquer. Usually, it is only one or two of the beneficiaries who have the gumption to assert control and spearhead the move, and other family members may not have similar financial or personal needs for independence. This also can be another good reason to go to separate trusts for different kinds of beneficiaries.

When trusts are set up for the benefit of a surviving spouse, a second spouse, or for various sets of children by different marriages, it is common for the income beneficiaries (the people who receive a current benefit from the trust) not to get along with those who receive the trust assets. It is difficult to see how you can move a trust without approaching both of these dissenting parties. If you represent the income beneficiary, how will you convince the remainder person who distrusts the income beneficiary to cooperate?

We suggest dealing with this issue by involving an outside attorney. The attorney will present the case to the principal remainder person that her interests are being hurt by the neglect or oversight of the current trustee. Choosing the correct third party is crucial when beneficiaries do not get along. Financial counselors who specialize in the emotional aspects of money are often skilled mediators. Sometimes going directly to a professional mediator works better than using an attorney. To take control of a trust, you must have one class of beneficiaries totally committed to making a change, or have a situation where your client is the only income beneficiary. This is a long process. The burdens and pressures generally rest on the person who is trying to effect the change. The trustee is going to be content to let things sit as they are, so a commitment aggressively to promote the move is essential. The SIP has to be clear that it will take time and some money to make the move a reality.

How Much Will It Cost?

It is difficult to know initially how long and how complex the moving process will be. It is possible that very little money will be needed. If the advisor does her homework properly, a compelling case can be presented to the trustee that things are best for everyone if there is a quick parting of ways. With a sufficiently researched case and acceptable alternatives lined up, even if the current trustee decides to fight, it generally does not last long, nor does it go to court.

One of the keys is finding the right attorney to represent the beneficiaries. There are attorneys in every city who, as opposed to being in the political circle of banks, for example, have made their reputations by challenging bank or private trustees successfully in the past. This can be a bank that has mishandled loans or specific trust attorneys who are cozy with upper management at banks. Litigation attorneys are helpful when dealing with uncooperative professional dynasties and individual trustees, because they know that you are serious when they hear from a well-known litigator

Approaching the Trustee

Everything is in place. The facts are lined up; the inheritors and beneficiaries are in agreement; an attorney has been engaged; and a successor trustee has been found. The strategy at this point depends on the individual circumstances. The person best qualified to approach the trustee to express the desires of the beneficiary must immediately convince the trustee that there will not be any turning back on the part of the heirs: Therefore, there is no point in the trustee trying to convince the beneficiaries to change their minds.

The beneficiaries and their advisors are armed with specific knowledge about how the trustee has erred. The new team has a plan in place to undo those mistakes and to do a better job for the beneficiary, and the heir has signed off on those plans. The current trustee will have to evaluate the difficulties he will face if it tries to keep the unhappy beneficiary in its fold involuntarily. If the trustee is successful in stopping the move, the fact is that it will be under microscopic scrutiny for the rest of its tenure as trustee. This will severely undermine the account's profitability. If a certain number of extra hours are required to constantly gauge beneficiary demands, the trustee will be in the hot seat. Mistakes that might occur in the future will be scrutinized and the trustee will be brought to task for them. This is not an ideal working relationship.

A brief outline of past transgressions and reasons for the dissatisfaction of the beneficiaries is sometimes helpful. It is important that this be transmitted in writing, with copies sent to as many people as possible. Trustees must know that in the absence of a clause in the trust document that gives the beneficiary the right to move the trust, the beneficiary is willing to make more trouble than it is worth if the current trustee is not cooperating. This message can be communicated in a variety of ways, both subtle and direct.

What to Do if the Trustee Doesn't Cooperate

You always need to understand the internal politics of the trustee. Who holds real power over the trust department? What image is the trustee trying to portray to the community? Don't be surprised in the least if the first attempt to move the trust fails to elicit cooperation. There is always a key issue in every trust situation. There is a unique way of unlocking access to trust assets, and it is different every time. That's one of the things I love about this work. It's like a detective story combined with politics and psychoanalysis! The advisor's job is to help the beneficiary find the key. The beneficiary is the one to turn the key, as it is her assets.

The politics of the trustee is one of the first keys to try if family members are involved with the trustee in other contexts or with other trusts. It is especially useful if family members have positions of stature in the local community. A trustee stands to lose a great deal in any fight with an unhappy beneficiary. There are many other potentially unhappy clients still in the trust department. The trustee definitely does not want his other clients to be aware of any dispute regarding the trust area. In a bank, for example, there are loan relationships, deposit relationships, future estate trust relationships—all of which can be used as leverage on the trustee. You can get what you want if you hold the key to something the trustee needs.

First, be aware that the current trustee wants to get the fees with as little trouble as possible. One approach is to say to the trustee, "Look, we want you to do this in order to satisfy our needs, and this is how we want you to do it." If the trustee is unable to change the standard operating procedures to accommodate your needs, he knows this and will look for a graceful way out of dealing with dissatisfied and vociferous heirs. The demands need to be reasonable and insistent. Beneficiaries can, at some point, offer to pay for costs of termination. The trustee will immediately be thinking about how large termination fees might be and when and how they can be collected. These amounts used to be set by law and are always buried somewhere in the trustee's published fee schedule.

You can be sure that when the family founder set up the trust, there was no such thing as a termination fee. Therefore, the need to negotiate or obtain a waiver was not part of the document. In order to raise income, banks interjected this fee, first as a reasonable way to cover their costs, then as a financial windfall to which deceased grantors could not object. In modern trust documents, it is essential to include a negotiated termination fee and portability language. Trustees need to understand that they have much to lose and little to gain by holding unhappy, discontented beneficiaries hostage to poorly drafted documents. Reasonable trustees with an eye toward their image in the community, and who want to do the right thing, will resign if given an appropriate out.

Final agreement to move a trust will include a release from liability to the resigning trustee concerning all actions. There will be a payment of some fee to the trustee for relinquishing the trust. If the trustee refuses to cooperate and attempts to strike back at the beneficiary with threats, innu-endoes, or worse, there are several strategies to use.

The Trust Buster's Arsenal

Let's look at six tools you have in your efforts to take control of the trust and talk about their possible applications. The first is management embar-rassment. Trust officers or trustee representatives, perhaps aspiring junior legal partners, have some pretty formidable goals in terms of bringing in new business and keeping current fee income on the books. If you find their administrative or investment errors, they quite naturally do not want their superiors to be aware of their mistakes. Most often, the mistakes go back through several generations of trust officers, especially in today's consolidated banking environment. How much time and attention does the trustee's middle or upper management want to spend on this particular account to control the damage? You have the ability to bring trust errors to the attention of people in uppermost management by complaining about systematic inadequacies. This is embarrassing for low-level trust officers and their immediate superiors.

The second tool is using the media to advance your cause. It is important to know what media connections are available in your community. You may need help in figuring out how to get the media to tell your story, if it becomes necessary. The trustee definitely does not want to be embarrassed in public. Is this intimidation on your part? Who knows? There are various ways to bring your situation into the public domain, some without divulging the particulars of your personal trust situation. Newspaper reporters, radio talk shows, magazine writers, financial bulletin ads on the Internet, the tele-vision media, local clubs, and professional associations are all venues in which you or your advisor can actively speak about your unhappiness with a trustee. Banks, for example, spend millions of dollars to create a finely crafted image in their communities. The last thing in the world they want is for someone to make it clear that one of their main purposes in life will be to discredit that carefully crafted image. This threat can have considerable weight in the trustee's decision regarding whether or not to fight your ef-forts to move the trust. Other trustees who are concerned about their repu-tations in the community also will not want a vocal detractor out stirring up trouble. No one does.

Third, litigation is always a possibility. Trustees do not want to spend time preparing for and going through litigation if it can be avoided. Even when the trustee threatens to use the beneficiary's own trust funds to fight the move, a finding of negligence will preclude this, and there is a possibility that the trustee will then have to reimburse you for any fees you incur as well. This can all be made clear to the trustee at the proper time. The threat of litigation is always present, but actually going to court is far down the list of probable tactics.

The fourth tool is request for monetary reimbursement for losses suffered as a result of administrative or investment blunders. Litigation also involves monetary damages. Trustees are not ordinarily responsible for losses incurred due to poor investment performance. But other types of errors abound. We have seen the failure to pay taxes on time, which caused interest and penalties. One Swiss bank even failed to liquidate an internal common trust fund because it closed the fund to redemptions! Inadequate disclosure of fees is often grounds to request reimbursement.

The fifth tool is the threat of a class-action suit. Beneficiaries have the right to band together to address unfair practices of a trust department if they so desire. This is a targeted public relations effort and is the last thing that a trustee wants to see happen. It is difficult to organize efforts for such a suit, but it is possible. When you connect with other dissatisfied people who are customers of a trustee, it increases your power considerably. One beneficiary in Pennsylvania organized a group of like-minded beneficiaries to fight a bank trust department over fees for moving trust money into and out of money market accounts. As in most legal battles, the lawyers always win. In this case, not much satisfaction was gained by either party in the final analysis. Nonetheless, the bank had to spend an inordinate amount of time, energy, and money to combat both the legal action and the negative publicity generated by this kind of confrontation.

Finally, there are the state or federal regulations that bind all corporate trustees. They are required to maintain a list of client complaints. You can make a case that you will be glad to provide plenty of fodder for the regulators, in effect assuring the trust department that a considerable amount of time will be needed the next time they are audited.

It is easy to make a nuisance of yourself to your trustee. Written demands after telephone demands after lawyer demands are tiring for both the recipient and the sender. Being a nuisance can be an effective way of getting attention. The trustee can be so worn down by persistence that it allows the trust to be moved to another established fiduciary.

Remember, in all of this you are holding out the carrot of absolving the trustee from their past misdeeds in addition to offering payment of a fee.

The trustee's continued good relationships with its other clients is also at stake.

How can you threaten the marketing efforts of stubborn trustees? If they are aware that you will be out to offset the goodwill they are trying to generate in the community, they will listen carefully. The key is having a well-defined plan of action that should be acceptable to any reasonable person. This holds out a ready alternative to fighting. It is interesting to note that all these devices will have more influence on corporate trustees than on professional dynasties. Lawyers, accountants, and individual trustees whose businesses are not solely dependent on trustee services have much less to lose by adverse publicity. They are also the worst offenders when it comes to abuse of power. Their professional associations are a possible venue for voicing concerns about incompetence.

Managing the Attack

Now you are ready to implement your strategy because the players are lined up and your documentation is in place. Timing is everything. Given the personal and financial situations of the beneficiaries, the financial advisor has to help the inheritor determine whether to move quickly or slowly. There will always be obstacles that come up, perhaps from unexpected sources. A family attorney may turn out to have ties to a bank. An heir you thought was committed to a change may get cold feet when the trustee threatens sanctions.

Have all parties check in regularly, and bring in the big-firepower items only when you need them. It is important not to let the process go on too long.

The Emotional Aspects

The final part of this chapter has to do with the emotional aspects of making the change. The beneficiaries and the advisor need to be strong, firm, and grounded in their desire for change. They have to have their eyes clearly set on the goal and understand what success would mean for their long-term financial future. Setbacks will occur; it will take longer than expected; it may turn out to be more expensive than originally anticipated. You really have to believe in the necessity of the change before starting.

Expect to hear "no" from attorneys, accountants, trust officers, bankers, and other family members, but not from your advisor. The advisor's job is to be a coach and a cheerleader to get out on the field and do the job. The beneficiary is the one who holds the key to success. It is only by his or her commitment that the job will get done. The current trustees will always be able to determine the level of commitment of the beneficiary because they will interact, threaten, cajole, promise, test, and probe the beneficiary. They will check out any opportunity or possible reason for not resigning. Because banks are totally driven by the bottom line, you can make the case that you will absolutely turn this account into an unprofitable one for them if they do not yield. This is the bottom line. Showing them a profitable way to resign is one sure way out of their clutches.

On the one hand, we have a trustee who can exert pressure monetarily, by cutting income or principal distributions, and psychologically, by contacting other family members and sowing seeds of family discontent.

The trustee is also capable of wining and dining possible defectors. He can promise to change to accommodate your expressed goals. Carefully examine your feelings about the trustee. Even if he could follow through on promises to you in this regard, do you want to continue dealing with him? Will the people who are talking and making promises to you today be there in five years? Does the trustee have the internal expertise to find, keep, monitor, and report on the best investment vehicles for your situation? If the answer is yes, it may be worth considering staying with the current trustee under a new arrangement. If the answer is no, you may decide to become a trust buster.

Conclusion

There can be a great emotional reluctance to take on a trustee. It means taking on family history, which can seem like taking on the weight of the world when life is stressful already. The advisor's job is to be the person who, upon the request of the heir, can step forward and say, "I'll take the lead now, but I'll check back with you at every step. I'll take care of shepherding the whole process and be available to take some of the heat." The advisor must be willing to be thought ill of by certain professionals and trust departments in order to be effective for the beneficiary. The beneficiary and advisor both have to be emotionally strong in themselves and in their trust in each other.

Trust Busting Made Easy

"I'm speaking to you now not as man's best friend but as your attorney's dog."

We have gone over the basics of how to take back control of a trust—how to get it moved. Now, we will give you some suggestions about how to make it a more expedient and less difficult process. As a seasoned investment professional, you need to have put into place the personal attributes and organizational strengths that we have previously described. You will be investing much time in this process, so you need to have clients who will recognize your investment in them. The beneficiary must be willing to ante up and prove that he or she also is serious about moving the trust. This raises again the issue of what needs to be in place before the trust-busting process begins. In this chapter we will cover whether a retainer is appropriate, how to choose the point person, how to get unanimity among beneficiaries, and how to set realistic expectations. Then we will provide items for discussion and information on how to choose a new trustee. We will give negotiation hints and suggestions on how to prepare to win freedom for the trust quickly and decisively.

Retainers

The first thing to keep in mind regarding retainers, or prepayment of fees for specific services, is that it is not really clear if they are advantageous or not. Clients are used to paying attorneys on a retainer basis with a certain amount up front, no matter what the outcome of their matter. In the investment field, investment advisors are used to working on a retainer basis when involved in financial planning, or on a percentage basis when managing assets. In any case, once the trust-busting process is successful, it will be more than worth the time and effort spent by all parties because the assets, if handled properly, should be much more productive for many years. What about unsuccessful attempts to move trusts? Should advisors get some sort of remuneration from beneficiaries in all cases? We think not. However, if beneficiaries can change their mind after time and effort have been expended, then the advisor and the beneficiary would be well served to have a written disengagement letter.

This is a sensitive and important issue. Having a rigid attitude about retainers could impact other inheritor-advisor relationships. A rule of thumb we use is that the farther the beneficiary's location is from the advisor, the weaker is the bond between the advisor and beneficiary, and the greater is the need for a retainer, since that need is inversely related to the closeness of the relationship.

Trust busting is more art than science. Being able to judge the level of commitment of beneficiary and knowing the likelihood of successfully moving the trust early on will save all parties a substantial amount of time and effort. It will also guide everyone in whether to put a retainer in place. Some clients will feel more committed to a process if they agree to pay a retainer. This is a very real psychological advantage because the advisor can be sure that the beneficiaries will not change their minds in the middle of the process, when pressure starts to build from the trustee or within the family. The beneficiary will also feel that the advisor will stay through thick and thin, a supportive and comforting thought.

If a retainer is appropriate, it should be borne equally by all of the beneficiaries, not just by the primary beneficiary who contacted the advisor. This will allow all beneficiaries a chance to examine the advisor's background and to clearly understand and sign on as part of the process. This will be helpful after the move is finished because the trusted advisor and the extended family will know each other. If the advisor is going to help to do the bulk of the work, supplanting the need for substantial legal and accounting professional time, it seems fair to ask for a retainer because the beneficiaries otherwise would be paying an hourly fee to someone else for the same work. If one of the beneficiaries is a current client of the advisor, this work may be considered as part of the advisor services for which the inheritor has already paid.

Drafting documents is not our specialty, nor do we practice law at our firm. We do have a set of forms that has been successfully used over and over again, obviating most of the need for an attorney except for the negotiation aspect of the move. An outside accountant could do the analysis of the account's history. Sometimes this is helpful from a political point of view because it gives the trustee an additional party to worry about in terms of their reputation. The accounting should cover past performance, fees, income and principal distributions, allocation fairness, tax return review, appropriate documentation, and so forth.

The Point Person

The responsibility for spearheading the process most often falls on the trusted advisor. This is because beneficiary tempers will flare and wills will be under pressure once the negotiations get tough. If a lawyer leads, it will be expensive—perhaps too expensive too soon to see the process through to its completion. The odds instinctively seem formidable because of the unique position trustees are in by virtue of their having the ability to use the client's own money to try to keep the account for their own company. Rarely will trustees who are being removed let go without some face-saving effort. They are highly motivated to make an energetic effort to dissuade the beneficiaries from making a change.

It is much easier on the client and the effort is more likely to be successful if everyone agrees to let the advisor lead the process, with a strong attorney as second. This takes the emotional aspect off center stage. It allows the lead to present the position and case for change to the current trustee in an objective and impersonal manner. Sometimes, however, it takes an attorney to lead the charge because the trustee will view the advisor as competition with a vested interest in moving the trust. The trustee will bring this to the attention of the beneficiary. In more complex cases, a team approach is best. We find the "good-cop-bad-cop" strategy works well if one of the team can befriend and empathize with the reluctant trustee.

Agreement among Beneficiaries

We previously talked about the necessity of having agreement among beneficiaries. The key question is whether this should be a verbal or written statement. The process of writing things down helps to clarify the issues involved, and we highly recommend it. We use several formats, which are essentially a formal business plan for the family. If people change their minds later, you can refer back to this mutual commitment, but having a plan will help beneficiaries to see and remember why they're doing what they're doing and where they hope to be headed. This can be most comforting when setbacks occur. When a client sees a written long-term investment plan that includes warnings about the inevitability of down markets, it helps him remember the emotional mind-set we tried to create through our educational work when we began the process, before the pressure was on.

Setting Realistic Expectations

As with investment returns, the trusted advisor needs to set realistic expectations, so that the beneficiary does not expect a quick and painless move. A realistic time frame is a minimum of two months and a maximum of two years. Trustees move slowly by design. Their policies and procedures are set up first of all to protect them from fiduciary liability, secondarily to receive fees, and thirdly to ensure that things stay the way they are for as long as possible. There is a limit to how fast one can push trustees.

Trust officers at banks are overworked and underpaid, and often out of touch with the investment world and the needs of their beneficiaries because of a lack of time, education, and experience in these matters. This is not due to lack of intellectual capacity or interest on their part. By and large, they are good people in situations not of their making. Bank trust officers have hundreds of clients, many of whom they have never met. They are required to adhere to the bank's established investment philosophy. Any changes, including discretionary distributions or agreement to transfer the account, must go through several committees.

The issue of court involvement should be addressed, even though it's unlikely to reach that stage. If the trust was created under a will that was probated in a state whose courts oversee the trust, then a summary examination and approval of the transfer by court is necessary. If the trust was registered for any reason and that is to be changed, then a withdrawal of registration is in order.

The court and the resigning trustee will look at the proposed successor trustee closely. Is it well-capitalized? Does it have enough management experience? Does it have the resources in place so that if future problems or disputes or dissatisfactions occur, the heirs don't have to come back to the previous trustee to make things right? This can be taken care of through a "release and hold harmless" clause absolving the departing trustee of any future liability.

Some claim that if a beneficiary has the unfettered right to remove a trustee and name a successor at will, then a true trust doesn't exist. This might remove the tax advantages afforded by some trusts. When there are beneficiaries who make unreasonable demands that might contradict the trust document, the trustee may be inclined not to hold to the basic terms of the trust. However, the interests of future beneficiaries have to be considered. Trustees can resign with notice to beneficiaries and successors, alerting both to potential tax problems.

Choosing a Successor Trustee

Find out what trust service providers are available in your area and who is best suited to the personality of the beneficiary. The following checklist will guide you to see which aspects of potential trustees are most important:

- The trustee-advisor relationship

- New trustee's location and charter

- Institutional or individual trustee?

- Find a trustee willing to work with the beneficiary-advisor relationship

- Trustees who allow for a wide range of investment vehicles

- Flexible and open to negotiation

- Price-competitive

The Trustee-SIP Relationship

In terms of the administration of the trust, a trustee should know ahead of time when and how much money a beneficiary needs. It is good to map out the reasons for requests for distributions at the outset of a relationship. The beneficiaries should be clear about their financial plans, and their demands upon the account should not change too often. Of course there are unexpected events in everyone's lives. It is a question of reasonableness and documentation. The reasonableness of demands on the new trustee depends upon the communication between the advisor and the trustee. This crucial communication has to be managed for the benefit of the client. "The client comes first" is an often heard, but too rarely practiced credo.

The successor trustee must have a comfortable relationship with the advisor. Good corporate trustees will visit the advisor's office to evaluate the tenor and quality of the services provided by the investment agent of the trust. Likewise, the advisor should regularly visit the trustee's office to make sure that the trustee's organization is intact. This ties into the new custodian/trustee's ability to give the advisor electronic information; to provide quick, efficient, and cost-effective transaction services such as block trading and pricing; and also to be a source of reliable administrative backup to the advisor in all trust-related matters. The trustee's job is to hold the inherited assets and provide reports plus provide administrative backup. The advisor's job is to manage the assets and get the beneficiaries what they need out of the trust.

New Trustee's Location and Charter

Is it important that beneficiaries have a personal contact person close at hand? Would they be satisfied with a national trust company that they might only speak with over the telephone? It is important to resolve this issue early. We work with trustees who are local, regional, and national. Every trust situation has a different requirement. There are pros and cons for each situation.

The geographic location of the new trustee, the size of the firm, and the experience of the staff are all factors that need to be reviewed. Even when trust documents don't mention the possibility of a successor, this should not discourage beneficiaries from thinking that they can move their trust. The fact is that most trust documents don't talk about removing trustees. If they do, they might only designate a successor as an organization that merges with the current trustee. Generally, it is not an appropriate arrangement for the needs of the beneficiary.

These clauses were put in place because it is in the trustee's interest to have the impression that choices are limited for the beneficiaries. The authors believe that the courts will reject the assumed right of current trustees to maintain control over their trust clients' assets without earning that trust through performance and service. Any private trust company can act as a successor trustee in any state. Currently it may not have offices or advertise, but independent trust companies can act in any state. National banks can also act as trustees on an interstate basis, but most are unwilling to do so. We have an established relationship with a state-chartered independent trust company whose business is to provide national trustee services for beneficiaries with their advisors at reasonable rates.

Institutional or Individual Trustee?

Does the beneficiary want an individual trustee or an institutional trustee? Most often, trust documents that speak about this issue require a corporate trustee to act as successor. This does not allow for family advisors, attorneys, or friends to become successor trustees. On the corporate level, there are various-sized trust departments, each with pros and cons. Local trustees are available and accessible, but they generally have little or no investment expertise. This can be acceptable if there is an investment professional available to act in that capacity. The local trustee most often has limited custodial capacity. This can present operational problems for executing trades and offering the widest available range of investment vehicles.

Regional trust companies are more sophisticated in terms of their technology, but they have a weak sense of local presence. The major drawback of regional trust banks is that they are likely to be bought out. The continued existence of the local trust organization is probably easier to ascertain than the possible tenure of regional trust banks. This issue can be important if you're concerned with the continuity of the trustee. National trust companies tend to be more expensive, more sophisticated, and sometimes much more rigid. They may be appropriate for very-high-net-worth individuals who move around the country.

Find a Trustee Willing to Service the Beneficiary-Advisor Relationship

Every advisor has an understanding of what the needs are in terms of custodial capabilities (that is, who will hold the records) and what kind of information flow is needed. We insist that our trustees give us the choice of various custodians and that they be able to download information electronically to our portfolio management system. The new trustee must be willing to operate under our client contact systems so that we can stay up-to-date on all financial events in our clients' lives. Unfortunately, many institutions are not willing to put systems in place to serve acting beneficiaries and their advisors.

Numerous trust organizations have been created over the last five years specifically to serve investment professionals. Our experience is that the larger they are, the more inflexible they are in terms of negotiating fees, terms of administration of the trust, investment vehicles offered, choice of custodians, and electronic information transfer capability.

Trustees Who Allow for a Wide Range of Investment Vehicles

This technical subject relates to what assets a trustee is willing or able to hold. For example, some Swiss banks will not hold U.S. corporate bonds and therefore are a poor choice of trustee for persons needing income. Regional banks will not hold some mutual funds or index funds, so trust companies set up by brokerage firms are poor places for persons wanting to hold low-cost growth vehicles.

Flexible and Open to Negotiation

We believe that trustees should be flexible. A set fee schedule or administrative procedure is not appropriate for all situations. If a trustee insists the fee schedule is nonnegotiable, it is a red alert signal that servicing liberated beneficiaries and their advisors is not this trust company's priority. An initially reluctant trustee can be downright rigid when an unexpected situation presents itself and the beneficiary needs something not previously discussed. You should steer clear of inflexible trustees. We believe that trustees should be willing to share financial information about the profitability of their services and provide backup documents if necessary. (We often need extra-customized statements and occasional personal visits with the beneficiary.) All of this means that there is a wide variety in the costs and capabilities of successor trustees.

Part of the taking control of inherited wealth is negotiating the best possible relationship. This includes negotiation of fees, ascertaining the experience and skill level of personnel to be dedicated to the inheritor's account, what control of distributions of income and principal will be exercised, what documentation will be required to change distribution amounts, and other matters regarding the cost level and service criteria that beneficiaries can expect. Asset allocation decisions are very important in the investment area. Trustees should not superimpose their own asset allocation models on the beneficiary. Their job is to supervise and ensure that the trust is not being invested totally to benefit one class of heirs.

The seasoned investment professional should be prepared to negotiate the following areas with potential successor trustees:

- Fees
- Level of service
- Control on distributions of income and principal
- Asset allocation decisions
- Reporting and communications
- Exit strategy
- Custody
- Electronic download of information capability

Price-Competitive

The trustee must price service competitively, based on the market and the amount of work involved. Negotiating trustee fees on behalf of beneficiaries is part of the advisor's job.

When negotiating fees, bear in mind that there is a baseline expense for having the account on the books and taking on fiduciary liability. This generally is quite low, 0.15% or $150 dollars per $100,000. A well-run trustee organization can make money on most any trust situation. Time is the crucial factor as far as the successor trustee's evaluation of whether to take on a trust and at what price to negotiate.

In our experience, when we act as a negotiating agent for another advisor with potential successor trustees, we are able to clarify for the trustee what expectations and demands will exist at the outset. We lay out the procedures for communications so that the beneficiary and advisor can feel that dealing with the new trustee will not be much different than managing his or her other accounts. The beneficiaries should feel that they have one solid contact person with whom they are comfortable. Simultaneously, the new corporate trustee must know that the requests that will be made will be formatted in such a way that they will fall under the guidelines of the trust. Thus, the new trustee's liability exposure is minimized. Trustees have to price their services based on many unknowns. The primary uncertainty is the time involved on their part. We plan out for the new trustee, our peer advisor, and the beneficiary how to bring the assets in, administer them, and finally—when the trust terminates—how to execute an efficient distribution.

As in all matters, size counts, but quality is the most important thing. High-net-worth individuals and competent financial advisors want the best quality at reasonable but not bargain prices. It isn't worth it to find a dirt-cheap trustee if you can't get accurate statements on a timely basis. Low commissions don't make up for losses suffered because of having to trade through a cumbersome mechanism. There are disadvantages for inheritors and their advisors if you trade off service for price.

Exit Strategy

The ability to move the trust again if the beneficiaries or advisors are not happy with the performance of the successor trustee should clearly be delineated. Any charges that might be levied for future movement of the trust should be prenegotiated as well. The beneficiary should not have to go through any trauma regarding portability of the trust more than once. The advisor's responsibility is to the client, and he should gracefully step down if asked, just as the new trustee's ability to take extraordinary fees should be constrained by a sort of prenuptial agreement.

The evaluation of successor trustees should be based on their flexibility to provide these kinds of agreements with the beneficiary. Part of taking control is to negotiate an exit strategy with the new trustee before the beginning of the relationship. We do not want to repeat the mistakes of the last generation of estate planners, who promoted trustees with lockholds on trust assets.

Full Disclosure

There must be full disclosure of the relationship between the advisor, the agents, and the new trustee. This is a very competitive business. Clients don't mind paying fees as long as they know what they are getting for their money. Beneficiaries must know how they are going to benefit from moving the trust. The level of fees should stay roughly the same as the trust moves from the old to the new trustee. The beneficiary also should be able to get considerably more income if the investments made under the investment professional's directions are more productive. All fee arrangements between any of the parties serving the trust should be disclosed to the beneficiary. The advisor's job is to interpret the fees in context of the net benefits to the beneficiary.

Document Preparation

The successor trustee should take on responsibility for preparing most of the draft documents of all transfer papers and then delivering them to the old trustee. The movement of assets is not complicated, but there is some coordination that has to occur between the old and the new trustee. Look for competent operations people who have experience in such arrangements when evaluating a successor trustee's capabilities.

The beneficiary's tax returns and the trust tax returns will, by necessity, be a combined effort of both trustees during the transition year. The beneficiaries will be penalized if this is not done in a cooperative spirit. Their personal tax returns must wait for the trust tax return to be finished so that they can include their K-1 forms as part of their income. Once the transfer documents have been completed and processed, you'll need an excellent trust administrator in the new trustee. Remember that flexibility and attention to detail save money in the long run, so don't automatically choose the trustee with the lowest fees.

Conclusion

The most important thing in getting a trust moved is to take enough time to make the right decisions. If your beneficiary has been well prepared and the advisor has done the research, the trust will be moved successfully. Remember that even if the document doesn't contemplate a move, you can still take control of it. We will be able to find shortfalls in the way the trust was handled because if there weren't any mistakes, the beneficiary wouldn't be dissatisfied. Although a few state courts still do not consider client satisfaction or psychological needs an important measure for evaluating fiduciaries, virtually all trusts can be moved.

The authors believe that eventually a beneficiary's bill of rights will be adopted throughout our country, perhaps influencing trust administration as much as the new restatement of the "prudent man" rule did in the area of trust investments.

Part 5

Trustworthy Advisors

By now, you know quite a bit about trusts. You know their history, the reasons they came into existence, how they operate, and the psychological nuances of their owners and trustees. You have guidelines and game plans for how to help bring them back under the rightful control of the inheritor.

The resources and expertise needed to accomplish these goals are immense, but so are the rewards. The next section of this book explains what it takes for the seasoned investment professional and beneficiary to embark on this journey with success. Chapter 17 describes the internal preparations an advisor's business must accomplish to become involved with trusts. Chapter 18 tells how to get into the thick of trusts, trustees, and beneficiaries. Chapter 19 is a working description of what a successful advisory firm for trusts needs to do on a daily basis. Chapter 20 is a further detailed description of how to find and choose the right corporate trust.

Is the Trust Business Appropriate for an Advisor?

"I realize, gentlemen, that thirty million dollars is a lot of money to spend.
However, it's not real money and, of course, it's not our money either."

N ow that you as seasoned independent professionals have a firm grasp of what kind of work is involved in moving trusts, you're no doubt wondering whether your current or future clients need this kind of service. If they do, then it's important to take a look at your own personal and business goals. In fact, most people in the financial advisory field go through considerable soul-searching on a regular basis. We regularly reevaluate our chosen methods in relation to the fast-changing world around us.

The authors believe that making money is not enough of a motivator to really excel in the trust field. What is needed is the kind of personal dedication that money can't buy, so that we can do the kind of job that inheritors deserve. Thus far the trust advisory business has played only a small part in America's financial history, but we believe that it will be a growing part of its future.

Estate planning to avoid taxes has become much more difficult over the years because Congress, through Internal Revenue Service regulations, has eliminated most strategies that Americans formerly used to avoid paying estate taxes. Life insurance trusts are no longer great ways for wealthy people to keep their fortunes intact. Such maneuvers as gifting, charitable trusts, and offshore trusts are evidence that people are having to search for solutions to estate tax problems.

The personal characteristics of a successful trust advisor involve a multiplicity of skills, a certain mind-set, and—above all—the ability to make a match with a particular kind of client. The purpose of this chapter is to help advisors to decide whether the trust area is right for them. If advisors have the interest and the know-how, they should gauge their personal readiness to go the distance.

In addition to possessing strong technical skills, advisors must have a keen interest in their clients' personal situations. The ability to establish close and meaningful relationships with beneficiaries depends more on character than technical skills.

There is a strong impetus to develop an ego about our abilities and to have a sense that we know more or are smarter than the next person. This is an unsatisfactory position for several reasons:

First, it is not true. Second, it can never be satisfactorily proven. Third, it doesn't make a difference in producing results for clients. Prospective clients who say, "I want to make x% per year over the indexes" are not the best kind of clients, even though we may want to achieve the same objective and occasionally even do it! If that was our business, we would start a mutual or hedge fund. But that is not our business. Trust clients want a fully human relationship. Trust advisors must be mentally, emotionally, and spiritually prepared to provide this relationship.

Where can we look for models in this area? Insurance sales people are a partial model. Because of the highly profitable commission structure under which they work, they have the time to cultivate strong client relationships. However, successful life insurance agents generally use an approach that emphasizes having a "surplus" to pay estate taxes or banking on every person's desire not to leave loved ones stranded. The technical goal of reducing estate taxes by setting up irrevocable life insurance trusts works but at an extremely high expense. Insurance companies don't give away money; in fact, they make so much money that they can afford to be intimately involved with the community and the details of their clients' lives. The question remains; "Is this in the client's best interest?" How can we do the right thing and be adequately compensated? Product sales is not the way nor have we seen anyone beat the market consistently.

The Trusted Advisor: Knowing Yourself

The central issue—serving trust clients—requires that we know ourselves first before we can help others. Socrates said that knowing one's self is a preparation for death. The Buddha said that it is a thousand times harder to know one's self, to investigate and discipline one's mind, than to do the most arduous physical task. This kind of effort is not for the fainthearted. Greatness is a lifelong effort—but luckily we do not have to be totally in touch with ourselves to do a good job.

Acknowledging personal inadequacies is an important first step in becoming an effective trust advisor. To use an analogy, how many of the people who are still married after fifteen years have been to marriage counseling? Very few couples whose relationships are strong and deep haven't had help from the outside. The trust advisor has to admit that he is not the greatest at everything. He cannot fully understand and articulate his own biases without outside help. In our business, we appreciate most employees who stand up and show the firm its inadequacies. This is akin to a spouse who, by being closest to us, is most able to assess our inadequacies, especially in terms of interpersonal communication. To work with trusts, we must first be willing freely to admit what we don't know. It is also important for us to understand how our own attitudes about money came into existence, because these kinds of issues come out in subtle ways when talking to clients.

For example, I am a workaholic. I am driven to work hard and to build an organization because no one else in my family ever accomplished this goal. As the youngest of four siblings, I always wanted to show my older brothers and sister that I was worthy of being noticed. It was and is my way of establishing a sense of self-worth. I realize that it was my habitual pattern of avoiding a sense of inadequacy—of not wanting to be lost in a crowd or swallowed up by forces more powerful than myself—that led me to the trust business in the first place.

There ought to be a confluence between business and personal characteristics. Knowing your characteristics and internal strengths and weaknesses is the first step. We will try to help you accomplish this by encouraging you to analyze your values, personal goals, lifestyle, interests, intellectual capabilities, and style under stress. Each of these areas involves self-examination as well as requesting assistance from others. Those who are close to us can tell us how they perceive our persona and where we are in our communication in these areas. We have also found that going through this process helps us to pick employees who work well with us. We want employees who share our attitudes so that we can build an organization that corresponds exactly to our chosen approaches to client relationships. The business of trust busting and trust building is primarily about client relationships; they are the alpha and omega of the trust business. Successful service depends upon a unified approach, which is why quantifying our personal and business quality is important.

Considering Personal Values

Before we can build relationships with others, we need to work at understanding and knowing ourselves. Take a moment and revisit your most important values—moral, political, social, familial, environmental, and spiritual. Our clients depend upon our judgment and trust us to help them. The more we understand our own values, the better chance we have of:

- Doing the right thing for the client and ourselves
- Making a better connection with our clients
- Knowing which clients are right for us

After we summarize the character development arenas, you will find a questionnaire that will help identify your personal values and those of your associates.

Considering Personal Goals

First, we evaluate our commitment as to how much time we want to spend on our business versus our home life. We try to identify what our targets for achievement might be and what we regard as personal success. Does the attainment of a certain goal give us satisfaction, or does it merely set up another more distant and higher mountain to climb? Can we enjoy the place where we are right now? If not, when will we find satisfaction? How important are fame and fortune to us? Do we expect to accumulate a certain amount of wealth? Do we hold this to be crucial to our own sense of self-worth? Is this what will give us a sense of definition and accomplishment in our life? If so, how do we reflect this to our clients in their own saving and spending patterns?

Considering Our Lifestyle

What kind of balance between money and time is important to us? What are our priorities regarding giving to the community through social service, spending time in the arts, or serving our chosen religious organization? Are our family lives set up so that our children see enough of us, and so that our spouses have adequate emotional support? All of these lifestyle issues emerge during our conversations with clients. This is especially true for trust clients, because they have the time and interest to deal with these matters for themselves. As one of their closest confidants, the trusted advisor must provide support and counsel even though it comes in the guise of financial issues. We either become a source of inspiration or of further problems for the beneficiary. Our clients need us to model what it is that they are trying to accomplish for themselves.

Considering Our Capabilities

What kind of clients can we serve? What are our capabilities for taking care of their multiple needs? For example, corporate executives require fast electronic transmission of information and constant modeling of comparative alternatives. This is the mode that they are used to in their daily lives. If our practice is set up in an old-fashioned, high-touch, low-tech way, then clearly we are not capable of handling this kind of clientele. Persons who have a sense of paranoia about the government and whose primary objective is to avoid taxation want investment professionals who are up-to-date on the latest shelter and asset protection devices. If our company's attitude is that people should pay their fair share of taxes because this is the price we all must pay to enjoy the fruits of our bountiful country, then we aren't right for that type of clientele. If clients feel that simplicity and lack of hassle are primary objectives, then we should not produce voluminous reports that require a high degree of sophistication to read. The capabilities of our various firms reflect our own attitudes about what we believe is important to our clients. These are really reflections of our own personal values, goals, and lifestyles. The authors believe that before entering the trust arena, you must define what kind of trust clients you want. Can you organize your services to deal with them in a complete way?

Considering Our Style under Stress

We all make mistakes, and the more we attempt to accomplish, the more mistakes we will make. Our office is organized so that no mistake should happen more than once. I am obsessed with taking responsibility for our clients so that even the smallest mistake draws my attention. We devote a great deal of time to establishing procedures that will prevent mistakes from occurring or reoccurring.

Everyone has a different style under stress. We surround ourselves with people whose styles under stress are different from our own. When a stressed client comes in, our office has multiple ways of assisting him or her, whether through empathy by a similarly oriented soul or through contrast by a staff member who exudes those character qualities that the client may lack. One of the greatest steps that we made in our firm was to acknowledge and recognize our various capabilities under stress and to develop an internal way of directing a client to the person with the appropriate style under stress.

Personal Values Questionnaire

The purpose of the exercise on the following pages is to enable you to begin to learn who you as an advisor are so that you can communicate your values, goals, lifestyle choices, capabilities, and style under stress. This is not a test, and there are no right or wrong answers. Focus on how each question applies to you and your life. You may find that some questions are easy to answer and that some are difficult. Focus on the easy ones first, and then return to the harder ones. It's best to write down exactly what first comes to mind. Don't hesitate—just put it down. Morning people will do best before everyone else is up; night-timers might be better off doing this exercise after everyone else is asleep. Solitude and quiet are essential. You may want to make a copy of these pages and write on the copies so that you can repeat the exercise later. The point of this is twofold. First, does providing trusted advisory services to beneficiaries fit in with the kind of personal and business life goals that you have articulated here? Second, will the demands of trust beneficiaries serve to increase your passion and love for work, or will it contribute to burnout? The process of taking control of inherited wealth and managing family trusts takes a peculiar combination of skills, talent, interests and lifestyle decisions. Do these all come together for you as the trusted advisor?

Worksheet 17.1 Personal Values Questionnaire

1. What do you want less of in your life?

2. Which part of your day do you value the least?

3. What are you doing that's not important to you?

List as many responses to the above questions as you can; put down at least five. Go back and look at each answer. How does each one of them make you feel? Identify the five most important things you want less of in your life and prioritize them.

Example:	**Event**	**Feeling**
	1. Noise in the office	Attacked
	2. Time in meetings	Impatient
	3. Commuting time	Aggressive
	4. Typing	Captive
	5. Worrying about mistakes	Obsessed
	6. Interruptions	Wasting time
	7. Time indoors	Restless
	8. Talking	Burned out

1. What do you want more of in your life?

(continues)

Take each of the top five items you want more of in your life and identify what is keeping you from having them. List the obstacles or barriers that you are encountering for each one.

Example: *I want time to play with my children from 5:30 to 8:30. What is keeping me from doing so is:*

1. I don't get home until 6:30.

2. I am too tired when I arrive.

3. We get interrupted by the telephone.

4. My kids haven't done their homework.

5. What do you value the most?

6. What's important to you?

List as many answers as you can. Go back and look at each answer. How does each one of them make you feel? Identify the five most important things you want more of in your life and prioritize them.

Example:	Event	Feeling
	1. Being in nature	Connected
	2. Time to paint	Relieved
	3. Play with children	Joyful
	4. Organized team sports (volleyball, soccer)	Young

Marketing Trust Services

By now you should have some sense of whether you want to be—and if you are capable of being—in the trust business. If your answer is yes, then you need to find out what it takes to be a player in this market. How do you position yourself so that in the minds of your community and potential client and referral sources you are the trust expert? You now need to create the perception that you are the person people should see when they need trust issue solutions. This chapter will cover how to target markets, publicize your business, distinguish yourself from the competition, and create a self-perpetuating marketing mechanism that will provide you with a steady stream of future business. Obviously, this chapter is written for advisors and not for clients. Still, the trust beneficiary may be interested in learning how seasoned investment professionals think about expanding their businesses, and this chapter may help evaluate the veracity and completeness of advisors' promotional materials as well as those sent by potential providers of trust services.

Your Market

What geographic area the advisor lives in determines the basic demographics of the potential kind of trust beneficiary clients. Southern California, with sunny skies, crowded freeways, and a fast-paced lifestyle helps define what kind of business tenor you will have if you decide to be a trusted advisor in this region. On the other hand, if you're in Bozeman, Montana, where a laid-back lifestyle is the norm and students, professors, farmers, ranchers, and refugees from the cities have come to reside, a whole different approach is required. There is a base of information you already have about local clientele and businesses. While studies have shown that most people like their advisors to be within 100 miles of their home, this is not the case with trust referral business, which can eventually become a large part of an advisor's work.

At least initially, a definition of a market segment is required. This is not just the traditional age, spending pattern, and educational levels kind of market segmentation, but a more in-depth, psychological one. In Santa Fe, New Mexico, for example (where the author's firm is located), there are few entrepreneurs. Entrepreneurs need access to a pool of highly moti-vated, educated workers who are risk-takers. Most people come to Santa Fe for the artistic, spiritual, and outdoors environment. As a result, there are not the kind of potential trust clients who are turned on by being the first to know about the latest hot stock or by following the market over the Internet. On the other hand, second- and third-generation beneficiaries who seek personal growth and distance from their families often come to Santa Fe. The age of the person in this case is not the most important fac-tor, nor is his or her level of education. Lifestyles vary from living in tepees to building multimillion-dollar homes. What *is* important for your work is to understand the personal aspirations and preferences and the family constellations of potential clients. In this way, we may segment peo-ple for trust services in a much different way than in other regions.

If we refer back to the personality types in Chapter 11, we find a mix-ture of people in all locations. However, we can focus in on certain lifestyle preferences that incorporate many of the choices listed. Let's take them in order and decide how to ascertain where people in your area reg-ister, and where you stand personally in relationship to their underlying motivational needs.

Santa Fe hosts numerous art shows and festivals oriented around tradi-tional crafts. There are many museums dedicated to the study of local, national, and international crafts, and the people that come to this area are extraordinarily sophisticated in their artistic tastes and habits. When I look at the array of organizations in Santa Fe dedicated to supporting artistic organizations, I find a clear indication of one very important market.

Another defining aspect of Santa Fe is the multitude of spiritual traditions represented here. We have visiting gurus, lamas, massage therapists, mediums, healing art institutes, polarities awareness practitioners, and Baptist conventions as well. Santa Fe also has a strong traditional Catholic community and representation in all of the other major religions, but the wealth is clearly skewed toward Eastern-type and new age religions, especially those oriented toward inner work and healing.

Looking more closely at these residents, we find that most are not living in traditional family constellations. We see a great number of single people, many with children from various partners. They are very well educated and want to help themselves and their children. As a result, there are many licensed psychologists and counselors in the area. In fact, there are several schools of counseling, acupuncture, massage, Chinese medicine, and so forth—far more per capita than most comparable areas. This is another strong clue for potential marketing efforts, but with one caveat: the seasoned investment professional must have a strong genuine interest in these areas herself.

Nothing is more obvious than a feigned interest in art, religion, sports, or anything else. Your interest has to be genuine, and there is either a match or there isn't. I happen to be a painter by predilection, and I still consider myself to be somewhat of an itinerant artist, even though the amount of time that I now spend on this pursuit is quite small.

Having a genuine interest in the community raises the point of tenure, which is to say that it is almost impossible to start a business in a new place without connections. Connections come from being grounded in one place for an extended period of time.

The next part of defining your market and the appropriate way of becoming involved in and establishing a reputation in a community in which you have tenure has to do with understanding the aspirations of potential trust clients. In Santa Fe, many people have counseling careers. The work habits of counselors and their clients are extremely variable, so one of the worst things that we could do would be to insist upon regular meetings at set times. We have a completely open-door policy, and clients can generally call and get an appointment for the same day. Likewise, we put no onus of burden or guilt on people who, for one reason or another, have a hard time showing up for appointments. We want them to know that if something comes up that makes the appointment inconvenient, they are welcome to pass and reschedule for another time. We have a philosophy of being accessible to our clients, and therefore we carry pagers. We pass our pagers from person to person as doctor groups do, because in a sense we are financial doctors. Though clients don't use this service much, they can find themselves thinking about their reports at off times and are welcome to check in, either via our voice mail or personally, if they have something that needs immediate attention. This is one solution to adjusting a trust business to its market.

Each advisor's market will be different, but focusing on the deeper values and psychological aspirations of people with inherited wealth in your community takes a particular kind of skill and an adaptable thought process.

Know Your Competition

The trust business is quite different from other financial services. It can involve such an array of disciplines and such an intimate familiarity with the client that traditional marketing won't work. The trust relationship is built on a one-to-one basis. You must know the other people in the field who are representing themselves as trust experts and know what their strengths and weaknesses are, just as you must acknowledge your own.

In our region, there are two new purveyors of independent trust services, as well as two local banks representing themselves as financial planners and investment managers. Almost every month, a new investment management firm is opened in Santa Fe by a broker who has seen how lucrative money management appears to be.

Some of our competitors have strengths that we do not possess. One advisor is handsome (while I am bald) and another's firm is staffed with esteemed professionals from all over the country who wear fancy suits. (In our office, my staff is lucky if I press my pants.) Down the street, two national brokerage firms have keyed in on our best-established markets—people with an interest in socially responsible investing. These companies have very articulate salespeople comparing mutual fund performances, brandishing sophisticated financial plans, and giving seminars on socially responsible investing. It's a crowded field in a small town. It's easy to feel under siege when you have only your own capital and people to rely upon versus name brand marketing and dedicated salesforces.

Nonetheless, we know that our hands-on expertise exceeds that of anyone else in our geographic area. This is true for the professionals recently arrived from out of state as well, because we know that they do not understand the needs of the local population. How then, do we parlay this into an advantage when we are outnumbered and outcapitalized, and when our voice is small compared with those all around us?

Getting the Word Out

We have now identified our competition. We know our advantages and want to communicate them as widely as possible with as little cost as possible. In our office, one person is assigned to surveying the community and understanding the images that are presented to people through advertisements, seminars, and professional networking. Contacting attorneys and accountants is nothing new in the field of financial advice. Everyone knows that referral networks are the best way of getting new business, but a referring professional also has needs. Clearly, the expertise we have gives us an established presence in the community. We are always gathering information about our competition, and we try to make this information known so that the referral sources can make a clean and clear choice, based on real facts. The benefit to the inheritor is in knowing the alternatives—not in our convincing them through media relations that we are the firm for them. The real facts consist of your firm's track record (i.e., how long you have been in the business and what your performance has been). This means *your* performance, and not the performance of a former employer or a network of mutual funds put together by a brokerage company. We point out how firms tend to suppress the records of their nonperforming funds, and how individuals may or may not have hands-on experience in actually getting the job done for the client.

Another way of getting the word out is contacting the competitors directly, establishing an understanding of what their strengths and weaknesses are, and presenting our own in an honest fashion. We contact all the potential providers of trustee services to see what their experience has been with these other firms. We regularly evaluate how we treat our employees to make sure that our motivations bring our employees in congruence with the clients' goals. This is not the case in many situations.

How to Find Trusts

There is good news and bad news: there is plenty of business out there, but it's hard to get people to move. We talked previously about how many trusts exist in the United States. You can find information in your current client base about who might have trusts by looking for K-1s included in their tax returns. We know that accountants and tax preparers can say which of their clients have large schedule As with interest and dividends and also which have K-1s from trusts. The interesting part about finding trusts is yet to come.

People often ask me how they can get a list of those having trusts at local banks. I respond by asking them, "What good would that do you?" "Cold-calling on trust clients is like trying to sell sand to the Arabs." Trust beneficiaries are pummeled by financial advertisements in TV, print, money magazines, phone solicitations, and mailings, all to no avail.

It is no secret that the people who are best suited to making introductions between beneficiaries and potential advisors are those who know that the trusts exist and who already have the confidence of those clients. That clearly points to attorneys and accountants as well as to psychological counselors.

The network that you as an advisor have already built up in your community may not be aware that you are considering yourself a trust advisor. Getting the word out to your referral sources that you have taken this tack requires some special effort and finesse. It is not merely mentioning, "Oh, by the way, I'm now interested in managing trusts," or "I have a relationship with a trust company so if you have any unhappy beneficiaries, please send them my way." You must firmly establish your reputation as a trust expert.

The trust business is the best of all financial businesses; it takes the longest time to nurture, and we consider that it requires the softest touch. Consider, for example, giving before you receive. How can you help lawyers and accountants do their work more efficiently and establish better relationships with their trust clients while you stay in the background? We have found that offering free assistance is an excellent approach. We always make a point of offering an anonymous review of any of their client situations without any pay or expectation of getting a new client. Accountants and lawyers are often asked questions that they are unable to answer without a great deal of research. We try to find these areas, and provide the answers to them, so that they can become familiar with our expertise in this area and our way of doing business. This builds credibility without pressure, which is the key to establishing a reputation as a trust expert.

We offer the same kind of assistance to potential inheritors. We are happy to help these inheritors analyze their family trust situations, with no commitment or compensation. Many times, we get involved, but do not get paid because trusts are locked up due to the family dynamic, which is not appropriate to changing the management of assets or trusteeship. Nonetheless, this establishes our reputation in one beneficiary's eyes, and we then have a good source of referral or can use that person as a reference when we are competing for trust business against someone else in our field.

Traditional seminars advertised in the media often bring in people who are interested in getting information but who have no serious intention of discussing their personal situations. In our environment, we prefer small "tea" situations, where there is a group sharing of questions in an informal format. The range of subjects that may come up is unpredictable, and we must be prepared to offer assistance on many topics as well as to admit our ignorance if we are unable to answer certain questions. We encourage people to bring friends to our teas, and we try to provide an informal, educational environment with as much interaction as possible. People do not learn much by just listening. They need to ask questions and be challenged and to challenge us as well.

This concept is carried much further in the weekend workshop concept, which has a decidedly different flavor than an afternoon tea. Weekend workshops are informative, challenging, and personal growth experiences for persons with inherited wealth. People derive much benefit from a weekend retreat in that it takes them out of their normal context and they are prepared to be challenged or to reflect in a new way while away from the time pressures of home, work, and family.

Weekend retreats, afternoon teas, and professional service support are ways of informing people that you are an expert in the field and that you are willing to spend the time and delve into a variety of issues. Once someone has become aware of your services and expertise, he or she may come in for an appointment to get to know you and to see if there is a match. The first appointment is crucial in establishing your credibility and your personality.

The issues that come up during the first meeting are crucial to establishing a long-term relationship. The first issue involves establishing your personal tone, and how you interact with the client. The person is looking to see if he can relate to you, not whether you are going to solve a specific problem. This causes difficulty, because most discussions revolve around particular problems. The authors feel it is important not to try solving problems at this initial encounter. In a way, this first meeting is like a first date. Both of you are feeling out on a subliminal level, through body language and other means, whether or not there is a genuine match. It is not primarily about numbers, charts, presentations, references, or anything other than the gut feelings and eye-to-eye contact that take place. Of course, numbers do matter, but they are not the determining factor.

We focus in our first meeting on fleshing out family stories. We try to understand the interactions between the potential client and his spouse, his feelings about children, and what aspirations, lifestyle decisions, goals, hopes, and dreams he has. This is a visioning session where the breadth of the advisor's vision must be exposed and his or her ability to listen and draw out a vision on the part of the inheritor is necessary.

We were recently introduced to a couple who came in to see us without any advance notice. A local trust officer thought that they might do well with outside investment counsel and so we had an opportunity to visit briefly with them. The woman started talking about the experience the family had with money and the kind of approach she liked, and I listened quite carefully, addressing questions and explaining our philosophy of investing. They seemed to be quite pleased, while the trust officer sat back, nodding and smiling. But after the couple left, we were informed that we had made an enormous mistake, because the man was in fact the decision maker and was absolutely terrified of any discussion of money. We had missed the boat by talking to the wrong person. In fact, we did try to solicit comments from the husband and involve him in the discussion, though he was unwilling to participate.

I was somewhat chagrined at my insensitivity in this situation, as well as annoyed at the trust officer, who should have informed me about the personal dynamics of this family. This happens infrequently, but it is an example of an account relationship opportunity that was over before it even started because of mistakes at the first meeting.

Advertising

"Does advertising work?" is a question often heard in our business. Beside establishing some general presence and name recognition, advertising doesn't seem to help a client decide between various alternatives. The fact is that the larger financial corporations will always have a more catchy phrase than a local seasoned independent advisor will. We must admit, however, that the few times we advertised in nonprofit journals whose causes we believed in, we did receive phone calls from people who were interested in our services and who turned out to be delightful clients. We thus believe that target advertising in the social, religious, or artistic organizational field is the most effective choice in our particular market area. The tone of any advertisement must match the image you are trying to portray. If you advertise performance, then you will get "hot money" that moves every few years to last year's best performer. If you advertise healing, you will get personalities only.

This brings up the question of publishing a newsletter. Almost every financial professional has a newsletter. It is considered essential to keep your name and the fact that you are an expert in some area in front of your clients at least once every three months. Everyone is doing this, including the brokerage firms and local banks. We have reviewed offers to write our newsletter for us and have concluded that no matter how expert the articles are, if they are written by someone else they betray this reason behind our commentary. By this I mean that clients want to know that you are the expert and that you have a particular approach that is well informed and well considered. Cutting and pasting articles written by someone else may save time and effort, but it does not establish and maintain true credibility.

Our marketing literature is limited. We have one brochure that describes our philosophy and approach, plus separate track record, and performance reporting examples. The purpose of the material is to help beneficiaries to establish a knowledge base about us before they come in for the first appointment.

One prospective client turned us down because our brochure included the words "socially responsible." He took this to mean "Socialist," and so we were out of the ball game; that was just fine with us. Most of the time, we find that sharing our internally written newsletter is the best way to keep our clients abreast of our thinking on the markets, on germane tax changes, and on other important estate planning ideas that we want them to be aware of.

Once we have established our persona, clients must judge for themselves whether it is truthful and appropriate. We use our own ways of communicating to get the word out that we are experts in the trust business and are trustworthy advisors. We have a system in place to deliver the service, and we love our work. That love comes across to the clients who are looking for what we have to offer.

Conclusion

Personal contact is the key to finding and keeping trust clients. The commitment we make to sitting face to face with each one of our clients and each of our prospective clients for however long they wish is the hallmark of our particular business. The advisor who knows the client is the client's best resource. In our minds, the definition of *trustworthy* is that you make a commitment, you have the ability to deliver on the commitment, and your goal is to be there when you are needed. The best kind of marketing is doing a great job for your current clients. Clients will send more business to you when you do a great job, when you let it be known that you are capable of doing more, and that you would like to do more.

With the exceptions already described, our firm has never advertised in its 17 years of history. We have never called upon professional clients or contacts, or asked them for their friends' names. Quite frankly, we haven't had to do this because we are so focused on doing a great job that our clients send other people despite the absence of these basic elements of marketing. We invite you to do the same.

Delivering the Goods

I f you are a financial advisor who has made the decision to deliver trust advisory services, a major shift in your firm may be necessary. This chapter is about the organizational attitudes and attributes that will need to be in place so that you and your associates can withstand the pressures that go with being a top-notch organization. Operating at the highest level of service and expertise when dealing with premiere clients such as trust beneficiaries is what will make your firm stand head and shoulders above the media-dominant national financial and investment firms.

Both the principals and employees of trust advisory firms must understand underlying principles of delivering comprehensive services with the kind of compassion and insight described in previous chapters. We will focus here on 14 key areas having to do with relationships within the organization:

- Time to do the job right
- Staff empathy
- Educational opportunities
- Company values
- Independence of thought

- Measurement of results
- Continuity within the firm
- Commitment to service
- Career opportunities
- Superb employee compensation
- Team-building efforts
- Maturity
- Systems and procedures
- Financial stability

Time to Do the Job Right

Do you and your staff have substantial extra time to spend on a few of your best clients, with no extra compensation for your work? Establishing a base in the trust market will take from 3 to 12 months, and during this process the outcome will remain unclear. Such an investment in time is necessary in part for interviewing clients to see if they are prospective trust candidates. Taking control of inherited wealth also will require you and your staff to develop relationships with various client family members, remain in communication with former trustees, and manage various professionals in their work so that things keep moving along. This commitment can be a money-losing operation for a seasoned investment professional. It will almost certainly look like a money-losing venture at the start, because in the eyes of beneficiaries and their professional advisors, you are not entitled to get paid for the process of establishing your organization's trust capabilities. Because of the risk involved, such an undertaking is easier for people to accept who are used to working on a contingency basis.

The time commitment required for dealing with various family members is the largest and most unpredictable component of this process. If there is more than one beneficiary, separate relationships need to be established so that each individual inheritor can feel that you understand his or her specific point of view. You must represent current and future beneficiaries, a crucial part of trust situations. Bank trust officers and individual trustees rarely take the time to contact family members, nor are they instructed to do so. As the trust advisor of the future, you must set a higher standard. The question remains, do you and your staff have ample time to do these things without becoming overstressed?

Becoming a trust advisor and building a successful organization is a wonderful challenge. You must have the time, however, to be adequately prepared and to be able to respond to clients with speed and accuracy. Effective management of time becomes a critical factor in making the transition from technical specialist to trusted advisor generalist. You must organize your time and personally take the steps to expand your business's vision to say, "This is who we want to be in the future for our clients."

Staff Empathy

In our firm, we establish criteria whereby each staff person demonstrates that he is keeping the client's comfort and convenience first in his mind. By establishing client service as the foremost criterion, people at every level of our organization become committed to maintaining relationships with clients based on responsibility, thoroughness, integrity, confidentiality, and empathy.

This means assuming more risk, both personally and professionally. Working with trusts means taking on many times the risk of an ordinary investment advisor, broker, or planner. Personal risk is increased in the sense that our firm's entire team is involved, with every staff member being vitally concerned about what is best for our clients and their families for generations to come. Actualizing this takes an incredible amount of time.

As strategic financial counselors, we are responsible for organizing our time and staffing our businesses so that the effort of entering the trust field does not overcome our capacity to do good work. For those of us who have a high need for activity, it is crucial that we do not overburden our associates. It's better to be overstaffed than understaffed when courting trust beneficiary clientele.

We go through exercises in which we place ourselves in the client's position. We ask staff members to look at a problem and ask, "If I were the client, what would I want out of this situation? Think ahead to what will happen if an issue isn't dealt with in its entirety." This is a new experience for most employees. It is hard to relate to what our clients are really asking us to do—which is to be totally responsible. Many employees naturally shrink from the responsibility of bringing their emotions into a business context. But no organization can deliver quality trust services unless it has the ability to relate effectively to its clients.

The staff must have empathy for some inheritors' occasional feelings of powerlessness and insecurity. The fact is that people who have more money than they need to live on can have difficulty in accepting that they are okay and that everything will be all right. We must intuitively grasp this and acknowledge our own anxieties. This establishes a common emotional ground. Of course, as professionals, we have solutions or ways of dealing with these anxieties, which we should be able to share with the inheritors.

We constantly reassure our clients that we are capable of carrying out the defined mission of protecting their family assets. We have the ability and expertise to discern what works in the long run. The trust client must know that we are committed to his or her happiness, and that our team is prepared to help regain the power from a trustee who is unresponsive, unapproachable, and controlling. The existing trustee seems to hold a place of irrevocable authority and to be backed up by the courts and tax laws. The trusts are armed with armies of lawyers, accountants, and investment strategies that seem impenetrable to the layperson. All of this makes taking control of family trusts a formidable and emotional job. One of the most powerful tools in the seasoned investment professional's camp is staff empathy.

Educational Opportunities

There are various contexts for which we must prepare our team in order to deliver excellent trust services. We occasionally exchange jobs with each other, so that all of us can see the difficulty in following anything less than crystal-clear instructions. We want all those on the staff to have a real understanding of what other people are going through when they try to get useful information out of an incomplete paper trail.

Such confusion is a daily experience for many of our trust clients. They do not possess the expertise to read reports sent to them by banks, brokers, or even by our firm! They don't always know how much they are spending, and financial issues make them uncomfortable. Because we educate our staff about how clients should be treated, even the receptionist can explain to a caller how to read his or her statement and can provide this assistance in a helpful way.

Company Values

Our firm's values are clearly outlined in our mission statement. Our strategic plan, which all staff members are aware of and into which they have had input, sets the tone for our values to be right up front and part of every process we do internally and externally. Our mission statement is shown below.

Mission Statement

Rikoon Investment Advisors, Inc.

Our mission is to help our clients attain financial peace of mind by:

- Building and preserving our clients' wealth through wise investments.
- Making life easier for our clients through handling the details of their financial lives.
- Helping our clients avoid personal and monetary problems through multi-faceted analysis and planning.
- Encouraging a sense of security in our clients by providing a friendly and practical education about financial matters.

To this end, we provide our employees with an enjoyable and challenging environment that affords long-term personal security, and we maintain our relationships with other professionals based on mutual respect, honesty, and goodwill. We are involved in these efforts in order to create a sustainable lifestyle, free from suffering, for all beings and our planet.

Independence of Thought

There are many situations in which we, as trust advisors, could well experience a conflict of interest with our clients. The most common opportunity for conflict is when our advice could be swayed by the choice of bringing assets under our management or having the client feel secure. Our ability to be in touch with and to communicate our own biases is crucial to maintaining our credibility. It is impossible to eliminate all possible conflicts, but we can definitely set strict limits regarding how much or little we or our staff may personally benefit from taking advantage of any aspect of the client/advisor relationship.

We were involved in a situation in which two siblings distrusted each other so much that we became a mediator in order to bring them together to oppose a Midwestern bank. On several occasions, we accompanied family members to see a counselor. Our motives were questioned by one part of the family, who asked if we were doing this work out of concern for the family or because of our desire to bring in a new account. It was a very good question, and we are the first to admit that we are not blessed with absolute purity of motives.

When we took ownership of our position, we felt exposed. But when we challenged the family's long-term trustee, the competing factions were all able to see that we were actually a participant with them in the struggle for retaking power over the trust. This bonding process varies each time, being as different as each trust beneficiary, each trust document, and each trustee. That's what makes this such an exciting and challenging field!

A final aspect of being a trustworthy advisor is willingness to take on uncomfortable subjects. We are often called upon to articulate to client family members the parents' deepest fears about their children, or one spouse's fear regarding the other spouse. This responsibility takes precedence over any discussions about budgets, financial projections, or discussions about relative investment performance.

One of our clients was continuously taking distributions from his family and purchasing real estate in Arizona. Although he had no idea what rate of return he was receiving on his properties, he was exceedingly pleased that his tax bill was so low. The fact is that he was in a terrible cash flow situation and had to come repeatedly to his 80-year-old mother for additional cash. He had never gotten a regular job and now, in his early 50s, was dependent on her for putting his son through college. Through some skillful third-party counseling, we got this individual to see that he was taking unjustified risks by being so undiversified. He wasn't paying taxes because he wasn't making any money. Overinvestment in real estate is the one area we constantly have to warn clients about.

As investment advisors, we have a vested interest in seeing that assets remain in marketable securities. Some clients are uncomfortable with the stock market. Our obligation is to point out why they shouldn't own either too much real estate or too many securities.

Measurement of Results

We believe that in trust services, whatever is measured will improve. This is practiced in our organization by evaluating our staff's performance regularly, as well as comparing it to the performance of our peers. There are service standards and criteria to keep score on responsiveness to client demands. We would never want a staff person to tell a client who asked something, "Well, that's not part of my job," or "Please take care of that unrelated item yourself." Even if these words aren't said, it's very easy to slide into this kind of attitude, which is inimical to exemplary trust advisory services. (See Figure 19.1.)

Knowing whether our staff members are happy is important to us, both for their sake and for our clients. We need to know if employees feel that they have the training and the procedures in place to do their jobs. With a constantly changing workforce, it is essential to have things written down in what we call "mind maps." The mind maps show the thought process of the person who is doing the job. While these conceptual descriptions don't go into detail about how to fill in specific paperwork, they do list the necessary steps to take to ensure that client service is being performed superlatively.

Continuity within the Firm

As trusted advisors, we purport to deliver multigenerational solutions to our clients. For that reason, it is essential for us to have a solid succession plan in place. Our firm has several plans ready should I meet an untimely demise. These include employee buyout options, standing offers to join up with a larger firm, and buy-sell agreements among several of our peers. All of these ought to ensure continuity of service. It doesn't matter what method you choose to provide for backup of client management services. It is only essential that your clients know that you have thought this issue through and have taken steps to provide adequately and care for them.

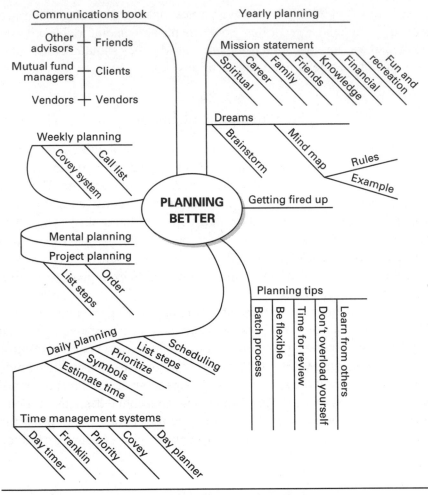

FIGURE 19.1 How to Plan Better

No one in our business thinks that succession planning is unimportant. On a regular basis, we hear people at every level of size in our industry recognize the need to establish continuity, though few have taken specific steps to address this issue. Our goal has been to engage the personal commitment of all of our employees to continue the kind of dedication under new management that our clients rely on now. Cross-training is difficult amidst the daily hubbub of business life; nevertheless we set aside one hour twice a week to cross-train in unrelated areas, and part of our review process and company retreat program revolves around our plans for middle management employees to rise in the firm.

Commitment to Service

Our firm's primary goal is to maintain the highest level of commitment to service that is humanly possible. Our associates, junior staff, clerical personnel, and even our part-time and temporary help know immediately what we do and how we do it, because they see our dogged efforts to give clients a wonderful, personalized service experience. We explain that when a client calls, our job is stop everything, listen to the client completely, and give him or her a realistic timetable for hearing back from us. Our job then is to follow up on anything that is of concern to the client. We have found that setting up our organization to reflect this commitment to service is extremely difficult. One prerequisite is that employee morale be high, so incentive plans need to be in place. We believe in taking care of all client matters at hand in a timely, unhurried, and noncrisis manner.

There is no set appearance for a trust advisory office, but the physical surroundings are somewhat a reflection of the firm's commitment to service. Clients will feel comfortable if there is a match between your firm and their perception of what trust and integrity look like. Different clients like various degrees of formality. Landscape paintings, modern playful sculpture, and plants set the visual tone in our office because they are a reflection of our community.

Career Opportunities

We are committed to expanding our staff members' opportunities for advancement. We need employees who are well-rounded and self-confident, because only then can they imbue the atmosphere with that sense of balance so important to being a trusted advisor. Every employee is unique; there is no limit to the amount of training or compensation that any employee can garner if it is deserved. Learning the operational ropes, becoming a valued client follow-up person, helping implement investment strategy, managing client relationships, initiating new clients—these are successive steps up the same ladder. One cannot leap to the top rung without first using the lower steps. Our employees know that as our organization matures and our identity becomes clearer in the trust service delivery area, ever higher levels of creative initiative on their part will be needed—and rewarded. We use a best-available athlete strategy, as when a pro football team finds an All-American sprinter and turns him into a championship receiver. It's not so much about past accomplishments as it is about future capability.

The educational and advancement policy of our organization is that every individual should have the opportunity to become a principal of the firm. It is difficult today for people to stay with a firm not just for 2 years, but for 20. If employees make a commitment, their contributions need to be recognized. Twenty years is a long time, but 40 years is actually more in keeping with the multigenerational perspective on service and relationships that we like to cultivate. If we take someone in during his twenties, and give him ample opportunity, why shouldn't that person stay until retirement if the pay is good, challenges are always present, and friendships formed with clients meaningful? This is our career goal for our organization.

A colleague of ours takes his staff on a retreat to a remote resort every six months. Once there, they work with a psychologist and therapist so that each staff member's feelings of insecurity can surface. Having released their feelings, these motives become less subversive, and when others get to see their coworkers' internal issues, acceptance and camaraderie naturally follow. This is what we are asking our clients to do: share with us their insecurities and let us help them as co-inhabitors of this wonderfully strange and difficult existence as human beings. We want to learn to enter their worlds so that they can come to trust and rely upon us. Hearing each employee speak his or her feelings equates with the ability to serve clients on a deep level.

We believe in hiring above the level of talent that we currently need. Unlike many large organizations that hire untrained people and teach them the ways of corporate life, we need people who are mature and responsible from the outset. Our clients entrust us with a great deal of money and sometimes psychic burdens regarding the private areas of their lives. They need to know that the people with whom they are dealing have a real awareness of the personal and emotional issues involved.

Superb Employee Compensation

We believe that paying above-market salaries, along with providing a generous profit-sharing plan, cash bonuses, and other nonmonetary types of acknowledgment are all extremely effective ways of compensating and enhancing employee performance. Employee stock options are excellent for connecting employees to the company's long-term performance. We have a system in our office whereby at the end of each year a portion of our firm's gross revenue growth is distributed, based solely on people's performance rising above the normal level of expected excellence.

Attitude is the key to everything. A positive attitude is an extension of an individual's passion or interest for the work and his feeling that compensation is more than adequate. If a staff member doesn't enjoy his work, he will eventually develop a bad attitude. If someone does not have a positive, upbeat attitude toward other employees or toward the clients, he isn't right for our organization. The group's mind and emotional states are extremely sensitive. One bad apple can spoil the barrel. We have had this experience in our organization, where the atmosphere was negative because of one person's bad attitude. It wasn't that this person didn't believe in our organization; he did not believe in himself.

We pay our staff members 10% over the prevailing salary rates as a way of impressing upon them the value we place upon doing an excellent job. We also have a client satisfaction gauge which, if met, results in an additional individual bonus, no matter what the rate of growth of the firm is or what our net income looks like. We have a special award for the top client service provider. The group profit-sharing plan, which comes into play after two years of employment, is the most generous retirement plan available. We believe that if we are trying to secure our clients' financial future, our employees need to see that their retirement needs are being met as well. Employees need to have a chance to garner wealth along with the principals if an outstanding job is done.

For those staff members who are committing the time and energy needed to become integral to our trusted advisor culture, we offer opportunities to obtain equity in our company. While the principals may be the ones who started the company, it is essential to bring in and retain quality people. This can be done by structuring a stock option plan based on the performance of the company and the amount of responsibility and dedication shown on the part of any individual associates. We provide a guaranteed buyback provision for our stock, so that it is really something of current value, not just a paper promise, sometime out in the future.

Team-Building Efforts

Concurrent with developing appropriate attitudes in individual staff members is team building. We insist that each person have not just one, but *two* backups for each portion of his or her job. Furthermore, we ask that all employees learn to delegate work when they have too much to do efficiently. It is important to know how to ask for help. We try to model this behavior from the top down. It is difficult because none of us is a perfect communicators.

We devote a great deal of time and money to maintaining clear internal communications. The prime focus for much of our staff's efforts relates to keeping track of our clients' lives and the related projects we take on to help them feel secure. We want everyone to be able to look at a client family and see what projects are going on, which staff members are involved, and what the status of any particular project is. Then, when a client calls, she can be assured that her issue has top priority and that everyone is capable and informed enough to be able to work on the account. Building such a team takes time.

We believe that company nonbusiness events are essential to create team spirit and camaraderie. Sharing regular lunch hours helps us to bond as a group and form personal relationships so that in particularly stressful times (which are many), people in our organization can feel safe to ask for help. The optimum situation is that when people understand that they are over their heads, they pause before acting, and then look elsewhere in the organization to get help.

Maturity

The maturity of a trusted advisory firm is measured by the quality of the people clients interact with. Our experience is that building an organization that can deliver trust services means not only having the organization, but also communicating our capability effectively. Making our organization's abilities available to other professionals is, as we have said before, the best way of showing our capacity to do the job. Our in-house expertise in investments and financial planning is secondary to our most valuable expertise, the ability to understand the minds and hearts of our clients. We want all of our staff to know what it is that clients want from their financial life. This takes a special kind of individual who does not get minted from business school programs. Nor is he or she created by corporate training programs.

Systems and Procedures

We believe that investing in the most up-to-date software is a necessity in the financial advisory field. For our firms, this takes the form of being able to integrate client contact management, portfolio data, accounting, asset tracking, and financial planning programs. The systems that are necessary to earn the trusted advisor the deserved reputation of being the best necessitates delivering what the clients want quickly and accurately.

Our vision of our company and its relationship to our clients revolves around systems and procedures. Every staff member has an interesting and challenging job. There is a system in place that verifies the accuracy and appropriateness of every action. This system can be checked both by the person doing the job and anyone else in the office. We operate on individualized schedules that are suited to our personal temperaments and lives. We have a simple philosophy—whatever equipment helps, we get.

Our trusted advisory company is run by dedicated, detail-oriented people who take pleasure in making sure that every "t" is crossed and every "i" is dotted. Some people with these qualities don't interact well with clients, and we are constantly looking for people whose skills represent a blend of both worlds: the left-brained compulsion to organize and accomplish, and the right-brained need to relate and empathize. Every detailed promise to a client must be kept and a record of its results preserved. Every problem that arises must be resolved and documented so that at the next client meeting we know exactly what events have transpired, no matter how seemingly insignificant they may be. Therefore we can also track the effort involved in servicing the client's account. Often, we overcommunicate with our clients so that they are aware of all the work being done behind the scenes. This is not easy unless you have a totally organized and accessible record of what has been done; of how it has been done; and of the time, effort, and commitment required to accomplish it. All of this is possible using relational databases.

The beneficiary wants to be as completely released from any anxiety about money as possible. For this to happen, he must be made aware that his financial affairs are being totally taken care of. We know how to take care of our clients, because we know how we want our own affairs handled. We have to communicate to our clients in brief, intense ways. We want them to see that there is an entire team of people standing behind every effort. When we hear from a client's accountant or attorney, we act as if the client himself is calling us. The accountant or attorney receives top-priority attention, and we try to do as much of her work for her as possible. Whether she takes credit for our portion of the work is not a concern. The result is that this person eventually says to the client, "I am really impressed with this advisor." That provides further confirmation to the client that his financial life is in good hands.

By investing in the top technology, hardware, and software, we enable all areas of our organization to enhance the personal quality of client interaction. This is the aspect of our work that is most fulfilling to all of us. We and our staff love our work because we have the satisfaction of knowing that we are helping people in a real sense. All of our technical skills are oriented toward this end. Our team-building efforts are directed toward sharing a vision of what we want to do for the client. The more often we articulate our vision, the better it is registered in our consciousness. We want to empower every staff member to change our systems and procedures if doing so will better provide what our clients need and eliminate what they don't need. This is a way of keeping the problems that might cause our clients concern out of their field of experience and in our back office, where they should be appropriately resolved.

The key to developing an efficient office environment is a commitment on everyone's part to developing procedures that are, when organized into a megaprocedure, referred to as systems. We use these procedures to run our company. Our staff runs these procedures, which are constantly improving over time. The best way to develop a solution-oriented client procedure is to focus on the most common frustrations. Take the frustration, analyze the situation, and determine as a team why it is happening. There is always a better way to do the task that will solve the issue and eliminate the frustration. Michael Gerber's *The E-Myth Manager* and *The E-Myth Revisited* are helpful books on these subjects.

Financial Stability

When a firm embarks on an expansion of services to include the trust field, the necessary commitment of time and development of technical expertise must be supported by ample capitalization. There are several ways to capitalize a company, all of which greatly affect the ability of a seasoned investment professional to get in to the trust business. We have seen companies start with inadequate capital and within six months be forced to issue additional shares and bring in new investors in order to keep their doors open. This happens when mass marketing is the primary focus of a new trust advisory organization.

In the last chapter we described the most effective trust marketing strategies. These start with outstanding service to a group of professionals and current clients. To go into the trust business, you must already be in the financial service business. In fact, we advise people with less than 10 years of experience to wait until they have a mature clientele base and solid reputation. There are many new corporate trust organizations that have been started by people with no trust experience and little actual trust business on their books, and whose contact with trust beneficiaries is based on a marketing concept. People like to own trust companies because they think it is a natural extension of their current services. This is correct in concept but off in reality. The actual delivery of trust services is a people-and-paper/systems-intensive business. The capital required to purchase or develop systems for trust work is 10 times that needed by a new broker, investment advisor, or insurance firm. The proliferating number of independent trust companies, formed by dissatisfied bank trust officers, must all have gathered considerable outside capital first. Venture capitalists, wealthy clients, and local banks with no trust department of their own are all possible sources of funding for start-up trust companies.

Capitalization is not an issue for trust companies started by wealthy families. Most financial advisors expanding into trusts start with some of their own money and additional capital from friends and/or relatives. Such firms are likely to grow in capital needs because of the increasing scope of services offered and the need to hire specialized professionals to run a trust division. Can the expanded services be provided by current personnel? The answer depends upon the size of the trust market, and what part of the market is your niche.

There are many excellent trust administrators, but very few good businesspeople who know the industry. Marketing trust services is a specialty that commands large salaries in major urban areas.

There are many excellent advisors who do an excellent job on financial planning, estate planning, and in making financial decisions. The strongest candidates for trust advisors are those who have the capital on hand to finance internally additional services for an existing customer base. A private, ultrawealthy family could afford the time and expense involved in buying the necessary expertise to be in the trust service business, but it takes much more to garner the reputation and referrals required for success. For trust advisors in the early stages of their careers, there may be a need for a line of credit and additional long-term financing to buy or lease top-of-the-line equipment.

The cash flow requirement for starting a trust advisory firm is at least one year of full operating expenses. The kind of fiscal strength necessary to become a trust advisor is much less onerous than the capital that is required to perform actual corporate trustee services. Corporate trusts need from $300,000 to $1 million if they are state charted. National charters require over $3 million of start-up capital. Trust advisors need up to $200,000 to start this kind of venture.

> To start an actual independent trust company, capital requirements range from the low end of $150,000 for a state charter up to $3 million for a national license. Do advisors need to have corporate trustee powers themselves? For successful financial advisory firms, it is natural to want to either start one's own trust company or to establish an association with a corporate trustee who specifically is set up to handle the trusted advisor's business referrals. We will talk about the delicate balance of power in this relationship between the advisor and the trustee in the next chapter.

Conclusion

Trustworthy advisory firms revolve around the following characteristics in client relations.

- *Time.* You must have the time available to give every client whatever it takes to complete the task at hand. In addition, you and your staff have to take the initiative to look at other possible ramifications and to anticipate other needs the client may have but is not articulating.

- *Empathy.* Each staff member must relate to the client with the same empathy he would give to a member of his own family. Concern, inquiry into emotional states, and sharing your own experiences are all necessary for the bond of trust to be established and to flourish.

- *Independence of thought.* This means having an atmosphere in which everybody in your company knows that you want them to feel that they have the permission and guts to say difficult things. The most valuable improvements happen when the fear of being wrong or embarrassed is overcome. Everyone who is intelligent ought to have his own ideas about better ways to deliver client service.

- *Depth of talent.* Continuity of personnel, formalized in a succession plan, is a key element when dealing with trust beneficiaries. If they feel that no one knows them personally, there is no way they will stay if someone else comes along and offers a more permanent connection.

- *Systems development.* This is an ongoing process in the best trust advisory firms. It doesn't mean, however, that you have to be in the software business. Consistency and follow-through are the two key elements that are impossible to deliver with systems. A two-person firm doesn't need systems; but three may; and four people do, absolutely!

- *Technical expertise.* This is the commitment to excellence in multiple areas that the client needs. Multiple skills and the cross-use of planning, counseling, investments, tax and legal knowledge will come into play when delivering trust services.

- *Measurement of results.* Ongoing evaluation of performance is the way the firm maintains its quality. The trusted advisor must delegate, in order to conserve time and energy for the truly strategic issues. Measurement is the closing of the loop between the client, the advisor, and the staff.

Within the trust advisory firm there are five elements that will help to ensure success:

- Team-building efforts
- Financial stability
- Common values
- Opportunities to advance education
- Compensation packages

Team-building efforts are needed to build a corporate culture. Without a uniform, consistent, articulated, and well-thought-out team plan, client service delivery will soon begin to look like that of the departing trustee—out of touch with the beneficiary's needs.

Financial stability takes the stress out of mishaps. You cannot focus on client service if the company bills are not paid on time. We are establishing a legacy for the clients and our associates in the firm. Adequate capital and freedom from daily money hassles set the right mood for the trusted advisory firm.

Common values are those beliefs that everyone in the company must share in order to articulate and accomplish the company's mission.

The challenge for personal growth and career advancement has two components—monetary and emotional. We want all of our employees' attention and talents. They in turn need nurturing and encouragement to grow.

The ability to be excited, interested, and committed to this difficult work is garnered by the firm's commitment to improve constantly the financial and intellectual lives of the employees, as well as of the principals.

The Trustee Connection

his final chapter of the Trustworthy Advisor section is about finding the right home for trusts. The choice of a successor trustee is crucial, and your part in this decision is pivotal. Let's look at the best way to find and work with successor trustees.

There are many issues to sort out when determining what kind of trustee is best for your client. Each trust situation is unique. Because it is so important that the personalities of the beneficiaries mesh favorably with those of the trustees, establishing rapport with a new trustee is an intensely subjective matter. Also, the new trustee has to be willing to follow the advisor's investment discretion and discretionary judgment. It is necessary to think long and hard about your ideal working relationship on behalf of this particular beneficiary distribution before you contact potential trust successors. The particular way that each trust document is written may constrain the choice of successor trustees. The size and character of the trust assets will affect to what extent a new trustee will negotiate with you in terms of reducing the standard fee schedule. Many trustees may even refuse to take a particular trust.

As the trusted advisor, your first job is to ascertain the reputations of the various available trustees. This is sometimes difficult to accomplish because you cannot talk to their dissatisfied or disaffected clients. The reality is that trustees run the gamut from excellent to terrible. Researching who is available takes time.

The most likely candidates are local bank trust departments, regional conglomerates, and national financial companies who have created new spin-off trust departments. Firms like Vanguard and Fidelity, some of the nation's biggest mutual fund companies, have trust departments as adjuncts to their main businesses. It is important that you offer as many viable options to your client as possible.

Inheritors will not necessarily know which option is the best for them. They will most likely turn back to their trusted advisor for help in making the final choice. Before approaching successor trustees, you need to know what range of fees is available from competitors and what is fair for both beneficiaries and trustees. You should define what kind of interaction you as the advisor will have with the trustee before the first meeting with the client and before any confidential information is divulged. If the trustee is interested, there is a set process to follow in terms of sending documents for review before the fee negotiations are finalized. Trustees need to see for themselves that the assets are ones that can be dealt with through their normal procedures and also be able to determine what possible complications might arise in the administration of the trust.

If this is your first interaction with a particular corporate trustee, the trustee will very likely not give you everything that you want. Negotiations take place throughout the process of reviewing documents while the trustee is calculating what the workload will be. It may only be after an appropriate fee schedule has been negotiated, the assets transferred, good communications established, and the complexity of the administration of the trust settled that you will know for sure that the right choice has been made.

As in most business dealings, the larger the size of the trust or the more trusts that you control, the more clout you will have in negotiating trustees' fees. It is important not to try to cut the trustee to the bone on fees. In the end, you will get no better service than what you pay for. A trustee who offers rock-bottom prices is likely to give a minimum of service. Nevertheless, in some cases an impersonal, far-off corporate trustee who will only contact the client upon the client's request may be the best choice. In other cases, such a choice would be a disaster. You must find out if the successor trustee is willing to play by the rules that you and the beneficiary lay out before any consideration is made of moving the account. This is when your negotiating and bargaining power is at its highest level.

Earlier in the book, we talked about the different kinds of fees levied on trusts. All of these should be clearly articulated and negotiated between the advisor, inheritor, and the new trustee. This can take several weeks or even months. The appendix provides a sample negotiating tool to be used with successor trustees. Get your potential trustee's feedback on your basic requirements early in the process, before putting in too much time and effort.

This chapter will investigate the following options available to the beneficiary and advisor.

- The advisor as private trustee

- Working with existing trustees

- The Swiss mystique

- Local and regional trust departments

- Independent trust companies

- National trustees—spin-offs

- Starting a new trust company

- Trust cooperatives

The Advisor as Trustee

The most obvious choice for successor trustee is for the advisor himself to act as individual trustee, if the document allows for it. This is a big decision with major consequences. To consider this option, the advisor must know how to fulfill a fiduciary's duties, understand the record-keeping obligations, and be aware of the potential liability of acting as an individual trustee. We do not recommend this option for most seasoned professionals because of the high degree of liability and the complexity of most irrevocable trust situations. As we have pointed out, in cases where attorneys name themselves as trustees, there is a strong possibility that sooner or later conflict of interest will arise. At some point during the trust relationship there will be intense scrutiny of the situation if he has named himself as trustee, even if he has done so at the strong urging of the client.

On the other hand, the benefit of being an individual trustee is that if you become established in the situation as trustee, you are then able to effect changes directly as the actual owner of the assets. Financial planners, investment advisors, and other persons in the financial service industry will be deemed to have custody of assets if they act both as trustee and advisor to a trust account. This is not an insurmountable obstacle. However, it does expose you to additional regulatory requirements.

It is often dangerous to wear too many hats. A trusted advisor who also acts as trustee needs to go to great lengths to document all interactions with his client. Every action needs to be considered with an express view of potential conflict of interest issues. We feel that it is better to have several pairs of eyes on trust situations rather than just one pair. For this reason we do not act as an individual trustee unless there is another professional such as an attorney/accountant acting as cotrustee with us. They serve to balance our power as investment advisors and also ensure our effectiveness as cotrustee. We only act as individual trustees in situations where the assets involved exceed $5 million. The cost of administering trusts as an individual trustee are considerable, therefore the high minimum threshold amount.

Our requirement that there be another professional acting with us as cotrustee is to give responsibility for accounting, administrative documentation, and maintaining official correspondence to someone we know is already in the liability management business. This is, in essence, the backroom part of acting as trustee.

We recommend that if an advisor decides to act as an individual trustee, a separate corporation be set up for this service. In this way the regulatory burdens will be kept separate from the normal requirements of the advisor's other business. It is important to keep fees collected and expenses incurred relating to trust administration separate from the advisor's other regulated activities and existing books. This will help when questions arise regarding the overlap of the trust business with other areas of the advisor's financial firm.

Working with Existing Trustee

First, let's look closely at working with the existing trustee. Changing a trustee/client relationship from a habitual mode is probably the most difficult option. The existing trustee has a relationship with the beneficiary based on a long history. The trustee will generally be unwilling to let investment discretion pass to an outside party. This is particularly true for banks, and their position becomes more rigid as they become larger and ownership passes out of local hands.

As a leader in the financial services industry in your community, you probably can secure an interview with the decision maker at the bank, especially if it is a small and locally owned operation. You then will have an opportunity to discuss the possibility of the bank delegating investment responsibility to you, along with some of the work involved in maintaining the client relationship. The bank needs to be willing to reduce its fees for playing this lesser role. Usually it will not agree, pointing to compliance considerations. Keep in mind that bank fiduciaries generally operate from a stance of fear of liability.

The main advantage of trying to work with an existing trustee is that from the beneficiary's point of view little has to change and continuity is preserved. The advisor has to make sure that there is an agreement regarding who will make the investment decisions and how requests are to be handled regarding distributions of income and principal.

We have found few banks acting as current trustees that are willing to allow an advisor to come in and manage the account as the result of a simple request by the beneficiary. There are few if any documents written before 1990 that specifically give the beneficiaries the right to do this. Hopefully, most attorneys drafting new documents are including this kind of provision, as well as provisions to remove the corporate trustee. Normally, corporate trustees are unwilling to grant flexibility regarding how to get the best investment advice possible. Nevertheless, it is important to offer beneficiaries the alternative of staying and negotiating with the current trustee. Make it clear that it probably won't work, and that other alternatives need to be lined up because of the likely unsatisfactory results of this approach.

It is important for the advisor to set a standard for the kind of relationship that would be satisfactory for the beneficiary to make the decision to stay with an existing trustee.

The Swiss Mystique

Let's look at the popular image of the private Swiss bank. Its office is comfortably located overlooking a broad lake on which boats placidly sail. In the distance, there is the sight of a snow-covered mountain. Walking through the hallways, you imagine the sounds of hushed voices in conference, with wine glasses clinking at a midday lunch. This gives a sense of assurance, along with the comfortable leather chairs you slide into while waiting for the trust officer to speak of the comfort, security, stability, confidentiality, and trust-worthiness of a centuries-old tradition. There is some reality in this image of Swiss banks—as well as some dangerous fantasy. We know through our own experience that Swiss bank dealings are confidential. However, the Swiss banks that have U.S. citizens as clients exhibit a markedly low level of client service. They also do not seem to care whether the clients' expectations are being met.

The Swiss are notoriously slow and rigid in terms of making investment decisions. They are unwilling to buy many types of U.S. securities. They are far behind the curve in terms of trading stocks and mutual funds with speed or any kind of cost effectiveness. It is unbelievably costly to have Swiss banks effect any kind of security transactions and their basic banking charges are very high.

One client of ours has his family accounts at a bank in Lucerne. The Swiss insist on doing all of their U.S. trading through a Canadian subsidiary. This involves two currency exchange transaction costs, a brokerage fee charged by the Swiss bank, and another brokerage fee charged in the United States. Furthermore, there is a special stamp tax levied by the Swiss on all non-Swiss transactions. A simple mutual fund purchase that might cost between $50 and $100 in the United States runs to almost $1,000 in fees for persons with Swiss trust accounts. The transactions also take two or three days to accomplish. It is difficult for the Swiss to identify their fees. A client recently changed his account from a managed relationship to a custodial one. He was told by the Swiss trust officer that it would take about six months to effect the new, lower fee rate because "that is how things are done here."

Swiss accounts do offer a huge advantage to non-U.S. citizens who do not have to pay taxes unless the money is sent to the United States and declared as income or capital gains. This is against IRS regulations for U.S. citizens but makes sense for foreign nationals with foreign income that is kept out of the United States. The Swiss are fully aware of the income and estate tax advantages of putting money with them. They know that once people make deposits into accounts in Switzerland, there is a huge disincentive to repatriate funds to the United States. Therefore, the Swiss fees are almost double those charged in the United States. Perhaps it is worth paying the fee, given our country's estate tax of 50% and high effective income tax rate on people in the top brackets. But buying an image of quality trust service has high costs. When our Swiss client needs money, it must be wired, which takes several steps to complete. Because of the increased time and expense of using Swiss trust bank services, we look to U.S. banks to see if they will respond more efficiently and cost effectively to meet our clients' needs for service.

Local and Regional Trust Departments

Generally speaking, most banks do a fairly good job of administering the more routine aspects of family trusts. Their ability to trade stocks, bonds, and funds at the request of an advisor depends on the bank's "corresponding" institutions or wholesalers that will actually execute these transactions. Some trust departments may resist giving an advisor all the investment options actually available, but all trustees are part of the Depository Trust Company system. Any publicly traded security, be it a stock or a bond, can be purchased by an advisor, who ends up holding trust assets at a local or regional bank. Security clearance is one area that advisors must clarify before choosing a particular successor trustee.

The new trustee's ability to produce performance reporting and to download information to the advisor's existing software system is another critical factor in the choice. The trustee needs to be willing to act on behalf of the beneficiary at the request of the inheritor's independent advisor. Some banks will do so, but most won't without a great deal of persuasion.

The ability of an advisor to keep track of a family trust's investment portfolio is problematic unless the trustee is willing to hold the trust assets at a custodian of the advisor's choosing. This can be a particular brokerage firm or a correspondent bank that will provide an electronic download to the advisor. This is important when an advisor goes to provide a complete, consolidated statement of the client's financial condition. It is cumbersome to enter manually large portfolios into a computer if they are kept with custodians that do not provide timely, accurate, and properly digitized data for input into the advisor's computer system. If the assets really are to be managed with clarity and control, assets inside and outside the trust must be considered together so the successor trustee's ability to link up electronically with the advisor is important.

One disadvantage of working with local or regional banks is that the issue of who really is in control is unclear. The bank legally owns the account because it is the named trustee. If an advisor brings an account to a bank, the bank always has the legal ability to fire the advisor, and also to turn around and reject any future request by the beneficiary to resign without another struggle. No matter what promises are made by the bank, a new bank owner can get out of abiding by a previously signed agreement. It can do this by relying on general fiduciary law, which states that as the fiduciaries, the bank's interpretation of powers and rights is the one that counts unless told otherwise by the court. By and large, using local and regional banks can work, but this is probably not the best long-term solution for inheritors and their advisors.

Independent Trust Companies (ITCs)

The independent trust company industry is in a situation similar to that of the investment advisory field in the late 1980s. This was when financial planners, insurance agents, stockbrokers, and smart institutional players like Charles Schwab realized that the big money to be made was not in commission-driven product sales, but through the personal service being provided by investment advice providers, be they big mutual funds, small independents, or business retirement plans. The best people left banks and brokerages in the 1990s and started their own firms, since the cost of doing so plummeted with the advent of microcomputers.

Independent trust companies are now in vogue, being formed by people who have mixed knowledge of the trust industry but who accurately see trusts as a way to extend the average life of their client relationships, perhaps for generations. There are also many wholesale independent trust companies, whose sole business is to provide trust services as a back-office and fiduciary solution for advisors.

It is not difficult to find good trust administrative officers or to find good trust companies. It is extremely difficult, however, to find good, flexible, and low-cost trust operations that can deliver what the beneficiary and his advisor need. The dollar volumes need to be high enough to make top-quality service available at a reasonable price. We foresee a consolidation in the independent trust company business. Independent trust companies that choose to serve as wholesalers for trusted advisors will be successful; however, there is room for only one or two in each state. We look forward to a leveling of the playing field when national trust laws are enacted. As in the other personal financial professions, there will eventually be uniform nationwide requirements for capital, compliance, education, and consumer protection in the trust field.

Let's look at the advantages and disadvantages of independent trust companies. The administrative capabilities of independent trust companies vary greatly. Some of them have experienced trust officers from banks who know how to administer trusts properly. Their ability to trade depends on to whom they contract their back-office functions. Their ability to communicate back to the beneficiary as well as the advisor is dependent on their software expertise.

We have not yet seen the development of an industrywide standard for coordination between trust accounting systems, custody services, and electronic download capabilities to advisor software. This will be accomplished in the near future, however, and then the benefits of using independent trust companies will be realized on a widespread basis. This will create a tremendous challenge to the banks, which have had a lock on most trust business until the development of this kind of alternate system. The banks will finally understand that the beneficiary, with the help of the advisor, is in the driver's seat. We have negotiated with independent trust companies all over the country. A handful of them hold client assets at a place of the advisor's choice. We have also been able to negotiate a lower fee, due to their playing only a custodial and back-office relationship to the client. This is the independent trust companies' big advantage over the banks. The independent corporate trustee is willing to take on more risk in terms of the kinds of assets it is willing to hold.

A main disadvantage of independent trust companies is that the ownership of the account is again called into question. We always negotiate a termination-without-cause clause for independent trust company services before the account is set up. There is, however, no legally binding way to hold the company to this agreement should the ownership change. The burden again is on the beneficiary's advisor to get the trust moved if a company goes back on its agreement. We do not perceive this to be a big problem, because enough documentation is in the file showing the corporate trustee's promise to resign. All trustees have a community image that they are worried about protecting. Having to go back on their promises would be severely embarrassing.

Because the name recognition of newly created independent trust companies is quite low, the trusted advisor's standing in her community is all the more important. When some family members are nervous about making a change of trustees, bringing in an independent trust company from another state may be a mistake. So far, we have been fortunate and have found ways to negotiate with local trustees who are known to one or more of the beneficiaries. As national independent trust companies become more common, it will be easier to overcome nervous beneficiaries' perceptual hurdle that they need to use a bank as the trustee.

There are no legal barriers to professional independent trust companies operating on an interstate basis (although perceptual difficulties may linger). A good sign that you have chosen the right successor trustee is the willingness of the trustee to take on the management of trust assets regardless of having to learn another state's laws, which must be followed in trust administration.

The lack of a recognizable name in a successor trustee has one advantage for the beneficiary and his advisor. It is clear that the client and his or her trusted advisor remain in the driver's seat regarding the administration of the trust. In this scenario, there is also no question about competition from the trustee. The ownership issue remains. The trusted advisor is retained on a contractual basis, renewing tenure based on performance and closeness of client relationship. The independent trust company remains in its position unless it really screws up and the trust has to be moved again. Where then is the professional benefit from the build-up of "equity" resulting from the gathering trust assets? This issue of equity—that is, receiving of some benefit from bringing trust assets to an independent trust company—is one that we have investigated. There is a potential conflict of interest if an advisor receives an advisory fee and also some kind of fee from a custodial or trust institution. We go to great lengths to make sure that these arrangements do not influence the decision of who will be chosen as successor trustee. Financial advisors can be compensated for referring trusts to corporate trusts if the relationship is disclosed.

National Trustees: Spin-Offs

Another option is to line up with a nationwide, highly recognizable company that has entered the trust business. In their relationship to advisor, these firms are more like money center banks than independent trust companies. Big companies, like Fidelity, Vanguard, and SEI, tend to act like banks in their lack of flexibility and impersonal service. They are driven more by the fear of liability and protection of their brand name than by commitment to excellent trust service.

We have investigated relationships with these national firms, and feel they may be appropriate for some accounts. The nationals put more constraints on the type of investments allowed. They exhibit much more rigidity than independent trustees in terms of fees charged. The delivery of trust administrative services is removed and somewhat distant when dealing with a national financial service company. In some cases, this may be to the financial advisor's benefit, again because of the issue of loyalty. National trust companies tend to have rigid administrative procedures, which puts them at a disadvantage to the local banks, which understand the needs of local people better than a big firm based far away in a major metropolitan area. National financial companies have strong name-brand recognition and an image of security. The difference between the trustee organization's security and the insurance coverage on actual trust assets was discussed earlier in the book. It is not uncommon for beneficiaries to initially feel more comfortable with a national company like Vanguard as trustee than an independent trust company in Taos, New Mexico. These feelings are not based on facts regarding safety, nor on the realities of service.

Starting Your Own Trust Company

The issue of whether to start your own trust company involves complex personal choices. Some states have reasonable capital requirements. National trust charters require enough capital to meet the Office of the Comptroller of the Currency requirements of around $3 million plus one year's operating budget cash needs. There are many decisions to make and factors to consider before deciding if it is worth the hassle to start your own corporate trust company. The time involved in obtaining a charter is between six months and one year. There is an annual audit procedure, which lasts two to four weeks. Each advisor in the trust market must decide for herself if she wants to pay these costs for the privilege of having her own trust entity.

The advisor must examine her organization's current compliance expertise and temperament. It is likely that you will need to hire someone specifically to take on these responsibilities in order to bring a new trust company into compliance with regulatory standards. Trust standards make running a broker-dealer subsidiary or investment advisory firm look like child's play.

When starting a trust company, you assume certain kinds of personal liabilities and problems. The barriers to enter into the trust business are high. This is intentional. It keeps fly-by-night operations out of the industry. It also tends to keep out of competition lawyers, who can operate de facto trust companies without the constraints imposed upon other businesspeople. The personal and corporate liability issues require some fairly expensive insurance and legal structures. There are burdensome weekly and monthly time commitments for corporate trustees. Unless you have some trust accounts ready to go into a trust company, our advice is to look for a joint venture arrangement with an existing corporate trustee.

Unlike many entrepreneurs who catch up on their corporate minutes occasionally, trust companies must have real, live administrative and investment meetings regularly. This is no joke, because trust companies still fall under banking regulations.

What are the benefits of starting your own trust company? The advantages have primarily to do with control and equity—and in your ability to deliver full service. You can assure your clients that they will get what you promise. For the advisor there is also the value of having another type of business to augment your current one. The value of building equity is that assets that are on someone else's books as trust accounts means they are, considered strictly as investment accounts, not really part of an advisor's transferable base. If you look to valuing your business, you get a higher multiple for trust assets as opposed to discretionary investment accounts. This is because of the perceived longevity advantage that trust relationships have over discretionary, agency, or investment management accounts. But is the increased multiple worth it?

The next decision, if you decide to be a trust company, is whether to apply for a state or national trust charter. This depends mainly on marketing issues.

New trust accounts from anywhere in the nation can be accepted by state-chartered institutions as long as certain restrictive guidelines are followed. No specific advertising can be done in national magazines by state-chartered trust companies. State-trust-chartered firms also are limited as to where they can physically be located outside their home state. None of these is an overriding rationale for not getting a trust charter, at least on an initial basis.

Trust Cooperatives

Another option is to start a trust company with a group of peers or to create an association of practitioners. This, in effect, is like starting a cooperative. There are many problems with this approach. These include cross-liability for errors on the part of associates, control and accountability responsibilities for expenses, divisional profits created unequally by members of the group, and conflicting managerial philosophies and styles.

We recently attended a meeting of a group of financial planners. They were attempting to start a national trust company. It seemed like a great idea, but the issues of who received what value in the business stymied the group. Its strategic purpose was also not resolved. If the trust company set out to become profitable, who would get the profit? Is the purpose to build a company that benefits the executive managers or is the point to provide the mutual owners with a low-cost corporate trust vehicle? When advisors try to join among themselves to start a trust company, there is a cross-responsibility for liabilities, which can be a tricky issue as well. Can and should advisors give up some of their independence to be part of this larger group? The issues of capital contribution, time, expertise, new-business production, and the questions of which assets and trust accounts take the most time to administer and which hold the greatest risk to the trust association are all germane if the venture is to succeed.

Does this kind of trust service venture have merit for even a small group of people who have worked together for years on an informal basis and who know and trust one another? The problems of management control always exist. Top-quality operational management, someone with trust experience, can be brought in. Is it possible without discord to allocate profits according to contribution and to allocate expenses according to effort and expenditures? Business ventures tend to have a life of their own. If a trust company is originally set up to service only a small group of advisors and their clients, it is unlikely to be worth the effort. There are other, simpler ways to increase account longevity than the trust structure. If you are going into the trust business to receive custody or fiduciary fees, be aware it is a new business effort entirely, and as such, has another total set of demands. It is not the business into which most advisors will want to put their best efforts.

For firms with assets under $500 million, there are trust specialists and wholesalers of trust services whose main business is to provide custodial, bookkeeping, administration, back-office trading, reports, compliance, and marketing assistance to advisors. These companies are willing to work with investment advisors but not on any kind of equity or revenue-sharing basis. Investment advisor and financial planning firms, when they pass the $500 million mark, should consider becoming trust companies on their own. At that stage, the cost of having one additional administrator with trust expertise is not that great, and it may well make sense to bring some functions in-house that were previously delegated to outside trustees. Before reaching this point, it probably doesn't make sense to start your own trust company or to take the time necessary to coordinate with peers to provide a similar service to those already available through wholesalers in the field.

Conclusion

Based on our interaction with trustees of various levels of expertise and in various geographic locations, we believe that corporate trustees should be able to make a decent profit at a fairly low level of charges to the client. The fixed cost of handling a trust account is somewhere around 20 basis points (0.20%) per year. We feel that it is worth paying 50 basis points to find a superior alternative to the local bank trust department. Adding in the advisor fees, the total new fees may be slightly above those levied by the traditional trustee, but the level of performance and results should be much higher, for a clear net benefit to the client.

The issues of control management and ownership are the next items of importance to the advisor. The way that trust business is being conducted is changing rapidly. The needs of people who are inheriting the family wealth that is coming out of bank trust departments or that is passing from one generation to the next over the next 20 years, due to the passing on of the World War II generation, are high. The advisor should anticipate these needs and feel motivated to hook up with an agreeable trust service provider or to start a trust company. Due to the stumbling of bank trustees as they consolidate, many trust beneficiaries are left paying more for less service. This situation does not seem to be diminishing. Large banking institutions are inevitable, due to the high cost of providing high-tech, sophisticated products. Only the megafirms will survive in many areas of traditional banking. This leaves many profitable niches open for the nimble niche player on a local level. This is where the family trusts and independent advisors exist. The market opportunity is there, and technical assistance is available. From the advisor's point of view, a trust account should not have to be treated any differently, from an operational point of view, than any other investment account of the client. As brokers, insurance agents, accountants, financial planners, attorneys, and investment advisors turn into trusted advisors, the back-office support and administrative options available to handle the needs of these situations will increase. We look forward to the day when the function of the trustee is just one more third-party service in an unbundled universe. As checking accounts and mortgage loans have become removed from association with their previously sole local banks, so too will trusts move into a different marketplace of competition.

Part 6

Taking Control of Your Inherited Wealth

Part VI is for beneficiaries who want to improve their trust situation. The first chapter of this section will help you get to know yourself financially. This will enable you to make better financial decisions, as well as business relationship decisions—which should save you a great deal of frustration in the future. Chapter 22, "Opening the Door to Change," will help you feel more comfortable in taking the necessary steps toward changing your financial life. Chapter 23, "If It's Working. . ." will help you identify the qualities you need in a trusted advisor. This chapter includes a comprehensive list of questions you'll want to ask before hiring anyone to help you. Chapter 24, "Keys to the Future," will assist you in finding the trusted advisor who fits your criteria.

21

Knowing Your Financial Self

The trust-busting and trust-building process will not be successful unless you, the beneficiary, have first engaged in several processes that build up self-knowledge and internal fortitude. Specifically, these processes involve looking inside yourself and discovering what makes you happy; defining the essential ingredients of both financial and personal health; establishing trust relationships; and developing mutual respect and integrity. We include a discussion of these preconditions as the first part of this last section because they are so crucial to the trust-busting and -building process. Many people will find it helpful to go through this chapter several times before approaching and evaluating prospective trust advisors and institutions.

The focus of our process is to help heirs grapple with the issues of how you want your assets to affect your lives. How do you want your inherited money to relate to each area of your interactions with other people?

Figure 21.1 is a graphic reminder that beginning with the self, we move out from the center to relate to:

- Family (in the center of the bull's-eye)

- Friends

- Career

FIGURE 21.1 Financial identity map.

- Advisors
- Institutions
- Community

In each part of the process, we ask the same questions: How is my identity in this realm influenced by our family's inherited money? Has my wealth had a positive or negative impact in the past? What can I do to make the influence of my assets a positive one?

Knowing Yourself

It is important that persons of inherited wealth be prepared for success and feel that they deserve a successful trust experience. We know that our clients must understand and be able to visualize clearly the desired outcome before we can plan a strategy for them to achieve a set of desired results. Most often, making more money is not the issue. The emotional character of the relationship with money begins with the beneficiary's attitude toward himself or herself. We ask our clients to go through a process of visualizing their past relationship with money and what the present looks like, and only then trying to imagine what true future financial health would look like.

What do you want more of in your life? What do you want less of in your life? What are your priorities? How much time do you want to devote to your family, your friends, and your career? All of these questions can be somehow slightly off the mark for people who have great wealth. You may not necessarily believe in the pervasive and culturally accepted maxim that more money will bring more time, more freedom, more love, less anxiety, and so forth. In our segmented society, the internal journey to self-knowledge is an important undertaking. Rearranging assets, breaking old trust relationships and establishing new ones, and putting your life together must wait for the outcome of the psychological efforts described below.

What Makes You Happy?

Most human beings have similar desires. We want to be happy and healthy, have a fulfilling career, engage in good relationships, help others, enjoy nature, and protect the environment. The big differences come into play when we try to prioritize our goals and establish a set of defined and attainable steps for reaching those goals. We all have a tendency to want to do more than is humanly possible. It is in the fabric of technological society that our exposure to so many opportunities, images, and possible experiences affects our minds in an unsettling way. We see good things and then want them—we can't help wanting to be artists, businesspeople, lovers, parents, friends, contributors to the arts and charities, athletes, dutiful children, school supporters, organizers of our homes, offices, and communities, and so on. No wonder so many people are unhappy. There is too much to do and nobody to blame for it not happening but ourselves.

Trust beneficiaries spend a great deal of time and money getting psychological help in becoming clearer because their priorities change with their emotional moods. Inheritors can have a particular problem in that some of the foundational elements for establishing goals and objectives, and for having the discipline to meet those objectives (and then feeling good about actually accomplishing some of them) may be missing from their lives. This has several implications. It can make it difficult for inheritors to feel good about themselves no matter what they do. It may seem impossible for them to get out of this bind, a result of privilege and over-protection from childhood. Guilt is often added to feelings of inadequacy. It can be difficult for inheritors to avoid having unrealistic, often high expectations about what they should be doing but cannot—which then leads to another cycle of self-deprecation.

The variety of roles that money plays in the lives of people is enormous. There are multiple layers of emotions present around the issue of money. These are common for everyone, no matter what his background, ranging from neglect to obsession; from constant fear about not having enough money to out-of-control spending. It is difficult to get a handle on these problems to address the issue of what can be done to make people—in this case, wealthy ones—feel successful.

Ingredients of Wealth

Underlying all of our emotional states are basic desires for security, free-dom, and love, and then to be a contributing member of some community. Our natural inclination is toward being spiritual and our desire to manifest compassion comes out in numberless ways. The authors believe that dur-ing the financial counseling process with beneficiaries, these issues are helpful when brought to the surface because they establish a commonality of purpose and meaning.

We organize into concentric layers our discussion of how beneficiaries can look inside to determine what their financial selves look like. Our inner relationship with money is complex and so affects every level of our lives that we have chosen to talk about it using the image of a concentric series of expanding bands, circles with self in the center and the commu-nity on the periphery.

First, we suggest doing some free association, asking what images come to mind relative to such words as "satisfaction," "happiness," "health," "success," and "freedom." Take freedom, for example. For you, does being free mean freedom from anxiety or freedom from the drudgery of a sched-ule? Or, perhaps, is it freedom to travel or having free time to help others without being concerned about other commitments?

People with inherited assets are usually not obsessed with multiplying their wealth, but rather are concerned with preserving it and using it wisely. With wealth comes a sense of responsibility. Sometimes it is also accompanied by an overwhelming apprehension. At this point, we ask inheritors to visualize for themselves what their lives would look like a year from now if the emotional contour of their existence could be anything they wished. The tension between where we are and where we would like to be is an important agent for change. We know that this kind of stress is important and useful, because it stimulates our biochemistry and helps us make sustained efforts to improve our lives. Later on we will talk about how best to communicate these realizations and discoveries to your advisor so that your financial life can follow your overarching personal plan.

What Do You Want Out of Life?

Personal Life

The development of character is said to be the highest and most difficult human aspiration. People of wealth have an unparalleled chance to deal with these issues. Perhaps our purpose in this life is to develop those aspects of our character that are hardest to deal with, and then to be tested over and over again in those areas in which we are weakest. Some of us need to develop patience and discipline; others need to exhibit compassion and to try to do some selfless sharing. We all lack complete development of some basic human attributes. Are our relationships with our siblings, parents, spouses, children, and neighbors satisfactory? Do we perceive patterns of dysfunctional codependency or unfocused anger? Do we wish to spend more time practicing art, playing music, doing charitable work, or helping the environment, but just can't seem to get organized? Or do we feel that we can afford to take the time, but don't have the energy to engage in these meaningful activities?

Low energy and depression are common syndromes for many people in today's world. Environmental illness and chronic fatigue syndrome are physical disorders that some psychiatrists feel may be symptomatic ways of dealing with the stress of our modern culture. Our world revolves around images of money and events that have to do with money. The alternative medicine and healing community is working its way into mainstream America, but many people already have a high level of interest in acupuncture, homeopathy, and massage therapy.

What is the order in which to deal with what interests us on the personal level, and what steps can we take to deal with the obstacles that stand in the way of health, happiness, and wholeness? The financial side of our lives should be helpful in accomplishing these goals rather than being a hindrance.

Financial Life

When it comes to dealing with money, our avoidance mechanisms are subtle and numerous. How many people know how much money they spend and exactly what it gets spent on? Very few—yet the process of analyzing our spending patterns and understanding where our income originates is an essential first step in attaining a sense of security and freedom. The preparation of budgets and analysis of past spending habits is a simple process. Everyone who has graduated from high school is fully capable of going through this process.

However, the emotional blocks to doing this are enormous. It takes special counseling skills to help people understand how many anxieties surface when it comes really to looking at our own spending patterns. This is a kind of reality check. No one is immune to a resistance to going through this painful exercise. For a practical guide to this process, see Fred Brown's book, *Money and Spirit.*

How many people know what tax bracket they are in? The ability to analyze our income, determine where it comes from, and to see how it is taken away by the tax authorities is an essential educational experience for every adult. The amount of paperwork and the difficulty of formatting this kind of material in order to understand our financial picture are formidable. According to *Kiplinger's 1998 "Cut Your Taxes,"* about half of all U.S. taxpayers have someone else prepare their tax returns. How many people go over their returns in detail with their tax preparer? If you don't, how can you have a feeling of connection with your money?

What Are Your Priorities?

All of these issues revolve around how much time and trouble you are willing to spend on managing your finances. Handling inherited assets can become a full-time job if you personally handle every aspect of it (i.e., investing, research, bookkeeping, tax preparation, etc.). Most people with inherited assets delegate these tasks, but there needs to be a balance. Informed people can understand that taking responsibility about your assets relieves deeper anxieties. Even among the ultrawealthy, some experience high anxiety about their money. The most common problem is in being in touch with their spending. Not dealing with this issue leads to the separation they feel from other people because of this overpowering and undirected abundance.

Discussions about how much to leave children, how many generations you want to provide for, and the reserves that may be needed for possible medical and housing issues during elder years are all issues that cannot be talked about intelligently unless a familiarity with budgets, taxes, and basic investment concepts is first obtained.

Additional issues regarding setting priority areas are as follows:

- How much money is enough to satisfy your personal lifestyle needs?
- What is needed to give a sense of security?
- How many homes are needed?
- How much travel is essential?
- How much charitable giving can occur?
- How concerned are you with estate taxes?

All of these require time and reflection on your part.

Let's move on to looking deeper at various areas of self-knowledge. These involve the relationship of the emotional self to money. Please reflect on how you personally would like to relate to these subjects. We are going over some of the psychological aspects of being an inheritor with the purpose that knowing and being able to communicate these motivations and priorities to your trusted advisor are essential for your future happiness and success.

Self

The self is the origin from which everything emerges. We all have wounds in the sense that when we were infants and children we did not receive complete, constant, and ever-present love and attention from our parents or primary caregivers. The disappointments that we experienced and the ways that we dealt with that pain were psychologically necessary for us to survive. These experiences determine to a large degree our adult personalities. There are ways to take us back to look at these childhood proverbial memories. The help that we can get in doing this contributes to our success in rounding out our personality. We need to come to peace with our deepest financial anxieties, which are reflections and reactions to these largely unconscious memories.

All human beings want and need love and affection. Rare indeed is the individual who gets that in ample measure as an infant and young child.

We have adopted individualized survival methods of compensating for the lack of attention and love in order to emotionally placate ourselves so we can go on as best we can. For our purposes, it is important to realize that on the financial side, our sense of inadequacy and the ways we learned to compensate for these feelings greatly affect our attitudes toward money. Those people who find help in dealing with these underlying complexities regarding the emotional aspect of money are the ones who as mature adults are most likely to end up enjoying what they have and who they are.

Without waxing philosophic, we believe that having a firm sense of self-identity and self-worth is essential to being happy. Accepting ourselves on various levels necessitates investigating how we have been wounded, and then bringing those wounds to the surface. Hearing about the wounds of others in confidential group settings can be a great assistance in promoting the healing process. Often a primary relationship with a spouse or significant other has healing power, as it gives us a chance to reopen and look inside these old wounds. It is a painful and humbling process because these wounds manifest themselves in the form of our habits and attitudes of unhappiness with our everyday lives.

Our true self is the most difficult aspect of our being to approach and directly experience. During almost every moment, whether asleep or awake, our minds are running "old tapes" about what happened to us in the past, as we try to figure out why something happened or to plan ahead for the future. It is difficult for the mind to relax and allow the experiences of childhood to bubble forth in full clarity. Many experiential psychology processes help our minds to come to a state in which this kind of experience can happen. The methods of interpreting and integrating these experiences into our normal psyche vary from tradition to tradition. All well-adjusted adults, no matter what their background or religious persuasion, go through some kind of process of uncovering, accepting, healing, and sharing of their journey to accept their own self-worth. The expression, "I'm okay, you're okay," can be taken on a deeper level to say that we truly are all okay just as we are, lacking nothing.

The Buddha, whose name literally means "one who is fully awake," first uttered after attaining complete enlightenment (to his true nature), "Wonder of wonders! All beings just as they are, are whole and complete, lacking nothing."

Family

The emotional experiences we had as children inside our immediate family constellations are too broad and too far from the main subject to be examined in detail in this book. To the degree that they relate to attitudes about money and impact our feelings of success (or failure), however, we would like to focus now on the likelihood that people who grew up in very wealthy families may have had a difficult emotional life around money. This is not to say that all children of wealth were not given a chance to become familiar with and to establish a healthy relationship regarding money. Many did and we want to reiterate that by no means do we wish to imply that most or even a majority of people with inherited wealth have any more deep-seated issues about money than any other class of people.

If a parent was a founding member of a financial dynasty, he may have spent little time at home. His absence was probably filled by surrogate caregivers who were paid money but may not have had much emotional interest vested in raising the children. Children of families with great wealth often have a sense that they don't deserve what they have or feel as if they deserve everything without having to work for it. Neither of these two extreme mental states is healthy, nor do they well serve inheritors as a model for building other kinds of self-esteem.

Many people who never have the chance to be challenged or forced by their environment to grow up and take on real responsibilities end up as perennial children. Inheritors who have childlike attitudes about wealth may be refusing to take responsibility for their money and are unable to look at their financial lives with any sense of being able to understand them. They have little motivation to go through what it takes to understand financial matters. The lack of continuity and absence of emotional engagement from a primary caretaker in families of extreme wealth can leave a sense of doubt about whether the inheritor is worthy of love. This then comes back later as a weak sense of self. This is similar in the end result to families where there is no father or mother present; that is, where two working parents have no time for a child during the majority of the child's waking hours. The child gets the sense that all is not right with the world and that everything that is needed for his or her life may not be there for the present and or even in the future.

The lack of intimacy inside a family where wealth has somehow replaced emotional expressions of love naturally leads to the substitution of money for attention. This results in more than a child who gets everything that he wants; it creates an unhappy adult who spends recklessly and who is unable to acknowledge his or her unbalanced view of the world. The profligate consumer feels a fleeting sense of satisfaction—and then a depressed sense of self-worth. People who go on these kinds of binges and don't have inherited money end up in bankruptcy. Trust beneficiaries caught up in this unsatisfactory but compulsive cycle end up at the door of the trustee, asking for more money but being unhappy with whatever they receive because it is never enough.

The difficulties that follow this kind of upbringing are enormous. There is a lack of "connectedness" with other people, because primary emotional bonds and the experience of genuine love are missing. As adults, such inheritors find it hard to establish relationships based on mutual need and trust. The sense of unreality and the disjointedness of not ever having to earn in order to receive makes it difficult to enjoy what you have. To feel a connection with others can be difficult when one has inherited substantial wealth. Further investigation of the family roots of emotionally dysfunctional behavior is well documented in the book *The Legacy of Inherited Wealth: Interviews with Heirs* by Blovin, Gibson, and Kiersted.

Friends

How do you, as an inheritor, relate to your wealth when dealing with friends? "Do my friends like me for who I am, or do they like me for what I have?" is an often-repeated question in inheritors' minds. You can begin to doubt the motives of your friends and even your spouse in those dark moments that we all have. This may lead to limiting your sharing of the important parts of your life with only those friends who come from a similar monetary background. When attention has always been received in the form of money and not through shared emotional experiences, even relationships with peers can become problematic.

The ties that bind friends together often are forged by adversity. We know that when we go through the traumas of young adulthood with close friends, the people and music that we relate to then often stay in our hearts for years to come. In college, sharing the stress of being away from home, challenging workloads, sharing bathrooms, standing in cafeteria lines, or being dumped by a date are all bonding experiences. It is possible to mix only with one's financial peers in an elite environment. If one has wealth and is accustomed to using it for protection against the pain of not having a close, warm, deep-loving family, then money can get in the way of making true and close friendships.

Our country is full of isolated people. Wealth and technology serve to keep us in our own worlds, replete with computers, TVs, automobiles, and the conveniences that serve to keep us from having to rely on other people's actual presence. Other than shopping for food, some people do not have to venture outside of their self-constructed cocoons. Making and keeping friends through the various stages of life is difficult in our segmented society. We do not often have a sense that we need friends for our physical support, so emotional support goes away as well. This is when our doubts about whether we are worthy of having friends can come into play. Sharing wealth used to be one criterion for being a good friend. In our culture of privacy and lack of openness about wealth, the way most of us deal with our financial assets creates barriers to closeness.

Wealthy people are often called upon to loan money or approached to invest in various ventures by so-called friends. This is usually devastating to genuine emotional relationships. It raises the issue of how much you want your friends to know about your financial situation. Keeping this important aspect of your life a secret may seem to help. However, doing this creates tension in that you always have this hidden world, and that an important part of who you are cannot be divulged to any but your most intimate partner—if one exists. The issues of loans, gifts, investing, or buying real estate together with friends are all fraught with danger. Relationships are easily sullied when money gets involved. There are peer group counseling opportunities for wealthy people where communication is not hindered by worry that someone might want to take advantage of your inherited money, make you ashamed of how much money you have, or how you obtained it.

Career

Very few topics for people of inherited wealth are more important to discuss than the difficulties in establishing and maintaining careers. Money is the primary motivating factor for most people in their pursuit of a career. Obviously this is not an issue for people with substantial inherited assets. Career choices for inheritors usually come later in life, and their paths often change.

Difficulty in finding a vocation or passionate avocation may be part of low sense of self-confidence that exists beneath a veneer of gaiety and social success because of money. Enjoyment of the world, which is not dependent upon your own actions, can feel rather hollow. It's like getting a free ride in school, where you receive A's because your parents own the school and teachers are afraid of your family's financial power. There is much shame and self-doubt in all of this. This is an extremely debilitating situation for young people and occurs again when undeserved employment is given to an heir who has not worked hard to deserve it. It is difficult to have a strong motivation to excel as an emerging adult when everything was always given to you. If you do try to excel, there may have been a put-down waiting because you can never measure up to the impossibly high standards established by the family founder's accomplishments. People with inherited wealth may learn to look for a sense of satisfaction in other things than what they themselves can accomplish.

When we are trying to learn to master new and difficult skills, the experiences of frustration and failure are important experiences. If we are insulated from suffering the consequences of our failures, it becomes impossible to develop the internal resources needed to overcome the many disappointments that are a normal part of life. Hardship is the basis of character development. If we are shielded or protected from hardship because there is always enough money to buy our way out of difficulties, and if we can always hire someone else to do the job, we develop a sense that we are incapable, a farce in our own and other people's eyes.

The sense of being able to encounter difficult situations and overcome them with our own internal resources is essential for establishing a career in the world. No matter how much money we have, there is going to be competition in any field—art, charitable giving, social work, teaching, and so forth. There will always be people who don't like us and people who stand in our way, and in whose way we may stand! There will be conflict with people who don't agree with our approach and who will try to manipulate situations so that their own sense of self-worth is enhanced at our expense. This is what we learn through competition in sports, at school, and while playing with a variety of friends from different backgrounds. For example, in public schools, there are roughnecks who make demands upon us that we can't be protected from. Most people with assets have to go through these and many other experiences in the course of their daily lives, and it is in this crucible that the fortitude to focus, establish, and excel in a chosen path is created. The ability to get back on our feet after suffering defeat or humiliation is another experiential learned skill. If we have never been exposed to the dangers of humiliation and competition, this lack of testing can lead to a low sense of self-confidence, which eventually inhibits establishing an identity in society as a contributing member through work-related activities.

Work is seen by most people as a necessary evil. In fact, work is as necessary for our well-being as are food and shelter. Work, like exercise, challenges us to use our abilities to their utmost rather than atrophying through languishing in a protected and "safe" environment. We most often encounter the meaning of life by experiencing our shortcomings, which is often painful. Pain in general is something that people can use money to avoid. Yet most of us do not really learn anything deeply except through pain and suffering. If a wealthy family has always been oriented toward having all kinds of ways to keep their children from encountering suffering, then their offspring's opportunities to grow in normal ways are limited. To some extent we all suffer no matter how well our families treated us, so we all know the experience of personal growth. Our ability to set out and master a career in the real world can be curtailed by being overprotected as children.

Our choice of a career can be greatly affected by how much money we need, and this, in the end, can turn out to be a very beneficial influence. People of inherited wealth can choose to go into the social services or arts for example. People that grow up poor may be driven to accumulate money to protect themselves and their progeny rather than going into lower-paying professions, such as education or nonprofit work.

The fact that persons with inherited wealth do not have the same kind of monetary pressures as most other people around them can lead to social and emotional isolation. It is easy for people to get depressed when they feel that they are unable to succeed on their own. Anxious about their own capabilities because they have never been tested, inheritors must consciously put themselves on a career track before they can achieve a sense of success.

The Trusted Advisor

In your financial life, you deserve a partner who promotes your happiness and well-being. The subject of inheritors' relationships with their advisors is a complex one and will be discussed more fully in Chapter 23. At this point, we will examine the emotional aspect of this relationship. It is based on both parties' emotional attitudes toward money. Inheritors often feel, unrealistically, that their advisors possess some kind of superior knowledge about business life. The advisor seems to be knowledgeable about the world of money and she is successful. Esoteric areas of finance are exactly those that cause the most anxiety in the inheritor's psyche. But this can have dangerous implications.

The advisor can perpetrate this unequal balance of power by acting like a know-it-all and seeming to have answers for every subject. Nothing could be further from the truth—every advisor we know has as many personal problems as any of our clients! Advisors must be humble and acknowledge their own shortcomings. They must search for and bring out the emotional strengths and talents of the inheritor. This kind of mutual respect between the inheritor and advisor is essential for a successful long-term relationship.

Advisors sometimes exhibit a kind of reverse snobbery. This is the unspoken attitude that says because the inheritors did not make their money, they are really not that valuable as individuals or as contributors to society, and that they are lesser people than the advisors themselves. An advisor can also commit the reverse error, looking up to the inheritor and thinking, "Here's someone who's special, who has something that I don't," and jealousy sprinkled with resentment can sneak in. In this case, the client is placed on an unwanted pedestal. Neither of these attitudes works in the long run.

All of us have similar motivations in our hearts and want the same kind of security. But fate and fortune have dealt us all different hands. The inheritor-advisor relationship must contain the acknowledgment that the advisor also has a need to be successful. Elsewhere in the book we speak about finding an advisor with career goals and motivations that will mesh appropriately with the inheritor's personality.

There is a dichotomy between wanting to establish trust with an advisor and fearing the advisor for her knowledge and power. How the advisor responds to these conflicting emotions is important, because inheritors can have a great fear that they are going to do the wrong thing and make a mistake with their money. This unconscious assumption that their lack of knowledge will lead to some kind of failure in this unchosen career (that is, managing their inherited assets) is another manifestation of low self-esteem. The advisor can be either a partner in this sense of dependency or she can take on the responsibility of helping to heal the wounds caused by family attitudes about wealth.

Employees/Servants

Inheritors sometimes have a sense that because of their money, they will have constant and complete access to every resource. The grown-up, poorly developed wealthy child can feel that everyone else's life revolves around their own. Since wealthy people are often not on a 9-to-5 work schedule, they can—and do—call on their advisors to do anything at any time. Some are unable to deal with any kind of paper. They are not able to sign and return any documents, and so become dependent on personal assistants who can handle this aspect of their lives.

This is debilitating because our world requires that we develop coping mechanisms and skills to survive everyday life. If inheritors stand outside the demands and can get away with being unreliable and irresponsible regarding even the smallest requirements, they become victims of their own wealth. Their feelings of self-worth can sink lower and a more pessimistic world view can begin to prevail. It is a terribly isolating circumstance in which to find oneself. Not having any compelling reason to deal with the issues that contribute to self-worth means that as adults, it may be excruciatingly painful to counter these dysfunctions that originated long ago. The advisor's job is to be willing to engage these issues, and to bare his own wounds and suffering, so as to give the inheritor equal ground to stand on in exposing his emotional history.

Institutions

Here we will cover some of the emotional aspects of your interactions with institutions. A song by Bessie Smith (redone by Blood, Sweat and Tears in the 1960s) says, "When you have money you have lots of friends, but when you don't, there's no one to be found." This reflects a common fear of people of wealth. Institutions provide a sense of security but they have little personality. If eating lunch at a fancy restaurant with sophisticated investment professionals or ingratiating administrators helps you feel important, then a certain kind of relationship with an institution can be very supportive. SIPs who operate out of their homes have a completely different kind of emotional feel to their service. Small firms' marketing materials and reports often seem unsophisticated and therefore less desirable than those from a larger organization.

The type of emotional relationship that you want to have with your financial institution should be reflected in your interactions with the representative of the institution. The following list of questions is an emotional interaction inventory:

- Is the administrator a friend, or a professional doing his or her job?

- Which do you want—a friend or a professional?

- Does the institution provide an incentive for that person to stay in his or her job, so that you won't have to reestablish your individuality and desired formal communication over and over?

- Is the institution asking about and listening to your needs?

- What kind of person do you prefer to deal with, (i.e., age, gender, level of experience, education, interests)?

- How available do you expect someone at the institution to be when you need to know something?

Answer these questions for yourself in the abstract first. What is your ideal relationship like? Then ask yourself if you think that your trustee would be interested in knowing and acting on your answers here.

Community

Inheritors have unique opportunities to relate to their communities. Some wealthy people have the time, the emotional strength, and the depth of interest to go into the community, which has a high need for them, especially now. With government pulling out of or cutting back on many social services areas, people need to have a sense of what kind of contributions they would like to make to communities of less fortunate people.

Some heirs are comfortable with the feeling that if they give money to the community, the world is better because of their gifts. Other persons with inherited wealth get more personal satisfaction when they become personally involved with community improvement projects. The emotional character of the relationship to your assets surfaces here in the choice of private versus public involvement, donation of time versus money, or in some combination of the two.

The surfacing of privacy concerns may indicate a psychological need to keep secret the reality of our wealth. This is an identity issue. Can our personal lives be kept separate from the source of our livelihood? For the most part, our culture is a primary source of identity. How do you want the community to relate back to you? What is your sense of self regarding your place in the world? People in large cities do not have to worry about this sense of personal identity as much as those who live in smaller towns. In retirement communities, it is a common and much talked-about subject—how much money does the neighbor have, and where did it come from? The rest of us usually don't have the time for such preoccupations, but we wonder just the same, don't we? To have a sense of self and identity totally independent of money is difficult. To extricate the financial aspects of your self and your relationship to others does not happen easily. Your involvement in community affairs has to be the product of a conscious decision about how to employ your assets and of how your identity is tied up in this expression. Our social selves are quite important to our happiness.

Conclusion

After reviewing these issues, you should have developed a sense of how you want your assets to affect your interactions with others. This is an outgrowth of how you wish to relate to your assets. The process of investigating your past history with money and being cognizant of how money affects your current relationships should be helpful. We suggest doing all this internal work so that you can visualize an ideal scenario for the future. There need to be clear goals for growth on both personal and financial levels. Time spent internally addressing these issues will have a direct influence on the success of your efforts to feel financially secure.

When we know our personalities, we know our wounds. We then move on to establishing our goals with consistency, and this in turn inspires discipline and the willpower to succeed. If there is a widespread interest in socially responsible investing, it will carry over into the financial industries, creating new products and services. In the long run, your personal sense of satisfaction, self-worth, and self-esteem will be passed on to others in your family. Your efforts will not go unnoticed by your peers.

Clear long-term financial goals are important because of the high estate tax rate and the great need for charitable organizations to deal with the acute social problems that pervade our world. It is easy to feel that there is nothing that we can do, that we can have no effect on the world. This is wrong because each of us—and especially those with inherited assets— has a great opportunity to help others. Our decisions today will affect generations to come. The vehicles we have for accomplishing good are limited only by our imagination and creativity.

Our emotional goal, then, is to develop a sense of well-being for ourselves, our families, our friends, and our communities, and to make a contribution to society. All of this flows from knowing your financial self and being able to communicate that to your advisor. Assistance can be obtained in setting up achievable and measurable goals. We believe that what gets measured gets better. This is a painful process, but, as Coach Vince Lombardi once said, "No pain, no gain."

Opening the Door to Change

"Are we there yet?"

I n the previous chapter we talked about how our emotional attitudes about money influence various aspects of our internal life. This process then translates into our relationships outward from the self to eventually encompass the community at large. In this chapter, we will try to help inheritors go deeper into understanding the underlying causes of their attitudes about money. The authors believe that in order to know the roots of our financial self, it is necessary to experience firsthand the emotional aspect of our present selves. We can do this through various means. The means are only expedient methods to get in touch with who we are. This journey can be exciting and wonderful, but it also has moments of pain and discomfort.

Just as any new beginning starts with an ending, inheritors experience a sense of sadness when embarking upon this kind of internal journey. This is normal. In fact, the greater the anxiety, the more likely the experience will be deep upon starting these kinds of experiential processes. All the money in the world doesn't make a bit of a difference when you sit down to look inside yourself. After every Zen meditation retreat I experience, I think that the value of the retreat is priceless. Literally it would be useless to pay money to get the true value of looking deeply inside. On the other hand, the process sometimes can be so excruciatingly painful that no one would ever take all the money in the world to go through this kind of tortuous experience. How strange!

All cultures have traditions of royalty, and inheritors are America's closest thing to nobility along with inventors and media personalities. When wealthy heirs leave their homes, families, and comforts to go out to discover what they are made of, it is the modern equivalent of the hero's quest. The creature comforts and sense of physical identities that are built upon money makes leaving home all the more difficult. But this is an essential journey for adulthood, and one that most people are motivated to undertake at some point in their lives. Whether it is precipitated by a crisis in a relationship, by health problems, or by existential angst, most inheritors realize that they need to look within, and they look for an appropriate guide to point the way.

We will describe one particular journeying method here. The point is to help you, the inheritor, to learn what the steps are in knowing your financial self. The first part of this chapter describes the general philosophy and concepts behind the 21 phases of a self-discovery process. This helps to reduce nervousness about taking the first step. We like to have a road map before embarking on a journey. The map is not the journey; and our description is a poor substitute for the experience itself. There are many variations on the processes presented here, but all are meant to reestablish connection with our past, and to acknowledge the shadows that exist inside all of us. These repressed personality traits have a valid place in our pantheon of spirit. We must consciously deal with them in order to attain some present and future security and serenity.

The Journey Within

Once a decision to make the journey within has been made, we embark on it with faith that something good will come out of the process. It is normal to experience fear and anxiety about descending into our dark places. But we have a strong motivation, because something is amiss in our lives. So, with a spirit of quest, we set out.

1. *Intention.* First, we state our intention as broadly as possible. We are challenged to come up with a mission for our lives and for the journey we are about to take. It can be as simple as, "I want to be happy, I want to get well, I want to get married, I want to meet someone, I want to be successful, I don't want to be afraid of so-and-so," and so forth. Stating our intention clearly fixes a purpose in our mind, so that when the journey is under way we have a psychological base to return to when our energy wanes or our discursive and doubting mind tells us it was a mistake to take this path.

2. *Context.* A context must be set for the journey. This includes establishing a different set of rules than exists in our daily life. It may involve being silent; it definitely involves a break from the routines and expectations of our normal surroundings. Our cherished supports are taken away: no telephones, no television, and no reading. The focus on the journey is established. This allows the mind to settle, but it also presents people with unfamiliar challenges. Our minds tend to run amuck when faced with the prospect of looking inward, and especially so when our normal supports and distractions are gone.

3. *Container.* Establishing a container is essential for diving into the deep personal past. A container is a safe, confidential environment where we have the knowledge and mutual commitment from everyone present that they are there for the same purpose as we are. There are no judgments in containers; there is nothing that is embarrassing, and our hidden stories can be shared without fear that the information will be divulged elsewhere or used against us in the future. The container has certain rules, which vary from place to place, but confidentiality is the bedrock of all containers.

4. *Accountability.* A sense of order must be established for inner work to take place. Accountability and consequences for not abiding by the rules have to be made up front so that commitment to the group's integrity can be achieved. Journeying is a strange phenomenon: it is individual work, but it takes place more easily in a group context. There is a kind of multi-

plying factor of human energy when people's minds come together in the same place to focus on similar issues. Regardless of whether there is speech or interaction between participants, just being present with others who are doing similar work seems to help.

5. *Teamwork.* Establishing mentors gives a sense that we are not alone in the work and that there are people we can personally relate to, who have trod the same path on which we are traveling. In intimate sessions along our journey, bonding occurs. A sense of continuity for efforts after the initial journey is over can be established. Continuity is not normal in our culture. Few of us who have found our way to new places on the planet have much contact with our parents and grandparents, or are included in any tradition practiced by our ancestors. They lived lives marked by different values.

Establishing multigenerational teams during this journey gives a sense of rootedness, like a young tree growing in the shade of an older tree. We know that the older tree will eventually die and that we, as the young sapling, will have our turn in the sun, and then we too will eventually die. Teamwork across generations allows us to see that the same struggles of human life are being repeated over and over. We are reminded that our culture has ancient wisdom for these internal journeying processes.

6. *Diet.* Generally speaking, a change in diet helps us to refocus our energy, just as does a change of location, and different sets of stimuli. Fasting is not essential, but a reduction of as much as two-thirds in the amount of food we eat changes our attitude and makes our minds sharper, clearer, and more insightful. When we are freed from the stressful demands of daily life, our physical and psychological needs for food are reduced.

7. *Visioning.* The next step in the process is establishing our intention in a more concrete sense. Visioning is creating a picture of the kind of person that we would like to become. It involves our emotions and our finances, as they need to support our human purpose or mission in this life. Sharing our vision by giving it voice and through songs, dance, and pictures is important because this process solidifies and connects our internal sense with your body and makes visible the undetermined. There is a common element to visions among most people. Sharing our own first efforts may help others to clarify or inspire their thinking, just as our listening to others often sparks insights into our own situation.

8. *Testing.* Testing returns us to the value and importance of context and container. We are given a taste of what it is like to be the focus of the entire group. This is preparing us to take responsibility for making the most of the internal journey soon to come. Support is necessary. The rules for the work are described again on a more detailed scale. Accountability is the structure for the context; testing is the establishment of the ground rules for the specific psychological steps to be used in looking inside ourselves.

9. *Psychodrama.* Psychodrama is a term for manifesting in playlike form a dialog or dilemma that is going on inside one of us. Any parent can recall hearing his or her own parents' words and tone of voice when reacting instinctively when their children do something that bothers them. Such a historical response is embedded in our neuron networks. Our habitual responses, especially in crises, are ingrained in ourselves, and far deeper than we can ever consciously remember. The psychodrama is setting the stage and gathering costumes and scripts in order to reenact one or more scenes from our past that greatly impact our present state of being.

10. *Remembering.* We all have vague feelings about what might be going on inside our heart of hearts—about what is influencing how we feel at the moment. We might feel sad, anxious, nervous, tired, or bored. If we look at any one feeling and follow it intently without judging it, our own sensations will lead us into our deeper selves, into our past, where we have a large storehouse of connected, intertwined, and emotional feelings about life in general and about our childhood in particular.

11. *Connecting.* Connecting is the phase where we identify and link our present emotion with a specific scene or occurrence in the past, most often having to do with our original family. We see, perhaps, that our general anger at ourselves and others is really a reenactment of our parents' anger at us. Perhaps it is our very real disappointment that we were not given what we really wanted and needed (e.g., affection, attention, or encouragement) at a particular point in our development.

12. *Physicality.* Physicality is the ability to remember consciously and direct our coparticipants in this process to take actions and use words that actually evoke the specific feeling of this emotional event. We can set up our actors to say specific words that connect us with our childhood. Using nicknames and specific phrases that may have been used to torment us for years, we elicit the long-suppressed sensations of being constrained, over-

come, or trapped in an unsatisfactory world. We create this feeling physically, using various props and moving into action to raise our energy level.

Raising energy is the process whereby we put ourselves back into this past event or feeling through some kind of isometric or physical exertion. This is a contained struggle on a physical level that doesn't hurt our coparticipants in the psychodrama process. It allows us to enter into the tunnel of infantile emotions and feelings.

13. *Emoting.* Emoting is the stage when we have reached the bottom of our disappointment, anger, frustration, hurt, or need. We experience this as if again we were children. The subject and object of our scene then disappears. We are left by ourselves, realizing that this is only a small piece of emotional energy that was left behind when we instinctively learned to stifle our hurt in order to move and socialize in the world. Whatever the circumstance, to some extent we all have been trampled on, torn asunder, somehow violated, or not given our full due. By bringing this wonderful kernel of truth back to the light—by giving it its due now in ourselves as adults—we can see it for what it is. This is something to acknowledge, to accept, and go on looking at for the rest of our lives. We do not change the past or consciously change our behavior in the present. But we can become more perceptive about what our underlying issues really are, and this has a liberating effect on our ability to change the course of our life.

14. *Acknowledging What It Is.* We know that this uncovering of one underlying aspect of our personality is only a piece of our work. There are many more stories and emotions still to uncover—many pieces of unfinished emotional business inside of ourselves.

15. *Peace.* Peace or contentment comes from knowing that we have uncovered, if not resolved, a previously buried issue from our past. We know how strongly each piece of unfinished business affects our current personality and sense of happiness. Sometimes the peace lasts; often it doesn't. But each time we work, the integration of these previously repressed issues helps us to gain new clarity and self-confidence.

16. *Releasing.* There is a release of happiness and energy as a normal consequence of going through a process that is both physical and emotionally challenging. The courage it takes to look deeply and to allow ourself to fall into something that is frightening is rewarded by an upsurge of optimism and pride.

17. *Trusting.* Trust is established when we realize that everyone in the container has the same basic issues, even though the stories are totally different. We learn to trust ourselves and to know that if we give energy to internal knots, they release themselves and eventually have less power over our lives.

18. *Ceremony.* Ceremonies are appropriate and necessary to celebrate the efforts that have been made. Ceremony is also a connection with our ancestors and teachers from the past. We know that there have been countless others who went through the same process of unraveling knots and discovering wholeness through traditions of introspection.

19. *Establishing a Group.* A group is set up so that there is support and continuation of our efforts. This helps us keep the focus on emotions in the forefront of our minds, and not to allow them to fade again into the subconscious and unconscious habits of normal life.

20. *Cleansing.* Cleansing is the ceremonial acknowledgment that our intentions and efforts will go out into the world. We take comfort in our commitment to become better people.

21. *Commitment.* The commitment to continue working on these issues in the future is a necessary part of the process, so that the benefits of our efforts will not be lost. It is said that deep experiences are the electricity; continued group efforts are the wires; and the telephone pole that holds up the whole system is daily activity in the same mode.

We have given a brief overview of one process that affords people the opportunity to confront the silent and pernicious voices inside all of us that tell us we are not good enough. These shadow aspects of our personality, if left to fester in the dark, will continue to inhibit our progress toward becoming fully functioning people. Our normal way of acting gives no light to these shadows and so they unceasingly do their work by sapping our energy and self-confidence.

Many of these processes serve to acknowledge and allow these parts of ourselves to show our pent-up power. It is scary at first to see the depth and strength of our anger and hurt. These wounds created the shadows inside of us that are the missing part of our wholeness. These foreboding and unpleasant shadows hold the key to our being able to enjoy a balanced, healthy lifestyle.

Our purpose in introducing these matters to a book on family trust and taking control of inherited wealth is that delving into the depths of our personalities is crucial for both inheritors and their advisors. Then we can do the work of trust building on a firm foundation.

Emotional Choices

When inheritors and advisors go through these processes, we realize just how much our childhood wounds and the shadows they create influence our attitudes toward money. We then can take an inventory of our ability to deal with the challenges that money presents to us now as adults.

When it comes to money, there are a wide range of emotional attitudes and many ways in which we manifest our shadows. Perhaps we have seen a few of these during our experience of internal journeying. In the following paragraphs we present various attitudinal choices that are assumed by people who have been greatly influenced by difficulties experienced inside their family of origin. In many ways, these choices are not really conscious decisions, but inherited response mechanisms. These mechanisms get passed down from generation to generation, in reaction to some ancient deep wound that created in one or both of our caregivers' own families a habitual pattern of repression. We know that giving a name to vague, unsettling feelings somehow helps to make our shadows more clear. This is important if we are trying to change our basic attitudes about money and then communicate our desired state of being to our loved ones or trusted advisors.

1. *Guilt versus Generosity.* Our caregivers created guilt in us by linking their expectations about how we were to behave to giving us what we wanted—food, attention, touch. All of the necessary nurturing ingredients for healthy souls, such as love, affection, caring, and encouragement, were tied up with our performing certain actions or assuming certain attitudes that somehow fit in with their ideal view of how a baby or child should act. There are endless variations on the guilt theme. There is the debilitating "Let me do it for you," which implies that you can't do it yourself, which leads to self-doubt. There is the "You're no good at anything" attitude, which yields low self-esteem. Guilt comes from an attitude on the part of a caregiver that something is owed to him or her. This "something" is totally unrealistic, and we bear the immediate crushing brunt of their disappointment. We are made wrong, inadequate, a failure early on.

In financial terms, guilt is created when money and material goods are given only in exchange for something else. This makes love part of a marketplace.

Generosity is the free giving of material support, be it emotional or spiritual. Generosity has a spontaneous and flowing quality, so that support is made available *when* it is needed and *in the way* that it is needed, which varies for every situation. Generosity is the free sharing of what exists at the moment.

2. *Anxiety versus Calmness.* Anxiety is produced when we avoid reality. Life consists of change, and it is the greatest of all unknowns. As the poet Byron said, "Life is a mystery to be lived, not a problem to be solved!" Anxiety comes from feeling uneasy because we don't know the future. It is impossible to know, yet we feel that we must prepare for it in some way. Anxiety is amplified when the world is seen as a threatening place. Some people assume that the future will probably be worse than the present or past—a negative attitude that is destructive.

Being anxious about money is so prevalent that we can mistakenly regard it as a natural condition of humankind. Anxiety is produced when our sustenance is dependent on others, whose expectations of us are unclear or which can't be met for other reasons. Ignorance about money is another major contributor to anxiety. What we don't know hurts us in subtle ways.

Calmness is the trait that comes from knowing what you own, how long it will last, and what it can and can't do for you. Calmness is accepting situations that you find yourself in, and knowing that if actions are needed, an appropriate course will present itself. On a deep level, you believe that everything will work out in the greater scheme of things. You have a sense that adequate support exists in the universe for what needs to be done or left undone.

3. *Anger versus Articulateness.* Anger/rage is the natural venting of strong personalities against a feeling of wrongdoing. Our desire to be loved, accepted, appreciated, nurtured, and acknowledged is where we come from as human beings. When we do not receive these emotional supports early on from our family, or later from people with whom we interact, we instinctively lash out because what we need is not being given to us.

If we understand the nature of our wounds and are committed to looking at them and healing them through forgiveness and acceptance, we can be articulate rather than angry. When my actions make my wife angry, her challenge is to have the presence of mind to tell me that she is angry. I then try to remember to ask her to tell me clearly how my behavior is affecting her. This does not right the wrong I may have done, but it does make me aware of what the effects of my actions are. Most of what goes on between people is unknown because of the lack of articulation about what we are really trying to do. It turns out that mostly we just want to be heard, acknowledged, appreciated, involved, or understood. This is key in what we expect money to do for us and how we wish to live. If we want money to affect our relationships in a healthy way, we need to learn to be articulate about highly charged emotional situations.

4. *Depression versus Contentment.* Depression is a common ailment among people with inherited assets. We have discussed the difficulties that wealthy heirs experience in feeling valued and appreciated, and in having a strong sense of purpose in life. Most people's self-identity is tied up with making money. Depression may be a result of the physical environment of inheritors, because an early life of luxury leaves little to discover in the material world. It is difficult to become motivated unless you have a strong sense of goals. There is a prevalence of anorexia and bulimia among wealthy teenage girls and a preponderance of drug experimentation among wealthy teenage boys. The higher incidence of suicide among wealthy people lends credence to the position that extreme wealth can be a contributor to depression. Depression about money takes on various guises.

In our culture, people judge each other based on what they do, how much they earn, where they live, and what they wear. It is extremely difficult for people of wealth to have an identity of their own if their lives are entirely provided for by their families, partially as a result of this identity crisis. Many wealthy people find an interest in spiritual pursuits or the arts. On closer examination, they are rarely satisfied and often move from one exciting possibility to another without persevering long enough in any one effort to become proficient. This leads to depression.

Progress in spiritual and artistic traditions only comes after long training. Training involves discipline and patience, forbearance, and the ability to delay gratification. Growing up wealthy can easily preclude developing the mental muscle needed to bring forth these personal attributes. Philanthropy has therefore become a very important focal point of inheritors' energies, and for good reason. Private and public foundation work, volunteering in soup kitchens, and supporting animal shelters and environmental groups are all roles where work and identity can come together for inheritors, giving a sense of meaning or contentment with life.

5. *Burdens versus Blessings.* Money can be a burden, whether we feel that we have too little or too much of it. When we have more than we need, there is the psychological onus of trying to fit into a culture in which the self-made person gets all the respect. The complicated nature of financial decisions, including whom to trust, what to give away, and how to invest, can become a burden to people who take seriously their responsibility of handling inherited wealth. There are not many people with inherited wealth who can sit back and say, "Gosh, I am fortunate and will spend my life enjoying my luck." The sense that money is a blessing comes only after we have learned to feel good about ourselves and what we are doing in life to help other people, and when family relationships are healthy (or at least open, honest, and real). Many people with inherited wealth are like this, and they are a pleasure to learn from.

6. *Scarcity versus Abundance.* Scarcity is not a feeling that depends on how much money you have, but is a result of your attitude toward wealth. Many very wealthy people are constantly worried that they won't have enough for their old age, for contingencies, or for highly likely emergencies. There is a need for some people to have two or three times the funds they actually need, to allow for the anxiety that they will be forced to live in scarcity if a crisis occurs. There is an insatiable part of each us that always needs just a little more protection. This felt sensation is rooted deep in our animal brain. Part of our survival as a species was well served by looking ahead, anticipating a dearth of edible items for the next week, or being fearful about the presence of lethal enemies that might be around the next corner.

Wealth does have the potential for creating a sense of abundance to be shared with other people. It is difficult for people without money really to get the point that money does not buy happiness. At most, it buys freedom from the time pressures of making money. People with inherited assets can attest to this fact—that having more free time is great, but being able to fill it up with ego-enhancing, constructive, healthy activities is a much different matter. A sense of abundance comes when you are able to say, "Yes, I am satisfied that I have enough for myself and that there is more than enough so I can share with others." This is an extremely beneficial state of mind, and one that is sought after by many people who use abundance as a spiritual milestone in their efforts toward full maturity.

7. *Entitlements versus Deserving.* Entitlement is the sense that, by one's very existence, others should be and will be there to serve. This comes

from an extremely strong emphasis on material satiation as a substitute for emotional closeness early in life. When you have servants and are not required to do any work or suffer any discipline, you develop a sense of entitlement. This is especially sad to see in children, whose lives are destined to be filled with great disappointment. No matter what our monetary status is in life, other people will never treat us the way that we desire or demand.

Development of an appropriate use of resources, which we call deserving, is the ability to express our desires and to understand ahead of time that they will not be—and should not be—totally fulfilled. It is the ability to understand that we have to give up on some of our desires, to work and sacrifice in order to get closer to what we believe in, and then to be happy with whatever is received. In this way, people learn that the process of giving up what we want is very healthy and beneficial to our long-term happiness.

8. *Resource versus Behavior Tool.* When money is used as a direct reward or punishment for children's behavior, the results are not good. Many studies on child-rearing have shown that allowances are best used as a normal part of life, and that a child should receive a set amount of money just to learn how to handle money wisely. When the child's allowance is spent, there simply isn't any more, and he has to do without unless extra work is done, just like in the workplace. When the allowance is tied to performing certain chores around the house in direct exchange for money, it becomes a power struggle. When there is anger about unrelated matters, chores aren't done and a fight ensues—confusing and muddling the issue because money was used inappropriately as a behavioral tool.

When money is withheld as punishment, our sense of personal autonomy and self-identity is slowly worn down. If our sense of self-worth is tied up with what we have done in exchange for money, the focus turns to the end and not the means. We work and accept society's morass because we all have to work together. We have to make a contribution in order for our lives to be sustained. Money is a resource and can be used to instill a sense of order and solid values that are healthy. Child psychology is not far afield from investor psychology. The proper use of money as a resource to create productive and happy lives is the goal of good financial relationships. Money should neither be withheld nor lavished on children (or adults). Its place in our financial lives should not be over- or underemphasized. Healthy families and healthy financial relationships are an acknowledgment of this balance.

9. *Obsession versus Balance.* When there is an obsession with money, it means that we are out of balance. The primary goal of many financial relationships is to make as much money as possible. The authors do not believe this to be in accordance with a healthy lifestyle. We believe that the basic proper use of money is to provide for material sustenance and to be useful in the interchange of ideas and excitement. Most working people are trying to make as much money as possible, in order to "get away and relax." The absurdity of this is that it is impossible to get away from our pressured society or to escape from the need to achieve, which is still inside us once the money has been made. It is a false promise based on an inaccurate premise.

Achieving a sense of balance is one of the primary focuses of people with inherited assets. Children of monied environments will sometimes try to make more money than the family founder or take shelter in other pursuits that deal with the guilt of not having made money themselves. For beneficiaries with careers, there is a balance between their professional aspirations which builds confidence that they can handle money well, along with giving back to the larger community through artistic or charitable efforts.

10. *Miser versus Spendthrift.* Some people who make or inherit great wealth can be miserly. This is a reflection of a deep fear that they will never be provided for adequately. No amount of reasoning or knowledge overcomes this kind of pain. Misers are caught in a cycle of self-deprivation. Somehow, they got a message that they were not good enough, and that no one really cared enough about them to give the love that was sorely sought for at that early stage of development. The need was born to improve continually and protect one's self, a quest symbolized by gathering money.

Spendthrifts, on the other hand, are people who can't hold on to money. They choose to remain ignorant about the effect of spending on their family and heirs. Losing themselves in spending, they figure uneasily that somehow tomorrow will take care of itself. Spendthrifts are afraid to find out about their investments because they will see the effects of their profligation. Spendthrifts usually come from a family background where the subject of money was taboo, never to be discussed. We believe there is a great deal of underlying anxiety when spending is out of control. It undercuts people's enjoyment of their lives on a spiritual level.

11. *Boredom versus Passion.* Boredom comes from having too many good things too quickly. When children are given every new toy and go to

the most exciting places on earth, a blasé attitude naturally develops. If people are constantly catered to, and given the best of everything without an effort on their part, how can they discover their own talents and abilities? A passion for money is not the same as a passion for life. There are many well-known figures in our culture who have a passion for money: Bill Gates, Ivan Boesky, Ivana Trump. Many deal makers and public personalities have somehow acquired a passion for money in exchange for giving up their passion for life.

12. *Fear versus Security.* Fear of loss exists in everyone. We all fear the loss of familiarity, of security, of friends, of family members, and of course death. Fear is a response to the great unknowns of life. We tend to appreciate the small aspects of life to a far greater depth once we actually delve into our fear.

The fear of loss is one of the most common threads explored by people on their inner journeys. A sense of security is usually achieved when we touch a piece of the ancient truth that the less we are attached to, the greater our happiness. To feel secure in our constantly changing and aging bodies is possible. Security is a state of mind not quantifiable in terms of financial planning or investment management. A sense of security can be aided by money—and also be impeded by it. It's all a matter of attitude.

13. *Excessive Sense of Responsibility versus Spontaneity.* An excessive sense of responsibility is a trait shared by those of us who are obsessed with doing everything right. As children, we may never have been told that we were good enough or given unmitigated credit for our efforts. Our desire to be loved and accepted spurs us on to greater achievements in the external world, while our internal sense of self-worth lags. There is a loss of flexibility when we have a need to be focused in on a particular task, long after the point that is necessary to accomplish a basic goal.

Some older people feel a need to be responsible for accounting by hand for their securities that have now been placed in electronic form. They were responsible, at one time, for tracking minutiae, and this may well have helped to make them successful. This is a manifestation of a desire to have a sense of self-worth, of purpose, of responsibility. We all need to be needed, but the issue is how much is enough and where are our efforts best directed.

Spontaneity is a trait enjoyed by few people, though some wealthy people have a pattern of deciding on the spur of the moment to go to Bali, or to Nova Scotia to see a total eclipse of the sun. Spontaneity can be a mask for narcissism, an avoidance of responsibility. It is not necessarily a sign of true enjoyment of your inherited assets. Spontaneity can take the form not of spending money, but of giving of your time and efforts to family, friends, animals, or the arts. Helping others as the need arises is one of the signs of true spontaneity, and the rewards of this state of mind and heart in quality of life are numerous.

14. *Competitiveness versus Self-Defined Boundaries.* Competition is rampant in our society. It is the accepted mode of behavior in sports and business. It is difficult to say that this is destructive, because some forms of competition are healthy, fun, and nondestructive.

Competitiveness for attention within families sometimes transforms itself into a need to achieve a higher level of income than is actually necessary for happiness. We all mentally compare ourselves to our peers, friends, neighbors, college roommates, or acquaintances. We instinctively evaluate our position in society to decide, in our own minds, whether we are better off or worse off than the people we meet. The fact is that everyone's internal personal and emotional lives are totally different. We really can have no idea what other people are experiencing in their own lives, but we tend to be competitive and judgmental toward ourselves. We evaluate our achievements on a social or material basis relative to others.

The ability to create our own boundaries and criteria based on nonmaterial status only comes after long periods of introspection. It is necessary to know our financial and emotional self, as well as ourself in relation to others, in order to establish boundaries that are healthy and that contribute to our happiness. Relatively few people have succeeded in matching their words with their performance, and in living up to their self-created ideals for setting boundaries, so that a balanced lifestyle is achieved. Why? We have much information and knowledge about the workings of the world— but little to go by in looking into our own minds as we investigate the interaction between money and spirit. People have a difficult time focusing on this issue. It underlies many of the emotional factors that quickly come to the surface in our everyday lives.

Untying the Knot

We have defined some of the attributes surrounding our emotional attitudes toward money. Hopefully, these brief descriptions have given you a sense of the ways that our characters are formed by the choices we make in how to adapt to the stresses of our upbringing. The issue now becomes how to change these attitudes, if doing so is one of our goals. Inherited wealth makes the process of change both easier and more difficult. It's easier because we can cordon off blocks of time to devote to this effort. On the other hand, as Tevya says in *Fiddler on the Roof,* having a great deal of family money usually means that we are not used to taking on difficult tasks.

Once we have uncovered and acknowledged our emotional heritage, born from our family circumstances, we want to know exactly how we can attain our goals for the development of our whole selves. The more understanding we have about the sources of our feelings about money, the less power our shadows will have indicating to us our future relationships. As long as our knots remain hidden in our subconscious selves, they will bind us to the habits of our past. If we can just bring these things up to our consciousness, our creative spirit and guidance mechanisms will help us in mysterious ways. As we become open to change, change happens to us. People appear to help us along our way.

In examining our lives, we find that we have reacted to the stresses of our childhood in different ways than our siblings did. We each have at hand certain tasks. Some of these involve money. We have to come to some kind of peace of mind concerning our values about money through working out these issues. Our spouses and partners are also drawn into this vortex of emotions.

When we analyze our upbringing around issues, we can have both a sense of gratitude and of dismay. We either received too much attention or too little, or we had too much money or not enough. Perhaps our parents educated us adequately about money, or perhaps they didn't. No parent is perfect, and the emotional scars from our childhood are unique, and to that we add differences in temperament. Brothers and sisters from the same family of origin can have vastly different attitudes about money. One sibling may have absorbed the mind-set of the mother, and another may have been more influenced by the father. The order of birth in a family is another important factor in how we are treated, both in emotional and monetary terms. Often the youngest gets spoiled while the oldest has had to do without, because the parents did not know how long their money would last and did not anticipate having a higher standard of living as they grew older.

Our culture exerts enormous influence on our attitudes about money. World War II–era parents were influenced by books that taught "proper" child raising procedures. These people split off from their own parents, the trust originators, and moved to the suburbs or across the country. The post–World War II modality was an emphasis on material goods versus spiritual pursuits, which had an enormous effect upon how baby boomers were raised, who in turn rebelled as young adults before becoming parents themselves.

Different kinds of expressions show how our attitudes have changed about money. The baby boomer generation that will inherit and then control the greatest amount of dispersed wealth in history has much different cultural morals than did their parents. Money still defines our identity, but less so now than before. We may have many interests, but the common denominator and common bond through which most people interact is money.

Our culture is built around media images of success. In a rather cruel way, our attitudes about money are influenced by commercial presentations of the world. The culture has fragmented into so many pieces that for any particular knot we may have there is a self-help movement, audiovisual cassette course of study, or expert healer available, for a price, to fix the malady. We live in an incredible time and have vast resources at our disposal. Still, when it comes to money, untying the knots of our emotional legacy requires constant awareness.

Conclusion

We have to make choices about the course of our personal lives. We know that we have the ability to change our attitudes toward inherited assets and opportunities to garner technical and emotional skills to let us become whatever we want to become. The choices available for people with inherited wealth and their advisors can be overwhelming. With the opportunities come the dangers of being spread too thin, and of not being able to focus on an appropriate lifestyle. Where do our financial assets and advisors fit into this picture? The next chapter is about using your discoveries about your true financial self to uncover the underlying truth of your current financial relationships.

CHAPTER

23

If It's Working . . .

Previous chapters have discussed how to discover and articulate who we are and what we want, both as inheritors and as trusted advisors. This chapter should help inheritors to determine if they will be able to get what they need from their current advisors.

The first step in this process is to define your needs on an emotional level, and then on a performance basis. Changing advisors is emotionally difficult and often is expensive, so most advisors are retained for at least several years. Changing course in midstream can be destructive to your assets, and so may be considered one of the cardinal sins in financial life. It is definitely worth the effort to go through the process of defining your needs and articulating them to your advisor. You will then be clear as to whether you are satisfied with the current situation, on both intellectual and gut levels.

Now is the time to know how to ask for what you need. We establish firm criteria at the beginning, so that later we can determine if we have actually received what we've asked for and if it is working for us. If not, is incremental change with our current advisor enough, or do we need to change to another, more suitably matched advisor?

Choosing an Advisor: The Emotional Connection

There are so many facets to our financial life that making a list of the important issues often helps to clarify them. In choosing an advisor, we recommend going into detail because this is an area where your preferences should be the guiding force. It is important to be able to justify to yourself the basis on which you can make your decision.

Fill in the lines that most appropriately describe your desired advisor:

1. Age

   20 to 30 _____   50+ _____

   30 to 40 _____   60+ _____

   40 to 50 _____   ANY _____

2. Gender

   Female _____   Male _____   Either _____

3. Location

   Within a 10-minute drive _____

   30-minute drive _____

   60-minute drive _____

   2-hour drive _____

   Doesn't matter _____

4. Size of firm

   Small (3 employees or less)

   Medium (4 to 20 employees)

   Large (20 to 100 employees)

   Institutional (over 100 employees)

   Doesn't matter

5. Accessibility of trusted advisor

   Is he or she available by phone when you call? _____

      Is this acceptable?

   How long does it take to set up a personal meeting? _____

      Is this acceptable?

6. Firm's Reputation
   List three people you know who would have recommended this firm to you

   Would you be willing to recommend this firm to someone else? _____

   Without hesitation? _____

7. Advisor's Ability to communicate
   Have you set goals with your advisor? _____
   Have you revised these goals, at least annually? _____
   Do you understand these goals well enough to explain them to someone else? _____

8. Advisor's Responsiveness
   Does the advisor call you back within 24 hours of your calls? _____
   Does the advisor write to inform you of changes in the firm's personnel outlook? _____

9. Accuracy
   Are the firm's returns consistent with the market? _____
   Are the firm's backup statements shown to you regularly? _____

10. Advisor's Philosophy
    Is it too conservative for your tastes? _____
    Is it too aggressive for your tastes? _____

11. Values
    How much do you want of each of the following? If it doesn't matter, leave blank. If it does, put in percentages so the total equals 100.
    Value investments _____
    Income investments _____
    Market timing _____
    Sector selection _____
    High yield investments _____
    Individual stocks _____
    Mutual funds _____
    New stocks _____

Now that you have some reactions to the business style of your advisor, let's look at the personality match. To evaluate whether you, your spouse, and eventually your children will get along with the advisor, answer the following questions:

1. Could you go out to dinner with your advisor and enjoy yourself?

    Y   N   N/A

2. If you and your advisor went on a picnic with children or senior citizens, would the advisor be comfortable in conversing with everybody?

    Y   N   N/A

3. Could you and your family go on a week's vacation with your advisor?

    Y   N   N/A

4. Does your advisor converse with you in language that you can understand?

    Y   N   N/A

5. Are your advisor's interests at all similar to yours?

    Y   N   N/A

6. Does your advisor know about your interests?

    Y   N   N/A

7. Does your advisor ask about your values and goals in life?

    Y   N   N/A

8. Does your advisor's body language project caring messages?

    Y   N   N/A

9. What do you like about the advisor?

10. What do you like about the advisor's staff?

11. What puts you off about the advisor?

12. What puts you off about the advisor's staff?

13. Have you ever discussed uncomfortable subjects with the advisor's staff?

        Y   N   N/A

14. If so, was the staff open and honest in response to your issues?

        Y   N   N/A

15. Is the staff willing to help you when you need it?

        Y   N   N/A

16. Do the staff members extend themselves personally to accommodate your needs?

        Y   N   N/A

Three objective criteria to use when considering advisors are their length of time in the business, their reputation in the community, and their long-term track record. There are many new advisors, and it is difficult to ascertain from resumes or marketing materials how much actual experience someone has in delivering trust services. Be wary of advisors who recently entered from other fields, as well as of those who have been in the field for 30 years and still hold the same stocks they held a decade ago. Both warning signs suggest that these people do not have adequate resources to deal with the demands of today's financial world. Look at a ten-year history of investment performance. Is it easily available and understandable?

Performance

One of the main objective criteria in addition to an advisor's length of time in business and reputation in the community is an audited track record of performance. Your advisor should have available at least a 10-year track record of her account returns, broken down by asset classes versus relevant indexes. We covered this earlier as a requirement of the current trustee. Here, we reiterate that unless you know how well an advisor does with investments over a long period of time in comparison with standard benchmarks, you can't know how well she has performed. In terms of service, you must have a strong sense that the advisor delivers on all promises that she has made. The questionnaires we have provided should help you think about and remember if she follows through in consistent, detailed, and accurate ways. This is one main way to determine if your current financial advisor is a fit with you.

An old maxim for businesspeople used to be, "don't discuss religion, politics, or sex." In our highly segmented culture, decisions to establish or keep relationships based on similarities of viewpoints regarding religion, politics, or sex generally do not work out to have monetary correlations, but these shared connections do add an element of comfort for most people. Do you feel that your advisor's lifestyle and concerns are similar to your own? Look at the following facets of his or her business:

What kind of dress code is there in the office?

Does it seem appropriate?

Is the office furniture too ostentatious for your tastes? Too austere?

What kind of art is on the walls? Are these original artworks or posters?

Is easy-listening music piped into the office? On the telephone waiting queue?

Does the advisor's firm have a distinct personality?

What kind of hospitality is extended when you enter the office? Are you offered drinks? Is there a place to sit? What kinds of magazines are on the table?

Is the advisor promoting himself on the premises or are there items of general interest?

From these subtle aspects, you can assess the degree of functionality of the advisor's firm. You are engaging an entire organization, so the more cognizant and clear you are about these intangibles, the better fit there will be if you choose to stay. On an interactive basis, ask the following questions:

How much contact does the chief decision maker have with your account?

How accessible is the decision maker regarding big questions?

Is the decision maker available to explain reports?

Is enough talent and expertise available in the firm to answer most of your administrative questions without bothering the trusted advisor?

Does the trusted advisor do his or her own research?

Do you have a sense of confidence in the administrative people who will be doing most of the work on your account?

Is their attitude positive and upbeat?

Do they talk in an understandable language?

Do the employees seem to be treated well?

Is there time and opportunity for education and advancement of bright people within the firm?

Are Your Needs Being Met?

In reviewing your trusted advisor's past performance, has he been willing to go the extra mile when you need help the most? Is he available on weekends, nights, or vacations if you ask him to meet with you? This is not to disrespect the advisor's boundaries, but in a crisis, would he be there? How do your advisor and his staff act under stress? If you came in on the last day of tax season or when the market is crashing, how would you be treated? Does your advisor, if you call and ask for him personally, return your calls even when he is traveling? Does your advisor have a sense of humor? Does he seem to be well adjusted to this kind of work for the long run?

Is your trusted advisor/financial advisor distracted when you see him? Does he seem chronically tired or overworked? Is he vacationing more than you? Is the advisor's firm growing too fast? Do you recognize any people in the firm from your last visit, or has everyone changed? Is a special effort made to introduce you to new people? Have you established rapport with several people in the firm so that you have personal contact at all times?

What kind of report card would you give your advisor in describing the performance level of your account over the last year or several years? Has your advisor approached you in a consistent fashion to determine whether your life circumstances have changed? Are the reports that she sends you informative and easily digested? Do they contain too much or too little detail? Does your advisor have knowledge about your other family members' circumstances? Is she keeping abreast of changes in your personal goals?

We were embarrassed once when a longtime client came in eight months pregnant and we didn't even know she was expecting! We had called her three times to try to stay in touch, but this person was ashamed of the fact that she had been taking far more money out of her account than was required for her budgeted needs. It turned out that her persuasive spouse was withdrawing funds so that he could speculate on hot stocks and real estate ventures; he had convinced her to spend her inheritance on his business ideas. This lack of communication with our client had allowed her husband to jeopardize her financial health seriously.

The authors feel that it is vital that a trust advisor be able to acknowledge an inheritor's feelings in an active way. This involves listening to and encouraging any expression of an heir's position and questions on any aspect of the financial relationship. Does your advisor solicit *your* feelings about what goes on in your account? Does he take time to disclose his own feelings, uncertainties, and doubts? This is a difficult area, but no one is omnipotent, and if no caveats are expressed about the vicissitudes of financial life, then beware!

What kind of service environment is right for you? If it were your health that was of concern, would you prefer the old-fashioned general practitioner who makes house calls, or the most high-tech, narrow specialist who has no "bedside manners" and to whom you have extremely limited access? Most of the time, for nonlethal ailments, you would prefer the old-fashioned approach—but there may be times when a specialist's knowledge is called for. Similarly, if your financial situation is precarious and in need of a specific remedy, a financial specialist may well be necessary for a short time. Financial maladies build up slowly, and are likely to improve only over several years.

Most advisors' philosophies slowly change, if they are thinking, learning, and becoming better at what they do. Some advisors develop a formula and put everyone's money into the same model. This is likely if all you receive are form letters regarding the investments that are held by all clients of the firm. Is this adequate for you, or do you need a customized portfolio? Has your advisor ever discussed with you the pros and cons of the investment options available to you—especially the ones that he does not follow? Has he owned up to his mistakes? Has he admitted to the bad things that have happened and shown you what he is doing now to prevent a recurrence of the errors?

Everyone makes mistakes. There is a real difference in personal character and integrity between people who can disclose their mistakes and those who never admit their errors. If an advisor admits to a mistake and offers to pay for it, she has honor. Has your advisor ever done this?

Relationship Vision

What criteria will allow you to know whether your relationship with your trusted advisor is moving in the right direction, toward where you want it to be in the future? Ask your advisor about his business plan for the next five years. Will he discuss it freely with you? It is important for an advisor to have a plan, to know how much growth is good, and how much time and energy and skill will be needed to keep the level of service extremely high. How will the personnel in his firm be developed, and what additional people will be hired? Ask your advisor to discuss his strategic business mistakes, why he made them, and what he has learned from them. All of this will give you a chance to see the human character of the advisor. Watch how he deals with your account and how your account fits in with his long-term business plans. In other words, how important are you to his future?

Does your advisor reinvest her own money into the business? Is there constant investment in new technology, new people, and in the education of current staff members?

Conclusion

Finally, ask your advisor how she spends her day-to-day time. Does she know, or is it a blur? Does she focus on new-business development, on the administration of the firm, on research, or networking? Does it seem that the advisor has balance in her life? Because after all, this is the quality you are looking for as an inheritor. If the advisor cannot model what you are looking for, how will she know how to help you find it?

The key to any great professional relationship is to know exactly what you want, and where to find it. Don't be afraid to ask your advisor anything you need to know. The most important thing here is to get to know her as a person. Afterward, take some time to ask yourself if you could be happy working with her. Does she have values similar to yours? Could you see her taking care of your financial needs? Can she make you happy? If so, try her out.

Keys to the Future

I n this final chapter, we hope to provide the person of inherited wealth with a map to find the right trustworthy advisor. The seasoned investment professional should be prepared to meet all reasonable expectations covered in this recommended interview and analysis process. We have had experience as individual trustees, corporate trustees, and (most of all) as agents for beneficiaries and their advisors. Finding and maintaining a healthy advisory relationship is possible and can even be interesting and fun. Remember to take your time, and don't be in a hurry just to get it over with. We will review the following aspects of the selection process:

- How to find potential "suitors" and sources

- What questions to ask—data gathering

- How to interpret your written, spoken, visual, and nonverbal impressions gathered from the interview

- Processing the information to turn yourself into a knowledgeable client

- How to articulate your needs to the potential trusted advisor and to reach agreement on service commitments and fees

- Making decisions—choosing with wisdom

Word of Mouth: Finding "Suitors"

Finding potential trustworthy advisors takes the same kind of effort as any-thing else important in your personal life. If you have looked for a mar-riage counselor, a tutor for your children, or a caregiver for your elderly parents, the steps to locate a trusted financial advisor are quite similar. In real estate, people say that picking the right piece of property depends on three things: location, location, and location. We feel that there are three important ways to find an advisor: First, ask someone you know; then ask another person you trust; and finally, ask a third person whose opinion you respect. Consult people with proven business acumen and insight. Find people who have worked with advisors themselves. Inquire as to the length of their relationships with their advisors, because you need an advisor who has been established for a considerable amount of time. The last kind of advisor that you want is a newcomer to the business.

The authors believe that you should look at advisors of different ages and with various interests. On the investment side, find someone who has been through several down markets, so that he or she will have developed the expertise and strategies needed to provide trust services in all kinds of eco-nomic conditions. Wait until a potential advisor's name comes up more than once. Some ineffective ways to find advisors are to go to free seminars or respond to advertisements in financial magazines. The best seasoned investment professionals don't need to advertise and don't want a torrent of public attention. Great advisors will come to your attention through word of mouth because of the high quality of their service and consistent investment performance. The people who tend to advertise are those looking to grow quickly without much regard to the appropriateness of the match between themselves and clients. Many firms want rapid growth and do not screen their clients for compatibility. They take on new employees and clients too quickly, and the quality of their service trends downward as the firm's growth is pushed upward. "Those who know, do not say, and those who say, do not know," is translated to "those who are great do not publicly broadcast their talents, and those who do use public means are not so great."

The Interview: Gathering Data

Once you have gathered names from reputable sources, you will want to arrange a personal visit with the advisor. The following questionnaire can be used when interviewing prospective trust advisors. Some questions may be more relevant to your situations than others, but all of them can be used. These questions are ones that advisors need to be prepared to answer:

About Your Firm?

- When did your firm start?
- How many clients does your firm serve?
- What is the average length of your client relationships?
- How many employees do you have?
- How long have they been with your firm?
- Where did they come from?
- How many have five or more years in the advisory business?
- How many professionals are there?
- What is the optimum number of employees for your firm now?
- How do you assign clients to professionals?
- How many clients are assigned to each professional? Why?
- What assurance is there for continuity in case a professional contact person leaves the firm?
- What succession plan do you have in place for the firm if something happens to the principals?
- What are your plans for the growth of your business over the next five years?
- How many employees will you need then?
- At what point will you close the door on growth?
- How will you ensure that I get top-quality service during this growth?
- What is the performance of your firm versus relevant indexes?
- Do you have an easy-to-read written explanation of how your returns are calculated?
- How many years have you been in the financial service industry?
- How many years have you been in this specific part of the business, (i e, being a financial advisor)?
- How many years have you been responsible for making financial investment decisions?

- What is your particular area of expertise in the market?

- What are the true after-tax returns to clients relative to the performance information being shown?

- By what means will you be contacting me?

- How often do you contact your clients?

- By what method will you communicate changes in my portfolio?

- Do you solicit input from your clients on changes in their personal lives that might affect the portfolio? How?

- What are the downsides to your particular approach to investing?

- What are your personal shortcomings on a technical side?

- How about on a personal level?

- What problems do you experience with clients due to poor communication?

- What are you doing to overcome these obstacles?

- What are your firm's weaknesses?

- How do you make up for these weaknesses?

Fees

- What kind of charges will be levied on my account?

- Are discounts available? What criteria are they based on?

- Are discounts available for my inherited stock? If it would create a big tax bill, are they to be sold and therefore they don't require the same level of management?

- What kind of consulting charges, if any, apply?

- Are there any set-up or termination charges?

- Are there any extra fees whatsoever?

- What is the average annual cost for trading in the account?

- What is the percent of the account that will change in an average year?

- What is included in the basic charge?

- Is financial planning included?

- Is tax analysis or insurance analysis included?

- If I want to negotiate on a house purchase or make other large financial transactions, are you available to help? Is there any extra charge for this help?

- Will I be talking with you, or will my account be assigned to someone else in the firm?

Other Questions

- How does the advisor make investment decisions?

- What do advisors do about their bad decisions?

- How do they communicate bad news to clients?

- What bad investment decisions have been made recently?

- What effect has it had on clients?

- Has the advisor been audited recently?

- What are the results of the examination made by the regulatory authorities?

- Can I see the audit report?

- How many clients have left their advisors during the last year? During the last three years? Why did they leave?

- Is the advisor forthcoming on the reasons? Are the reasons plausible?

Interpreting Your Impression

You have gathered much data during your interview. Now, you must take some of the responses to your questions and make sense of them. We have discussed the longevity and reputation of the firm. Chances are that you will not deal with the chief investment officer but rather with a midlevel person. What is your sense of her match with you? Is she the kind of person you will enjoy dealing with 90% of the time?

In the advisor's responses to your questions, was there any testiness in her tone of voice? This is your first opportunity for assessing how patient and plainspoken your advisor might be if you engage her. Was she able to produce the information on the portfolio's performance, trading costs, and after-tax returns in written form, or was it pulled out of the air in a generalized statement? This will show her degree of technical expertise in tracking investment returns.

When inquiring about the firm's goals, determine whether it has a written plan in place. Are its promises backed up by quantifiable measurements created to gauge whether client service quality is being maintained? What kind of questionnaires about your personal views and overall financial situation were given to you? These will be representative of how well the advisor can think from your point of view. If you are given many forms to fill in (homework so to speak), does this mean that the responsibility to gather information and spend time on your affairs at home is an expected part of the relationship?

Does the advisor seem flexible on fees? How about her format for reporting to you? Is she able to look at and spend time with you on many different issues, or did it seem that she only wanted your money to invest, or that a certain canned approach with set parameters was presented to you?

Finally, how honest and forthright was the advisor about her past mistakes, audit results, and explanations of why some of her former clients have left? Honesty and openness are the keys, and saying at least some noncomplimentary things about oneself is a good sign.

Following Up: Processing Information into Knowledge

Your visit to the advisor's office can provide you with a wealth of information. Recall the attitude of the people working there. Were they chatting, or working hard? Did they look up and greet you in a friendly way, or did they seem harried and hassled? We look at advisor workplaces in the same way that we look at a car repair shop. How clean is it? Is it neat, orderly, and organized? Is the pace hectic, or is the workload under control? All of these things contribute to the quality of the work that will be done on your behalf. During the interview, ask the advisor for other client names as well as professional references in the community. Ideally you will find someone you know personally who can give you feedback concerning the advisor. This is the reverse process of asking friends or people whose business acumen you trust to give you potential advisors' names. Find someone whom you can talk to "off the record" about the advisor, so that informal information can surface.

During the interview, ask the advisor for some specific recommendations for you—something particular to your personal situation. See if he is willing to prove himself in terms of the quality of the service, and test his technical expertise. This should not cost you anything. It will also give you a chance to determine whether the advisor satisfactorily follows up on promises made in the initial interview.

Articulating Service Commitments and Fee Agreements

Let's figure that you are now satisfied that this "partner" and you could work together. The next phase is yet another test of the advisor's compatibility and suitability for you. In the follow-up on promises made during the interview, you should have received a taste of his commitment to follow up. Ask now for a written plan of action, with timetables and criteria, that will be used to see if the advisor is accomplishing his goals. The benefits of using his service should be formatted into contract schedules, projected income levels, reporting desires, and communication points that all keep you informed as to how things are proceeding. In your inquiries, if appropriate, ask for a fee discount on inherited assets that will most likely not be sold except in extenuating circumstances. If the advisor refuses, it indicates a closed mind and rigid management style. Ask for a long-term written agreement that says that fees will not be raised at all or will be raised only by a small percentage after considerable time. Remember, you are now responsible for your family's wealth and the advisor will have a major impact on your financial future.

Negotiation on fees is an accepted part of the trust business. Look ahead and anticipate changes in your family's composition and needs. Likewise, the advisory firm may go through various permutations. You have a right to ask it to anticipate these changes and assure you that the agreement now being made is as good and fair as possible. This is where honor and integrity will become evident.

Making Decisions: Choosing with Wisdom

You have concluded your negotiations, and the agreements are in place. Your advisor and her staff are enthusiastic, helpful, knowledgeable, providing you with the exciting possibility that one of your life's great burdens—doubt about making the right financial moves—is about to be shared with someone who seems to fill the bill for you. In this final phase, which we compare to a honeymoon, keep a close eye on your emotional reaction to giving up control. Trusting your advisor has everything to do with trusting yourself. You should meet frequently during the first year. Try to speak on the telephone with the advisor at least biweekly for the first three months. Is your advisor carrying the burden of making contact with you, going over every unplanned item that may have come up? There are always complications and delays, especially when it comes to moving money and implementing a new, more productive regime. Your advisor should be anticipating your questions and concerns. She should be taking care of your assets as if you were a member of the family, which in a sense you are. Is there a deep feeling of satisfaction within you? Can you release some of the anxiety you have carried around regarding money and the place it has in your life? If so, then you have made a wise decision. Although life is full of risk, you have a reliable guide in your inner voice.

Conclusion

The importance of a good match between you and your advisor cannot be overemphasized. You should and will have gut feelings about these people, who will be an important part of your family's financial life and peace of mind. More often than not, your first impression will be accurate, but we do change over time. A proven investment and service record needs to be present. Your feelings of trust and the combination of communication, a commitment to personal service, and proof of performance should be sufficient for you to make a wise decision. We recommend that all seasoned investment professionals consider their current clientele. Life is too short for any of us to have a poor marriage present in our financial lives. Sometimes, with work, our partnerships can come alive again, or we gain the courage to move on and begin anew. So it is with gaining control over family trusts. We believe that you will find it rewarding to give it a chance.

Appendix

The charts (A1–A8) on the following pages should help beneficiaries, advisors, and trustees. Beneficiaries and advisors can use them to evaluate the performance of their trustees. Trustees, in turn, may want to review them as they evaluate their own business practices.

The following charts are provided courtesy of Heirs®, Inc., a nonprofit organization that offers practical advice to dissatisfied beneficiaries of irrevocable trusts. Heirs® advises trust creators who want to be sure that the needs of their beneficiaries are well served, especially when the trustee will be a bank. Heirs® publishes the *Heirs® Personal Trust Handbook* and a newsletter called *Fiduciary Fun*. For more information, contact Standish H. Smith at P.O. Box 292, Villanova, PA 19085, (610) 527-6260.

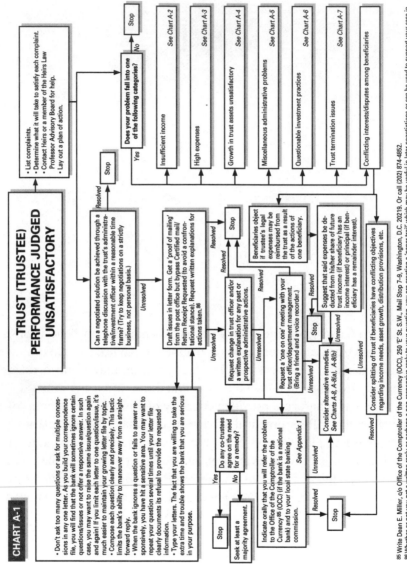

CHART A-1

TRUST (TRUSTEE) PERFORMANCE JUDGED UNSATISFACTORY

- List complaints.
- Determine what it will take to satisfy each complaint.
- Contact Heirs or a member of the Heirs Law Professor Advisory Board for help.
- Lay out a plan of action.

Does your problem fall into one of the following categories?

No → Stop

Yes ↓

- Insufficient income — *See Chart A-2*
- High expenses — *See Chart A-3*
- Growth in trust assets unsatisfactory — *See Chart A-4*
- Miscellaneous administrative problems — *See Chart A-5*
- Questionable investment practices — *See Chart A-6*
- Trust termination issues — *See Chart A-7*
- Conflicting interests/disputes among beneficiaries

Can a negotiated solution be achieved through a telephone discussion with the trust's administrative/investment officer within a reasonable time frame? (Try to keep negotiations on a strictly business, not personal basis.)

Resolved → Stop

Unresolved ↓

Draft issues in letter form. Get a 'proof of mailing' from the post office but bypass Certified mail/ Return Receipt Requested (to avoid a confrontational stance). Request written explanations for actions taken.[86]

Resolved → Stop

Unresolved ↓

Request change in trust officer and/or a written explanation for any past or prospective administrative actions.

Resolved →

Unresolved ↓

Request a 'one on one' meeting with your trust officer/department management. (Bring a friend and a voice recorder.)

Resolved → Stop

Unresolved ↓

Beneficiaries object if trustee's legal expenses may be reimbursed from the trust as a result of the actions of one beneficiary.

Resolved → Stop

Unresolved ↓

Suggest that said expenses be deducted from his/her share of future trust income (if beneficiary has an income interest) or principal (if beneficiary has a remainder interest).

Consider splitting of trust if beneficiaries have conflicting objectives regarding income needs, asset growth, distribution provisions, etc.

Consider alternative remedies.
See Charts A-8, A-8(a), A-8(b)

Unresolved ↓

Do any co-trustees agree on the need for a remedy?

Yes → Stop

No ↓

Seek at least a majority agreement.

Indicate orally that you will refer the problem to the Office of the Comptroller of the Currency[85] (OCC) (if the bank is a national bank) and to your local state banking commission.
See Appendix 1

Resolved → Stop

Unresolved ↓

Consider alternative remedies.
See Charts A-8, A-8(a), A-8(b)

- Don't ask too many questions or ask for multiple concessions in any one letter. As you build your correspondence file, you will find that the bank will sometimes ignore certain questions/issues or not offer a responsive answer. In such case, you may want to raise the same issue/question again and again! If you limit each letter to one question/issue, it's much easier to maintain your growing letter file by topic.
- Compose each question clearly and precisely. This tactic limits the bank's ability to maneuver away from a straightforward reply.
- When the bank ignores a question or fails to answer responsively, you have hit a sensitive area. You may want to repeat your question several times until your letter file clearly documents its refusal to provide the requested information.
- Type your letters. The fact that you are willing to take the extra time and trouble shows the bank that you are serious in your purpose.

[85] Write Dean E. Miller, c/o Office of the Comptroller of the Currency (OCC), 250 'E' St. S.W., Mail Stop 7–9, Washington, D.C. 20219. Or call (202) 874-4852.

[86] Whether or not you get a written reply or perhaps a non-responsive reply to your question, you are creating a 'paper trail' which may be useful in later negotiations or can be used to support your case in court should you elect to litigate.

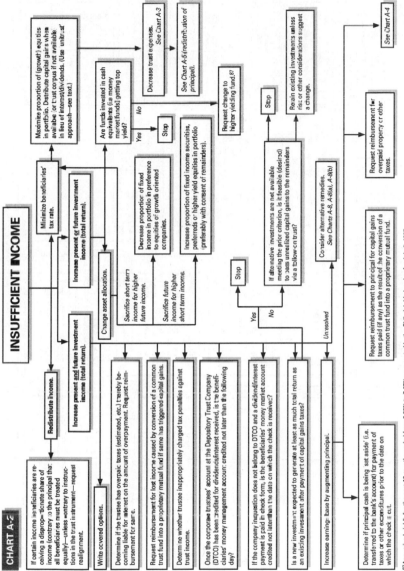

CHART A-2

INSUFFICIENT INCOME

87 Annualized yields for the past 12 months varied from 2.83% to 5.67% as reported in the *Philadelphia Inquirer* for July 3, 1997.

347

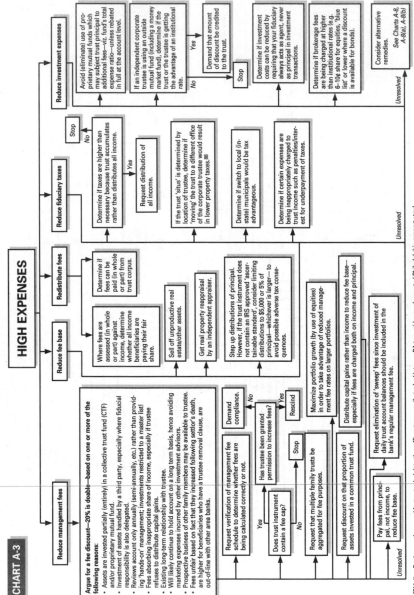

CHART A-3

HIGH EXPENSES

Reduce management fees

Argue for a fee discount—20% is doable—based on one or more of the following reasons:

• Assets are invested partially (entirely) in a collective trust fund (CTF) and/or proprietary mutual fund.
• Investment of assets handled by a third party, especially where fiducial responsibility is also delegated.
• Reviews account only annually (semi-annually, etc.) rather than providing 'hands-on' management; investments restricted to a master list!
• Fees absorbing inappropriate share of income, especially if trustee refuses to distribute capital gains.
• Existing long-term relationship with trustee.
• Will likely continue to hold account on a long term basis, hence avoiding marketing expenses incurred by other investment advisors.
• Prospective business of other family members may be available to trustee.
• Fees unfair based on fact that they increased following settlor's death, are higher for beneficiaries who have a trustee removal clause, are out-of-line with other area banks.

Request verification of management fee schedule to determine whether fees are being calculated correctly or not.

Does trust instrument contain a fee cap? → *No* → Stop

Yes ↓

Has trustee been granted permission to increase fees? → *No* → Demand compliance.

Yes → Rescind

Request that multiple family trusts be aggregated for fee purposes.

Request discount on that proportion of assets invested in a common trust fund.

Request elimination of 'sweep' fees since investment of daily trust account balances should be included in the bank's regular management fee.

Pay fees from principal, not income, to reduce fee base.

Unresolved

Reduce fee base

Where are fees assessed (in whole or part) against income, determine whether all income beneficiaries are paying their fair share.

Sell off unproductive real estate/other assets.

Get real property reappraisal by an independent appraiser.

Step up distributions of principal. However, if the trust instrument does not contain an IRS approved 'ascertainable standard', consider limiting distributions to $5,000 or 5% of principal—whichever is larger— to avoid possible adverse tax consequences.

Maximize portfolio growth (by use of equities) in order to take advantage of reduced management fee rates on larger portfolios.

Distribute capital gains rather than income to reduce fee base—especially if fees are charged both on income and principal.

Redistribute fees

Determine if fees can be paid (in whole or part) from trust corpus.

Reduce fiduciary taxes

Determine if taxes are higher than necessary because trust accumulates rather than distributes all income.

Yes ↓

Request distribution of all income.

If the trust 'situs' is determined by location of trustee, determine if 'moving' the trust to a different office of the corporate trustee would result in lower property taxes.[88]

Determine if switch to local (instate) municipals would be tax advantageous.

Determine if certain expenses are being inappropriately charged to trust income such as penalties/interest for underpayment of taxes.

Unresolved

Stop ← *No*

Reduce investment expenses

Avoid (eliminate) use of proprietary mutual funds which may subject trust principal to additional fees—viz. fund's total expense ratio—unless rebated in full at the account level.

If an independent corporate trustee is using an outside mutual fund (including a money market fund), determine if the trust or the trustee is getting the advantage of an institutional rate.

No / *Yes* → Demand that amount of discount be credited to the trust.

Stop

Determine if investment costs can be reduced by requiring that your fiduciary always acts as agent, never as principal in investment transactions.

Determine if brokerage fees are being charged at higher than institutional rates (e.g. 6–10¢ share for equities, 'blue list' or lower where a discount is available for bonds).

Consider alternative remedies.

See Charts A-8, A-8(a), A-8(b)

[88]Mellon Bank recently moved its trust administration offices temporarily to Jenkintown, PA to avoid a newly created Philadelphia property tax!

348

GROWTH IN TRUST ASSETS UNSATISFACTORY

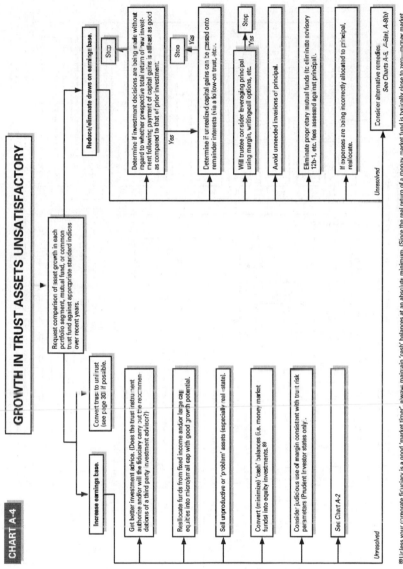

Request comparison of asset growth in each portfolio segment, mutual fund, or common trust fund against appropriate standard indices over recent years.

Increase earnings base.

Convert trust to unitrust (see page 30 if possible).

Get better investment advice. (Does the trust instrument authorize and/or will the fiduciary carry out the recommendations of a third party investment advisor?)

Reallocate funds from fixed income and/or large cap equities into micro/small cap with good growth potential.

Sell unproductive or 'problem' assets (especially real estate).

Convert (minimize) 'cash' balances (i.e. money market funds) into equity investments.[89]

Consider judicious use of margin consistent with trust risk parameters (Prudent Investor states only).

See Chart A-2

Unresolved

Reduce/eliminate draws on earnings base.

Determine if investment decisions are being made without regard to whether prospective total return of new investment following payment of capital gains is at least as good as compared to that of prior investment.

Yes → Stop

Determine if unrealized capital gains can be passed onto remainder interests (via a follow-on trust, etc.).

Yes → Stop

Will trustee consider leveraging principal using margin, writing call options, etc.

Yes → Stop

Avoid unneeded invasions of principal.

Eliminate proprietary mutual funds (to eliminate advisory 12b-1, etc. fees assessed against principal).

If expenses are being incorrectly allocated to principal, reallocate.

Unresolved

Consider alternative remedies:
See Charts A-5, A-8(a), A-8(b)

[89] Unless your corporate fiduciary is a good 'market timer', always maintain 'cash' balances at an absolute minimum. (Since the real return of a money market fund is typically close to zero—money market rates track inflation—there are no compelling reasons to do otherwise other than for the corporate fiduciaries' administrative convenience.)

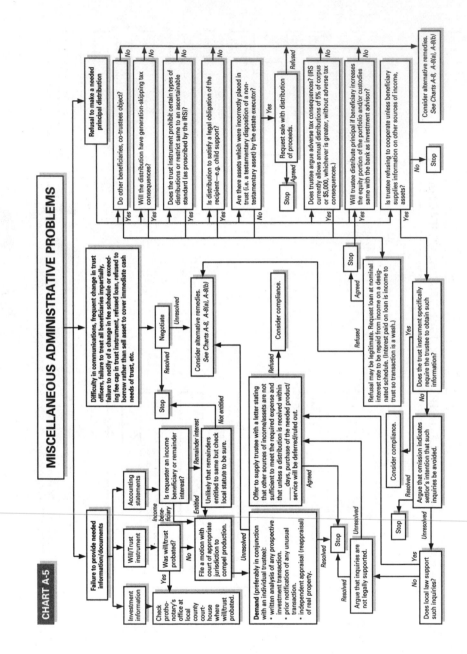

MISCELLANEOUS ADMINISTRATIVE PROBLEMS

CHART A-5

350

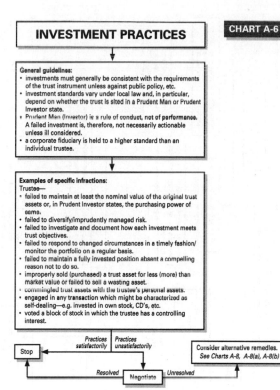

INVESTMENT PRACTICES

General guidelines:
- investments must generally be consistent with the requirements of the trust instrument unless against public policy, etc.
- investment standards vary under local law and, in particular, depend on whether the trust is sited in a Prudent Man or Prudent Investor state.
- Prudent Man (Investor) is a rule of conduct, not of performance. A failed investment is, therefore, not necessarily actionable unless ill considered.
- a corporate fiduciary is held to a higher standard than an individual trustee.

Examples of specific infractions:
Trustee—
- failed to maintain at least the nominal value of the original trust assets or, in Prudent Investor states, the purchasing power of same.
- failed to diversify/imprudently managed risk.
- failed to investigate and document how each investment meets trust objectives.
- failed to respond to changed circumstances in a timely fashion/ monitor the portfolio on a regular basis.
- failed to maintain a fully invested position absent a compelling reason not to do so.
- improperly sold (purchased) a trust asset for less (more) than market value or failed to sell a wasting asset.
- commingled trust assets with the trustee's personal assets.
- engaged in any transaction which might be characterized as self-dealing—e.g. invested in own stock, CD's, etc.
- voted a block of stock in which the trustee has a controlling interest.

Practices satisfactorily | Practices unsatisfactorily

Stop

Consider alternative remedies.
See Charts A-8, A-8(a), A-8(b)

Resolved | Negotiate | Unresolved

351

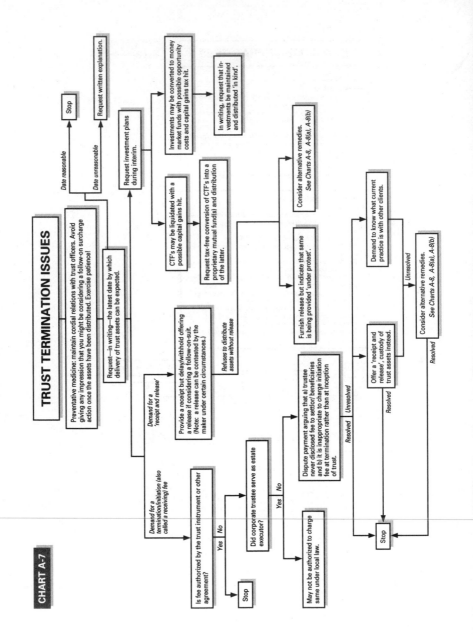

TRUST TERMINATION ISSUES

CHART A-7

Preventative medicine: maintain cordial relations with trust officers. Avoid giving any impression that you might be considering a follow-on surcharge action once the assets have been distributed. Exercise patience!

Request—in writing—the latest date by which delivery of trust assets can be expected.

Date reasonable → Stop

Date unreasonable → Request written explanation.

Request investment plans during interim.

CTF's may be liquidated with a possible capital gains hit.

Request tax-free conversion of CTF's into a proprietary mutual fund(s) and distribution of the latter.

Investments may be converted to money market funds with possible opportunity costs and capital gains tax hit.

In writing, request that investments be maintained and distributed 'in kind'.

Demand for a 'receipt and release'

Provide a receipt but delay/withhold offering a release if considering a follow-on-suit. (Note: a release can be contested by the maker under certain circumstances.)

Refuses to distribute assets without release

Furnish release but indicate that same is being provided 'under protest'.

Consider alternative remedies. *See Charts A-8, A-8(a), A-8(b)*

Demand for a termination/initiation (also called a receiving) fee

Is fee authorized by the trust instrument or other agreement?

Yes → *No*

Stop

Did corporate trustee serve as estate executor?

No → *Yes*

May not be authorized to charge same under local law.

Dispute payment arguing that a) trustee never disclosed fee to settlor/ beneficiaries and b) it is inappropriate to charge initiation fee at termination rather than at inception of trust.

Resolved | *Unresolved*

Offer a 'receipt and release', custody of trust assets instead.

Resolved → Stop

Demand to know what current practice is with other clients.

Unresolved

Consider alternative remedies. *See Charts A-8, A-8(a), A-8(b)*

Resolved → Stop

Stop

ALTERNATIVE REMEDIES

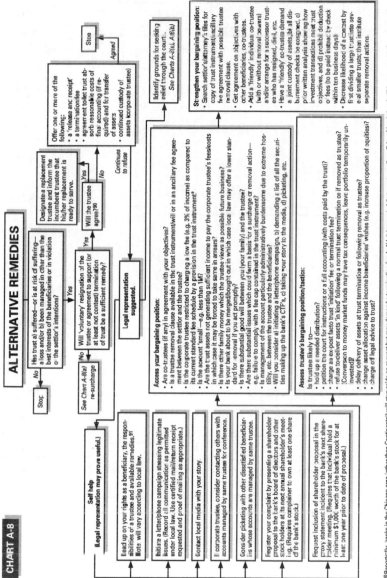

Self help

(Legal representation may prove useful.)

Read up on your rights as a beneficiary, the responsibilities of a trustee and available remedies.[91] Note will vary according to local law.

Initiate a letter/phone campaign stressing legitimate issues. (Record all communication as permitted under local law. Use certified mail/return receipt requested and proof of mailing as appropriate.)

Contact local media with your story.

If corporate trustee, consider contacting others with accounts managed by same trustee for conference.

Consider picketing with other dissatisfied beneficiaries whose accounts are managed by same trustee.

Register your complaint by presenting a shareholder proposal to the bank's board of directors and other stock holders at its next annual shareholder's meeting. (Requires that individual hold a minimum $1,000 worth of the bank's stock for at least one year prior to date of proposal.)

Request inclusion of shareholder proposal in the proxy statement incident to the bank's next shareholder meeting. (Requires that individual hold a minimum $1,000 worth of the bank's stock for at least one year prior to date of proposal.)

Has trust a) suffered—or is at risk of suffering— a loss and/or b) been managed in other than the best interests of the beneficiaries or in violation of the settlor's intentions?

No → See Chart A-8(a) re-surcharge

Yes ↓

Will 'voluntary' resignation of the trustee or agreement to support (or at least not contest) termination of trust be a sufficient remedy?

Yes → Designate a replacement trustee and inform the incumbent trustee that his/her replacement is ready to serve.

No → Legal representation suggested.

Will the trustee agree?[90]

Yes → Offer one or more of the following:
- a 'release and receipt'
- a termination fee
- agreement to let trust absorb reasonable costs of final accounting (if required) and for transfer of assets
- continued custody of assets corporate trustee)

→ Agreed → Stop

No → Continues to refuse

Assess your bargaining position:

- Are co-trustees (if any) in agreement with your objectives?
- Is a trustee removal clause available in the trust instrument/will or in an ancillary fee agreement between the settlor and the trustee?
- Is the corporate trustee restricted to charging a low fee (e.g. 3% of income) as compared to its current standard fee schedule by a provision in the trust instrument?
- Is the account 'small'—e.g. less than 1M?
- Are the trust assets not generating sufficient income to pay the corporate trustee's fees/costs in which case it may be forced to take same in arrears?
- Is there other family money which the trustee views as possible future business?
- Is your bank about to be merged/bought out in which case local law may offer a lower standard for removal if you act promptly?
- Is there substantial good will between you (your family) and the trustee?
- Are there substantial issues which could form a basis for a surcharge or removal action— e.g. failure to comply with a fee cap contained in the trust instrument?
- Is management of the account particularly administratively burdensome due to extreme hostility, etc. between the trustee and the beneficiaries?
- Will you consider a) initiating a letter/phone campaign, b) demanding a list of all the securities making up the bank's CTFs, c) taking your story to the media, d) picketing, etc.

Assess trustee's bargaining position/tactics:

Is trustee likely to—
- hold up a needed distribution?
- petition the court for instructions or a full accounting (with costs paid by the trust)?
- charge a ex-post facto trust 'initiation' fee or termination fee?
- refuse to deliver assets 'in kind' following a normal trust termination or if removed as trustee? (Conversion to money market funds may have tax consequences, leave portfolio temporarily uninvested?
- delay delivery of assets at trust termination or following removal as trustee?
- change asset allocation against income beneficiaries' wishes (e.g. increase proportion of equities)?
- charge of legal advice to trust?

Identify grounds for seeking relief through the court.
See Charts A-8(a), A-8(b)

Strengthen your bargaining position:

- Search settlor's/attorney's files for copy of trust instrument/will and/or any ancillary fee agreement with possible trustee removal clause.
- Get agreement on objectives with other beneficiaries, co-trustees.
- Add a 'friendly' individual co-trustee (with or without removal powers) and/or arrange for a successor trustee who has resigned, died, etc.
- Have a 'friendly' co-trustee demand a joint custody of assets, b) all disbursement checks be cosigned, c) prior written analysis showing how investment transactions meet trust objectives, and d) prohibit deduction of fees (to be paid instead by check within ten business days)
- Decrease likelihood of a contest by first dividing a large trust into several smaller trusts; than institute separate removal actions.

Stop

---

[90] Reportedly banks in the Chicago area (other than Continental) will step aside on request but may demand a termination fee. In NJ, it is reported that courts are 'beneficiary friendly' and will honor requests for a change of trustee. Further, a St. Louis based practitioner finds that local banks "...will resign (or decline to serve) if requested," but may also charge a termination fee. See Loring, A Trustee's Handbook, Rounds, Charles E. Jr., Little, Brown and Co., NY, NY. Or dial (617) 573-8185. See also Restatement of the Law Second, American Law Institute, American Law Institute Publishers, 1959, St. Paul, MINN.

[91] See Loring, A Trustee's Handbook, Rounds, Charles E. Jr., Little, Brown and Co., NY, NY. See also Restatement of the Law Third—Trusts, Prudent investor Rule, American Law Institute, American Law Institute Publishers, 1992, St. Paul, MINN.

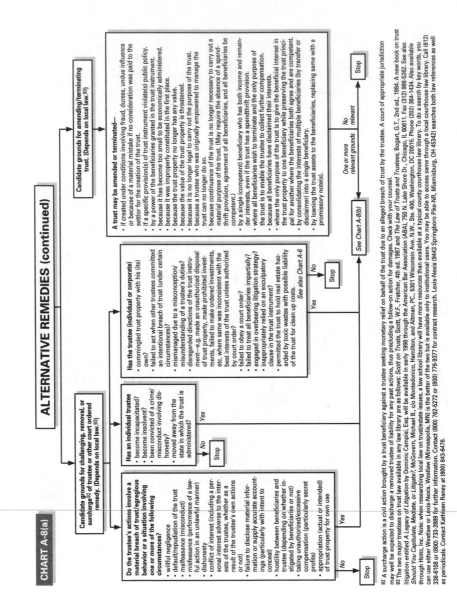

ALTERNATIVE REMEDIES (continued)

CHART A-8(a)

Candidate grounds for challenging, removal, or surcharge[92] of trustee or other court ordered remedy. (Depends on local law.[93])

Do the trustee's actions involve a material breach of trust/egregious behavior or a situation involving one or more of the following circumstances?
- willful negligence
- default/repudiation of the trust
- malfeasance (misconduct)
- misfeasance (performance of a lawful action in an unlawful manner)
- dishonesty
- conflict of interest (including a personal interest adverse to the interests of the trustee, whether as a result of the trustee's own actions or not)
- failure to disclose material information or supply accurate accountings (particularly with intent to conceal)
- hostility between beneficiaries and trustee (depending on whether instigated by beneficiaries or not)
- taking unauthorized/excessive compensation (particularly secret profits)
- appropriation (actual or intended) of trust property for own use

No → **Stop**

Yes ↓

Has an individual trustee
- become incapacitated?
- become insolvent?
- been convicted of a crime/misconduct involving dishonesty?
- moved away from the state in which the trust is administered?

No → **Stop**

Yes ↓

Has the trustee (individual or corporate)
- commingled trust property with his (its) own?
- failed to act when other trustees committed an intentional breach of trust (under certain circumstances)?
- mismanaged due to a misconception/misunderstanding of a trustee's duties?
- disregarded directions of the trust instrument—e.g. made an unauthorized disposal of trust property, made prohibited investments, failed to make ordered investments, etc. where same was inconsistent with the best interests of the trust unless authorized by court order?
- failed to obey a court order?
- failed to treat all beneficiaries impartially?
- engaged in overbearing litigation strategy?
- inappropriately relied on an exculpatory clause in the trust instrument?
- permitted the trust to hold real estate hazarded by toxic wastes with possible liability of the trust for clean up costs.

See also Chart A-6

Yes ↓   No → **Stop**

Candidate grounds for amending/terminating trust. (Depends on local law.[93])

A trust may be amended or terminated—
- if created under conditions involving fraud, duress, undue influence or because of a material mistake if no consideration was paid to the settlor for the creation of the trust.
- if a specific provision(s) of trust instrument violate(s) public policy.
- by a power of the beneficiaries granted in the trust instrument.
- because it has become too small to be economically administered.
- because it was improperly constituted in the first place.
- because the trust property no longer has any value.
- because the value of the trust property is threatened.
- because it is no longer legal to carry out the purpose of the trust.
- because a trustee who was originally empowered to manage the trust can no longer do so.
- because continuation of the trust is no longer necessary to carry out a material purpose of the trust. (May require the absence of a spendthrift provision, agreement of all beneficiaries, and all beneficiaries be competent.)
- by a single (competent) beneficiary who has both income and remainder interests, even if the trust has a spendthrift provision.
- where all beneficiaries wish to terminate and the only purpose of the trust is to enable the trustee to collect further compensation.
- because all beneficiaries have disclaimed their interests.
- where the only purpose of the trust is to give the beneficial interest in the trust property to one beneficiary while preserving the trust principal for another where the beneficiaries both agree and are competent.
- by consolidating the interests of multiple beneficiaries (by transfer or disclaimer) into a single beneficiary.
- by loaning the trust assets to the beneficiaries, replacing same with a promissory note(s).

One or more relevant grounds → **See Chart A-8(b)**

No relevant → **Stop**

---

[92] A surcharge action is a civil action brought by a trust beneficiary against a trustee seeking monetary relief on behalf of the trust due to an alleged breach of trust by the trustee. A court of appropriate jurisdiction may well be expected to discharge a removed trustee of liability for any past actions, thus precluding a follow-on action for damages. Check with your counsel.

[93] The two major treatises on trust law available in any law library are as follows: *Scott on Trusts*, Scott, W.F. Fratcher, 4th ed. 1987 and *The Law of Trusts and Trustees*, Bogart, G.T., 2nd ed., 1984. A new book on trust litigation entitled *A Legacy of Litigation* by Dominic Campisi, Esq. will be available in early 1998 through the American Bar Association (ABA), 750 N. Lake Shore Dr., Chicago, IL 60611, Fax (312) 988-5262. See also *Should You Capitulate, Mediate, or Litigate?*, McGovern, Michael B., c/o Montedonico, Hamilton, and Altman, PC, 5301 Wisconsin Ave. N.W., Ste. 400, Washington, DC 20015, Phone (202) 364-1434. Also available through Heirs, Inc. Note: when researching local law on trust/estate issues, a law school library will have more resources than available at a typical county courthouse law library. To do a search by key words, you can use either Westlaw or Lexis-Nexis. Westlaw (Minneapolis, MN) is the better of the two but is available only to institutional users. You may be able to access same through a local courthouse law library. Call (612) 338-6108 or (800) 733-2889 for further information. Contact (800) 762-5272 or (800) 776-9377 for contract research. Lexis-Nexis (9443 Springboro Pike-NR, Miamisburg, OH 45342) searches both law references as well as periodicals. Contact Kathleen Raney at (800) 843-6476.

ALTERNATIVE REMEDIES (continued)

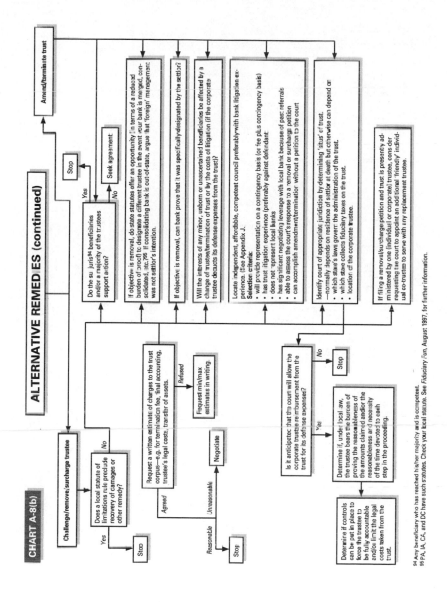

94 Any beneficiary who has reached his/her majority and is competent.
95 PA, IA, CA, and DC have such statutes. Check your local statute. See *Fiduciary Fun*, August 1997, for further information.

Index

Accountants:
  as business source, 252
  compensation for, 42
  job satisfaction of, 41
  tax, 21, 59
  in trust busting, 227
  as trusted advisors, 37–39
  as trustees, 149
Accrual, 90
Accumulator-type trust beneficiary, 158, 162,
  163, 169–170, 192
Adjustment of income, 90
Advertising:
  as marketing tool, 254–255, 338
  by state-chartered trust companies, 286
Advisor. See Financial advisor; Trusted advisor
Advisor-client relationship, 58–66, 69, 125, 137,
  303–305
  communication in, 230
  conflict of interest in, 261, 262
  duration of, 75
  establishing, 71–73, 132, 253–254, 258
  example of, 117–119
  mismatch in, 164–174
  psychological match in, 145, 152–164, 177,
  249, 253–254, 343–344
  qualities needed in, 124–139, 240
  and retainers, 226–227
Annuities, 37, 85
Asset protection trust, 85, 88
Association of Independent Trust Companies
  (AITCO), 7, 148
Attorneys:
  as advisors, 21, 39, 163
  business equity for, 40, 41

  as business source, 252
  compensation for, 37, 39–42
  and local bank trusts, 177
  in trust busting, 218–219, 227–228
  as trustees, 10, 25, 40, 146, 149
Avoider-type trust beneficiary, 153–154, 160,
  161, 192

Baby boomers (BBs), 5, 11–12, 170
  as inheritors, 6, 14, 100, 143, 325
  and socially responsible investing, 70, 171
  take-charge attitude of, 40, 173–174
Bank(s). See also Bank trust departments
  acquisitions/mergers of, 10, 22–25, 36, 148,
  206
  drawbacks of, 27, 178–180
  historical role of, 9–10
  as investment product distributors, xii, xv, 12
  liability of, 24, 26, 181, 279
  as money centers, 145–146, 160
  and philanthropy, 171
  private, 146, 163, 171, 178
  public images of, 221
  regional, 148, 160, 163, 171, 173, 281–282
  trusts held by, 7, 11, 27, 91, 144, 281–282
Bank trust departments, xiv, 24–28, 35–36, 148,
  172
  disadvantages of, 151–152, 229
  and investment underperformance, 212, 213
  segmentation of, 178–179
  unfair practices of, 222
Blind trust, 85
Blue-chip stocks, 9, 10, 173, 211
Bonds:
  flower, 92

Bonds *(Continued)*:
  income from, 93
  and interest rates, 9
  investment in, 32, 94, 172
  municipal, 10, 214
  quality ratings for, 188
  and Swiss banks, 232
  U.S. Treasury, 10
  wealth based on, 4
Brokerages, xii, 20–21, 32, 33, 36
  as advisors, 17, 28, 34
  as nominees, 83
  personal attention from, 44
  as trustees, 9, 232

Capital, 9, 63, 93
Capital gains, 91, 93, 95, 96
Capitalization:
  for trust advisory firm start-up, 271
  for trust company start-up, 285
Caretaker-type trust beneficiary, 153, 160, 161,
    164–166, 192
Case studies:
  of beneficiary types, 164–172
  of persons of wealth, 100–120
  on trustee evaluation, 193–194
Certified public accountant (CPA), 38
Charitable trusts, 14–16, 85–86, 240
Charles Schwab and Company, 20, 36, 110
Chartered Financial Analysts, 58
Class, social, xiv, 5, 128, 144
Class-action suit, as trust-busting tool, 222
Commissions:
  of brokerages, 20, 28, 36
  in car sales business, 35
  for CPAs, 38
  disadvantages of, 46, 59
  profit margins with, 37
  succeeding on, 33
Common trust fund, 172, 180, 188, 211, 213
Communication:
  between client and advisor, 51–53, 56, 58, 62,
    133
  to establish trust, 139
  format of, 63
  frequency of, 79
  nonverbal, 124
  style of, 55, 135–136
  success at, 69
  within trust advisory firm, 268
  with trustee, 233, 234
Compassion, 67, 70, 294
  business, 76–79
  personal, 71–75
Compensation. *See also* Fees
  to accountants, 42

  to attorneys, 37, 39–42
  to financial advisors, 68
  hourly rate as, 37–39, 42, 46, 59
  revenue-sharing, 38
  to trust advisory employees, 267–268, 274
Competition, 6–8, 36
  and compassion, 67, 70, 75
  in trust business, 250–251, 288
Computers:
  advantages to attorneys, 41
  for client management, 51–54
  limits of, 56
  and productivity, 4
  to track investment histories, 38
Conflict avoidance, 176–177
Conflict of interest:
  and accountants, 39
  and blind trusts, 85
  in car sales business, 35
  and trusted advisor, 33, 261, 262, 278, 284
Conservatorship, 82, 83
Consumer spending patterns, 5
Cotrustee(s), 82
  with advisor as trustee, 278
  beneficiaries as, 97
  written consent of, 98
Credibility, establishing, 69, 252, 253
Credit shelter trust (CST), 86–87

Decedent's trust, 87
Depository Trust Company system, 281
Descendant, 82, 84
  adopted, exclusion of, 96
Disability, 82, 84, 98
Disclaimer, of trust, 96
Distributions:
  determination of, 97, 215, 233
  discretionary, 91, 94, 95
  mandatory, 97
  of principal, 94, 212
Diversification, 10, 76, 91, 94, 263
Driver-type trust beneficiary, 154–155, 160,
    161, 166–167, 192
Dynasty trust, 87

Economy, U.S., 5, 8–9, 108–111
Education trusts, 87
Electronic information transfer, 232, 233, 243,
    281, 283
E-mail investing, 171
Embarrassment, as trust-busting tool, 221,
    283
Emotional connection:
  between advisor and beneficiary, 69, 136,
    138, 260, 327–331
  between beneficiary and trustee, 192, 217

Emotional issues about money, 120–121, 294, 298–300, 316–325. *See also* Family issues
E-Myth Manager, The (Gerber), 270
E-Myth Revisited, The (Gerber), 270
Entrepreneurship, 5, 6, 8, 14
  and money center banks, 145–146
  in Third World, 15, 16
  and trust advisory firms, 270–272
  and trust companies, 285–286
Entrepreneur-type trust beneficiary, 156, 161, 163, 169, 192
Equity, building of, 57, 60
  for financial advisor, 40, 41, 44, 46, 284
  in trust company, 286
Estate planning, xiv, 37, 77, 240
  revocable trusts in, 144
  trustee help with, 215
Estate tax, 91–92
  establishing reserves for, 96
  and flower bonds, 92
  and gift taxes, 92–93
  and irrevocable trusts, 89, 144
  and life insurance, 37
  and personal residences, 90
  rate of, 280
  trusts to avoid, 13, 86, 87
Excellent Investment Advisor, The (Murray), 137
Executor, 83

Family issues:
  for advisor, 243
  and changing trustees, 181, 183, 217, 224
  in first client contact, 254
  and money, 73, 75, 100, 134, 176, 299–300, 316
  resolving, 134, 324
Family office, 42, 43, 147–149, 178
  beneficiary type match with, 160, 162–164
Family tree, 210
Family trust, 87, 93
Fee(s), 32–46
  of banks, 24, 28, 179
  clarification of, 145
  evaluating, 191, 193, 211
  extraordinary, 92
  full disclosure of, 235
  hourly, 37–39, 42, 46, 59
  inflexible, 232–233
  legal, for moving trust, 207
  negotiation of, 275–277, 343
  paid from principal, 94
  retainer, xv, 39, 41–43, 70, 226–227
  at Swiss banks, 280
  termination, 94–95, 168, 169, 174, 182, 220

transfer, 174
  of trustees, 91, 92, 95, 212, 213, 232–234, 288, 348
  for "wrap" accounts, 34
Fiduciary, 82–84, 212, 282
Financial advisor(s), 22–24, 28–36, 43–44. *See also* Seasoned investment professional; Trusted advisor
  compensation of, 68
  qualities of, 46, 67
  relationship with client, 58–66
  shift to trust service, 257, 270
  and trustee choice, 176
Financial markets, 4, 32
Financial security, 63, 75, 76, 178, 310
Financial service industry, xii, xvi, 3, 14, 22–27, 61
  alliances in, 78
  compensation in, 32, 37–38, 45
  distrust of, 35
  job satisfaction in, 41
  number of workers in, 144
  profits in, 37
Financial statements, as trust-busting tool, 198–199, 210–216
Fixed-commission schedules, 20
Flower bonds, 92
Foundations, 84, 130, 160
Full acquittance and discharge, 97
Furnishing bonds, 97

Generation-skipping trust, 88
GI Bill, 9
Gift(s), xv, 159, 171, 240
  annual exclusion for, 91
  to education trusts, 87
Gift taxes, 89, 92–93
Golden Ghetto, The (O'Neill), 102, 120
Good faith acts, 95
Grameen Bank Coalition, 15, 16
Grantor, 83
Grantor retained annuity trust (GRAT), 88
Great Depression, 8, 9, 111
Gross domestic product (GDP), xiv
Guardians, 83

Heirs, xv, 83, 173, 176. *See also* Persons of inherited wealth
  support groups for, 177, 193
Heirs®, Inc., 177, 345
Heir's Handbook, The (Smith), 177

Income, 93
  and capital gains, 96
  and trust distributions, 212

Income beneficiary, 83
Income fees, 92
Income tax, 8, 95, 280, 296
    Schedule K-1 for, 94, 199, 215, 235, 252
    state, 211, 214
Inflation, 110, 111
Influence peddling, 85
Information:
    from advisor to client, 55, 130–135
    electronic, 232, 233, 243, 281, 283
    legal right to, 96, 179
    about trustees, 198–201, 212
    as wealth-building commodity, 4
Inheritance tax, 91
Insurance, 21, 178
Insurance agents, 22, 23, 37, 59, 240–241
Insurance companies, xii, 17, 241
Integrity, 44, 46
    in advisor-client relationship, 67–68, 135
Interest rates, 114, 165, 213
Internal Revenue Service, 8
    and estate planning, 240
    returns filed with, 94, 144
    and Swiss accounts, 280
    trust thresholds of, 215
Internet, 4, 51, 54
    as trust-busting tool, 221
Interstate commerce, 9
Investment trustee, 83
Investment without being limited by statute, 93
Irrevocable trusts, xiii, 7, 17, 89, 143–144, 277
    trustees of, 173
Issue:
    definition of, 83
    ensuring financial future of, 134
    lawful, 97

Kiplinger's 1998 "Cut Your Taxes," 296

Legacy of Inherited Wealth, The (Blovin, Gibson, and Kiersted), 300
Liability:
    of accountants, 42
    of attorneys, 42
    of banks, 24, 26, 181, 279
    of financial advisors, 23–24
    and offshore trusts, 89–90
    in trust company start-up, 285
    in trust cooperative, 286, 287
    of trustee, 93, 97, 229, 234, 277
    and trustee resignation, 220
Life insurance, 21, 37, 215
Life insurance trusts, 59, 89, 117, 240, 241
Lifetime interest in property, 93
Limited partnership, 20
Litigation, as trust-busting tool, 221–222

Living trust, 17, 89
Loans, 178, 179
Low-cost-basis property, 93

Majority determination, 97
Mandatory distributions, 97
Marital trust, 89
Marketing, of trust services, 247–256
Media:
    as marketing tool, 251
    as trust-busting tool, 221, 222
Meditation, 74
Merrill Lynch, 36, 143
Microbanks, 179
Minors, 83
    education trusts for, 87
    and special-needs limitation, 98
Mission statement, 260–261
Mistakes:
    admitting, 64, 68, 126–127, 139
    by advisors, 244, 334
    paying for, 139, 222
    by trustees, 209, 210, 216, 219, 221, 236
Money and Spirit (Brown), 121, 296
Money center banks, 145–146
    beneficiary type match with, 160–163
    and philanthropy, 171
Money managers, 22, 32, 38
    and banks, 145, 173
    relationship to clients, 17, 58
    and "wrap" accounts, 33
Money markets, 110, 211
Mutual fund(s):
    common trust, 172, 180, 188, 211, 213
    from money center banks, 145
    1970s crash of, 110
    no-load, 33, 34, 36
    on-line rating services for, 38
    selection management for, 60
Mutual fund companies, 17, 276

National trustees, 284–285
Natural resources, 4, 8, 15, 16
Net income, 93, 97
Net worth statement, 199, 201, 215
Newsletter, as marketing tool, 255
New York Stock Exchange, 20
NIMCRUT/NIMCRAT, 89
No-load mutual funds, 33, 34, 36
Nominee, 83
Nonprofit organization, 85

Office of the Comptroller of the Currency, 7,
    144, 284
Office of Thrift Supervision, 144
Offshore trusts, 89–90, 240

On-line investing, xii, 37
On-line rating services, for mutual funds, 38

Paper profits, 93
Performance, 63
  of advisor, 145, 263, 331–333
  and asset loss, 178
  of banks, 179, 180
  and expectation, 76
  of investments, 212
  and marketing, 251, 255
  responsibility for, 222
  short-term, 66
  of trustee, 188–191, 193, 201, 203, 210–211,
    345–355
Personal contact, 56, 78–79, 148
  evaluating level of, 191
  as marketing tool, 255–256
Personal representative, 83
Personal Values Questionnaire, 244–246
Persons of inherited wealth (POWs), xi–xiv, 50,
    61
  acceptance of, 124–125
  and careers, 301–303
  case studies of, 100–121
  counseling for, 136, 173, 293, 301
  emotional issues of, 100, 193, 299–300,
    316–323
  friendships of, 300–301
  goals of, 136, 292–293, 307
  guilt felt by, 106, 127, 294, 316
  illness prevalence among, 103, 318
  priorities of, 296–297
  and relationship to community, 306–307
  self-knowledge of, 310–316
  self-worth of, 129, 304–305, 307
  and sense of entitlement, 134, 319–320
  shame felt by, 106
  validation of, 126
  values of, 127–129, 250
  weekend retreats for, 253
Philanthropist-type trust beneficiaries, 159, 162,
    164, 171–172, 192
Philanthropy, 129, 159, 171, 318
Portability language, 214
Portfolio management, 91, 94, 129, 281
Power of appointment, 97
Principal, of trust, 84, 90–91
  and capital gains, 95, 96
  distributions of, 94, 212
Principal fees, 94
Private foundations, 84, 130, 160
Probate, xv, 40, 97, 144
Professional associations, as trust-busting tool,
    223
Professional dynasties, 146–147

beneficiary type match with, 160–164, 170
  and investments, 173, 212
  and philanthropy, 171
  pitfalls of, 182, 183, 223
  and trust assets, 178
Property:
  disputes about, 97
  distribution of, 91
  lifetime interest in, 93
  low-cost basis, 93
Protection from creditors, 89
Prudent investor rule, 94, 236

Qualified personal residence trust (QPRT), 90
Qualified terminable interest property (QTIP)
    trust, 90

Rabbi trust, 90
Reagan administration, 111
Real estate:
  baby boomer effect on, 143
  income from, 93
  as investment, xiv, 5, 8, 68, 110, 263
  in trusts, 213
Referrals, 65, 248, 251–253, 272
Regional banks, 148
  and community philanthropy, 171
  service at, 173
  as trustee, 160, 163, 281–282
Registered Investment Advisors, 32–33, 38
Regulation:
  and advisor as trustee, 278
  and bank as trustee, 10
  of independent trust companies, 149, 284–286
  on new advisors, by states, 34
  of professional dynasties, 147
  as trust-busting tool, 222
  in trust industry, 25
Remainder person, 84, 95, 217, 218
Reputation, 63, 77, 272
  establishing, 252–253
  of seasoned investment professional, 46
  of successor trustee, 275
  of trustees, discrediting of, 221–223
Retainers, xv, 37, 39, 41–43, 70, 226–227. *See
    also* Fees
Retirement planning:
  by baby boomers, 5
  as investment need, xiv
  and rabbi trust, 90
  trustee help with, 215
Revocable trust, 90, 144
Revocation, 97
Risk:
  capital, sharing of, 63
  distributing, in portfolio, 91

Risk *(Continued)*:
  tolerance for, 199–201, 216
  in trust advisory start-up, 258, 259
Risk-tolerance questionnaire, 199–201
Roaring 2000s, The (Dent), 5
Rule against perpetuity, 87, 97

Sales:
  by brokers and agents, 39
  cold calls, in trust business, 252
  of financial services, 20–22
  versus service, 57
Schedule A, 94, 252
Schedule K-1, 94, 199, 215, 235, 252
Seasoned investment professional (SIP), xi–xiv,
    36, 63. *See also* Financial advisor; Trusted
    advisor
  advantage of, 25, 44, 45, 67, 70
  integrity of, 67–68, 75
  negotiation by, 233
  reputation of, 46
  as team coordinator, 119
  in trust-busting process, 226
Securities, 94
Securities and Exchange Commission, 34
Self-actualization, 72, 129
Self-knowledge:
  for advisor, 241–242
  for beneficiary, 291–294, 297–298
  process of, 310–316, 323
Seminars:
  to find advisor, 338
  as marketing tool, 251, 253
Service(s):
  advisor standards for, 263
  from banks, 27, 173, 177–179
  and compensation, 65, 66, 234, 276
  comprehensiveness of, 59–61, 70
  computer role in, 37, 51–54
  continuity of, 263–265
  convenience as, 136
  emphasis on, 6, 57, 77, 265
  evaluating, 191, 193, 202
  and marketing, 253
  from national companies, 284
  personalized, 42–44, 53, 69, 133, 265
  success in, 242
  by Swiss banks, 280
  and trust asset value, 25, 65
Sharing of risk capital, 63
Socialite-type trust beneficiaries, 157–158, 162,
    163
Socially responsible investments, 15–16, 113,
    250, 307
  environmental, 70, 127–128, 171
  as validation, 126

Software. *See also* Computers
  evaluating, 54
  for trust advisory firm, 269
  upgrades of, 53
Specialization, 20, 58
Special-needs limitation, 97–98
Special needs trust, 90
Spendthrift provision, 98
Sprinkle, 98
Status seeker–type trust beneficiaries, 156–157,
    162, 163, 192
Stock market:
  downturn in, 76–77
  income from, 93
  increased investment in, 32
  record returns on, xiv, 10, 44, 77
Stress:
  advisor handling of, 244
  in modern culture, 295
  reduction of, 131–132, 136
Substitute trustee, 84
Succession plan, from advisor, 263–264
Successor trustee, 84, 214, 219
  advisor as, 231, 277–278
  choosing, 230–234, 275–276, 284
  document preparation by, 235
  exit strategy from, 234–235
  and security clearance, 281
Support groups for heirs, 177, 193
Swiss banks, 232, 279–281

Tax returns:
  preparing, 296
  for trustee evaluation, 199, 201, 214–215, 235
  on trusts, 93, 144
Teamwork:
  in self-knowledge process, 312
  in trust advisory firms, 268, 270, 273
Technocrat-type trust beneficiaries, 158–159,
    162, 164, 170, 192
Technology, 4, 5, 14, 32
  evaluating, 54
  and professional dynasties, 173
  for serving financial clients, 50–56, 270
Termination fees, 94–95, 168, 169, 174, 182, 220
Terminology, 81
  on parties involved, 82–85
  on rules, 94–98
  on trust assets, 90–95
  on types of trusts, 85–90
Time management, 258–259
Transfer documents, 235
Transfer fees, 174
Transfer tax, 89, 91
Trust(s):
  corpus of (*see* Principal, of trust)

court involvement in, 229
definition of, 7, 62
distributions from (*see* Distributions)
evaluating investments of, 199–201
expenses of, 92, 93
family, 87, 93
income from, 93
irrevocable, xiii, 7, 17, 89, 143–144, 173, 277
locating, by advisor service, 251–254
longevity of, 10, 13, 87
number of, 144
origins of, 8–9
purposes of, xv
records from, 95
renunciation of, 96
revocable, 90, 144
revocation of, 97
rules concerning, 95–98
splitting of, 94, 217
tax advantages of, 13, 85–90, 229
types of, 85–90
Trust advisory firms:
    conflict of interest in, 261, 262, 284
    education within, 260, 265, 273
    empathy as quality of, 260, 272–273
    employees of, 242, 251, 265–268, 273, 274
    marketing for, 247–256, 271
    maturity of, 268–269
    performance of, 263, 273
    physical surroundings of, 265
    priorities of, 259
    procedures for, 269–270, 273
    service by, 257–259, 263–265, 270
    software for, 269
    special needs, 90
    start-up of, 271–272
    team building in, 268, 270, 273
    time invested by, 258–259, 272
    values of, 260–261, 274
Trust amendment, 98
Trust assets, 90–95
    allocation of, 188, 199, 233
    disputes about, 97
    and investment performance, 212
    as loan collateral, 178
    multiple claimants to, 96
    protection of, 97
    and special-needs limitation, 97–98
    value of, and service level, 25, 65
Trust beneficiary (TB). *See also* Advisor-client relationship
    access to technology by, 53, 55
    agreement among, 228
    annual reports to, 95
    baby boomers as, 12, 173–174

and banks, 27, 183, 283 (*see also* Bank trust departments)
best interests of, 96, 188, 201, 241
case studies of, 164–172
contingent, 82
as cotrustee, 97
current, 82, 94, 97
definition of, xi, 82
demands on, 28–29
of education trust, 87
financial needs of, 230
full disclosure to, 235
goals of, 204
income, 83, 96, 218
objectives of, 293
overspending by, 300
peer group support for, 193
personality types of, 152–164, 177
principal, 84, 96
and retainer payment, 227
rights of, 183, 198, 212, 214, 222, 229, 236
sources of income of, 94
trustee change by (*see* Trust busting)
trustee evaluation by, 186–194
Trust building, xii, xiii, 68. *See also* Trust(s); Trust advisory firm; Trusted advisor
Trust busting, xi–xiii, 11–12, 62
    basis for, 173, 213, 215, 216
    checklist for, 201
    costs involved in, 207, 218, 220, 226
    court involvement in, 229, 236
    document preparation in, 235
    emotional issues in, 223–223
    family issues in, 217, 228
    on friendly terms, 206–207
    full disclosure in, 235
    information needed for, 198–202, 210–216
    initiating, 197–198, 216–221
    leader in, 227–228
    negotiating in, 206, 219–221
    questions to ask, 202–206
    retainer for, 226–227
    timing in, 223, 228–229
    tools for, 221–223
Trust charter, 286
Trust companies, independent, 40, 148–149, 282–284
    depository accounts for trust assets, 178
    increase in, 25, 28, 144
    interstate operation by, 284
    and philanthropy, 171
    start-up of, 285–286, 288
    as successor trustee, 231
Trust cooperative, 286–287
Trust document, 62, 84
    access to, 96, 176

Trust document *(Continued)*:
  amendment of, 98
  court interpretation of, 97
  distribution guidelines in, 91
  on fees, 168
  language of, 213–214
  and mandatory distributions, 97
  outdated, 134
  and successor trustee, 84, 231, 275
  and trustee evaluation, 199, 201
Trusted advisor, xii–xiv, 22–23, 29, 63. *See also*
    Financial advisor; Seasoned investment
    professional; Trust advisory firm
  accountant as, 37–39
  approach of, 58–61
  attorney as, 21, 39, 163
  benefit of, 16–18, 71
  compensation of, 33, 37–43, 65, 226–227
  and conflict of interest, 33, 278
  evaluation of, 327–335
  and finding trusts, 251–255
  goals of, 60, 242–243, 255
  interviewing, 338–343
  motivations of, 68, 75, 240
  and moving a trust, 216, 220, 223–224,
    227–228
  negotiation by, 206, 219–223, 233, 283
  qualities of, 57, 67, 124–139, 145, 240–242
  role of, 63, 121, 129, 135, 137, 231
  selection of, 337–338
  service level from, 44, 45, 131–132, 243–244
  and trustee evaluation, 188–190, 192, 197–207
  values of, 241–246, 260–261
Trustee, xiii, 62, 84. *See also* Bank trust depart-
    ment; Successor trustee; Trust companies,
    independent
  accessibility of, 203–204
  administrative, 82, 206
  advisor as, 231, 277–278
  attorney as, 10, 25, 40, 146, 149
  benefit to, 198
  changing (*see* Trust busting)
  choice of, 159, 186–188
  corporate, 13, 91, 223, 231–232, 276, 288
  delegation of duties by, 96
  evaluating, 186–194, 198–206, 345–355
  expectations of, 190–193
  fees of (*see* Fees)
  individual, 149–150, 178, 212, 231–232, 258
  investment by, 93, 94, 212–213, 232
  liability of, 93, 97, 229, 234, 277
  location of, 231
  mistakes by, 209, 210, 216, 219, 221–222, 236
  national company as, 284–285

  negotiating with, 206, 219–223
  nominal, 149
  and philanthropy, 171
  resignation of, 98, 220, 224, 229, 283
  as third-party service, 143, 288
  trust donor as, 96
  working with existing, 278—279
Trustor, 85
Trust originator (TO), 8, 9, 13–14, 176
  death of, 147
  negotiation by, 28, 92
  and termination fees, 220
Trust service providers. *See also* Bank trust
    department; Trust advisory firms; Trustee
  evaluating, 186–190, 230
  finding, 288
  mismatches with, 164–174
  personality match with, 151–164
  and philanthropy, 171
  standards for, 188
  types of, 145–150
Trustworthiness, 62, 68, 256

Unrealized growth, 93
U.S. Treasury bonds, 10, 213

Values, 73–74
  acknowledgment of, by advisor, 127–128
  of advisor, 242
  alignment of, 128–129
  questionnaire on, 244–246
  of socialites, 157
  of trust advisory firm, 260–261, 274

War veterans, 8–9, 11
Wealth:
  emotional issues about, 120–121, 294,
    298–300, 316–325
  entrepreneurship as means to, 5, 6
  transfer of, in United States, 3, 7, 143
Web sites, as tool, 171
Will:
  codicil to, 98
  executor in, 83
Women:
  asking for inheritance advice, 119
  paternalism toward, 120
  postwar educational opportunities for, 11
  and socially responsible investing, 15, 16
Workshops, as marketing tool, 253
Worrier-type trust beneficiary, 155–156, 161,
    163, 167–169, 192
"Wrap" accounts, 33–34

About the Author

Robert Allen Rikoon has been a Registered Investment Advisor in Santa Fe, New Mexico, since 1983. After receiving his BA, with honors, from Harvard University in 1977 and an MBA from the University of New Mexico, Rob managed trust departments for two regional banks. His company, Rikoon Investment Advisors, provides investment advice and supervises financial affairs for individuals and nonprofit organizations. He specializes in advising trust beneficiaries and financial professionals on how to regain control over family assets in irrevocable trusts.

Rob is also an accomplished painter. One of his works, a six-part, egg tempera mural, is on permanent display in the Rotunda of the New Mexico State Capitol. He currently is working on painting a 62-panel ecumenical chapel. For relaxation, Rob enjoys participating in summer triathlons and winter quadratholons (bike, run, cross-country ski, and snowshoe). His community activities have included serving as President of the Los Alamos Study Group, a think tank dedicated to pursuing alternative strategies for national defense, and Treasurer of the Mountain Cloud Zen Center, a Buddhist meditation retreat center.

Rob lives in Santa Fe, New Mexico, with his wife, Deborah, and his two daughters, Robyn and Hannah.

pg 10   acquiescing